50 Years of
Urban Planning
in Singapore

World Scientific Series on Singapore's 50 Years of Nation-Building

Published

50 Years of Social Issues in Singapore
  edited by David Chan

Our Lives to Live: Putting a Woman's Face to Change in Singapore
  edited by Kanwaljit Soin and Margaret Thomas

50 Years of Singapore–Europe Relations: Celebrating Singapore's Connections
with Europe
  edited by Yeo Lay Hwee and Barnard Turner

Perspectives on the Security of Singapore: The First 50 Years
  edited by Barry Desker and Cheng Guan Ang

50 Years of Singapore and the United Nations
  edited by Tommy Koh, Li Lin Chang and Joanna Koh

50 Years of Environment: Singapore's Journey Towards Environmental Sustainability
  edited by Tan Yong Soon

Food, Foodways and Foodscapes: Culture, Community and Consumption in
Post-Colonial Singapore
  edited by Lily Kong and Vineeta Sinha

50 Years of the Chinese Community in Singapore
  edited by Pang Cheng Lian

Singapore's Health Care System: What 50 Years Have Achieved
  edited by Chien Earn Lee and K. Satku

Singapore–China Relations: 50 Years
  edited by Zheng Yongnian and Lye Liang Fook

Singapore's Economic Development: Retrospection and Reflections
  edited by Linda Y. C. Lim

Singapore and UNICEF: Working for Children
  edited by Peggy Kek and Penny Whitworth

Singapore's Real Estate: 50 Years of Transformation
  edited by Ngee Huat Seek, Tien Foo Sing and Shi Ming Yu

The Singapore Research Story
  edited by Hang Chang Chieh, Low Teck Seng and Raj Thampuran

The complete list of titles in the series can be found at
http://www.worldscientific.com/series/wss50ynb

World Scientific Series on
Singapore's 50 Years of Nation-Building

50 YEARS OF URBAN PLANNING IN SINGAPORE

Editor

Heng Chye Kiang

National University of Singapore, Singapore

World Scientific

NEW JERSEY · LONDON · SINGAPORE · BEIJING · SHANGHAI · HONG KONG · TAIPEI · CHENNAI · TOKYO

Published by

World Scientific Publishing Co. Pte. Ltd.

5 Toh Tuck Link, Singapore 596224

USA office: 27 Warren Street, Suite 401-402, Hackensack, NJ 07601

UK office: 57 Shelton Street, Covent Garden, London WC2H 9HE

Library of Congress Cataloging-in-Publication Data
Names: Heng, Chye Kiang, 1958–   editor.
Title: 50 years of urban planning in Singapore / Chye Kiang Heng (NUS, Singapore).
Other titles: Fifty years of urban planning in Singapore
Description: New Jersey : World Scientific Publishing Company, 2016. |
   Series: World Scientific series on Singapore's 50 years of nation-building |
   Includes bibliographical references.
Identifiers: LCCN 2015044561| ISBN 9789814656450 | ISBN 9789814656467
Subjects: LCSH: City planning--Singapore--History. | Urban policy--Singapore--History.
Classification: LCC HT169.S55 H46 2016 | DDC 307.1/216095957--dc23
LC record available at http://lccn.loc.gov/2015044561

British Library Cataloguing-in-Publication Data
A catalogue record for this book is available from the British Library.

Desk Editor: Shreya Gopi

Typeset by Stallion Press
Email: enquiries@stallionpress.com

Foreword

Mr Khaw Boon Wan

Coordinating Minister for Infrastructure & Minister for Transport

As Singaporeans celebrated our Golden Jubilee last year, our beautiful skyline and the Marina Bay made us proud. They also reminded us to reflect on our remarkable achievements. In its 2015 Quality of Living ranking, Mercer placed Singapore top in Asia for quality of life, ahead of other well-established cities such as Tokyo and Hong Kong.[1]

This collection of essays, by those who played a part in Singapore's nation-building, contains insights into the strategic considerations behind the city's transformation. They also inspire us to imagine what the future may hold for us.

Today, Singapore's economy is vibrant, creating good jobs and opportunities for our people. Almost all Singaporeans have a home. Most live in quality public housing, with parks and water bodies in the vicinity. Our heartlands are lively with community activities. Our people move around with ease and peace of mind.

Against this backdrop, few remember our humble beginning of homelessness and joblessness in a city littered with slums and squatters. The achievements of today were the results of bold vision and dogged determination of our founding leaders and the pioneer generation.

From day one, our urban planning policies and redevelopment strategies paid close attention to holistic economic, social and environmental outcomes. This is the only city we have. If we mess it up, with pollution, congestion or disamenities, we get an unattractive, unpleasant and unliveable home, period. With these absolute constraints, we got off on the right footing and planned for Singapore's long-term sustainable development. Our strong emphasis was on providing a good quality of life for our people. These fundamental principles continue to play a pivotal role in shaping Singapore today.

---

[1] Mercer Quality of Living Rankings, March 2015. Accessed at https://www.imercer.com/content/quality-of-living.aspx.

Our physical handicap requires us to constantly look for innovative ways, out of the box, by investing in research and technology whilst trying out new urban solutions to enhance our living environment. We look out for good solutions proven elsewhere and are ready to adopt them. We are also bold to be first movers, once we have thought through the risks and the implications. We recycle used water for consumption. We were the first to apply road pricing.

One success factor is our strong partnership with the private and people sectors. Active participation from across the sectors allows for the generation of ideas, and helps to engender a sense of shared ownership to drive positive change.

As our founding Prime Minister Mr Lee Kuan Yew said: "The good things of life do not fall from the skies. They can only come by hard work and over a long time. The government cannot produce results unless the people support and sustain the work of the government ... There may be times when, in the interest of the whole community, we may have to take steps that are unpopular with a section of the community. On such occasions, remember that the principle which guides our actions is that the paramount interest of the whole community must prevail."

Going forward, we will face fresh challenges, evolving needs and higher aspirations. We can, however, take heart that the strong foundation laid over the past 50 years by our pioneers will give us the confidence to move forward. Above all, we must continue to place our people at the heart of our plans. That way, Singapore will always be an *endearing home and distinctive global city*.

I thank the authors for their invaluable contributions and Chye Kiang for bringing together these diverse perspectives through this book.

Preface

Singapore's urban landscape has been shaped over 50 years by unique conditions. These conditions either facilitated or compelled the island-state to take certain directions in its development. What are these conditions and how have they influenced urban planning in Singapore?

First, as an island with a limited land area, Singapore faces the perpetual issue of land scarcity. Despite (or, perhaps, because of) the smallness of our island-state, Singapore manages its land constraints through strategic long-term planning, high-density development, and technological innovations—all this, while also aspiring towards high standards of urban liveability. The challenge of land scarcity, however, will become more and more complex in the near future given the need for economic progress and population growth in the face of an ageing population. As a small nation with limited natural resources, Singapore's economic well-being is not only contingent on our competitiveness and relevancy on the world stage but also the size and diversity of our human capital. It is difficult to separate one from the other given that both issues are arguably two sides of the same coin. The question to ask is: How can we achieve a sustainable balance between economic progress and population growth in the long-term?

Second, Singapore is simultaneously a city and an independent state. There are only a handful of such sovereign city-states in the world, much less an island city-state. In this way, Singapore stands apart from most cities. Unlike cities, it has to plan for all the functions of a sovereign state. For instance, to the extent that is possible, Singapore has had to develop water self-sufficiency and build up its national defense capabilities. Within Singapore's limited territory are 17 reservoirs and a number of military airbases and training grounds. Again, more than a city-state, closer scrutiny reveals an urban core around the historic centre connected by rail and road networks to 26 housing estates and new towns across the island—an island which accommodates the nation's population of some 5.5 million people.

Third, Singapore is also different from other metropolitan areas in that our island-state is entirely administered by a centralised government. A single-level central government system enables a coordinated and integrated approach to long-term planning, scaling from the local to national level. This avoids the conflicts of interests encountered in planning decision-making across the levels of city, province and state and, by the same token, eliminates any excuses for accountability and lack of coordination across the different governmental functions. Additionally, enacting intermediary changes to plans as part-and-parcel of a long-range planning framework is afforded by a single-level system of governance and the efficiencies it provides in terms of implementation. This nimbleness in planning actions and processes is, undoubtedly, also enhanced as a result of Singapore's small territorial size.

Fourth, the state's high ownership of land in Singapore and its legal instruments also facilitates the planning of the island-state. The Land Acquisition Act (LAA) is a significant example of central planning powers at work in Singapore. Since 1967, the LAA has enabled the government to acquire and amass land through compulsory and compensatory means for strategic development that meets the planning objectives of the state. In this way, the LAA affords the government greater control and coordination in the timing and planning of land development for public projects while keeping costs affordable, particularly in the case of public housing and mobility infrastructure. On the other hand, Singapore's pro-market policies have created opportunities in recent years for private sector involvement in large-scale urban projects.

Fifth, the longevity of a political system and government dominated by a single political party contributes to the continuity of the country's planning and urban plans. Where change of governments in other cities often precipitates the revision and even abandon of urban plans and efforts made by previous administrations, Singapore's 50 years of uninterrupted rule by a single political party has made the island-state an urban laboratory of sorts. Here, ongoing planning decisions and methods could be fine-tuned from one plan to the next in order to achieve an ultimately desirable outcome. The impact of Singapore's single political party landscape towards the endurance of long-range planning is equally matched by the effect of a whole-of-government approach towards complex policy issues and multi-agency initiatives. Adopting a whole-of-government mode of operation creates opportunities for the Singapore public service to exchange expertise and leverage resources across organisational lines, thus creating a culture of collaboration towards shared strategic goals.

Sixth, Singapore's urban transformation is as much a consequence of geography as it is an outcome of historical and political circumstances. Strategically positioned along an active maritime route in the South China Sea, Singapore had an advantageous start as a colonial entrepôt. Two hundred years later, Singapore's port is one of the busiest transshipment harbours in the world, playing a key role in both domestic and global economies. At the same time, Singapore thrives not only as a trading hub but also a cultural hub. Parallel to the movement of goods is the flow of people and ideas. As an immigrant society situated in a diverse region, Singapore has long been associated with the notion of multiculturalism. Our foods, languages, social practices, and religious customs are reflective of the nation's plural ethnicities—they, in turn, have shaped our built heritage, identity and openness to cultural diversity.

Indeed, the combination of geography and globalisation has helped to accelerate Singapore's transition from a fledgling entrepôt to a world city. As a business-friendly and knowledge-rich destination, Singapore's industries have continued to attract educated and mobile professionals from the region and beyond. Today, 30% of Singapore's total population comprises foreigners living in Singapore to work or study on a non-permanent basis. By 2030, the numbers of foreigners living in Singapore could be as high as 40% of the total population—this strategy to step up immigration is proposed by the government as a means to supplement Singapore's shrinking and ageing population. Sociocultural diversity and an ageing populace are anticipated to be the twin demographic challenges of our future. What might be the physical implications of such a population scenario for Singapore's urban environment, and how might it impact our culture and identity as a city in Asia?

As Singapore celebrates 50 years of nationhood in 2015, we are presented with a timely and significant opportunity to review, reflect, and rethink the past, present, and future of urban planning in our island-state. *50 Years of Urban Planning in Singapore* explores the unique conditions that have made our island-state distinct, while also questioning how these very conditions could change over time to create new challenges and opportunities for Singapore in the future. This book presents a collection of perspectives by a diverse group of industry experts, academics, and public intellectuals whose life's work has touched on the manifold aspects of urban planning in Singapore. The chapters of this book are organised into three sections, beginning with a macro picture of Singapore's urbanisation experience and planning framework, followed by a comprehensive overview of the key constituent parts of land use planning and, lastly, an interdisciplinary focus on contemporary issues affecting urban planning.

In *Part I: Paradigms, Policies & Processes*, the first chapter by Alan Choe describes the tumultuous early years of nation-building and how Singapore, then a newly-minted country, rose above the challenges to become a modern city and First World nation. Liu Thai Ker's chapter navigates the complex field of urban planning from a theoretical standpoint, while providing in-depth real-world insights into the principles and objectives that have shaped the urbanisation process in Singapore. Philip Yeo's chapter on economic planning traces the five phases of Singapore's industrialisation trajectory and discusses the transformative impact of industrial development on the urban landscape. Closing this section is Tan Yong Soon's chapter on the successes and future challenges of environmental planning for sustainable development in a small city-state like Singapore.

In *Part II: The Built Environment as a Sum of Parts*, Ng Lang launches the section with a chapter on Singapore's planning philosophy and urbanisation solutions in addressing our island-state's unique set of land constraints. Khoo Teng Chye and Remy Guo's chapter provides a detailed discussion on Singapore's integrated urban systems framework, presenting the key guiding principles of such a planning approach. The subsequent chapters in this section each cover a major land use sector. Collectively, these chapters demonstrate the comprehensive nature of long-term strategic planning in Singapore. Cheong Koon Hean's chapter navigates through five decades of Singapore's public housing programme in order to map out the evolution and highlight the significant milestones in town planning, development, and renewal. The role of transportation planning in urban development is discussed by Mohinder Singh in his chapter, which looks at the fundamental principles that have underpinned Singapore's land transport policies and key projects since independence. Tang Hsiao Ling's chapter provides an overview of industrial land development trends in the past 50 years with case studies illustrating how constraints and opportunity costs are deliberated in industrial planning. On the green environment, Tan Puay Yok's chapter investigates the importance of parks and greenery while highlighting the emerging challenges of greening Singapore alongside increasing population and urban densities. In Pamelia Lee's chapter, tourism is discussed for the influential role it plays in urban planning decisions and contribution to the transformation of Singapore's physical landscape. This section concludes with Goh Hup Chor and Heng Chye Kiang's chapter on urban design and public space, demonstrating the relationship between design, people, and the city with case studies of significant projects from the past 50 years.

In *Part III: Urban Complexities & Contemporary Issues*, we look at four interdisciplinary areas of urban planning today that concern the future of Singapore's urban landscape. Lily Kong's chapter discusses the evolution of Singapore's conservation programme and highlights the rise of diverse, and sometimes divergent, societal views towards urban heritage sites in a developmental city-state. In Tan Ern Ser's chapter, the implications of social heterogeneity for community building are examined in the context of public housing estates where government intervention and civic participation are discussed for their roles in creating opportunities towards social interaction and community development. Ho Kong Chong, in his chapter on the new urban economy, explores the shifting nature of industry and work and considers the consequences of this shift for Singapore's urban development and positioning as a world city in Asia. Concluding this section is Heng Chye Kiang and Yeo Su-Jan's chapter, which identifies emerging sustainability issues related to globalisation and urbanisation in Asia with a specific focus on Singapore and the strides within governance and research to develop our nation's resilience and responsibility towards a sustainable urban future.

In the *Epilogue*, a panel of eight distinguished personalities share their thought-provoking views on Singapore's urban outlook. Each panelist was asked to write a short essay in response to a big question: *Given the unique circumstances of our city-state in these exceptional times, what fundamental changes to Singapore's planning systems and processes might be necessary, if at all, to achieve greater peace, prosperity, and progress for our urban future?* The insightful essays not only demonstrate the diverse perspectives and disciplinary proficiencies of the panel but also illustrate the multidimensional approach required to tackle complex planning issues in the Singapore of tomorrow and beyond. Essays by Peter Ho, Low Teck Seng, and Kishore Mahbubani point to the need for bolder experimentation in aspects of strategic planning, mobility, and technology development—in other words, forward-thinking urban innovation. From the social science angle, David Chan and Melissa Kwee emphasise in their essays the importance of a people-centric approach to urban planning that duly integrates the human dimension in processes of policy development and city-making. With a focus on the physical environment, Shawn Lum, Tay Kheng Soon, and Wong Mun Summ and Alina Yeo examine in their respective essays the notion of 'systems'—ecological, architectural, and design theory—and the value of re-thinking deep-rooted systems through new paradigms in biodiversity conservation, architectural standards, and design education.

Spanning sixteen chapters and eight short essays, *50 Years of Urban Planning in Singapore* is a comprehensive and informative volume on the broad field of urban planning and its sub-themes of architecture and design, economic and environmental planning, urban sociology, and urbanism. The compilation of this book is made possible by the generous time and commitment of the featured contributors—it is an honour for me to be joining them on this bold project. I thank Professor Phua Kok Khoo, founder of World Scientific Publishing, for the invitation and opportunity to shape and edit this book. I gratefully acknowledge Ms Shreya Gopi, Editor at World Scientific Publishing, for her invaluable guidance on the publication production. Lastly, I am especially thankful to Dr Yeo Su-Jan for her unstinting research contribution and editorial assistance in the planning, coordination, and preparation of this book.

The collection of voices in *50 Years of Urban Planning in Singapore* demonstrates the range of local knowledge and experiences entwined with the transformation of Singapore, thus providing a richly-layered understanding of our built environment. Such a diversity of perspectives illuminates the complex textures of Singapore's urban landscape past, present, and future. Hence, this volume aims to engage with readers on an intellectual level as well as from an emotive front—for the conditions that make a city endearing and convivial, in addition to efficient and functional, are ultimately shaped by our shared hopes and aspirations.

Heng Chye Kiang
Lum Chang Chair Professor and Dean
School of Design and Environment
National University of Singapore
21 March, 2016

About the Editor

Heng Chye Kiang is Lum Chang Professor and Dean of the School of Design and Environment, National University of Singapore. He teaches architecture, urban design and planning at its Departments of Architecture and Real Estate. His research covers sustainable urban design and the history of Chinese cities. He serves as a member of several editorial boards of international journals and as a jury member of many international design competitions in Asia. He is currently on the Boards of the National Museum of Singapore, Centre for Liveable Cities, Singapore Institute of Technology and the Housing & Development Board; and was formerly on the Boards of the Jurong Town Corporation, Urban Redevelopment Authority and Building and Construction Authority. Chye Kiang consults on urban planning internationally and is the conceptual designer of several international urban design/planning competition winning entries in China. He publishes widely on urban history and design. His books include *Re-Framing Urban Space* (2016), *On Asian Streets and Public Space* (2010), *A Digital Reconstruction of Tang Chang'an* (2006), and *Cities of Aristocrats and Bureaucrats* (1999).

About the Contributors

David CHAN is Lee Kuan Yew Fellow, Professor of Psychology & Director of the Behavioural Sciences Institute at Singapore Management University (SMU), Adjunct Principal Scientist at Agency for Science, Technology and Research (A*STAR), and Co-Director of the Centre for Technology and Social-Behavioural Insights jointly established by A*STAR and SMU. He has received numerous international awards and served as Editor or board member on several journals. His works have been cited over 3000 times in various disciplines. He serves on various national councils, boards and advisory panels in Singapore and United States. He is Elected Fellow of several international psychological associations.

Alan CHOE Fook Cheong graduated as an architect and town planner from the University of Melbourne. In 1962, Alan joined the HDB as its first architect/planner. During his tenure at the HDB, he was involved in establishing public housing standards, developing Toa Payoh New Town, and activating urban renewal. Alan helped to set up the Urban Renewal Authority and became its first General Manager in 1974. He left the URA in 1978 to become a Senior Partner in a large architectural firm. In 1985, Alan was appointed Chairman of Sentosa Development Corporation where he transformed the old military island into a major tourist attraction and established Sentosa Cove Pte Ltd. Alan was a recipient of the Gold Medal, Meritorious Service Medal, Distinguished Service Order, and Outstanding Contribution to Tourism Award for his services.

CHEONG Koon Hean is the CEO of the Housing and Development Board (HDB), overseeing the development and management of 1 million public housing flats in 26 towns/estates. She was also previously the CEO of the Urban Redevelopment Authority, in charge of strategic land use planning, conservation of built heritage, promotion of design excellence and the real estate market. Koon Hean is on the Boards of the HDB, the National University of Singapore, the Civil Service College, as well as the International Federation for Housing and Planning. She is a member of the World Economic Forum's Real Estate and Urbanisation Global Agenda Council and serves on the nominating committee of the Lee Kuan Yew World City Prize and several international expert panels.

GOH Hup Chor is an architect, urban designer and planner. He held key positions in the Housing & Development Board (1968–1984) and Urban Redevelopment Authority (1984–1996), and is widely recognised as one of the key figures involved in the shaping of today's urban Singapore. In 1979, he was conferred the Public Administration Silver Medal by the Government of Singapore for his outstanding work in public housing. Hup Chor joined RSP, one of the largest and most established multidisciplinary planning and architectural firms in the region, as a Director in July 1996 and retired from RSP in 2003. Hup Chor has served for many years as a design critic and external examiner to the Department of Architecture at the National University of Singapore, and is also an adjunct Associate Professor in the Masters of Urban Design programme since 1995.

Remy GUO is Senior Assistant Director at the Centre for Liveable Cities, where he is involved in planning and development related research. Prior to joining CLC in 2013, he was a practicing urban designer and architect in the private sector and completed various local and overseas projects ranging from district level master plans, urban design proposals, to architectural construction projects. Remy graduated from the National University of Singapore with Master of Architecture with Specialisation in Urban Design.

HO Kong Chong is Associate Professor of Sociology at the Faculty of Arts and Social Sciences, National University of Singapore. Kong Chong's research interests are in the political economy of cities, urban communities, and higher education. He is an editorial board member of Pacific Affairs and the International Journal of Comparative Sociology. Kong Chong is co-author of *City-States in the Global Economy: Industrial Restructuring in Hong Kong and Singapore* (1997, Westview); and co-editor of *Service Industries, Cities and Development Trajectories in the Asia-Pacific* (2005, Routledge); *The City and Civil Society in Pacific Asian Cities* (2008, Routledge), "Capital Cities and their contested roles in the Life of Nations" (2009, *CITY* volume 13(1)); *New Economic Spaces in Asian Cities* (2012, Routledge), and "Globalising Higher Education and Cities in Asia and the Pacific" (2014, *Asia Pacific Viewpoint* volume 55(2)).

Peter HO was Head of Singapore's Civil Service, concurrent with his other appointments of Permanent Secretary (Foreign Affairs), Permanent Secretary (National Security and Intelligence Coordination), and Permanent Secretary (Special Duties) in the Prime Minister's Office. Before that, he was Permanent Secretary (Defence). He is now Chairman of the Urban Redevelopment Authority of Singapore. He is also Senior Advisor to the Centre for Strategic Futures, where he continues to pursue his interests in good governance and strategic foresight, and a Senior Fellow in the Civil Service College.

KHOO Teng Chye is currently the Executive Director for the Centre for Liveable Cities, Ministry of National Development (MND), Singapore. He was formerly the Chief Executive of PUB, Singapore's National Water Agency (2003 to 2011), Chief Executive Officer/Chief Planner at the Urban Redevelopment Authority (URA) (1992 to 1996), Chief Executive Officer/Group President of PSA Corporation (1996 to 2002), President and Chief Executive Officer of Mapletree Investments and Managing Director (Special Projects) of Temasek Holdings (2002 to 2003). Teng Chye graduated with First Class Honours in Civil Engineering from Monash University, Australia. A President-cum-Colombo Plan Scholar, he also holds a Master of Science in Construction Engineering and a Master of Business Administration from the National University of Singapore.

Lily KONG is Lee Kong Chian Chair Professor of Social Sciences and Provost at the Singapore Management University. Her main research areas include religion, heritage, cultural economy, and cultural policy. Recent publications include *Arts, Culture and the Making of Global Cities: Creating New Urban Landscapes in Asia* (2015), *Food, Foodways and Foodscapes: Culture, Community and Consumption in Post-colonial Singapore* (2015), and *Religion and Place: Competition, Conflict and Violence in the Contemporary World* (2016).

Melissa KWEE is a well-known social activist and volunteer leader who has served as Chair of Halogen Foundation, a youth leadership organisation. President of UN Women Singapore, and founder of Beautiful People, a volunteer mentoring programme for girls. Melissa is currently on the boards of Crest Secondary, a specialised school for technical education in Singapore; 70x7, an initiative by the Prison Fellowship Singapore, Pontiac Land Group and Honestbee. Melissa was recognised with the Singapore Youth Award in 2007, Asean Youth Award 2008, and has received several other awards for leadership and service. She was educated at Harvard College and was a Fulbright Scholar to Nepal. Melissa was appointed CEO of the National Volunteer & Philanthropy Centre in September 2014.

Pamelia LEE began her career in 1977 with the Singapore Tourism Board. There, she initiated and served as Chief Coordinator of a S$1 billion Singapore Tourism Product Development Plan, which resulted in concerted efforts to preserve Raffles Hotel, Fullerton Hotel, Singapore River, Civic District, Chinatown, Little India and Kampong Glam. Today, as a Senior Tourism Consultant, Pamelia extends her experience and passion related to heritage conservation and tourism on projects that have included: saving Singapore's two remaining Dragon Kilns, building Hua Song Museum, and enhancing the recreational potential of the Southern Islands. More recently, Pamelia purchased for Singapore a 9th century Tang Shipwreck Treasure

xviii   *About the Contributors*

of over 54,000 rare artefacts that provide living proof that the Maritime Silk Route thrived 1,100 years ago. Pamelia is the author of *Singapore, Tourism & Me* (2004) and co-authored *The Greening of Singapore, A Legacy of Lee Kuan Yew* (2014).

LIU Thai-Ker, Architect-Planner, has been a Director of RSP Architects Planners & Engineers Pte Ltd since 1992. He is the Founding Chairman of the Centre for Liveable Cities, since 2008. He is also Adjunct Professor of the National University of Singapore and Nanyang Technological University. He served the Housing and Development Board from 1969 to 1989, the last 10 years as its CEO. He oversaw the planning and design of 23 New Towns and the development of half a million dwelling units and facilities. From 1989 to 1992, as CEO of the Urban Redevelopment Authority, Thai-Ker led the major revision of the Singapore Concept Plan. He was also the Chairman of the National Arts Council from 1996 to 2005 and Chairman of the Singapore Tyler Print Institute between 2000 and 2009. Thai-Ker is also a planning advisor to over 30 cities in China.

LOW Teck Seng is a tenured Professor at Nanyang Technological University and the National University of Singapore. He is a Fellow of the IEEE and an International Fellow of the Royal Academy of Engineers, UK. He is currently the CEO of the National Research Foundation, Singapore. Prior to his appointment at the NRF he was the Managing Director of the Agency for Science, Technology & Research. He is the founding Principal of Republic Polytechnic and had served as Dean of Engineering at the NUS. He also founded the Data Storage Institute. He was awarded the National Science and Technology Medal and the Public Administration Medal (Gold) in 2004 and 2007 respectively. Teck Seng was conferred the Order of the Legion of Honour with the grade of Knight (Chevalier) by the French Government in Paris on 17 March 2016.

Shawn LUM is a botanist and plant ecologist at Nanyang Technological University. He currently serves as the president of the nature conservation NGO Nature Society (Singapore), and feels that civil society can and should contribute to the safeguarding of natural heritage. Originally from Honolulu, Hawaii, Shawn has spent his entire working career in Singapore, when he joined the NTU's National Institute of Education in 1993. He now lectures at the university's Asian School of the Environment. Shawn is an advocate of public participation in nature study and conservation at both formal and informal levels and spends time serving schools, community groups and corporations to those ends.

Kishore MAHBUBANI has been the dean of the Lee Kuan Yew School of Public Policy at NUS since August 2004. Before that, in his thirty-three-year career as a diplomat, he served twice as ambassador to the UN and as President of the UN Security

Council. He has published articles in leading global journals and newspapers, including *Foreign Affairs*, *Foreign Policy*, *National Interest*, *Financial Times* and *New York Times*. He has also authored five books: *Can Asians Think*, *Beyond the Age of Innocence*, *The New Asian Hemisphere*, *The Great Convergence* and *Can Singapore Survive*. *The Great Convergence* was selected by the *Financial Times* as one of the best books of 2013. Professor Mahbubani was listed by *Foreign Policy* as one of the top 100 global thinkers in 2010 and 2011; and by *Prospect* as one of the top 50 global thinkers in 2014.

NG Lang was appointed the Chief Executive Officer (CEO) of the Urban Redevelopment Authority in August 2010. Before this, Lang was CEO of the National Parks Board for 5 years, where he played a key role in implementing major infrastructural programmes to achieve the "City in a Garden" vision. This includes the development of the park connector network, streetscape greenery masterplan, skyrise greenery, the expansion of the Singapore Botanic Gardens and the Gardens by the Bay. He also championed community outreach efforts to enhance public appreciation and participation in Singapore's greening and biodiversity conservation programmes. Lang is currently board member of the Singapore Tourism Board, the Jurong Town Corporation and the Science and Engineering Research Council.

Mohinder SINGH is the Advisor of LTA Academy in the Land Transport Authority of Singapore. He was the Dean of LTA Academy from 2006 to 2014 before assuming his current appointment in July 2014. Before this, he was the Director of Planning of the Land Transport Authority from 1996 to 2007. Before joining the Land Transport Authority in 1996, he served in various senior positions in the Ministry of National Development overseeing urban and transport planning in Singapore. He holds a Bachelors degree in civil engineering from Queen's University, Canada and a Masters degree in Transportation from Birmingham University, United Kingdom.

TAN Ern Ser is Academic Adviser, Institute of Policy Studies Social Lab, and Associate Professor of Sociology, National University of Singapore. He received his PhD in Sociology from Cornell University, USA. He is author of "Does Class Matter?" (2004) and "Class and Social Orientations" (2015). He is also co-investigator of Asian Barometer-Singapore, World Values Survey-Singapore, and the Singapore Panel Study on Social Dynamics. Ern Ser has served as research consultant to government ministries. He is Research Adviser, Ministry of Social and Family Development, and Chairman, Research Advisory Panel, HDB. He was appointed a Justice of the Peace in 2013.

TAN Puay Yok is an Associate Professor in the Department of Architecture at the National University of Singapore. Prior to joining the academia, Puay Yok held senior positions in public service in the areas of urban greenery management, policies and research. His research, teaching and professional activities focus on the policies, science, and practices of urban greening and ecology of the built environment. In addition to teaching and research, he also serves in the editorial board of a number of international journals, as a reviewer for national and internal grants, jury member for design competitions and as advisory committee member for a number of land use developments in Singapore.

TAN Yong Soon is an Adjunct Professor at the Lee Kuan Yew School of Public Policy, National University of Singapore. Prior to his retirement from the Singapore Public Service in October 2012 after over 35 years of service, he has held appointments of Permanent Secretary (National Climate Change) in the Prime Minister's Office, Permanent Secretary in the Ministry of the Environment and Water Resources, Deputy Secretary in the Ministry of Finance, Deputy Secretary in the Ministry of Defence, CEO of the Urban Redevelopment Authority and Principal Private Secretary to the Prime Minister.

TANG Hsiao Ling is the Director of Land Planning Division of JTC Corporation, Singapore's leading industrial infrastructure specialist spearheading the planning, promotion and development of a dynamic industrial landscape. The Land Planning Division focuses on master planning for industrial developments, planning for redevelopment of existing sites, development of innovative solutions and products, and devising land use policies which optimise land use. Hsiao Ling graduated with a Bachelor's degree in Arts (Architecture) from The University of Sheffield in 2000 and a Diploma in Architecture from the University College London in 2004.

TAY Kheng Soon, Adjunct Professor and architect, is from the first cohort of locally-trained architects, graduating in 1963 from the Singapore Polytechnic which later relocated to NUS. As such, he is acutely concerned that architecture and the living environment must be rooted in climate and culture while modernising and humanising. He thus became Chairman of SPUR and later president of SIA, receiving its Gold Medal in 2010. His design research extends beyond architectural scale to urban planning and finally to the global scale. The Maximally Deployable Modular City of the 21st Century uploaded on YouTube.com is his latest output.

WONG Mun Summ is the co-Founding Director of WOHA, an internationally-acclaimed architectural practice in Singapore. WOHA received the 2007 Aga Khan Award for Architecture for their first tropical high-rise tower, 1 Moulmein Rise in Singapore and more recently, the 2015 CTBUH Urban Habitat Award, for PARKROYAL on Pickering hotel. WOHA are currently exhibiting an invited, solo exhibition at The Skyscraper Museum in New York until September 2016. They are also participating at the 2016 Venice Architectural Biennale. In conjunction with their installation in Venice, WOHA has launched a new book, titled *GARDEN CITY MEGA CITY*, which shares strategies for the burgeoning mega cities of the tropical belt. A travelling exhibition devoted exclusively to their works opened at the Deutsches Architekturmuseum, Germany, in December 2011, and four substantial monographs—*WOHA: The Architecture of WOHA*; *WOHA: Selected Projects (Vol. 1 and 2)*; and *WOHA: Breathing Architecture*—have already been published.

Alina YEO has been associated with WOHA for the past 12 years. She first joined WOHA as an intern in 2002 before returning permanently upon completion of her Master of Architecture in 2005 from the National University of Singapore and was made Associate in October 2014. Alina's portfolio with WOHA encompasses design and project management, including institutional and high-rise condominiums. She was instrumental in the design of the School of the Arts, has authored numerous published papers and leads in many of WOHA's design competitions, monographic exhibitions, research work and building contract matters.

Philip YEO is the Chairman of SPRING (Standards, Productivity and Innovation for Growth) Singapore whose mission is to enable and grow local small and medium enterprises. In 2013, he set up Economic Development Innovations Singapore (EDIS), a company which plans, develops, and manages overseas Technology Parks. He is the Chairman of several companies, including Hexagon Development Advisors, which provides economic and industrial development advice to overseas governments and government-related entities. From 2010 to 2013, Mr Yeo served as a member of the United Nations Committee of Experts in Public Administration, which promotes and develops public administration and governance among Member States. He was formerly Chairman of the Agency for Science, Technology & Research (A*STAR) and of the Economic Development Board. He has previously served as Senior Adviser for Science and Technology in the Ministry of Trade & Industry, and Special Advisor for Economic Development in the Prime Minister's Office.

YEO Su-Jan is a researcher, writer, and collaborator on contemporary urban topics. Su-Jan completed her Ph.D. in Architecture from the National University of Singapore where she is currently a Research Associate at the School of Design and Environment. She is a recipient of the Rotary Foundation Ambassadorial Scholarship (2004–2005), National University of Singapore Research Scholarship (2009–2013), and World Future Foundation Ph.D. Prize (2014). Su-Jan has published in peer-reviewed journals that include *Urban Studies*, *Town Planning Review*, and *International Development Planning Review*. Prior to her academic work, Su-Jan was an urban planner at the Urban Redevelopment Authority in Singapore.

Contents

Foreword   v
Preface   vii
About the Editor   xiii
About the Contributors   xv

Part 1   **Paradigms, Policies & Processes**   **1**

Chapter 1   The Early Years of Nation-Building: Reflections
                      on Singapore's Urban History   3
                      Alan F. C. Choe

Chapter 2   Planning & Urbanisation in Singapore: A 50-Year Journey   23
                      Liu Thai Ker

Chapter 3   Economic Planning for Productivity, Growth,
                      and Prosperity   45
                      Philip Yeo

Chapter 4   Environmental Planning for Sustainable Development   59
                      Tan Yong Soon

Part 2   **The Built Environment as a Sum of Parts**   **69**

Chapter 5   Planning to Overcome the Constraints of Scarcity   71
                      Ng Lang

Chapter 6   Making Singapore a Liveable and Sustainable City:
                      Our Urban Systems Approach   81
                      Khoo Teng Chye and Remy Guo

Chapter 7   The Evolution of HDB Towns   101
                      Cheong Koon Hean

Chapter 8   Transportation: Mobility, Accessibility, and Connectivity   127
              Mohinder Singh

Chapter 9   Industry Planning in Singapore   153
              Tang Hsiao Ling

Chapter 10   Greening Singapore: Past Achievements, Emerging Challenges   177
              Tan Puay Yok

Chapter 11   50 Years of Urban Planning & Tourism   197
              Pamelia Lee

Chapter 12   Shaping Singapore's Cityscape Through Urban Design   211
              Goh Hup Chor & Heng Chye Kiang

Part 3   Urban Complexities & Creative Solutions   235

Chapter 13   Conserving Urban Heritage: Remembering
              the Past in a Developmental City-State   237
              Lily Kong

Chapter 14   Public Housing and Community Development:
              Planning for Urban Diversity in a City-State   257
              Tan Ern Ser

Chapter 15   Era of Globalisation: Singapore's New Urban Economy
              and the Rise of a World Asian City   273
              Ho Kong Chong

Chapter 16   Towards Greater Sustainability and Liveability in an Urban Age   287
              Heng Chye Kiang and Yeo Su-Jan

**Epilogue   Perspectives on the Future of Urban Planning
              in Singapore   305**

              Challenges for a New Era   307
              Peter Ho

A City in Time for the Future   309
Low Teck Seng

Singapore: The Smartest City on Our Planet   311
Kishore Mahbubani

People-Centric Approach to Urban Planning   313
David Chan

Singapore: From Liveable to Lovable City   315
Melissa Kwee

Accommodating Nature in Singapore   317
Shawn Lum

Garden City Mega City   319
Wong Mun Summ and Alina Yeo

Top Down Bottom Up?   321
Tay Kheng Soon

Part 1
Paradigms, Policies & Processes

CHAPTER 1

The Early Years of Nation-Building: Reflections on Singapore's Urban History

Alan F. C. Choe

Introduction

Singapore has one of the most striking and ever-evolving skylines in the world, created through a process of rapid urban development (Figure 1). In the short span of 50 years, the city-state has transformed from a third world to a modern global city. Today, Singapore ranks as one of the top 10 most livable cities in the world. Singapore's success in urban development and infrastructure efficiency has also elevated the nation's position as a desirable country for economic development, coupled with sound economic policies and a stable political environment, thus spurring greater urbanisation and development.

This transformation from a "fishing village" to a modern world-class metropolitan city was beyond the imaginations of many, given, some 50 years ago, slums and squatter settlements were rampant. Lack of modern sanitation in tandem with poor public health and safety standards were then the norm. Today, we often take for granted the privileges of health, safety, and modern conveniences that include an accessible and operational mass rapid transit (MRT) system at our fingertips. It is therefore useful to reflect where we came from and the progress Singapore has made in a post-independence era. Today's Singapore, particularly our model of urbanisation, is the envy of many countries.

This chapter is an attempt at reflecting the history of Singapore's early years, when extremely poor living conditions were part and parcel of the everyday urban experience. Improving such dire living conditions involved intense struggles and passionate efforts towards modernisation and urbanisation. The strategies, methods, and improvisations for urban development needed to compensate for the lack of readily available resources and information on the subject as televisions, publications, and the Internet were non-existent then. By shedding light on our trials and tribulations, it is hoped that the experiences of my generation will offer some useful and thought-provoking considerations for future successive generations.

3

Figure 1.   Singapore's modern urban skyline featuring Marina Bay and the Central Business District.

Source: Urban Redevelopment Authority.

In this chapter, I would like to explore how urban planning was introduced to Singapore during the colonial era and why urban renewal was incorporated into the nation-building process following Singapore's independence. This moment of urban change was led by the clear vision and determination of fearless political leaders and government officials. Through cooperation, innovation and courage, a city was developed and a nation built in two generations. In order to value the fruits of this labour we must start at the beginning.

The Colonial Legacy: An Urban Story of Inheritance and Loss

The story of Singapore's urban history traditionally begins with the arrival of Sir Stamford Raffles in 1819 and the strategic establishment of the island into a colonial entrepôt serving the Straits Settlements trade route. During this 140-year colonial reign, the British rulers sought to imprint their Eurocentric urban planning principles on the physical terrain of Singapore. Under the colonial administration, Singapore inherited a development strategy that favoured a system of planning to promote economic development and bolster development growth. Thus, Singapore's earliest detailed town plan (1822) (Figure 2), prepared through a Town Planning Committee formed by Sir Stamford Raffles and led by Lieutenant Philip Jackson, served as the blueprint for the spatial organisation of the future town of Singapore.

The "Plan of the Town of Singapore", as the planning document was called, set forth three proposals for the layout of the new settlement sited at the gateway of the Singapore River. Firstly, a gridiron street pattern was imposed on the land as a means of inculcating a rational sense of uniformity and orderliness. Land was then subsequently divided into narrow lots which private individuals could purchase on a freehold basis or on a leasehold term of up to 999 years, as was the liberal policy then towards land ownership and tenure. Construction at the time consisted mainly of low-rise shop-house-style buildings of one- to two-storeys with commerce permitted on the ground

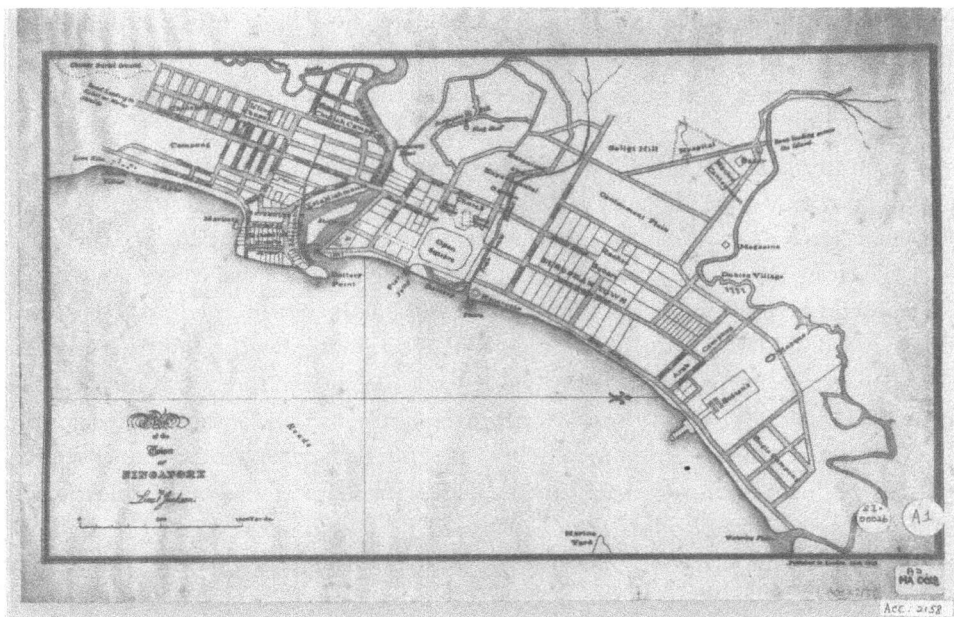

Figure 2.   Plan of the Town of Singapore, 1822.
Source: Survey Department Collection, Courtesy of National Archives of Singapore.

floor to support the expanding mercantile activities along the Singapore River. Secondly, land was assigned functional specialisation with areas carved out for administrative, educational, recreational, and religious activities. This initial zoning of land led to the provision of infrastructure and amenities such as civic institutions, schools, and parks for use by the growing numbers of Europeans settling in Singapore. These places, however, ostracised the local inhabitants. Thirdly, and in relation to the local populace, the town plan concentrated and segregated the various racial and ethnic groups into designated residential enclaves. Some enclaves, such as Chinatown, were further divided according to clan dialects with the Hokkien, Teochew, and Cantonese communities occupying various parts of the Chinese district.

The ethnic enclaves created social and spatial divisions; at the same time, they attracted newly-arrived migrants who naturally gravitated to areas that resembled the familiarities and kinship of their homelands. These migrant settlements soon became more and more populated as demand for labour coincided with Singapore's growth from a fledgling trading outpost to a major commercial seaport. In the early days of development, a massive influx of foreign capital and enterprising immigrants entered Singapore, thereby contributing further to the acceleration of economic growth and transforming a once sleepy town into a bustling city. During this growth period, Singapore inherited from the colonial predecessors a modern system of planning which laid the foundations for urban development. The colonial legacy also included the inheritance of a physical morphology characterised by its fine-grained compact urban fabric and a human-scaled streetscape consisting of low-rise shophouse architecture.

A century later, the urban scene in Singapore became a stark contrast of its early days. By the 1920s, the city core (Central Area) was experiencing severe issues of residential overcrowding, poor sanitation, and street congestion. Many European settlers were relocating from the Central Area to the outlying urban fringe, where larger estate homes could be built in more open space settings. This transition led to the gradual blurring of boundaries and overlapping of functional zones within the Central Area, as earlier settlement patterns conformed less and less to the intentions of the 1822 town plan. In 1927, the Singapore Improvement Trust (SIT) was formed by the British colonial administration to help with progressive environmental improvements such as the introduction of backlanes—for service maintenance and collection of refuse—between shophouses that once existed back-to-back. The SIT was later granted greater authority to build low-cost public housing, the first being the Tiong Bahru Estate in the 1930s. However, the SIT did not produce sufficient numbers of units to mitigate the rising need for adequate housing made more acute following the Pacific War (1941–45). Urban conditions in the Central Area dramatically worsened.

The shophouse, which was designed to accommodate a single household, was partitioned into smaller living quarters which, in many cases, were further subdivided into cubicles and sublet by tenants or the landlord. This practice of absorbing multiple families in shophouses, many of which had been indiscriminately altered with extensions and additions, resulted in severe overcrowding. These densities ranged from 1,200 to 1,700 people per hectare with occasional instances of densities on some blocks reaching approximately 2,500 people per hectare (Chua, 1989). The overcrowding situation severely aggravated the health and safety of those living in the dilapidated shophouses. Ironically, the Rent Control Act of 1947, which sought to protect tenants from exorbitant rental increases arising from the acute shortage of housing following the Pacific War, contributed to the physical deterioration of buildings as landlords were no longer incentivised to maintain and upkeep their properties. Elsewhere, slums and squatter settlements were proliferating in open spaces where salvaged materials such as *attap* leaves, corrugated iron sheets, and wooden planks were used in the construction of makeshift dwellings and ancillary spaces for unregulated businesses. These unauthorised developments posed tremendous risks to the inhabitants and the surrounding environment, especially when activities involving the use of fire, such as cooking, could not be properly contained and controlled.

It became increasingly obvious to the colonial government that Singapore's urban situation would spiral into a vicious cycle unless an intervention was made to regulate growth and development. This intervention was introduced in the form of the

Singapore Improvement Ordinance (1952), which required the SIT to convene a work team that would carry out a detailed island-wide survey to help guide future development. The study was conducted over a period of three years, after which the team produced a Preliminary Island Plan (1955). This draft plan, which was conceptualised by colonial officers at the time, was based mainly on British town-planning practice and was predicated on assumptions of slow managed growth. In terms of land use, the draft plan proposed to retain a clear distinction between the core functions of the Central Area for industrial purposes and peripheral functions of outlying suburbs for self-contained residential communities. The draft plan also favoured low-rise buildings over high-rise constructions, citing cost and traffic congestion as liabilities. The draft plan was further refined and formally approved in 1958 as the Master Plan (Figure 3)—Singapore's first statutory land use document.

The 1958 Master Plan provided a comprehensive island-wide development framework for a projected population of two million in 1972, by identifying three new town sites in Jurong, Woodlands, and Yio Chu Kang as well as prescribing maximum permissible net residential densities (in persons per acre) for planning districts within the Central Area. The architects and planners of the 1958 Master

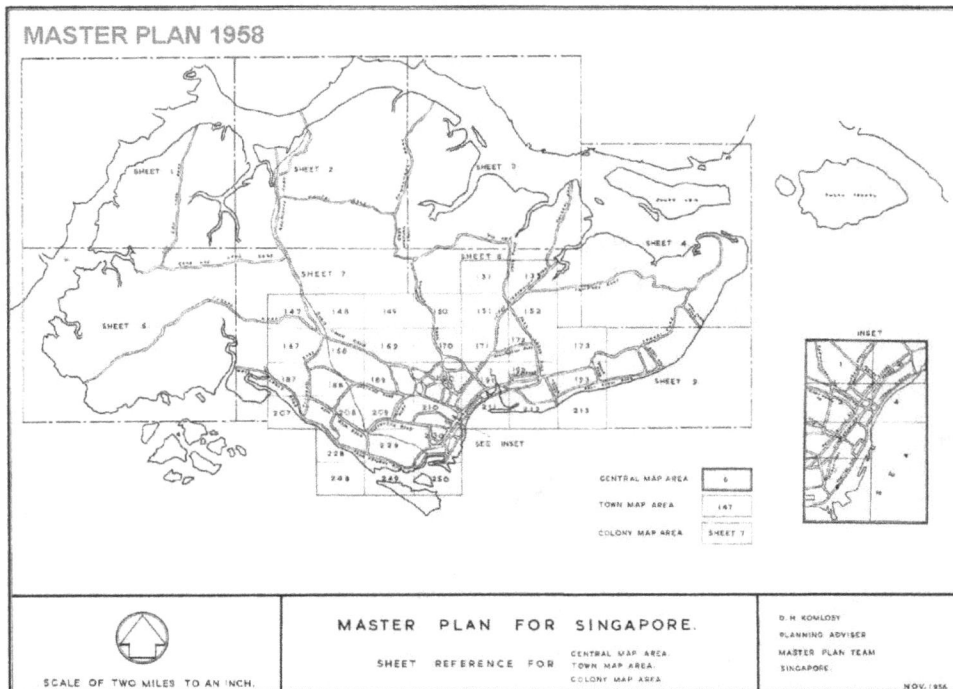

Figure 3. 1958 Master Plan—Singapore's first statutory land use plan.
Source: Urban Redevelopment Authority.

Plan, however, did not anticipate that Singapore's rate of growth would quickly outnumber their projections, nor did they envision the series of political developments that would alter the course of Singapore's colonial history and consequentially pave the path towards full independence as a Republic.

The Road to Independence: Challenges and Opportunities

In 1959, I returned from my architectural and town planning studies in Melbourne to Singapore at a time of transitional change. Singapore had achieved status as a self-ruling State through a democratically-elected government in 1959. The newly-established government was confronted with several major challenges, but the focus on three key priorities would set the stage for Singapore's breakaway from poverty and disorder. The first and most immediate priority was to resolve the acute housing problem. The SIT could only manage an average of 1,700 housing units per year during the post-war period when the population had already exceeded one million (Teh, 1969). A new institution named the Housing and Development Board (HDB) was therefore created in 1960 to replace the SIT.

Secondly, Singapore could no longer depend on her natural hinterland or rely solely on her regional port activities for sustained economic stability as more land was required to accommodate the growing population. In addition, unemployment was on the rise, resulting in a burgeoning informal sector comprised of itinerant hawkers and petty traders working in precarious conditions (Figure 4). Economic advancement therefore

Figure 4.   Illegal hawkers and traders once plied the streets of Chinatown (left). A specially-designed shopping environment at People's Park Complex, a URA sale of site development, provided modern facilities for vendors (right).

Source: Urban Redevelopment Authority.

became a priority which set in motion the creation of a statutory board, the Economic Development Board (EDB), in 1961. As I will later illustrate, there was to be great strategic cooperation between the domains of urban planning and economic development that helped spur Singapore's progress from third world conditions to a developed nation.

Lastly, when Singapore gained full independence as a Republic in 1965 following her separation from Malaysia, the newly-established government led by then Prime Minister Lee Kuan Yew focused on nation-building for a population that was approaching two million. Paradoxically, this pressure drove the government to new heights of courage such that opportunities could be grasped and bold visions adopted, in this way, allowing dynamic and effective changes to ensue. In the next section, I relate my experiences on three bold urban programmes that I believe paved a critical path for Singapore's transformation and modernisation.

A Young Nation with Bold Urban Plans

In Singapore's early years as a young nation, there were hardly any trained architects. For the most part, the transfer of design and planning knowledge was passed down from colonial administrators to local technicians and draftsmen. When the SIT dissolved upon the establishment of the HDB, a large number of British architects and town planners left Singapore. However, a small cohort of freshly-qualified architects had just returned to Singapore. I also returned along with this cohort as a graduate of architecture and town planning, and I initially joined a private architecture firm where I was seeking to develop my professional career. Shortly after, however, I was headhunted and invited to join HDB in 1962 as I happened to be the first and only architect then with town planning qualifications in Singapore.

A dynamic team was appointed by the government to steer the newly-established HDB. The team included Lim Kim San (HDB's first Chairman) and Howe Yoon Chong (HDB's first CEO), both of whom were neither architects nor planners. Moreover, Lim Kim San and Howe Yoon Chong had no prior building experience nor a successor from whom they could take over the reins of SIT's public housing mandate. But they were courageous visionary leaders with strategic ideas. Under their directorship, I was empowered to carry out bold and sweeping public housing programmes, new town developments, and urban planning ideas never before experimented in Singapore or elsewhere. Although faced with immense challenges, I was emboldened by the fact that we were all learning together without recourse to sources of information and we had to improvise and devise our own strategies and methods. My only advantage is that I was the only one trained in city planning then.

My initial HDB experience was daunting, as the responsibilities borne were unlike other earlier duties I had held in town planning. The overseas training that I underwent involved the planning of only small European towns with populations of 10,000 to 30,000 people. At HDB, one is thrust into real world conditions with national implications—this proved to be a tremendous learning curve. The real world conditions of Singapore then were indeed extraordinary and a far cry from any of the case studies I encountered in my University studies. Information on public housing was sparse then, as few cities in the world had embarked on such daring and massive public housing initiatives.

Public Housing: Reinventing the Way-of-Living

Immediately after its formation, HDB was tasked with not only eradicating chronic overcrowding by clearing slums and substandard dwellings in the Central Area, but also providing permanent homes for people affected by resettlement as well as for future population growth (Figure 5). Upon surveying the extent of the housing problem, HDB assessed that 147,000 dwelling units (some of which would include market housing built by the private sector) would be required to meet their objectives by 1970 (Yeung, 1973). Thus began an ambitious 10-year programme with a target of over 50,000 public housing units to be constructed within the first Five-Year Plan between 1960 and 1965. Recognising the severity of the housing shortage, HDB delivered basic accommodation with speed and quantity without compromising on liveability such that, by the end of 1965, the target figure was exceeded with the completion of nearly 55,000 public housing units (Ibid).

How did HDB achieve the construction of a maximum number of units in minimum time and with the least cost? Firstly, by constructing larger numbers of small units of one- and two-room flats, HDB was able to meet the housing demands in terms of quantity. Secondly, by standardising the floor plans as well as sourcing for affordable and easy-to-assemble construction materials, HDB not only saved on construction time but also cost. The second Five-Year Plan concluded in 1970, raising the total stock of public housing units under the management of HDB to over 118,000 (Ibid). In those years, attention to fanciful communal facilities and architectural design details was a luxury that speed and monetary constraints simply did not permit, but that was to change as Singapore progressed and advanced with experience and confidence gained. Today, HDB has pushed the frontier for public housing and estate planning through demonstration projects such as Treelodge@Punggol and Pinnacle@Duxton which feature environmental design elements and the integration of public facilities for social, recreational, and commercial activities.

Urban Renewal: A Formula for Conservation, Rehabilitation, and Rebuilding

My initial years at HDB were steeped in the design of prototype public housing units and planning and development of new towns that included Queenstown

Figure 5.   Poor, unhealthy, and dangerous living conditions of a slum quarter in Singapore's early history (top). New HDB one- or two-room flats offered to families affected by resettlement (bottom).
Source: Urban Redevelopment Authority.

and Toa Payoh, both iconic public housing projects through which I gained much experience. The government and HDB soon realised that providing public housing alone, however, cannot completely eradicate the acute source of poor housing and living conditions. Slums and squatters had to be cleared. But such actions could only be undertaken when sufficient public housing was available to adequately resettle affected residents.

The Singapore government, through the auspices of the United Nations Development Programme (UNDP), deployed Erik E. Lorange in 1962 as an expert to evaluate Singapore's readiness for urban renewal. Being the only trained architect and town planner at the time, I was again tasked by HDB to study, shadow, and assist Lorange in his three-month study in Singapore. At the end of his review, Lorange submitted a report to the government outlining Singapore's readiness to embark on an urban renewal programme.

In 1963, a second UNDP team of three experts in urban renewal visited Singapore after the government accepted Lorange's report. The three experts were Otto Koenigsberger, an architect-planner, Charles Abrains, a legal advisor on land issues, and Susumu Kobe, a traffic economist. At my request, I was given two more architects to study and assist the three experts. Despite the short two-month stay, they were able to outline a report with the boundaries of the central areas to be renewed. Accordingly, in 1964, HDB formed an Urban Renewal Unit and I was tasked to head this special unit. As the importance of slum clearance and urban renewal gained momentum, the Urban Renewal Unit upgraded two years later to a full-fledged Urban Renewal Department (URD) within HDB. The URD was responsible for undertaking land requisition, resettlement, urban renewal, conservation, and sale of sites for private development.

To better understand how urban renewal was carried out in the developed world, I embarked on study trips to Britain, Germany, Japan, and the United States. Other than the United States, the other countries barely carried out or experimented with urban renewal. The American urban renewal experience was the most revealing; here, urban renewal received harsh domestic criticisms for its blatant demolition of buildings and indiscriminate destruction of neighbourhoods that resulted in the displacement of people, for its development of urban ghettos, and a non-transparent sale of sites process for private development. Returning to Singapore, I prepared a report with strong convictions that Singapore would need to approach urban renewal in a different fashion from that which I had witnessed in the United States. Singapore had to create her own formula of urban renewal—a formula of sensitive clearance, resettlement, conservation, rehabilitation, and careful sale of land for private participation and rebuilding.

Government Land Sales: Private Participation and Economic Development

In order for urban renewal to be impactful at a comprehensive level, contiguous parcels of land needed to be transferred legally to the government, cleared, and re-parcelled for redevelopment opportunities. However, much of the land in the Central Area was subdivided under the earlier colonial planning system into many small narrow lots that were individually owned by private persons. This fragmented patchwork of proprietorship complicated the process of land purchase and clearance. Hence, the Land Acquisitions Act, which was legislated in 1966, enabled the government to acquire private land, in support of national development programmes, at market value compensation to the owner. Within the Central Area, two precincts better known as South 1 (bounded by Havelock Road, Outram Road, and New Bridge Road) and North 1 (bounded by Crawford Street, Beach Road, Jalan Sultan, and Victoria Street/Kallang Road), served as pilot sites for land acquisition and urban renewal.

One of the earliest land parcels to be redeveloped for public housing for resettlement was the former Outram Prison site situated at the foot of Pearl's Hill in precinct South 1 (Figure 6). Built during the colonial period, Outram Prison served as the largest penitentiary facility until the construction of Changi Prison in 1936. Given the prime real estate on which Outram Prison was situated and the urgency faced by a young nation to allocate land in the Central Area for housing resettlement, the rational decision then was to transfer the functions of Outram Prison to a location outside the Central Area and to develop the site for higher intensity residential use. In 1966, the Queenstown Remand Prison was constructed to replace Outram Prison and, with the site freed up, HDB proceeded to develop 1,000 public housing flats and a multi-storey shopping complex at Outram Road specifically to resettle a whole community cleared from People's Park (Figure 6). Other sites in precincts South 1 and North 1 were identified for redevelopment potential. By 1968, 85% of the land in South 1 and North 1 had been acquired for public redevelopment, which resulted in

Figure 6. Outram Prison (left) occupying a strategic site was relocated to make way for development of public housing and shops (right) for a whole community affected by URA's resettlement programme.

Source: Urban Redevelopment Authority.

the completion of 3,200 units of flats and shops with a further 3,000 units under construction (Choe, 1969) for resettlement and private development.

Following the success of the South 1 and North 1 pilot projects, the subsequent planning strategy was to redevelop the Central Area in phases. Thus, 15 precincts were demarcated with seven precincts north of the Singapore River and Central area (North 1 to North 7) and eight precincts south of the central business district (CBD) (South 1 to South 8). The strategy was to develop progressively the less complicated parcels of land at the fringes and advance towards the more challenging sites within the Central Area. In particular, the strategic location of the Central Area called for a variety of commercial buildings that would promote economic development. Such projects needed to be viable in order to attract private participation, which was vital to the success of urban renewal. In this way, private participation in commercial developments allowed the government to concentrate mainly on public infrastructure projects such as public housing.

For a long time, however, the fragmented subdivision of land, with narrow frontages for shophouses with multiple ownerships, prevented private development of any significant value to be built on such plots. The private sector is unable to buy, assemble and clear such small lots into sizeable plots of significant projects. Only the government, through the URD, can acquire, clear, and assemble such small plots into sizeable parcels for major commercial projects. In addition to making available amalgamated land, the URD also offered incentives—such as reduced property tax, easy repayment of land cost, and accelerated approval of plans—to attract private sector participation. The URD also embarked on publicity campaigns to educate the public on the needs and opportunities of urban renewal.

In 1967, 14 sale sites on 99-year leases in the Central Area were selected and launched publically for tender to the private sector (Choe, 1969). The first sale site, incidentally, was made available as a result of a fire in 1966 which destroyed an open-air makeshift market that once occupied the grounds we know today as People's Park Complex. People's Park Complex—the first mixed-use podium and tower block construction in Singapore, opened in 1973—was designed and developed by private enterprises following a successful tender bid for the site. In determining the land use for such sale sites, the URD consulted readily with the Planning Department. Right from the beginning, the URD was to not only clear slums and rebuild the CBD but also to generate economic development. Hence, projects offered to the private sector had to warrant demand in and of itself, which also ensured the success of the private sector. As such, the EDB was consulted to ascertain industry trends and market demands which could be developed to spur economic growth. Projects identified for the 14 sale sites ranged from hotels and shopping complexes to offices and residential apartments. By 1973, this initial pilot scheme led to further successive sales, resulting in a total of 45 sites released through the tender system and attracting $466 million worth of investments (Chew, 1973). It soon became clear that, as the number of sale sites amplified in conjunction with the rapid pace of urban renewal, the URD's workload would not only outgrow its staff but the scope of work would also diverge more and more from the mandate of HDB.

I was convinced that the URD needed greater independence and flexibility in order to effectively and efficiently implement urban renewal programmes beyond the current scale and pace; thus, I began to advocate for the URD's autonomy. Accordingly in 1974, the government established the Urban Redevelopment Authority (URA) to become a statutory board under the Ministry of National Development (MND). I was appointed as the first General Manager of the newly-formed URA, where I intended to serve a brief term after I had completed setting up the rules, procedures, and launch of the first three sale of sites. Thereafter, my intention was to return to private practice. However, I agreed to stay at the request of the Board and I continued on as General Manager of the URA until my resignation in 1978.

The Significant Role of URA and HDB

The government's sale of sites programme for private development was the most important and significant instrument in promoting Singapore's urban development as well as economic growth. Under this initiative, URA would identify potential sites then acquire, clear, and assemble the sites into substantial parcels for major developments. URA would also conduct research on market demands for particular commercial projects that would contribute to Singapore's economic growth—for example, promoting tourism by building hotels or generating financial services by constructing offices. In addition, URA would lay down very specific planning and design requirements for each parcel of land sold. The sale of sites programme by URA also offers much financial incentive to attract bidders for the sites.

The tender documents clearly stipulate that, aside from the price offered, the URA panel also places great emphasis on the design when deciding on the winner of a tender bid. In this way, the process aims to promote good design, nurture and help discover talented architects, as well as educate developers to appreciate good designs. The sales programme sprouted a new generation of designs never before seen in Singapore at that time. For example, the first sale of sites resulted in the People's Park Complex (the first large multi-use building with a large atrium) and three large international class hotels on Havelock Road. Subsequent sales resulted in strikingly large and well-designed high-rise buildings of various commercial and residential types in the precincts of Golden Mile, Central Business District (Figure 7), and Shenton Way (Figure 8).

Figure 7.   The early launches of URA's sale of sites programme introduced skyscrapers and modern architectural styles to Singapore's urban skyline. International Plaza in the Tanjong Pagar district (left). OCBC Building in the Raffles Place district (right).

Source: Urban Redevelopment Authority.

Figure 8.   Shenton Way before URA commenced a major sale of sites effort to create a Financial Centre (left). Shenton Way after redevelopment gave rise to six modern well-designed office towers along a stretch of former warehouse sites (right).

Source: Urban Redevelopment Authority.

Since its inception, URA has operated independently and alongside the Planning Department (then under the Prime Minister's Office) and Research and Statistics Unit (under MND) to carry out the multifaceted work of nation-building. Over time, however, there was stronger impetus for the centralisation and streamlining of planning, development control, sale of sites, and conservation functions that resulted in the merger of the URA, Planning Department, and Research & Statistics Unit. Maintaining the name Urban Redevelopment Authority (URA), the new statutory board became operational in 1989.

URA and HDB were and still are significant organisations that have contributed directly to Singapore's urban development. The striking, attractive, and dramatic skyline bears testimony to our very rapid growth, elevating Singapore to one of the most liveable cities in the world.

Long-term Planning for the Future: Genesis of the 1971 Concept Plan

Most of the discussion thus far has dealt with the intricacies of Central Area redevelopment and urban renewal. On a grander scale, planning in Singapore is also an island-wide endeavour. In order to ensure optimal and judicious use of limited land resources to accommodate future economic and population growth, Singapore has systematised a comprehensive and long-range guiding plan for island-wide development. In 1967, a Plan of Operation was signed between the Singapore government and the UNDP for the preparation of a Concept Plan under an initiative called the State and City Planning Project (SCP).

The SCP drew from the expertise of a multidisciplinary team comprising the HDB, Planning Department, Public Works Department, and the assistance of the United Nations. In 1969, the SCP released a draft Concept Plan that made Singapore's approach to planning more strategic and forward-looking, gradually supplanting an otherwise piecemeal and corrective stance towards nation-building. The draft Concept Plan proposed a long-term vision for the allocation of land and investment of infrastructure, thus providing strategic directions for the physical development of Singapore over a 20-year forecast. After two years of further refinements—which included a special topics study carried out by the URD for the preparation of a Central Area Structural Concept Plan that would extend on the island-wide scheme—the Concept Plan was adopted by the government in 1971.

The 1971 Concept Plan (Figure 9) mapped out a vision for the future development of Singapore that can be abstractly represented as a 'ring' pattern of self-sufficient new towns encircling the green Central Catchment area and an East-West corridor along the southern coast of Singapore connecting major employment hubs such as Changi Airport (East), Central Business District (Central Area), and Jurong Industrial Estates (West). The 1971 Concept Plan imparted three urban growth strategies which, today, are visible components of Singapore's physical landscape. Firstly, in terms of spatial organisation, the 1971 Concept Plan promoted a form of urban development and expansion structured around a ring pattern of circulation. This ring helped to ensure the safeguarding of land for essential transportation infrastructure such as the island-wide expressway system, MRT network, and Changi

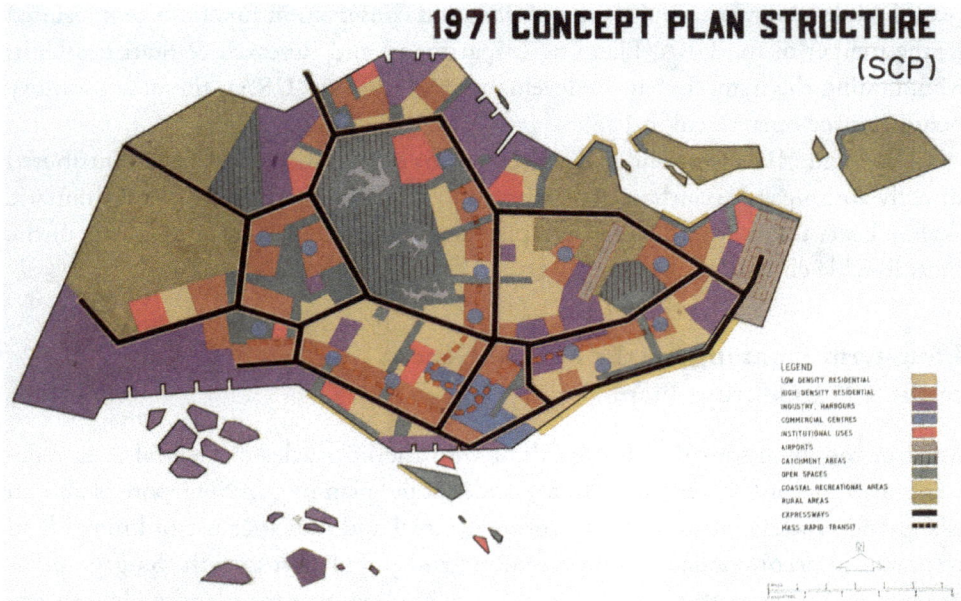

Figure 9.   1971 Concept Plan.
Source: Urban Redevelopment Authority.

Airport. Secondly, the nodes along the ring provided a spatial framework for the integrated planning of major land use sectors, namely, high-density residential areas served by commercial centers, industrial estates, and green spaces, resulting in the coherent development of self-sufficient new towns. Thirdly, the 1971 Concept Plan identified the Central Area—situated at the historic city centre and where the two proposed MRT lines would intersect—as a significant commercial hub for business and financial activities, which then prompted the series of urban renewal programmes described earlier.

The 1971 Concept Plan laid the necessary foundations for Singapore's growth and promoted a rational planning approach based on grounded calculations and population forecasting. Thereafter, subsequent reviews of the Concept Plan would be undertaken every 10 years to build successively upon the broad strategies and development policies of earlier Concept Plans. With each new version of the Concept Plan, we learn more about our past and, in turn, this learning creates new lessons for our future.

Today, URA has evolved its capacity to include many new functions relating to land development and control. At the same time, URA is continuing the essential traditions of its predecessor by identifying and conserving architectural heritage while also charting the urban future of Singapore by building on the successes of earlier plans. The 1971 Concept Plan is the earliest long-term land use plan whose foundational principles continue to manifest in the physical landscape of Singapore. The story of Singapore's urban history, therefore, would be incomplete without illustrating the contribution of the 1971 Concept Plan—a hallmark blueprint and a keystone in the making of modern Singapore at that time. The URA of today, comprising a highly developed and extremely talented team, has adopted an action oriented plan that can quickly adapt to the ever-changing demands and needs of society and businesses but with careful consideration on long term land use, availability of land, and population and economic growth.

Conclusion: Lessons from the Past are Lessons for the Future

Singapore's rapid progress of nation-building and urban development is the envy of many countries. Within 50 short years as an independent city-state, Singapore has developed into a global hub with modern amenities rivalling advanced urban economies such as Hong Kong, London, and New York. Today's image of Singapore, however, is a sharp contrast against the Singapore of yesteryear. That a small island-nation emerged from near destitute urban conditions to become one of the world's wealthiest countries is indeed a remarkable feat involving cooperation, innovation, and courage. It is these three qualities that, time and time again, resonate in the story of Singapore's urban history.

Cooperation was a vital work ethic during an era of limited financial resources and scarce knowledge capital. In those days, government agencies learnt to adopt a consultative and collaborative attitude towards their counterparts in the public sector. By leveraging on the multidisciplinary skills of civil servants and sharing knowledge across agency lines, a whole-of-government approach to planning was formulated so as to achieve the best all-round results on public projects for which many lives and multiple stakeholders were affected.

In the early years, innovation was rampant despite the lack of resources, due to the necessity for functional housing, amenities, proper sanitation, and efficient traffic circulation. Such urgent matters served as a powerful driving force for advancements in planning. Much of the innovation was derived by way of studying and learning from precedents. Public housing, for example, has gone through a series of design innovations with each new era producing better improvements over the previous one. During my initial years with HDB, I studied the early generation of SIT flats in housing estates such as Tiong Bahru where kitchens and lavatories were communal facilities shared by multiple households in the one-room units built. The HDB flats that immediately superseded the SIT flats were not only much taller buildings, in order to maximise the use of land, but also designed such that each dwelling unit was equipped with its own private kitchen and lavatory as a result of changing social demographics. Such quantum leaps continued as public housing evolved over the decades with the introduction of the Build-to-Order and Design, Build, and Sell schemes.

Courage has served as the resilient axle for every pivotal turning point in Singapore's urban history. The courage to draw up ambitious visions and bring to reality bold urban plans through committed implementation enabled Singapore to overcome challenge after challenge. In the early years, such courage stemmed from strong political will, good governance, and pragmatic foresight, which were instrumental in gaining public support for projects that at first seemed too radical and ahead of their time. Projects such as high-rise living in HDB flats, acquisition of private land for urban renewal, and transportation by means of the MRT network were initially confronted with public hesitation and scrutiny. However, through sound planning, rational goals, and testing of pilot studies, the government sought the support and confidence of the public. In this respect, it could be said that Singapore's pioneer generation visibly wore courage on their sleeves.

Singapore's path was paved 50 years ago with clear intentions and ambitions. The direction of Singapore's progress and development was charted early on, allowing key action programmes to be identified and swiftly carried out: eradicate poverty; provide safe and permanent housing for the masses; revitalise the city centre; and inject new economic opportunities that would simultaneously create jobs and raise the employment rate. In those early years, the objectives were discernable and the will to achieve them was fervent. As we now ponder the urban fate of Singapore in the next 50 years, we need to ask ourselves if we should continue forging on the path which we have trekked for five decades, or venture on a trail yet to be marked. The road ahead is laid with complexities and uncertainties, but by gleaning insights from Singapore's urban history, we learn anew the ways through which cooperation, innovation, and courage can take the future of urban planning in Singapore to heights never before imagined.

Acknowledgement

I would like to thank Professor Heng Chye Kiang for the invitation to participate in this book project. I also wish to thank Dr Yeo Su-Jan and the editorial team for assisting in the preparation of this article. Lastly, my appreciation to the Urban Redevelopment Authority and National Archives of Singapore for extending their help and information on the images used in the chapter.

References

Chew, C. S. (1973) 'Key Elements in the Urban Renewal of Singapore' in: Chua, P. C. (Ed.) *Planning in Singapore*, pp. 32–44. Singapore: Chopmen Enterprises.

Choe, A. F. C. (1969) 'Urban Renewal' In: Ooi, J. B. and Chiang, H. D. (Eds.) *Modern Singapore*, pp. 161–170. Singapore: University of Singapore.

Chua, B. H. (1989) *The Golden Shoe: Building Singapore's Financial District*. Singapore: Urban Redevelopment Authority.

Singapore Economic Development Board (2014) *Future Ready Singapore: Facts and Rankings*. [http://www.edb.gov.sg/content/edb/en/why-singapore/about-singapore/facts-and-rankings/rankings.html, accessed on 31August 2014]

Teh, C. W. (1969) 'Public Housing' in: Ooi, J. B. and Chiang, H. D. (Eds) *Modern Singapore*, pp. 171–180. Singapore: University of Singapore.

Yueng, Y. M. (1973) *National Development Policy and Urban Transformation in Singapore: A Study of Public Housing and the Marketing System*, Research Paper No. 149. Chicago: University of Chicago, Department of Geography.

CHAPTER 2

Planning & Urbanisation in Singapore: A 50-Year Journey

Liu Thai Ker

Introduction

This year we celebrate the 50th anniversary of our nationhood. In a relatively short span of time, we have transformed from a backward British colony into a modern metropolis. While we are officially 50 years old, our urban upgrading work actually began five years earlier, in 1960. By 1985—within a time span of 25 years, or one generation—the basic groundwork of this transformation was by and large complete. Several key signs of progress had already emerged. All squatters were gone, our city was seen as clean and green, with flowing traffic and universal supply of water, electricity and gas. As pollution control was introduced almost from Day One, the overall quality of environment met world standards, and every citizen or permanent resident had a roof over his or her head. On top of that, our education system had greatly improved. Not surprisingly, our GDP multiplied 20 folds. Fast-forward to this day, our GDP per capita is slightly higher than that of the United States. The Singapore Story gradually attracted attention from around the world, first from other Asian cities, then the Middle East and more recently Eastern Europe, Africa, South America, and even developed nations.

Our achievements can be summed up in three words: Speed, Quantity and Quality. Like many other cities, we wanted the transformation to be fast, the extent to be broad so as to benefit as many people as possible, and the quality to be world-class. While these achievements are often credited to planners, architects, engineers and other professionals, in reality, our success is due more to the close collaboration between political leaders and professionals in a manner often referred to as Whole of Government, and indeed Whole of Society.

When a government passes regulations and legislations and where the results are not entirely satisfactory, it is sometimes feasible to make adjustments along the way. However, I can think of three areas which are rather intolerant of mistakes. First, if education policies were unsound, an entire generation of young people would lose

23

their precious youth, which is impossible to recover. Second, if ecology was damaged, it would be gone forever. Third, if the built environment had been poorly planned and developed, it would be extremely costly to modify massive concrete and steel structures, when mistakes are discovered some 20 or more years later. Yet, despite the gravity of this situation, urban decision makers can get away with giving subjective or experimental directions. For, by the time mistakes surface decades later, they would have either been promoted or moved on, and can no longer be held accountable for their actions. Fortunately in Singapore, we have managed this problem with extreme care, and therefore experience few regrets. On the occasion of our 50th anniversary, I look back at our carefully calibrated hard work indeed in great wonder and feel compelled to write about how we had done it.

Close and Compatible Collaboration

In the area of planning and urban development, the manner of collaboration between political leaders and professionals can be described in Figure 1.

To begin with, (Fig. 1, Step 1) our planning ideas came from two main sources, the first being problems that had already emerged and require urgent attention, and the second being potential problems anticipated by political leaders who went the extra mile, taking early action to nip them in the bud before they surfaced. In both cases, the Whole of Government characteristically never failed to face hard truths, looking at real causes rather than at superficial symptoms. Parallel to problem spotting, our political leaders meticulously took time to observe the strengths and weaknesses of urban strategies, asking serious questions about urban issues while studying and learning from the successful experiences of other cities. This approach required time and effort, especially when pains were taken to adapt findings to our local conditions. However, though tedious, it proved much more rewarding than simply copying seductive images from other cities, as it enabled us to explore new solutions and ultimately contribute to the world's body of knowledge on urban planning.

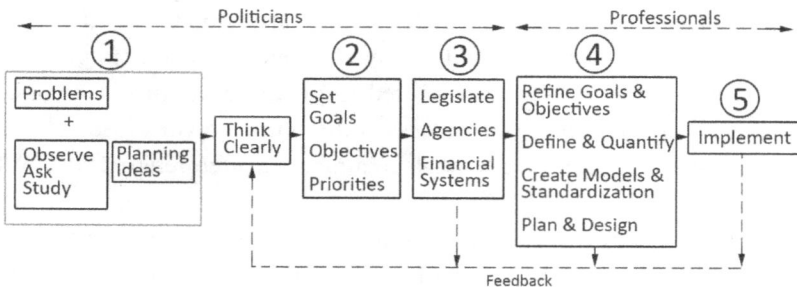

Figure 1.　Culture of governance.
Source: Author.

Critical for a good start, ideas alone do not assure solutions. The next step was to think through the ideas carefully and clearly in order to set effective goals, objectives and priorities (Fig. 1, Step 2). For example, the key problem encountered in the 1960s was that out of 1.6 million citizens, about 1.15 million lived in squatter settlements. If Singapore was to become a world-class liveable city, it was necessary to move these squatters into decent housing. Given the large population size, low income and relatively high land price, the only way to meet this goal was to have a massive public housing programme, subsidized by the Government. The Housing and Development Board (HDB) was thus formed on a high priority basis in 1960, even though the entire construction industry then could barely cope with work of such a scale.

In this context, many who had worked closely with the late Mr. Lee Kuan Yew appreciate the fact that he was a worrier. He worried about problems long before they surfaced, and proceeded to find ways to tackle them way before they became serious. For example, in as early as the 1970s, glass curtain walls on high-rise buildings became popular, but heat transmitted through the glass panels into interior spaces required additional energy to cool down. At the same time, the heat reflected off the glass surface raised the temperature of the surrounding environment. To address these concerns, the Overall Thermal Transmission Value (OTTV) of curtain walls was introduced. This mandatory requirement took place well before the world raised the alarm on CO_2 emission or urban heat islands.

Parallel to solving fundamental urban issues, Mr. Lee and his colleagues were also eager to transform the image of the city in the shortest possible time. To this end, they put in place several quick-fix measures which proved highly effective. For one, they pushed for the Garden City concept through systematic tree planting and ground turfing, including on wastelands and brown fields. In Mr. Lee's own words, this was the cheapest and most effective way to transform the look of a city. At around the same time, a Walkway Committee was set up to improve all footpaths, making them comfortable for walking. Again, this idea appears to be ahead of its time, before 'Walkability' attracted world attention. On another front, a car parking standard was introduced for every new building, while a small number of common garages were built to address car parking needs of older buildings. This way, roadside parking mostly disappeared. Subsequently, by around the late 1970s, five-yearly repainting became a requirement for every building. Within a few years, dirty looking facades became a thing of the past. Thus, the image of Singapore improved dramatically without the aid of iconic architecture.

Having set clear goals, objectives and priorities, the government, almost without fail, proceeded to pass legislation and set up dedicated agencies responsible for the delivery of the various tasks, while providing financial and manpower support (Fig. 1, Step 3). Regarding legislation, both the Land Acquisition Act and the Resettlement Act had been critical in enabling the government to compulsorily acquire land for specified public purposes, thereby successfully resettling squatters into flats, shops or factories developed by HDB. Although many cities do have these acts enacted, the Singapore government had been able to use them quite widely and effectively for the purpose of urban regeneration. This was possible by virtue of the fact that the government had been highly disciplined in using the land so acquired strictly for the stated purposes, besides ensuring that squatters were compensated fairly, thus earning the trust of citizens. This hard earned trust proved critical for our successful long-term redevelopment efforts.

In addition, the authority of the plan is crucial for its eventual execution. In Singapore, there is only one Master Plan, not several, as seen in some cities. There is also only one planning authority, the Urban Redevelopment Authority (URA), which has the clear mandate to require all development proposals, whether public or private, to comply with the Master Plan and its relevant detailed plans, rules and regulations. This effective arrangement, though often taken for granted by Singaporeans, has ensured a well-coordinated urban system, and therefore a functional and orderly city. Besides, given such an authority, pressure is exerted on politicians and planners to ensure that all plans and regulations introduced are fair, beneficial and highly credible to the people so affected. The Singapore Concept Plan or Master Plan must therefore be, and indeed was, carefully and Intelligently thought through.

With regard to the provision of financial and manpower resources to public agencies, it is noteworthy that every government proposal was put through a careful evaluation process, so as to ensure that it would be well used, especially where subsidies had been required. Clear priority was set to implement government plans on a just-in-time, just-in-need basis, minimizing wasteful investment. A virtuous cycle of funds thus became possible, enabling the government to embark on other new projects.

Next, it was up to the professionals to deliver their assigned responsibilities (Fig. 1, Step 4). We were given reasonable opportunity and time to refine and even to counter suggest goals and objectives to our political leaders. In the 1960s and 1970s, the professionals, myself included, were young and inexperienced. Hence, extensive research was required before we embarked on a planning assignment. For example, in the area of New Town planning, my colleagues and I spent several years conducting on-the-ground research and interviews while exploring written sources. This enabled us to gain a better grip on definitions, scales, dimensions and land use mix for New Towns, neighbourhoods, precincts, town centres, and so on. Various prototypes were thus created. Later, when I became the Chief Planner of URA, we repeated the same process, this time encompassing the entire island. At that time, the government wisely saw the need for the standardisation of urban components, thus came guidelines for tree planting and road sections across categories, to name but two examples. Both prototyping and standardisation were effective ways to ensure quality control when carrying out our tasks. Working under these circumstances, our planners, architects and engineers were better assured of creating a city both functional and beautiful.

While strong government support is important, planning as a profession also requires solid skills. Unfortunately, the importance of solid skills is often underrated or unappreciated in many parts of the world. As a master plan essentially consists of a few lines and colour patches on a flimsy piece of paper, it tends to suggest that anyone can do the job. As a result, architects or landscape architects, rather than planners, have been called upon to produce so-called master plans. This would hardly be conceivable in the medical field. If we liken a planner to an urban doctor, such a doctor would have spent years acquiring skills and knowledge which enable him to bring a sick city back to health. Nobody would think of asking a dentist to operate on his eyes or a chiropractor to extract his teeth, and no patient would think of dictating the diagnosis to a doctor. Yet, planners are often told what to draw. While the plan may seem innocent, its content would eventually be converted into nearly indestructible concrete and steel. When unsound decisions have been made and damage done, it would be very costly to rectify. To reinforce this point, I predict that there would always be two types of cities, one in which cars are driven on the right-hand side of the road, and the other with cars driven on the left. To convert either system to the other requires massive demolition of concrete and steel structures, which is simply unthinkable.

During the years when I was in the civil service, Singapore's government took urban planning matters very seriously and thus circumvented unfortunate errors. Politicians set clear directions and let the professionals work out solutions. In return, the professionals were expected to deliver their tasks at world standards. With a high degree of self-discipline, politicians respected the professionalism of planning, avoiding intervention on technical matters. Conversely, as professionals, we had sharpened our skills to become confident enough to stand firm on sound principles in the interest of the state. Therefore I often tell our overseas visitors that in Singapore, the highest authority of the land is not the Prime Minister, nor the President, but the Truth. Even the President or Prime Minister would bow to the Truth, so that the best ideas would triumph for the benefit of the country.

With the plans ready, the next task was to devise methods for implementation (Fig. 1, Step 5). This will be elaborated upon later when we discuss Figure 4.

The Four Main Objectives of Urbanisation

The four main interconnected objectives of Singapore's urbanisation are: to look after the Basic Needs of People; through infrastructure projects to maximise the Function of Land; to ensure Land Sustainability; and to Enhance Liveability. There is a strong complementary relationship between the construction of the physical environment (hardware) and the creation of supporting policies (software) in the formation of a city.

1. *Basic Needs of People*

City planning, especially for a small city-state like Singapore with limited land, requires both foresight and continuity. Thus the Concept Plan of Singapore is a legal blueprint for land use allocation and infrastructure development, which is never discarded but reviewed periodically and updated every 10 years.

Singapore's first Concept Plan was put together with the help of the United Nations Development Programme (UNDP) in 1971 for an estimated population of 3.4 million by the year 1992. A key strategic feature of this plan is the system of four urban corridors, with the inner two encircling the central catchment area and outer two extending to the city's east and west along the southern coast line. Along these corridors, high-density satellite towns were earmarked, mainly for the development of public housing. These towns were to be linked by Mass Rapid Transit lines (MRT), complemented by a comprehensive network of expressways.

However, Singapore's population had grown much faster than anticipated, reaching 2.9 million by 1982, thus necessitating an update of the 1971 Concept Plan. Between 1985 and 1989, quantitative studies were carried out by all ministries in order to estimate the population size, urban land required for development and the floor area needed for respective activities of all residents in our city. This heroic effort provided a solid quantitative basis for the preparation of the 1991 Concept Plan (Figure 2) for a projected population size of 5.5 million by year X, approximately 100 years later, to ensure a liveable environment for the future.

The aim of the 1991 Concept Plan was to alleviate congestion in the city core through decentralization, which requires the creation of a hierarchy of urban centres outside the central area. In the plan, the island-city was carved into five regions–Central, West, North, North-East and East. Each region was to accommodate around a million or more inhabitants, and was further subdivided into several highly self-sufficient New Towns featuring a mix of high, medium, and low density housing forms. Besides the Central Business District (CBD), the areas identified to become regional centres were Jurong East, Woodlands, Nee Soon and Tampines. To further decentralize, the plan also identified several sub-regional centres, namely Buona Vista, Bishan, Serangoon, Paya Lebar, and Marine Parade. Moreover, along the fringe of the CBD, a number of "fringe centres" were introduced to complement and enhance its functions. These include the Singapore River, Outram, Newton, Novena, Lavender and Orchard. Besides commercial centres, industrial developments were also hierarchically dispersed across the island, with light industries strategically located near homes for easy commute to and from work. Also, under the 'Green and Blue Plan', a framework was introduced to safeguard nature reserves while enhancing leisure opportunities through the creation of a comprehensive system of open spaces and waterways.

It must be noted that the Concept Plan was enhanced by a series of extremely sound decisions made by the government regarding the location of major installations. A good example would be the location of petro-chemical plants on Jurong Island, a

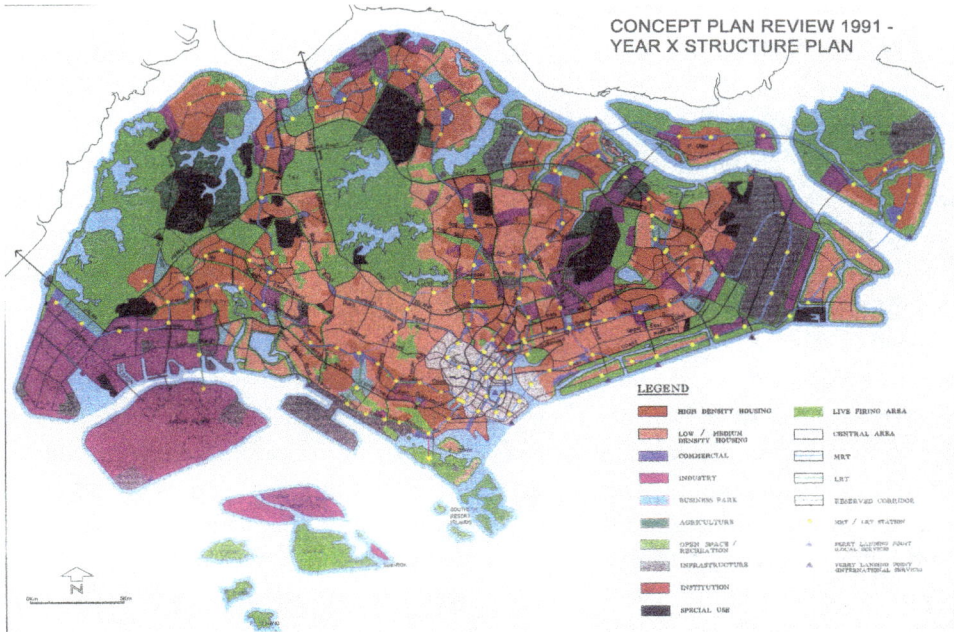

Figure 2.   1991 Concept plan.

Source: Urban Redevelopment Authority.

safe distance from heavily populated areas. Military training grounds, as another example, serve not only defense purposes but also conserve large tracts of tropical jungle. While the Central Catchment Area located in the middle of the Island was the choice of the British Colonial Government, the Singapore Government later expanded it northwards for better assurance of water supply. Moving further East, in the interest of spatial allowance for long-term expansion, Paya Lebar Airport was moved to Changi, at the extreme East of the Island. In so doing, the built-up area affected by noise disturbance and height restriction was minimized. These decisions, taken together, contributed to making Singapore a city where everything functions well with minimal disruption to daily life.

Under these circumstances, the 1991 Concept Plan was able to achieve its vision of 'A Tropical City Of Excellence', defined as "a city within an island which balances work and play, culture and commerce; a city of beauty, character and grace, with nature, water bodies and urban development weaved together".

To effectively cascade these macro visions and goals to the micro level, a total of 55 planning areas were carved out and their respective detailed local plans, called Development Guide Plans (DGPs), were prepared over a five-year period between 1993 and 1998. Data of every land plot was obtained to ensure that the final plans would be both forward looking and fair to private land owners. The completed DGPs were then incorporated into an Outline Plan, complete with control guidelines for plot-specific parameters such as land use, development intensity and building height. This formed the legal base which guided decision-making on planning applications and appeals for specific development proposals.

In both the 1971 and 1991 Concept Plans, New Towns clearly played a key role as the city's basic urban building block, effectively solving the housing needs of the people while ensuring liveability of the environment. At the beginning, HDB's battle cry was 'Break the Backbone of the Housing Shortage'. By the late 1970s, when the government saw that HDB had managed to build up sufficient capability to move a large number of squatters into high-rise flats, the theme changed to 'Home Ownership for All'. By looking squarely at the desperate housing needs, the government decided that in order to house everyone, we had to make two choices that were contrary to world trends. The first was to build high-rise, high-density housing, a housing form condemned all over the western world in the 1960s and 70s because of its many associated social problems. Having made that decision, our task was to identify the problems brought about by such a housing form before proceeding to overcome them through urban planning and building design supported by human-centric rules and regulations. The second decision, made around 1964, was to build public housing for sale rather than for rent. In those days, and even today, such housing was built mainly for rent in many parts of the world. This decision was prompted by three factors: first, to encourage residents to take better care of their home environment; second, to make it worthwhile for them to upgrade their apartments as their economic positions improved; and third, to help citizens become strong stakeholders on this tiny multi-ethnic island. Through these policies, together with setting the selling prices at very affordable levels, over 90% of citizens and permanent residents own their homes today. This is clearly a world record.

To produce a good urban plan for successful urbanisation, I cannot emphasize enough the importance of "Intelligent Planning", by which I mean meticulously and rationally studying and thinking through urban issues. What happens typically is that the government of a certain city finds the will to create a good city, and then leaps straight into iconic architectural design, bypassing the fundamental planning process in between, with no careful translation of ideas into plans, and plans into built environment. This sort of hasty process, to a large extent accounts for the many poorly assembled cities that we see around us today. The more appropriate process of Intelligent Planning is shown in Figure 3. Step 1, setting a vision, includes sieving through ideas and finding the vision and needs of both the government and the people. Concurrently, the top city leaders and their planners must quantify the components of the urban plan, as shown in Step 2. They have to determine the population size of the city, its suitable density and land area. These processes have been discussed earlier.

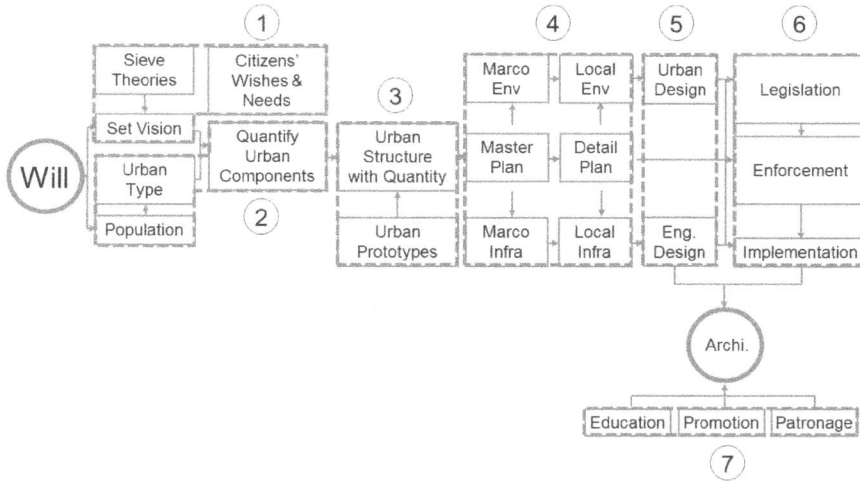

Figure 3. Intelligent planning.

Source: Author.

This brings us to Step 3 where a planner is to work out a logical urban structure for the city, guided by relevant information such as urban components (or land use), the numbers required, and the dimensions expected. Before embarking on this task, the planner will be well advised to determine for himself an ideal urban prototype as a point of reference. This is important, yet often neglected. I have, for instance, asked many experienced planners about the optimal distance between two parallel express-ways. Only a very small handful had a credible answer. If we do not even know these requirements, how can we plan a city? With a workable prototype, we shall then decide on the planning approach and determine the general urban structure, taking into account the population size, density, the requisite urban components, their respective quantity and dimensions, as well as the characteristics of the terrain.

Having devised our strategies, we start formulating the Master Plan followed by Detailed Plans as shown in Step 4. As we do this, we must carefully consider and incorporate the social, economic, environmental, ecological, and other factors into the plans. Thereafter, we begin working on Step 5, urban design. At the next and final stage, Step 6, we introduce legislation to guide the enforcement of the urban plans and devise an effective implementation system for the governing authorities to ensure that every individual project complies with the requirements of the Master Plan, Detailed Plans and Urban Design Guidelines.

As shown in Table 1, it is gratifying that despite the substantial population increase and the accompanying higher population density, our urban environment has actually improved. By 1985, virtually all squatters were cleared, with 81% of the population living in public housing and the unemployment rate lowered to an

Table 1. Scale and dimension: land, population, economy.

Source: Centre for Liveable Cities.

	Year	Units	1965	1985	2005	2014
Land	Population	Persons	1,886,900	2,735,957	4,265,762	5,469,724
	Land Area	sqkm	581.5	620.5	696.9	718.3
	Urbanized Area	sqkm	177.4	298.8	NA	518[*1] (2015)
	Density	Persons/sqkm	3,245	4,409	6,121	7,615
Population	% of Resident Population living In HDB Housing	%	23	81	83	82
	Home Ownership (Total, including HDB, private apartments, landed properties)	%	29.4[*2] (1970)	58.8[*3] (1980)	91.1	90.5
Economy	GDP	Mil USD	974.2	18,554.6	127,402.4	307,859.8
	GDP Per Capita	USD	516	6,782	29,866	56,284
	Unemployment	%	8.9 (1966)	4.1	3.1	2.0

[*1]http://www.demographia.com/db-worldua.pdf
[*2]http://www.singstat.gov.sg/docs/default-source/default-document-library/publications/publications_and_papers/population_and_population_structure/population2014.pdf
[*3]Ibid.

acceptable level of around 4%, strongly indicating that, by and large, the basic needs of the people had been adequately met.

2. *Basic Functions of Land*

In the preparation of the Concept Plan, or each New Town Plan, the essential urban functions such as infrastructure, municipal functions, amenities and transportation system have to be simultaneously incorporated and integrated.

For our city to thrive economically, in addition to the domestic transportation system, external linkages like airports, seaports, cruise terminals and ferry terminals to nearby islands are vital. We are not just congested on land, but equally congested at sea and in the sky. We need sufficient seafront area for our port development and relatively clear skies for flight and microwave paths. These services were invariably planned for the long-term for at least two reasons. The first is to minimize any negative impact these plants or facilities may have on surrounding areas; the second to prevent the need to relocate these facilities as the city expanded into outlying areas.

In addition to creating Intelligent urban plans, it is equally important to devise an Intelligent implementation process. This was another exhausting but necessary task. As shown in Figure 4, through this process, we were more likely to create a city both functional and beautiful. We began by spelling out our vision. This was followed by creating the Master Plan, then Detailed Plans, and Urban Design Guidelines. Concurrently, we worked on the Infrastructural Master Plan and Detailed Plans to ensure that the city's infrastructure would function well, be integrated with the Land-use Plan and delivered on a timely basis. Further, as we work on urban design, engineering design should come on board too. Thereafter, we systematically passed legislation, carried out promotion, and finally, began development.

A very important contributor to our urban development process was, again, our Public Housing Policy. The ambitious construction programme comfortably met the

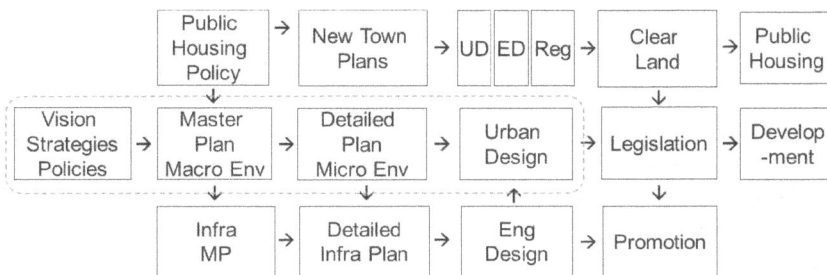

Figure 4.   Intelligent implementation process.

Source: Author.

rehousing needs of squatters. Through massive resettlement, it became possible to clear large tracts of land, not just for public housing, but also for commercial, industrial and infrastructural developments.

The delivery of these tasks required the input of many governmental departments. Fortunately, all of us worked closely together. 'Silo Syndrome' was hardly known at that time. In fact, visitors to Singapore often envied this close collaborative working relationship. For instance, while infrastructural projects were designed by engineers, aesthetic sensitivity was very much required. While in the government, I worked with engineers on their designs to achieve the multiple goals of being functional, user-friendly and beautiful. In doing so, many of these engineers became and remain good friends until today.

Table 2 speaks volumes for the steady upgrading of infrastructure provision. We had managed to achieve full utility provision to every home and business premise by the time we cleared all squatters in 1985. Public transportation also continued to improve and our international transportation linkages expanded continuously to the extent that our seaport became the largest transshipment port in the world. The only unfortunate aspect is that Singapore was a slow starter in the promotion of cycling.

3. *Sustainability of Land*

While we depend on the land for various functions, we must ensure its sustainability. Singapore is often described as a city in a garden, with gardens in the city. Such an accolade does not come about without some serious planning and hard work. In the preparation of the 1991 Concept Plan, one of our first tasks was to identify all historical buildings and natural areas worthy of protection. Since the early 1990s, some 7,000 buildings have been gazetted for conservation. With regard to the conservation of nature, our Water Catchment Plan immediately comes to mind, incorporating Bukit Timah Nature Reserve, Labrador Nature Reserve, Telok Blangah Hill, Bukit Gombak Hill and Mount Faber Park.

Further, we managed to protect most, if not all, the rivers in their natural state, except where they ran through urbanized areas and embankments became necessary. As for land reclamation, in as early as the mid-1960s, long before rising sea levels became a global issue, our government decided to set the platform level of the East Coast reclamation area at eight feet above sea level at high tide. With virtual simulation, we could envision the effects of wave action on the shoreline over time. During the preparation of the 1991 Concept Plan, my colleagues and I also decided to conserve a stretch of the original beach near Changi Creek so that future generations could know and understand the appearance of Singapore's original shores. Moreover,

Table 2. Transportation, utilities.

Source: Centre for Liveable Cities.

Year	Units	1965	1985	2005	2014
Transport-Domestic					
Private Cars (excluding taxis)	No.	104,723	221,279	432,287	600,176
MRT Lines/Length	Kilometres	NA	67 (1990)	109.4	154.2
MRT Average Daily Ridership	'000 passenger-trips	NA	740 (1995)	1,321	2,762
Bus Average Daily Ridership	'000 passenger-trips	NA	3,009 (1995)	2,779	3,751
Bicycle Path	km	NA	NA	NA	230
Transport-External					
Airport: Number of Passenger Arrivals	Million passengers	0.8	4.32	15.36	26.67
Seaport: Annual No. of TEUs handled	Million	NA	1.6	23.2	33.9
Cruise	Thousand passengers	NA	NA	6,526	6,820
Utilities					
Electricity Generation Capacity	MW	NA	2,571	NA	11,283
Electricity Consumption	GWh	913	8,821	35,489	44,923
Length of public sewer system	km	561	1923	3100	3400
Domestic Water Use	Litres per day per capita	197	104	155	151

a number of islands are still kept in their original condition, namely St John's Island, Kusu Island, Pulau Tekong and Pulau Ubin.

Besides nature conservation, new parks and water catchment ponds were created all over the island. Neighbourhood parks, New Town parks and a number of Regional or Citywide parks were added. To name a few, they are East Coast Park, Bishan Park and Sungai Seletar. During the preparation of the 1991 Concept Plan, the land area of Bukit Timah Nature Reserve was increased to encompass the entire hill. While preparing the Bukit Batok New Town Plan, a disused stone quarry was converted into a park with a stone cliff and a deep-water pond. The scenery is so picturesque that it has been fondly nicknamed Little Guilin. We can also speak of a few beautiful gardens such as the historical Botanic Gardens, which first appeared during the British colonial times, as well as newer entries like the Chinese Garden, Japanese Garden, Gardens by the Bay, the Mandai Zoo and Jurong Bird Park.

The quality of the physical environment depends not just on well-conceived new urban areas or the conservation of heritage and green areas, but also on the quality of air and water. In this respect, the government started pollution control basically from Day One. Although we were extremely poor and desperately in need of foreign investment, there was an instance when a multinational corporation looked to set up a factory right in the middle of the city in the Golden Mile area. While the government badly wanted this investment, it stood firm on its principle against this choice of location. In the end, through negotiation and tax incentives, we managed to convince the investor to locate the factory in the Jurong Industrial Area. This incident, with a host of other government measures, reinforces the point that good environment does not happen without a clear understanding of important principles. The end results are very gratifying, as shown in Table 3.

Table 3. Conservation, Ecology.   *Source*: Centre for Liveable Cities.

	Year	Units	1965	1985	2005	2014
Conservation	Heritage Buildings	No.	0	3,200	NA	7,100
	Total Green Coverage*[1]	%	NA	35.7 (1986)	46.5 (2007)	42.2 (2012)
	Total Park Area*[2]	Ha	NA	3,720	1,841.9	2,363
Ecology	CO_2 emissions per capita*[3]	Metric tons	1.34	12.21	7.12	4.32 (2011)

*[1] A City in a Garden, Developing Gardens—Unpublished internal document, (S:NParks).
*[2] Parks, playgrounds, open spaces, fitness corners and park connectors, excludes nature reserves.
*[3] Data from the World Bank.

4. *Liveability for People*

In addition to getting the big picture right in areas such as employment, education, housing, transport and so on, the quality of life of the people should be enhanced with excellent facilities and amenities located at convenient distances from homes. At the city scale, schools, universities, public libraries, and cultural institutions are considered high priority amenities. Over the years, these facilities have been incrementally upgraded to reach world standards. Our new National Gallery is now able to permanently exhibit works of Singaporean and Southeast Asian artists while the Performing Arts Centre at the Esplanade has become an attractive venue for world-class performers.

In the push for citizens to keep themselves healthy, the government also introduced sports grounds and indoor stadia in every New Town. To maintain the traditional lifestyle of eating hawker food and buying fresh produce in markets, we invented the cooked food centre as well as the wet market. Over time, our eating houses and coffee shops have become icons of our traditional way of life, not unlike the open air cafés of Paris. They may look old fashioned but are very much loved by locals and foreigners alike.

In view of the massive resettlement of people from squatter colonies, the government, together with its planners, was looking for ways to nurture community spirit in the new high-rise environment. New towns were therefore sub-divided into neighbourhoods, which were in turn further sub-divided into precincts. Each precinct, at about 3-5 hectares in size, could give the residents a sense of attachment to the land as well as neighbourliness with surrounding households. To reinforce this objective, town centres and neighbourhood centres were designed for the dual purposes of commercial and civic activities. Residents can not only shop in these areas, they can also meet friends and relatives in eating outlets and small squares. Other facilities such as institutional sites, religious sites for different religions, and petrol stations were also carefully studied and incorporated into each New Town. The prototype of a New Town can be seen in Figure 5. When such a prototype is applied to the actual site to blend in with local historical and geographical characteristics, each can look very different from another, as shown in the Bishan New Town Plan in Figure 6.

Conceived as a basic urban building block, every New Town was planned to be highly self-sufficient through the provision of a wide, highly comprehensive range of amenities. Liveability was thus ingrained throughout the city and a form of high-rise, high-density housing emerged without its associated urban ills, despite the rapid pace of development in the 1960s, 70s and 80s.

A quick overview of the provision of facilities for health, education and culture is shown in Table 4. One can easily see that there has been a steady improvement for the ever growing population, with perhaps one exception. That is, with the lower birth rate, the number of primary and secondary school students has dipped slightly in recent years.

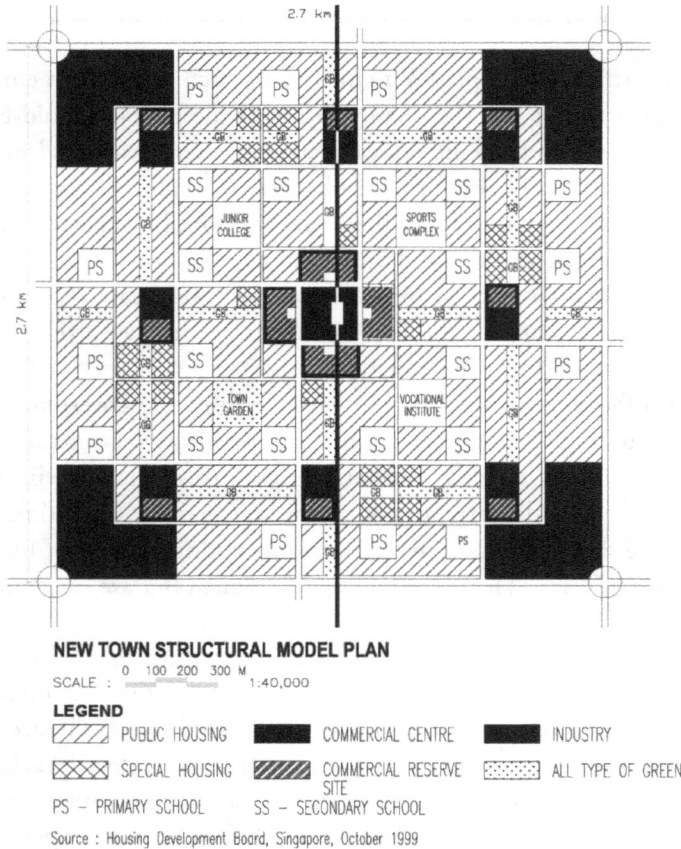

NEW TOWN STRUCTURAL MODEL PLAN

SCALE : 0 100 200 300 M   1:40,000

LEGEND

Symbol	Description	Symbol	Description	Symbol	Description
▨	PUBLIC HOUSING	■	COMMERCIAL CENTRE	■	INDUSTRY
▩	SPECIAL HOUSING	▨	COMMERCIAL RESERVE SITE	░	ALL TYPE OF GREEN

PS – PRIMARY SCHOOL   SS – SECONDARY SCHOOL

Source : Housing Development Board, Singapore, October 1999

Figure 5. HDB New town prototype.

Source: Housing Development Board, Adapted by RSP.

A Rewarding Journey

I am more familiar with Singapore's planning and urbanisation efforts up to 1992 when I left the government. In looking back, I am thankful that we had started on sound footing. We had focused more on solving real problems and meeting basic needs of the people and land, rather than allowing ourselves to be seduced by glamorous projects. Tackling basic needs is often both unglamorous and requires much more hard work, while embracing the superficial and glamorous may earn one instant praise, and can be done with relative ease. It is now fashionable to say that we must look to the future. However, if we do not understand the past and the present well, how can we really know the future?

Figure 7 summarises the handsome rewards of our arduous urbanisation journey. Imagine the triangle as an iceberg. The portion in grey is below sea level and cannot

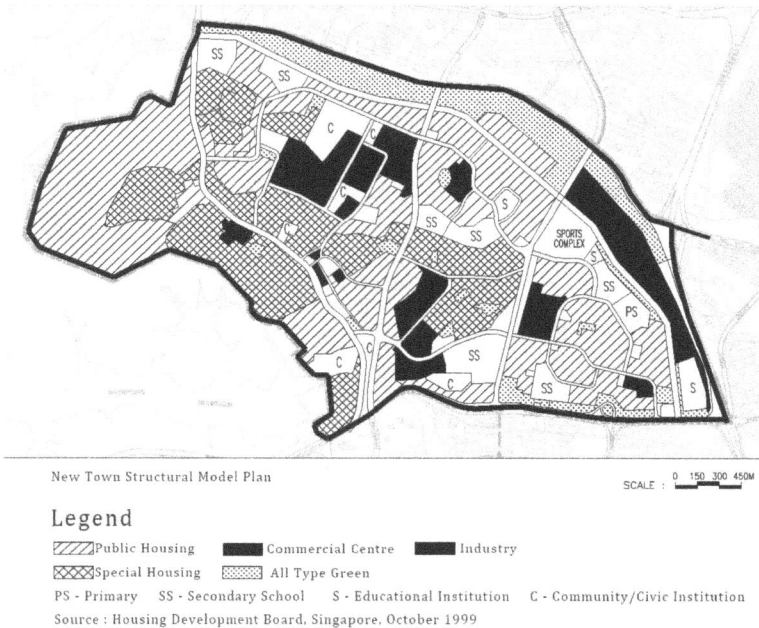

New Town Structural Model Plan

SCALE :   0 150 300 450M

Legend

//// Public Housing   ■ Commercial Centre   ■ Industry
XXX Special Housing   ░ All Type Green

PS - Primary   SS - Secondary School   S - Educational Institution   C - Community/Civic Institution

Source : Housing Development Board, Singapore, October 1999

Figure 6.   Bishan new town plan.

Source: Urban Redevelopment Authority, Adapted by RSP.

be easily seen, whereas the portion in white is above sea level and can be readily appreciated. The foundation of our urbanisation effort rests on having a group of pragmatic, far sighted and disciplined political leaders. They developed our city according to sound principles with an effective system of delivery.

At the beginning, our government was very concerned with the issue of survival. How could our tiny island, with multi-ethnic groups and without a clear sense of nationhood, survive? To make matters worse, the industrial and service sectors were practically nonexistent. But survive we must. It was not a choice. The government then set goals and priorities for the physical development of projects according to the urgency of needs and availability of resources. At the same time, the physical environment was supported by corresponding legislation, education and requisite resources. In moving forward steadily and surely, by 1985, Singapore was accepted by people around the world to be a modern metropolis. Having gained a stronger sense of nationhood, not only were we more confident of our survival, we had also managed to nurture a creative and highly energised citizenry which in turn attracts global talents to Singapore.

With these measures and developments in place, the world could clearly see that Singapore took excellent care of its ecology, urban environment and education, resulting in economic prosperity. However, I feel that the highest reward for having a city planned and developed well is earning unconditional esteem from people around the

Source: Centre for Liveable Cities.

Table 4. Health, education, culture.

	Year	Units	1965	1985	2005	2014
Health	Hospitals	No.	14	16	22	29
	Clinics	No.	NA	NA	NA	3404 (2013)
	Public Swimming Pools	No.	4	14 (1982)	NA	25
Education	Universities	Institutions	2	2	3	5
		Students	NA	16,958	59,441	77,619
	Polytechnics	Institutions	2	2	5	5
		Students	NA	21,610	64,422	87,183
	ITEs	Institutions	NA	15	3	3
		Students	NA	18,894	21,603	26,288
	Primary & Secondary Schools	Institutions	NA	385	342	336
		Students	NA	441,465	503,324	414,534
Culture	Performing Arts Venues	No.	NA	8 (1984)	NA	65
	Annual Performances	No.	NA	2,510 (1997)	6,102	8530 (2012)
	Audience Sizes	No.	NA	721,500 (1990)	1,190,000	1,950,100 (2012)
	Museums	No.	NA	1 (1984)	36	55 (2012)
	Libraries	No.	1 Central 2 Branch 3 Mobile	1 Central 8 Branch 8 Mobile	1 National 22 Community 16 Children's	1 National 26 Public (2015)

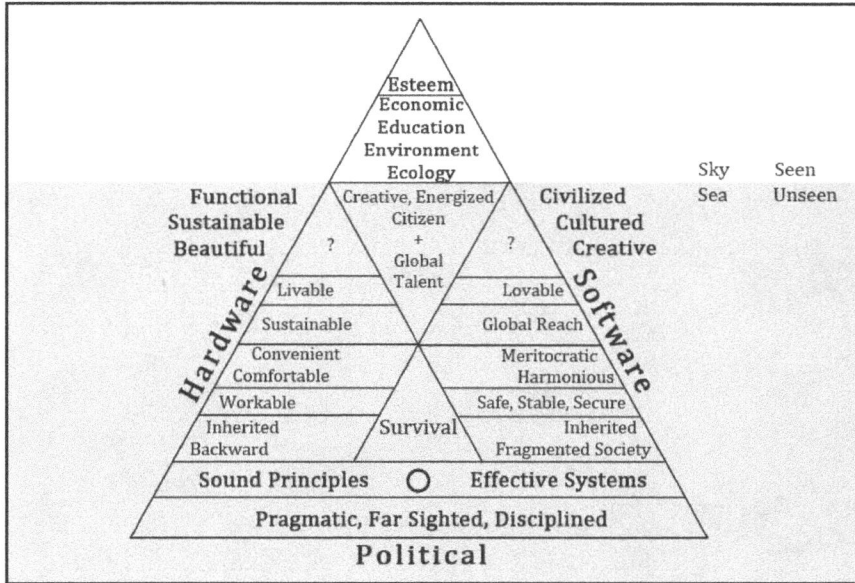

Figure 7.   Hard work pays off.

Source: Author.

world, for the people living in the city. I would like to add that the concern for survival and the need to continue planning ahead for our physical environment and our software support should be deemed as a perpetual and unending process. The fact that Singapore seems to have arrived does not mean that we can afford to take things easily. We must not forget the key lessons learned in the last 50 years. They are: good governance, effective collaboration between politicians and professionals, Intelligent Planning, Intelligent Implementation, with an Intelligent approach. To add an important footnote, both the politicians and professionals obtained their ideas from listening to the people as well as experts, learning from successful examples in other cities and sieving out good principles through rigorous research as described in Figure 1.

Further, I would like to elaborate on the issue of an Intelligent approach as shown in Figure 8. In the preparation of urban plans, three considerations are critical. First, setting goals and objectives with the right values requires the heart of a humanist. Second, the planning of a city is akin to assembling a large machine for living, which requires the head of a scientist. Third, making a city beautiful and in harmony with nature and heritage requires the eye of an artist.

When I was a student of architecture, we were taught: Form Follows Function. I would suggest that the word Form applies to both architecture and city planning. Function, it would seem to me, means enabling people to have a fun experience in a city or a building. We could therefore rightly say: Form Follows Function Follows Fun.

| Vision Strategies Policies | Master Plan Macro Env. | Detailed Plan Micro Env. | Urban Design |

Value Humanist Heart

Science Scientist Head

Art Artist Eye

| Art | Science | Value |

| Form | Follows | Function | Follows | Fun |

✓

| Form | Follows | Fashion | Follows | Fame |

✗

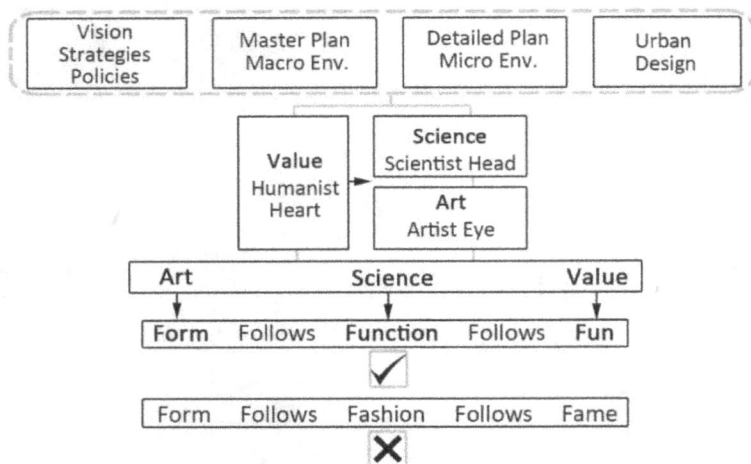

Figure 8.   Planning and design philosophy.

Source: Author.

In this case, Fun is related to Value, Function to Science, and Form to Art. However, I am concerned about the prevailing trend today, in both architecture and city planning. A fair number of practitioners lean more towards the practice of Form Follows Fashion Follows Fame. In other words, if a person plans a city or designs a building according to the prevailing fashion, he is more likely to enjoy instant fame. This is certainly very tempting, but not necessarily done in the best interest of the people or the land.

In both city planning and architecture, the word Design to my mind suggests producing a clever and simple urban solution which is convenient, comfortable and easy to use, while satisfying the complex needs of our lives today. This task is not unlike a doctor's; having felt the pulse of the patient, he would have to find the single most appropriate treatment to help the patient become healthy and beautiful again, with minimum fuss.

In this respect, many of us involved in the urban planning of Singapore do feel that we had been offered a very good Urban Laboratory to carry out research in order to find the most appropriate and effective urban solutions for our needs. Undoubtedly, we had picked up many urban theories from the west. However, after going through the test of our urban laboratory, something rather different emerged—our own 'Asianised' theories.

This shows that when there is a will to get things done right, there will be success, regardless of geographical location. In the case of Singapore, while we have used our city as an urban laboratory and to some extent experimented on ourselves, our research has become valuable know-how, to be shared with other cities. Besides, the need for good urban planning seems to be particularly great in Asia. As of today, 60% of the world's population lives in Asia on only 30% of its total land. The urban density in Asia is therefore unavoidably high. The rate of urbanisation is also very high, due to massive and rapid rural-urban migration. In the next few decades, if Asian cities can plan and develop well, it will contribute significantly to a better environment for the world. On the contrary, if this is not done well, it may accelerate the further deterioration of our global environment. The implication is immense.

I will conclude by looking briefly at Singapore's future. We should begin every urban planning effort with a long term projection of population size over a period of around a century. On the issue of population growth, we can learn valuable lessons from the growth trends of other countries. The respective population sizes of Scandinavian countries have been growing continuously for at least the last 60 years, despite their remote location on the world map. Based on these trends, and considering how Singapore sits in the middle of a highly populated continent, it would be unrealistic for us to think that our population growth can be effectively curbed. Further, the more limited the territory of a country, the more one must plan for the long-term. Therefore, I propose that we project our population size from the current 5.5 million to 10 million persons, over a time frame of at least 100 years. This growth rate can sustain our economic growth for the next century, and hopefully beyond.

The harsh fact is that if we aspire for Singapore to remain a sovereign country forever, we have to plan our city for a longer term than that of other cities. The sooner we make this bold decision, the more options we will have to keep our jungles, hills, lakes, rivers, military grounds and golf courses; to protect our historical areas and landed properties; and to disperse the requisite land area of higher density over a larger area, including land yet to be reclaimed. In doing so, we may be able to avoid being forced at a later stage to squeeze developments of very high intensity in remnant corners of our tiny island. If we act fast and boldly, we may still retain the quality of our urban environment, despite the much larger population size and higher overall density. Good urban environment, after all, contributes to economic prosperity.

To ensure the survival of our country, in addition to physical planning, we also need the support of our whole society, especially in areas such as better education for a value-added economy, economic restructuring for higher productivity and so on, to try to reduce, but not to stop, population growth, thereby enjoying the twin benefits of economic prosperity and higher quality of life.

In addition, it is also my wish to enhance our urban environment with great streets, parks, plazas, architecture and works of art that make Singapore a great city like historical London, Paris, Rome, Beijing, etc. To do so, we must not only maintain, but transcend, rationality. To this end, a bolder vision, stronger cultural tradition and greater intellectual depth would come into play. At the same time, we must never forget to keep the rigour and good practices behind our success story.

Finally, if I were to use two words to describe Singapore's urbanisation experience over the last 50 years, they are simply CLARITY = COURAGE.

Acknowledgement

I would like to thank Prof. Heng Chye Kiang and Ms. Poh Hui Min for their assistance during the preparation of this paper.

CHAPTER 3

Economic Planning for Productivity, Growth, and Prosperity

Philip Yeo

Introduction

Singapore is an island-nation with very limited land area and no natural resources. Nevertheless, Singapore has leveraged exceptionally on its geographical location, industrial infrastructure, and intellectual capital to drive economic growth. How did Singapore, a small city-state with no natural resources, advance from poverty in a Third World region to become a global city on the world stage? What has been the role and contribution of economic planning in sustaining this transformation? Singapore's rapid makeover, while relatively fast-paced by global standards, was by no means an easy feat.

Throughout my 45-year public administration career, I have engaged first-hand in building Singapore's defence systems and technology (MINDEF, 1970–1985), developing industrial sectors (EDB, 1986–2000), promoting scientific research (A*STAR, 2001–2007), and more recently cultivating economic innovation (SPRING, 2007-present; EDIS, 2013-present). Needless to say, I have participated in the successes and struggles of planning for Singapore's competitiveness and resilience in an increasingly volatile global climate. With each passing decade, newer and more complex considerations, challenges, and opportunities emerged. Singapore's economic progress in the past 50 years was made possible by a pragmatic approach toward economic development. There were three key facets: (1) industry creation, (2) infrastructure development, and (3) talent investment. By exploring the motivations and rationale behind industry creation, infrastructure development, and talent investment, we can better understand the Singapore approach to economic planning that has contributed to the efficiency and proficiency of our nation's engine of production.

Singapore's Industry Phases Over the Decades

1960s: Labour-Intensive

The 50-year evolution of Singapore's economy can be divided into five distinct episodes. During the 1960s, there were the twin challenges of an uneducated population and high unemployment. Work was not only gruelling and labour-intensive but also often carried out under precarious conditions in shipyards, construction sites, and quarries. Some were self-employed as hawkers, rickshaw pullers, and petty traders, but the business risks and uncertainties of survival were high given the low wages and general level of poverty which inflicted the urban poor. Moreover, during this era, Singapore was constrained by its small domestic market with regional export limited within the boundaries of the old colonial British Empire. Singapore's GDP during the difficult years of the 1960s amounted to around S$8 billion (Lim, 2014)—a very low figure compared to 2013 when our GDP grew to about S$373 billion (Singapore Statistics, 2015a).

There was great urgency, therefore, to develop and spur the growth of Singapore's economy by cultivating skilled labour, creating employment opportunities, and exploring international relationships with global partners. In 1961, Singapore established the Economic Development Board (EDB), a government agency given the legislated mandate to plan, coordinate, and direct the nation's industrialisation. The earliest economic strategies paid particular focus on labour-intensive industrialisation. Jurong Industrial Estate was the first initiative to jumpstart Singapore's progress as an industrialised nation.

Formerly an area of swamps and small fishing villages, Jurong—with its flat terrain, coastline geography, and proximity to the Keppel Harbour in the south of Singapore—was identified as the site for a modern industrial estate (Figure 1). National Steel & Iron Mill Ltd (today known as NatSteel) was the first manufacturing company in 1962 to establish its factories at the Jurong Industrial Estate. Occupying a site of 30 acres, these factories were one of the largest industrial undertakings at the time (NatSteel, 2013; Jurong GRC, no date). In its initial years, the Jurong Industrial Estate experienced slow progress. This changed after Singapore attained independence and the newly formed Housing and Development Board commenced plans for Jurong Town. The comprehensive town plan for Jurong included improvements to the rail and road networks as well as development of public housing for a thriving residential population.

1970s: Skills-Intensive

By the 1970s, the economy was taking off as Singapore initiated an industrialisation program that would create jobs and raise the skills of the local workforce. Two major industrial sectors flourished during the 1970s: electronics and energy. Manufacturing

Figure 1. Left: View of Jurong in the early 1960s prior to urbanisation and industrial development. Right: Construction of Jurong Industrial Estate (foreground) and islands yet to be amalgamated into the present day Jurong Island (background), circa 1968.
Source: JTC Corporation.

gradually evolved to higher-end products shifting from garments, textiles, and toys to electronics such as computer parts and peripherals, software packages, and silicon wafers. At the same time, energy products such as petroleum and gas were also contributing increasingly as generators of revenue for Singapore's economy. In these two industries, the Singapore government saw an opportunity to upgrade the economy from one based on low-cost, labour-intensive industries to one which could create higher value-adding skilled jobs and businesses. At the same time, Singapore recognised that its small domestic market could not, by itself, support the newly industrialised economy. Hence, these industries focused on producing goods for export. Moreover, as a participant in the global marketplace, Singapore needed to adopt a proactive model for engaging and attracting foreign investors.

Significant efforts were made to, firstly, position Singapore as a global business hub with the capabilities to cater to a company's entire value chain of activities and, secondly, attract multinational companies (MNCs) to establish manufacturing operations as well as research and development activities in Singapore. Texas Instruments, for example, was one of the pioneer MNCs to set-up their manufacturing facility in Singapore during the late 1960s. It produced semi-conductors and integrated circuits—a major investment highlight in the coordinated push toward developing the electronics industry. Other MNCs soon followed suit in the 1970s, namely Hewlett-Packard (USA), SGS (Europe; known today as ST Microelectronics), and NEC (Japan). The energy sector also benefitted from foreign investment. The set-up of oil refineries in Singapore by foreign energy companies, such as Shell and Esso, not only provided the foreign investment necessary to purchase capital equipment, thereby allowing Singapore's funds to be allocated for public infrastructure projects (such as housing), but also transferred knowledge and skills in management and production.

The electronics and energy sectors created jobs for Singapore's population and upgraded the skills of the local workforce. Technicians, engineers, and managers could also obtain specialist training at various EDB industrial training institutes such as the French-Singapore Institute, German-Singapore Institute, and Japan-Singapore Institute. In the 1970s, manufacturing surpassed trade for the first time. Through a combination of bold and pragmatic policies on housing, education, and economic development, Singapore rapidly left Third World conditions behind in the 1960s and 1970s. Singapore society became increasingly affluent, mobile, and skilled.

1980s: Capital-Intensive

The 1980s saw a leap toward capital-intensive manufacturing amidst rapid globalisation. This decade marked Singapore's 'Second Industrial Revolution' and the government recognised the need for land to be set aside for clean, higher value-added industries. However, accelerated economic growth during the first half of the 1980s was short lived. In 1985, Singapore was affected by a global economic recession: companies folded, unemployment rose, and the economy shrank. It was during this time that the then Minister of Trade and Industry, Tony Tan, asked me to join EDB as Chairman. I consulted Dr Goh Keng Swee—then Chairman of the Monetary Authority of Singapore and with whom I had worked at the Ministry of Defence since 1970. I learnt that Lee Kuan Yew, then Prime Minister, advised that I go over to help EDB.

In 1986, I started work full-time at EDB where I focused on turning the economy around through economic diversification. This would build resilience against future volatilities. New strategic areas of growth were identified that would enable Singapore to carve a greater competitive edge in the next phase of development. One of these economic strategies was to position Singapore as a 'Total Business Centre' where industry is combined with technical expertise to forge business relationships and attract international service corporations in the financial, educational, lifestyle, medical, information technology, and software sectors (SEDB, 2014a).

1990s: Technology-Intensive

By the 1990s, Singapore was on the path to modernising its industrialisation output based on higher value-added science, technology, and research and development (R&D) innovations in the chemicals, electronics, and engineering sectors (SEDB, 2014b). The earliest key initiative of this technology-intensive decade was the 1991 establishment of the National Science and Technology Board (NSTB). It replaced Science Council which was formed in 1967. NSTB's range of responsibilities included: fostering and promoting R&D; coordinating the formation of research institutes and their activities; dispersing research funding; evaluating manpower needs in the science and technology fields; and organising collaborations with overseas counterparts. In the same year as its formation, NSTB launched a $2 billion 5-year National Technology Plan to shape Singapore's development of science and technology and boost R&D activities and investments. Twenty-five years since the inception of the first national science and technology (S&T) plan, four more S&T plans have been rolled out resulting in the steady growth of R&D expenditure as a percentage of GDP from 0.8% in 1990 to 2.3% in 2009. By 2015, this percentage is targeted to increase to 3.5% of GDP (ASTAR, 2011).

During the 1990s, there was also a strategic focus on growing the R&D capacities of foreign MNCs and local companies through the provision of business park developments. In 1992, the International Business Park in Jurong East was launched, providing the facilities and incubator opportunities to grow knowledge-based enterprises. Five years later, Changi Business Park in Changi South was completed to accommodate high-technology businesses, data and software enterprises, and R&D activities. These business parks, together with the Singapore Science Park, which was initiated and built earlier in the 1980s, are part of a growing inventory of national infrastructure assets for the promotion of R&D, support of emerging tech industries, and enhancement of human resources through employment of skilled workers. There are still new opportunities for the future of business park development as demonstrated by the launch of CleanTech Park in 2012—Singapore's first eco-business park with a focus on the environmental sustainability industry.

2000s and Today: Knowledge- and Innovation-Intensive

In the 2000s, the tide turned toward a knowledge- and innovation-intensive economy. In 2001, I was appointed as Executive Chairman at NSTB and re-aligned its focus on two key areas: biomedical sciences research, and development of human capital. That same year, NSTB was restructured into the Agency for Science, Technology and Research (A*STAR) with a specific mission to advance the nation's R&D capabilities and human resources. This directed focus on enhancing the economic potential of R&D and human capital was achieved by transforming Singapore into an innovation hub that would attract highly-skilled people. In turn, this drive toward innovation-based industries has contributed to the diversification of Singapore's economy by introducing new technologies, products, and services to the market both domestically and internationally. In 2013, Singapore's GDP reached S$373 billion wherein the services-producing industries (e.g. wholesale and retail trade, business services, finance and insurance) generated more than 70% of the nominal value-add while 25% was generated by the goods producing industries (e.g. manufacturing, construction, utilities) (Singapore Statistics, 2015a).

Within the goods-producing industries, manufacturing—which includes sectors such as chemicals, electronics, precision engineering, transport engineering, and biomedical sciences—accounted for 19% of the total GDP in 2013. This shows the evolving, high-tech, and knowledge-based nature of manufacturing today. The biomedical sciences cluster is a new pillar in the Singapore economy that is generating complex knowledge and precise applications. In 2013, this cluster contributed 8.2% to the national GDP with a value-add of 20.5% (Singapore Statistics, 2015b). The two significant areas of the biomedical sciences cluster are pharmaceuticals and medical technology. Pharmaceuticals manufacturing investments were enabled by a reclamation project at the western tip of Singapore to form the Tuas Biomedical Park. As of 2013, the park is home to seven of the top ten big pharmaceutical companies, including 29 commercial-scale manufacturing plants for API (active pharmaceutical ingredients), biologics, cell therapy, and nutrition. Meanwhile, the medical technology sector currently comprises 30 manufacturing plants with over 10,000 sector employees and has established six R&D centres in Singapore. The next phase in growing the biomedical sciences industry aims to achieve commercialisation that will take research from 'bench' (laboratory) to 'bedside' (service delivery to patient) through financing and support such as start-up seed grants and co-investment with strategic partners under the Biomedical Sciences (BMS) Initiative.

Over the decades, Singapore has developed and accrued expertise knowledge and technical skills on various aspects of economic planning. Today, this set of invaluable knowledge and skills is our competitive advantage. In recent years, the Singapore government has worked with other countries at forming international partnerships and joint opportunities for knowledge exchange and enterprise. Initiatives include Batam Industrial Park (Indonesia), Suzhou Industrial Park (China), Wuxi-Singapore Industrial Park (China), and Vietnam-Singapore Industrial Park.

Industry Creation and the Singapore Approach

Through each decade of change, three key strategies have defined the transformation of Singapore's industrial development. Firstly, each decade of industrial advancement is an attempt at producing *value-added* results over the previous decade. Such value-added outcomes may be seen in skills upgrading, resource efficiency, technological capacity, and so on. Secondly, *innovation* resides at the core of such quantum leaps—the will to go into emerging industries has opened opportunities for Singapore's economy. Thirdly, every successful innovation introduces new commodities into the market, thereby promoting horizontal *diversification* across industrial sectors. These three approaches—value-add creation, innovation, and diversification—characterise the 50-year evolution of economic planning in Singapore from low-cost labour-intensive trades to high-value knowledge-intensive industries.

Economic planning, however, not only involves foresight and vision but also coherent and coordinated implementation of hardware and software elements. Why is infrastructure provision for industry creation necessary? How does the physical set-up of such infrastructure influence and shape the urban environment? Who are the people that work, live, play, and learn in these environments? Why is human capital an indispensable ingredient in economic development? Hardware (infrastructure) and software (talent) are both crucial to economic planning.

Strategic Investments in Hardware and Software Development

Good infrastructure is a key agent of urban modernisation and economic progress in today's networked cities. Singapore's continuous provision of and investment in infrastructure not only facilitates the creation of industries, thus broadening and deepening the nation's economic base, but also affects the physical landscape of the city-state in terms of land use effects on growth and distribution. I will briefly highlight two significant industrial infrastructure projects—'Jurong Island' and 'one-north'—and explore their impact on Singapore's development and economy.

Hardware Development: Infrastructure

Prior to Jurong Island, there existed seven small islands located off the southwest coast of mainland Singapore: Pulau Ayer Chawan, Pulau Ayer Merbau, Pulau Merlimau, Pulau Pesek, Pulau Pesek Kecil, Pulau Sakra and Pulau Seraya. In the 1960s, Pulau Ayer Chawan, Pulau Merlimau, and Pulau Pesek were sites for the oil processing facilities of Esso, Singapore Refinery Company, and Mobil Oil respectively. It was on a helicopter flight back to Singapore from the Indonesian island of Karimun (where a shipyard was being planned for Sembawang) that I saw the seven islands in a new light and questioned the possibility of linking them to create one large offshore island on which to grow and expand the petrochemical industry. The idea of Jurong Island, a global petrochemical hub, was seeded. The government approved a budget of S$7 billion to amalgamate the seven islands and reclaim land from the sea to create a single island of 3,000-hectares (double the size of Ang Mo Kio HDB estate) (JTC, 2000). A challenge was then presented to EDB officers—sell potential investors the promise of land yet to be created from the sea. There was scepticism in the beginning but, as one company after another began setting up their operations on Jurong Island, Singapore's credibility to deliver on bold and ambitious plans became our greatest strength.

Figure 2.   Jurong Island today is a thriving petrochemicals hub.
Source: JTC Corporation.

Premised on a 'plug and play' development model, Jurong Island today provides a vertically-integrated structure where activities spanning the petrochemicals spectrum (oil refineries, crackers, gas synthesis, petrochemicals, and specialty chemicals) are co-located (Figure 2). In this way, the catchment area served by infrastructure is intensified, thus simplifying logistics and generating possibilities for partnerships among the stakeholders on Jurong Island. By its official opening in 2000, 60 companies had invested more than S$20 billion on Jurong Island (Goh, 2000). Today, the economies-of-scale effect at Jurong Island has attracted more than 100 companies resulting in over S$47 billion in investments.[1] Following the success of Jurong Island, the Singapore Government in 2010 announced the next phase of development—'Jurong Island Version 2.0' (JIv2.0). The JIv2.0 initiative, a 10-year masterplan with a focus on five core areas (energy, logistics and transportation, feedstock options, environment, and water), aims to increase the competitiveness of Singapore's petrochemicals industry and advance the development of research activities while promoting innovations in sustainability.

The clustering of industrial activities on Jurong Island not only supports the burgeoning petrochemicals industry, allowing cost-sharing and synergistic relations to develop between companies located there, but also enables land on the main island of Singapore to be optimised for other industrial sectors that contribute as significantly to economic productivity, growth, and prosperity. The one-north development, a 200-hectare purpose-built high-tech zone located seven kilometres west of

Figure 3. Satellite image of one-north, 2014.
Source: JTC Corporation.

the Central Business District, houses the biomedical, information and communications, and media industries within state-of-the-art facilities. Designed as a self-sustaining development, the complementary range of infrastructure at one-north not only includes laboratories, offices, and business space but also educational institutions, housing, retail, and recreational amenities to enable integration of work-live-learn-play (Figure 3).

Launched in 2001, one-north was then a pioneering project — the next generation science park—which the Singapore government envisioned as a strategic means to capitalise on an emerging new economy in the science and technology sector. This new economy, based on knowledge- and innovation-intensive activities with emphasis on collaboration and flexibility, would set the stage for the restructuring of work and labour skills in the 21st century. Today, one-north comprises three emerging industry nodes—within zones named Biopolis, Fusionopolis, and Mediapolis—that have been

Figure 4.   Top: Biopolis, biomedical cluster at one-north.
Source: Agency for Science, Technology and Research.
Bottom: Fusionopolis, information and communication technologies (ICT) cluster at one-north.
Source: Author.

identified to foster the next wave of knowledge production and innovation in Singapore.

The vision for a biomedical research hub in one-north has been realised through the development of Biopolis (Figure 4), a cluster of seven buildings housing well-known companies in the biomedical industry that are conducting R&D activities ranging from pharmaceutical and clinical development to medical technology research. The information and communication technologies (ICT) hub at Fusionopolis is yet another industry that is establishing itself on 30-hectares of land in one-north (Figure 4). Consisting of five construction phases, Fusionopolis and its state-of-the-art facilities will grow to accommodate the expanding ICT sector including complementary disciplines such as physical sciences and engineering. Mediapolis, the latest addition to one-north, was initiated in response to the burgeoning media sector. Content development, interactive digital media production, and ancillary media services are some of the activities of the media ecosystem that will be carried out. Although many of the completed buildings in one-north are today optimised and operational, the one-north masterplan is expected to be fully implemented in 2040; thus, generating over two million square metres of space for value-added scientific knowledge and technology production.

Investment in world-class infrastructure and R&D hubs, such as one-north, has helped to create a vibrant precinct at the urban fringe. This precinct, in turn, is not only boosting the economic value of Singapore's homegrown industries but also attracting and cultivating a pool of higher-skilled workers and creative talent. Industry creation, after all, is people-led. Investment in raising the capabilities of a nation's human capital, therefore, is as important as investment toward revitalising the stock of a nation's infrastructure assets.

Software Development: Talent

For a nation with no natural resources, it is vital that we elevate our *human* resources to levels that will become our competitive advantage. I therefore initiated the government-funded National Science Scholarships (NSS) in 2001 during my Chairmanship at A*STAR to create a way for committed young scientists to advance their research careers through education and job placement—in this way, breeding and retaining talent. The NSS enables the nation's brightest and most promising youth to develop their science careers by sponsoring their academic studies from the Bachelor to Doctoral level. Upon graduation, NSS scholars work at A*STAR for a period of five to six years so as to learn from, engage with, and ultimately contribute to Singapore's scientific community. Since its inception, the NSS has produced more than 1,200 local scholars with PhDs who are today productive members of the knowledge economy in Singapore, helping to shape the future of science and technology from their diverse roles within industry, academe, and administration (ASTAR, 2009).

Constructing a pipeline of highly-capable and ambitious young scientists is only one arm of a two-pronged strategy to develop R&D talent capital. The other arm involves recruiting internationally-acclaimed scientists to Singapore to lead cutting-edge research in their respective fields. The presence of high-profile thought leaders in science serves two purposes for Singapore. Firstly, as well-respected senior figures, these top scientists are linked to invaluable overseas networks—the scientific work that they conduct in Singapore would not only help to raise the profile of Singapore's R&D capabilities but also help Singapore build on their connections. Secondly, as experts in their scientific fields, the scientists have the experience to establish and direct research institutes and laboratories with full financing from the Singapore government. These research institutes and laboratories would not only be places of employment and learning for the next generation of scientists but also centres of knowledge and innovation creation.

Human capital development promotes upward social mobility by equipping individuals with the skills and financial capabilities to move up the social strata. As Singapore society becomes more educated, affluent, and aspirational, the marketplace will need to accommodate the demand for a greater variety of goods and services. This demand, in turn, generates jobs across the range of industrial sectors from manufacturing and services to R&D and knowledge creation. Additionally, the combination of technical expertise, innovation, good governance, and financing opportunities creates an environment conducive for entrepreneurship. Singapore nurtures enterprising innovators and provides the resources that enable local start-ups to one day become global brands. A dynamic entrepreneurial landscape produces new businesses, creates jobs, spurs competition, and enhances productivity through innovations in methods and processes—thus, enriching the economic health of a city-nation for successive generations.

Conclusion: The Future of Economic Planning

Singapore has enjoyed a steep development trajectory over a relatively short 50-year period. Such achievement, however, also raises questions about the possible future directions of this accelerated economic growth. This raises important questions for us all to consider. What might the industries of the future look like and how can economic planning today ready Singapore for that change when the time arrives? As globalisation continues to generate new sets of challenges as well as opportunities, how can Singapore's industries continue to be relevant and competitive? And, as the dynamics of the population evolve and the pressures of urbanisation increase, what characteristics might typify the new marketplace 50 years from today?

If there is one lesson that we can learn from Singapore's history of economic planning it is this: to secure our future, we must go out and create it. For the past five decades, the economic future of Singapore has been built by identifying and creating new industries, reviewing regulations and policies, and coordinating the implementation of strategies. Singapore's capacity to create a future based on a robust, sustainable, and vibrant economy has long been the nation's competitive advantage. This competitive advantage has enabled Singapore, a small republic with no hinterland and natural resources, to compete with a league of much larger developed nations. Developing and retaining talent will remain vital to Singapore. We need people who not only possess the expertise and knowledge to perform their work, but also the passion and courage to take risks and persevere for the betterment of Singapore. We will also need world-class infrastructure to support industry. Together, the twin engines of quality infrastructure and talent will enable Singapore to progress and prosper beyond tomorrow.

References

ASTAR (Agency for Science, Technology and Research) (2009) 'Scholarships and Attachments: For Graduate Studies' [http://www.a-star.edu.sg/Awards-Scholarship/Scholarships-Attachments/For-Graduate-PhD-Studies.aspx].

ASTAR (Agency for Science, Technology and Research) (2011) 'Science, Technology & Enterprise Plan 2015' [http://www.a-star.edu.sg/portals/0/media/otherpubs/step2015_1jun.pdf].

Goh, C. T. (2000) Speech by Prime Minister, Goh Chok Tong, at the Official Opening of Jurong Island on 14 October 2000 [http://www.nas.gov.sg/archivesonline/speeches/view-html?filename=2000101403.htm].

JTC (Jurong Town Corporation) (2000) *The Making of Jurong Island: The Right Chemistry*. Singapore: Epigram Pte Ltd.

Lim, H. K. (2014) Speech by Minister for Trade and Industry, Mr Lim Heng Kiang, for the Ministry of Trade and Industry Pioneer Generation Tribute Event at Raffles City Convention Centre, 27 November 2014 [http://www.news.gov.sg/public/sgpc/en/media_releases/agencies/mti/speech/S-20141127-1].

NatSteel (2013) 'Our Heritage' [http://www.natsteel.com.sg/about_heritage].

SEDB (Singapore Economic Development Board) (2014a) 'Our History, The Eighties' [http://www.edb.gov.sg/content/edb/en/why-singapore/about-singapore/our-history/1980s.html].

SEDB (Singapore Economic Development Board) (2014b) 'Our History, The Nineties' [http://www.edb.gov.sg/content/edb/en/why-singapore/about-singapore/our-history/1990s.html].

Singapore Statistics (2015a) 'Visualizing Data: GDP 2013' [http://www.singstat.gov.sg/docs/default-source/default-document-library/statistics/visualising_data/GDP-2013.pdf].

Jurong GRC (no date) 'Tribute to Dr Goh Keng Swee, the "Father of Jurong"' [http://www.juronggrc.sg/goh_keng_swee].

Singapore Statistics (2015b) 'Principal Statistics of Manufacturing by Industry Cluster, 2013' [http://www.singstat.gov.sg/statistics/browse-by-theme/manufacturing#sthash.GfYYsbPo.dpuf].

CHAPTER 4

Environmental Planning for Sustainable Development[1]

Tan Yong Soon

A clean and green environment offers a high quality of life for its residents as well as enhances economic growth. Singapore, a tiny island state with very limited land and resources, has been able to achieve a good balance between economic growth and environmental protection. This requires clear visions, long-term environmental planning and effective implementation.

Land Use

Long-term and integrated land-use planning plays a major role in protecting the environment. At the macro level, Singapore's development is guided by the Concept Plan, a strategic, long-term land use plan that maps the land-use vision for Singapore over the next 40 to 50 years, and is reviewed every ten years. This process is spearheaded by the Ministry of National Development and Urban Redevelopment Authority, but is really a collaborative effort involving all relevant agencies, especially environment and economic agencies, working together to ensure that the environment is protected in tandem with development. Consequently, land resources are used optimally so that quality of life improves even as Singapore continues to develop and its population grows. One level down, the Master Plan translates the broad, long-term strategies of the Concept Plan into detailed plans, even to the extent of specifying the permissible land use and density of development for every parcel of land.

Environmental controls are factored into land-use planning to ensure the developments are properly sited. Major land users with potential to cause extensive pollution are grouped together and located as far away as possible from residential areas and town centres. Through the process of developmental control and building plan approval, a developer of a project has to satisfy the planners and environment agencies

---

[1]An earlier version of this chapter was first published in *50 Years of Environment: Singapore's Journey Towards Environmental Sustainability* (World Scientific Publishing, 2015).

of its environmental pollution controls to limit its impact on the environment and ensure the compatibility with the surrounding land use.

Environmental pollution control requirements have to be incorporated into the design of the development, particularly with regard to environmental health, drainage, sewerage, and pollution control. Industries with the potential to cause extensive pollution and major developments that are likely to have major impacts on the environment are required to carry out pollution control studies covering all possible adverse environmental impacts, as well as the measures recommended to eliminate or mitigate these impacts.

Pollution control for industries goes beyond the planning and development phase. Even after approval is given, pollution levels are closely monitored. Pollution standards are reviewed over time and adjusted with improvements in technology.

As many green spaces as possible are set aside for recreation and the protection of the environment and biodiversity. Some nature areas, designated as national parks or nature reserves, are protected by legislation enacted by the Parliament. These nature areas are limited in land-scarce Singapore. Where areas rich in biodiversity are not protected by legislation, they are kept from development for as long as possible. Chek Jawa, a 100-hectare wetlands with different ecosystems and biodiversity located on the southeastern tip of Pulau Ubin, an island off the northeastern coast of the main island of Singapore is an example. Most land parcels are however open for multiple use. To enhance green areas, where appropriate, the drainage reserves along roads and canals are turned into green corridors and park connectors. The offshore Semakau landfill, Singapore's only remaining landfill, has been designed and operated to conserve the biodiversity of the surrounding areas and protect and preserve the marine ecosystem. It is also an idyllic and scenic attraction, open for activities such as educational tours, guided intertidal walks, bird watching, sport fishing or overnight stargazing. As a result of such careful planning, Singapore's green cover has grown from 35.7% to 46.5% between 1986 and 2007.

Land will always be a scarce and precious resource in Singapore. Going forward, Singapore will have to continue putting in significant effort to explore innovation in land and space optimisation. Aiming to take advantage of R&D to develop groundbreaking and pioneering technological solutions to increase Singapore's land capacity for its long-term development needs and to create alternatives for future generations, the National Research Foundation has allocated S$135 million from 2013 to 2018 for a land and liveability national innovation challenge that would "create new space cost-effectively and optimise the use of space to sustain Singapore's long-term growth and resilience".[2]

---

[2] National Research Foundation, Singapore (NRF) (2014), National Innovation Challenges. Retrieved 10 January 2015 from http://www.nrf.gov.sg/about-nrf/programmes/national-innovation-challenges?

Critical Environmental Infrastructure

Land also has to be set aside for critical environmental infrastructure such as drainage, sewerage, water supply as well as waste disposal facilities. Projections of future land requirements for such infrastructure are also factored into the Concept Plan so that adequate land is safeguarded for these needs. Selected areas that are ecologically rich will also be safeguarded. Having a good infrastructure in place is important.

Drainage

Singapore is located in the equatorial belt with abundant rainfall. Regular and severe flooding will occur if the storm water drainage infrastructure is not adequate. Managing flooding from heavy monsoon rains is important as floods cause not only great inconvenience and disruption to people's lives but also potentially tremendous damage to properties. In some flood incidents, lives might even be lost. Adequate storm water infrastructure requires setting aside extensive land parcels to build the drainage system. Hence the environment and water agencies, in consultation with URA, HDB, JTC and other development agencies, prepared and put into action a comprehensive Drainage Master Plan, taking into consideration current and future land use as well as intensities of developments. The Drainage Master Plan also sets aside land for widening existing storm water drains and canals as well as for building future drains, canals and detention facilities to minimise future flooding in tandem with developments. New policies are also introduced, such as requiring higher platform levels for developments, and getting new developments to implement on-site detention measures to reduce peak runoff discharged from their sites during intense rainfall. As a result, flood-prone areas have been reduced to 36 hectares at the end of 2013, from about 3,200 hectares in the 1970s.

Sanitation

Sanitation is another critical infrastructure, as otherwise diseases will spread. A Sewerage Master Plan was developed drawing from the apportionment of proposed land uses under the Concept Plan. The Sewerage Master Plan served as a detailed guide for the development of sewerage facilities, specifying corresponding projected sewage flows based on pre-determined zoning, and even micro-level design considerations of sewers and the layout of the sewerage facilities. Under the Sewerage Master Plan, Singapore was divided into a number of sewerage catchment zones, based on the contours of the island. A centralised sewage treatment plant served each zone, where the sewage was treated to international standards before the treated effluent was discharged into the sea. Pumping stations were installed to transfer sewage flows to the plants.

The design of Singapore's sewerage management system requires a clear separation of storm water and sewage streams and systems. Ensuring sewage goes into a central sewerage system and is kept separate from storm water has been critical in keeping waters in and around Singapore clean. This separate sewerage system is a more effective and economical approach in the long run as it ensures that the inland waterways, reservoirs, and the sea surrounding Singapore are not polluted by the discharge of untreated or semi-treated sewage and industrial effluent; and ensure all wastewater is collected for treatment before discharge into the sea or further processing to produce industrial or potable water. The separation of the systems also prevents storm water from entering the sewerage systems and causing overflows during heavy storms, as may happen in the case of combined sewers.

All premises are required to connect to public sewers. Developers of housing and industrial estates have to incorporate a sewer network to collect and convey sewage and industrial wastewater effectively into the public sewerage system. Proposals for development are scrutinised to ensure that they do not encroach on the public sewerage system (i.e. sewers, pumping, mains, etc.). This helps to avert any potential damage to the public sewerage system and, in turn, prevents pollution resulting from overflow or leakage of sewage. In addition, stringent sewer pipe laying and sanitary work requirements are also imposed through legislation.

With the development of NEWater (potable water reclaimed from treated wastewater, but is mostly used by industries as high purity water), sewage and industrial wastewater becomes used water, a resource that can be reclaimed for re-use. A deep tunnel sewerage system was built to consolidate the collection of used water into a central water reclamation plant for treatment and conversion to NEWater, freeing for redevelopment a number of parcels of land previously used for sewage treatment plants and pumping stations.

Water Supply

Achieving water sustainability is a strategic goal. Inland streams were dammed to form reservoirs, which were expanded. Estuarine rivers were also dammed up, the salty water flushed out to create large bodies of freshwater. The water catchment areas had to be protected to ensure storm water collected meets raw potable water quality. Where developments were necessary, such development was limited to residential estates and industries with clean and light uses. In addition to land-use planning, stringent pollution control was also required. Yet land scarcity does not allow us to have all water catchment areas to be protected. In fact, two-thirds of the island's land mass are water catchments areas, most of which are unprotected. Proper sanitation and strict regulation of sewage and industrial wastewater allow development in these unprotected water catchment areas.

NEWater or reclaimed water, the purification of used water to drinking water standards, and desalinated water combined can now meet up to 40 per cent of Singapore's water demand.

Waste Disposal

Land must also be set aside for an effective solid waste management infrastructure to ensure no potential threats to public health. Initially refuse were disposed of at sanitary landfills located on the main island, in areas that were not suitable for development without intensive preparation such as swampy areas, and far away from heavily populated areas. As land became increasingly scarce and with ever increasing solid wastes, Singapore introduced incineration in the late 1970s to reduce the refuse to be dumped into landfills to about 10% of its original volume. The closed landfills could be cleaned up and re-zoned for other uses. Heat from refuse incineration is recovered as electricity. However, land has to be allocated for refuse incineration plants and ash from refuse incineration is still required to be disposed of at a landfill, although the landfill requirement is much reduced. With no more swampy land available on the main island, an offshore landfill at Pulau Semakau was built for disposal of incineration ash and solid wastes that could not be incinerated.

Critical Success Factors: The 4 Ps

While the physical planning aspects—land use planning and critical environment infrastructure—are important, a good environment can only be achieved through the critical success factors of the 4P's—political leadership, public sector efficiency and effectiveness, private sector competitiveness and social responsibility and people participation and ownership.

Political Leadership

Political leadership is key to achieving a good balance between economic growth and environmental sustainability because there must be a clear vision from the very top that a clean and good quality living environment is important; a strong commitment to implement such a vision; and the ability to communicate that vision so that it can be shared and supported by everyone.

In the first 50 years, Singapore has had political leaders who possessed the foresight to see beyond economic development—that preserving the environment and growing the economy are not only not mutually exclusive, but complementary. Our leaders had the resourcefulness and mettle to take the long view and build capabilities, and also the skills to communicate the vision and persuade the people and businesses to suspend some of their immediate needs that the foregone economic development could have met.

Public Sector Effectiveness and Efficiency

In addition to sound political leadership, an effective and efficient public sector is critical to achieving success. The political leadership must be ably supported by a public sector that helps to design good policies and implement them effectively. It has to organise and work as an effective integrated government, develop and manage infrastructure projects well, innovate, continually set high environmental standards and regulate judiciously. The public sector would also have to introduce the right mix of market mechanisms to deter polluters and to encourage the development of a vibrant private sector which can produce environmental goods and services efficiently.

Private Sector Competitiveness and Social Responsibility

The private sector is certainly in the position to contribute to new environmental goods, as business is often good at innovating and searching for opportunities. Thus the desalination plants and the latest NEWater plants and incinerator plant are all privately owned and operated on a Public-Private Partnership arrangement with the relevant government agencies. In fact, Singapore based companies such as Keppel, SembCorp and Hyflux have also made successful forays overseas, for example into China and the Middle East, to help deliver environmental and water services and supplies competitively.

The private sector must also be socially responsible. Companies have to abide by the environmental standards set up by the government. Businesses are encouraged to provide feedback to proposed new regulations and standards so that they can be introduced effectively, in a reasonable timeframe.

People Participation and Ownership

People must want a better environment for themselves and their children. Public participation and ownership are critical to a better environment. The first national public education effort was a month-long "Keep Singapore Clean" campaign in 1968. It took many years of public education to enable the public to develop a sense of civic consciousness, social responsibility and discipline. Such government led platforms have now been replaced largely with mass participation, sharing of long-term plans and bottom-up initiatives by a healthy civil society.

Initially people may be more attuned to their immediate needs and need to be persuaded of the benefits of a clean environment. But once people have reaped the benefits of a clean environment, they would be inclined to desire it and may even be a few steps ahead of the government, if the government is slow in delivering a clean environment.

People have started to desire a clean environment, but they also have to organise and educate themselves, and to be motivated to assume the role of stewards of the environment for their children, to modify their behaviour, to help and not rely solely on the government to deliver a clean environment.

New Environment Challenges

Singapore has done well to protect its environment through effective environmental policy, planning and implementation. As a result of the good environment and concomitant economic progress, Singaporeans are better educated, widely travelled and hence, more environmentally sophisticated and demanding. We must continue to upgrade our environmental infrastructure and raise our standards to give our people a better quality of life. This is particularly important when climate change will pose tremendous dangers and unpredictable risks. We will need to take the necessary measures to mitigate and adapt to climate change.

We must move from the mindset of environmental protection to one of environmental sustainability. Sustainable development, as defined in the 1987 UN World Commission on Environment and Development report Our Common Future, is "Development that meets the needs of the present without compromising the ability of future generations to meet their own needs".[3] Singapore has already embarked on an environmental sustainability programme. It is an ongoing journey. The top-down approach to protecting the environment is still necessary but increasingly insufficient. An effective bottom-up approach is even more important now.

A Higher Quality of Environment

As Singapore progresses, Singaporeans will come to better understand the linkages between the environment and our health and social wellbeing, and that the quality of the environment is an important contribution to our quality of life. Good basic public hygiene and human health will no longer be sufficient. Our environmental infrastructure and standards must constantly be upgraded to truly meet first world standards. The challenge is to introduce and incorporate innovative environmental

---

[3] UN World Commission on Environment and Development (WCED) (1987), Chapter 2: Towards Sustainable Development, in *Our Common Future: Report of the World Commission on Environment and Development*. Switzerland: WCED. Retrieved 8 December 2014 from http://www.un-documents.net/ocf-02.htm

infrastructure/measures and make such facilities efficient and convenient for residents to practise environment-friendly programmes like waste recycling and energy conservation.

New forms of pollution threats and causes of environmental degradation need to be tackled effectively. The public deserves and will demand a higher quality of the environment.

Climate Change

Climate change, with the resultant rising sea level, extreme weather with very intense rainfalls and energy requirements, poses new challenges, not just infrastructural and economic, but also has tremendous important environmental, social and health impacts. We need to be able to address these issues and keep in mind the impacts in the future. More and more, we need long-term planning and policy and technological innovation to find effective and efficient solutions.

Environmental Sustainability

Singaporeans must want to live sustainably—environmentally, socially and economically. While many Singaporeans want a better quality of the environment, they must also be willing to pay, either in improving behaviour and habits so as to keep public places clean and reduce energy consumption, or footing the higher immediate economic costs required to safeguard the environment for future generations. Strong political leadership and committed public ownership will be needed to persuade and bring along the public to support a good environment. There will be a cost to improving the environment, but there is a greater cost to inaction.

Environment: Singapore's Competitive Advantage

Singapore has placed so much importance on the environment from our early days. Because of our unique circumstance as a city-state with no natural resources and hinterland, taking good care of our environment and making the most efficient use of our resources, is a necessity for us and not a choice.

Singapore environment agencies from the Anti-Pollution Unit (set up in 1970) to the Ministry of the Environment (set up in 1972 and later renamed as the Ministry of the Environment and Water Resources in 2004), and its agencies, PUB, the national water agency and the National Environment Agency, have always planned for the long term, innovated constantly and implemented effectively and pragmatically to help Singapore to develop in a sustainable way.

Land-use planning has always and will continue to be important to ensure that environmental considerations are incorporated in urban planning in Singapore. Environment agencies have and will continue to work with the urban planning authority to ensure integrated land-use planning. Critical environmental infrastructure must also be planned and implemented.

Our clean and green environment is our competitive advantage in ensuring a good quality of life for our residents as well as for attracting investments. As Singapore develops and grows into a first world country, it is even more important that we move successfully from the mindset of environmental protection to one of environmental sustainability. The political leadership's vision, the public sector's ability to help facilitate the execution of that environmental vision, the vibrancy of the private sector and the people's support for a good environment and taking personal responsibility and ownership, these are all factors which have brought us where we are today and are sources of great strength that will continue to propel Singapore forward.

Acknowledgements

The author wishes to thank his former colleagues in the Ministry of the Environment and Water Resources, especially Loh Ah Tuan, former Deputy CEO and Director General of Environment Protection, National Environment Agency (NEA), Foong Chee Leong, former Director General Meteorological Services and Director Pollution Control, NEA and Yap Kheng Guan, former Director Drainage and Director 3P (Public, Private and People sectors) Network, PUB for their comments and suggestions.

Part 2

The Built Environment as
a Sum of Parts

CHAPTER 5

Planning to Overcome the Constraints of Scarcity

Ng Lang

Planning for Singapore's land use and urban development is fundamentally about overcoming the physical constraints of a land-scarce island city-state. After independence in 1965, we started with 580 sq km of land, and only managed to expand it to the current modest 719 sq km after many years of land reclamation efforts. On this small island, besides having to cater to the wide-ranging land demands of a city, we also have to put aside land to meet the needs of a state, such as land for defence.

Yet, we have not done too badly despite the constraints. Within five decades, we have produced a dramatic transformation of the living environment. When we achieved independence in 1965, we had almost two million people crammed in the city centre, with serious problems of unemployment, squatter colonies, overcrowding in the city centre, and shortage of basic utilities and housing. 2015 was Singapore's 50th anniversary, and we celebrated a very different outcome with a population two-and-a-half times bigger. Singaporeans live in clean, lush and beautiful housing estates supported by world-class infrastructure. We are one of the most competitive economies in the world, and are linked to the world through a well-connected aviation hub and one of the world's largest ports. We are also regularly ranked as one of Asia's most liveable and greenest cities.

Planning Philosophy

Without doubt, we owe much of this success to the vision, values and ideas of Mr Lee Kuan Yew and his team of founding leaders in the 1960s. Post-independence, their first priority was to provide a safe and liveable environment, where the population could aspire to have decent jobs, good housing, and a clean and green environment. This was achieved through respecting the rule of law, embracing meritocracy and racial diversity, supporting an open economy to welcome foreign trade and investment, and building good schools and universities to train a skilled workforce. From the nation-building efforts, we inherited a planning philosophy that places emphasis on people and their quality of life, underscored by good governance that makes plans possible.

This was also a generation of visionary leaders, with an uncanny ability to look beyond the many pressing preoccupations of the day to plan for the long term. Before sustainable development became fashionable, our planning governance already incorporated long-term sustainable principles that delicately balanced economic, social and environmental outcomes. For instance, the Air Pollution Unit was set up in Singapore in 1971, and we only welcomed investment in industries that passed the environmental tests of the unit. It must have been a difficult decision then for a poor economy that was in desperate need for jobs, but an important one that kept our environment clean for the long term.

A Long-term Land-use Planning Framework

These governance principles are encapsulated in a strategic long-term land use plan known as the Concept Plan. Besides being a spatial land use plan, the Concept Plan is an important planning framework to ensure there is sufficient land to meet long-term growth while providing a good quality living environment.

The first Concept Plan was drawn up in 1971 (Figure 1). This was the first strategic long-term land use plan that decided where land would be set aside for future

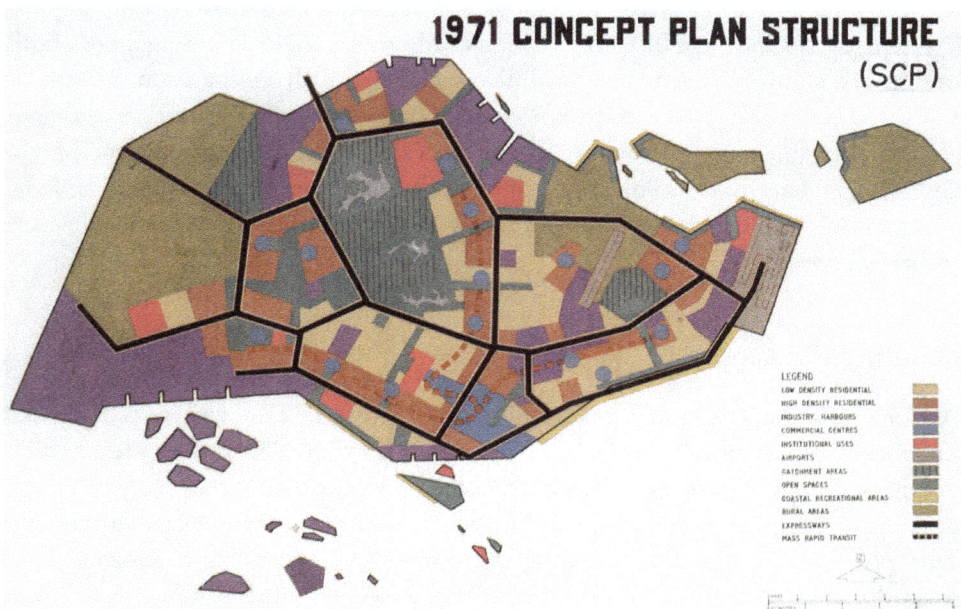

Figure 1.   Singapore's 1971 Concept Plan.
Source: Urban Redevelopment Authority.

townships, industrial parks, the financial centre, the airport, port, etc. It was a simple but powerful plan that defined the skeleton of Singapore's urban structure today.

The 1971 Concept Plan went through successive reviews and revisions in 1991, 2001 and 2011. These reviews involved many Ministries and agencies, and provided a Whole-of-Government platform to make strategic decisions on the long-term deployment of land. While the Urban Redevelopment Authority administers the Concept Plan, long-term land use decisions are taken collectively in government.

For this reason, the Concept Plan review process has inculcated within the government the discipline of constantly re-assessing Singapore's long-term needs, and always looking out for opportunities to create and safeguard land for the future, and for future generations. A vivid illustration of the significance of this approach is the land reclamation at Marina Bay, which started in the 1970s. In the early 2000s, at a time when the Singapore economy was going through a sluggish phase of growth, the land provided space for a seamless extension of our existing Central Business District (CBD), and gave Singapore a "second wind" to boost its ambition to become a global financial centre. The Marina Bay story reminds one of the Chinese saying—前人种树, 后人乘凉—one generation plants the trees, while later generations enjoy the shade.

This tradition of planning for the future continues with the current intention to eventually move the City Terminals and Pasir Panjang Terminal to Tuas, and the more recent announcement to re-locate the Paya Lebar Airbase. These are big moves which will free up large tracts of land; 1,000 ha of land along the southern coast in the case of the ports, and 800 ha of land in the case of the airbase. The latter will also lift the height restrictions for future developments in the eastern part of the island. The two areas will probably not be needed until beyond 2030, but the massive work needed to make them available has already been set in motion.

This ability to plan and implement land use for the long term is the hallmark of Singapore's urban planning, and the envy of many city planners. In essence, this is what sustainable development means—that we safeguard important resources to meet the needs of future generations. The same discipline extends to our land sales programme, where sale proceeds are locked up in the national reserves as a resource for the future, and not in the budget of the current government. This effectively removes the temptation for any government of the day to use land sales as an instrument to grow its budget.

The Concept Plan also serves an important function to balance the distribution of land among future competing economic, social and environment needs of Singapore. This way, despite the pressing needs of land for development, it gave us the confidence to protect land for both conservation districts and nature reserves for the future. In the 1980s, during a period of rapid urbanisation, the ability to project our long-term land needs allowed the government to conserve seven significant historic areas—Chinatown, Kampong Glam, Little India, Boat Quay, Clarke Quay,

Figure 2.   Preserving our built heritage in the heart of our city.
Source: Urban Redevelopment Authority.

Cairnhill, and Emerald Hill, and saved 3,200 heritage shophouses from the wrecking ball. Similarly, we have been able to set aside 9% of our land for parks and green spaces, including four nature reserves. Notably, the Central Catchment Nature Reserve is one of the very few protected tropical forests in the heart of a city. The reserve is a source of rich biodiversity, and it is fascinating that we are still finding new and unnamed species in the area. How we plan our city is a reflection of the collective values of our society. The land we set aside for conservation and biodiversity is a significant expression of the importance that our society attaches to heritage and the environment.

Transparency in Implementation

The strategies in the Concept Plan are implemented through the Master Plan. This is a comprehensive and progressive document that maps out in detail the permissible land uses and intensity of all land in Singapore. While the Master Plan is not uncommon in other cities, the transparency with which the Master Plan is implemented is another distinction of our planning governance framework.

The Master Plan is an open document easily accessible online, and more recently through mobile applications. It is backed by statute and, together with a set of clear development control guidelines and development charges, ensures transparency in our development approval process and proper governance for the State to have a fair share of development gains. The Plan is reviewed every five years to ensure that we factor in changes arising from local and global trends, and that our plans remain relevant to address future challenges and meet the needs of Singaporeans. The Planning Act states that it is mandatory to exhibit the reviews and open them to public views and comments. The review of the Master Plan in 2013 was exhibited over an eight-week period both at the URA City Gallery and online. The exhibition attracted 71,000 visitors, while the online version received almost 160,000 visits. While it is not always possible to have planning solutions that satisfy everyone, these public engagements are important to help us make more informed decisions to strike a balance among the diverse interests of society. It is also an avenue for government to garner public support for difficult, but necessary, planning policies and decisions.

Finding Our Own Solutions

Singapore occupies a unique position as the only island city-state in the world. Unlike most countries, we have only one city and nowhere to sprawl beyond our island's boundary. Ironically, this gives us an ideal environment for urban innovation. Our only way to succeed is to have the courage to find our own solutions to our problems, even if it means having to face some short-term pains for long-term good. Some of these solutions may even seem draconian because they have never been tried anywhere else before.

In 1975, we became the first city in the world to successfully implement a road congestion pricing scheme. To avoid the traffic gridlocks seen in many cities, we imposed a fee on vehicles entering the CBD to moderate the demand for road space. This was replaced in 1998 by the current Electronic Road Pricing (ERP) system. Many visiting policy makers have seen and expressed admiration for the system, but would always concede that it is politically impossible to implement it in their own cities. The ERP remained a uniquely Singapore solution for many years, and has only been adopted in recent years in cities like London and Stockholm.

With this same spirit of innovation, we have found our own solutions in other areas. These are some examples:

Public Housing

Over 80% of the Singapore population lives in public housing today. The public housing scheme started in the 1960s with the intention to resettle slum dwellers in the congested city centre. It also served to provide affordable home ownership to help a disparate migrant population of diverse racial background sink roots in Singapore and develop a national identity. Today, it has evolved to provide citizens with sophisticated housing nestled in vibrant and inclusive towns that offer a good quality and attractive living environment.

The newest public housing town in Punggol offers a glimpse of the future of public housing. It is designed to be much more environmentally-friendly than our older towns, and is immersed in a beautiful environment with lush greenery, canals and water bodies. At a time when citizens in cities globally grapple with the high cost of housing, the public housing scheme in Singapore offers a range of good, affordable housing to citizens from different income groups.

Greenery

Despite rapid urbanisation, Singapore is rich in greenery and urban biodiversity. The provision for greenery and biodiversity has been key in our urban planning and development approach, and stems from the conviction that nature and biodiversity can play an instrumental role in uplifting the human spirit within the urban environment. We do not have a hinterland to provide respite from the city, and so we integrate greenery deeply into our urban landscape. The sustained work done in this area over almost five decades has produced in Singapore a distinct identity, and few visitors would today challenge our claim to be a tropical City in a Garden. In 2010, in an acknowledgement of Singapore's achievement in this area, the UN Convention for Biodiversity partnered Singapore to conceive the Singapore Index on Cities' Biodiversity as a tool for cities to monitor and assess the progress of their biodiversity conservation efforts.

However, what we have achieved in this area cannot be taken for granted. The city is an artificial construct, and maintaining nature in the urban environment requires continued resolve, ingenuity and hard work. The current network of park connectors is an example of the continued efforts in innovation that is required in this area. The network is now 300 km long, and has expanded our space for greenery and leisure substantially using very little land.

Given our land scarcity, the continued efforts to green Singapore will have to depend to a large extent on such strategies to "borrow space" for greenery. Two areas of innovation will be key. The first is to closely integrate greenery with our waterways and reservoirs, and transform them into beautifully-landscaped streams and lake parks to expand our space for leisure and havens for biodiversity. The second is to weave greenery into our buildings. In the past 10 years, thanks to rising demand from a society that appreciates nature, the adoption of skyrise greenery in new developments has increased in tandem. We have also stepped up our policies to incentivise the adoption of skyrise greenery or to mandate it in some areas. The greatest impact of this effort is making it mandatory in selected parts of the city for affected landscape to be replaced as skyrise

Figure 3.   Bishan-Ang Mo Kio Park—transforming our environment through green and blue integration.

Source: NParks.

greenery on new developments. When Japanese architect Mr Toyo Ito was interviewed in Singapore a few years ago, he asked this question: "Is the building of the future one big tree?" This is certainly something that we hope to work towards.

Water Management

Our water scarcity has ironically made us one of the most advanced cities in the area of water management. In the 1960s and 1970s, Singapore relied heavily on imported water from Malaysia. By investing in water technology and adopting an integrated approach to water management, we have developed a diversified and sustainable water-supply strategy that significantly extended our water catchment areas, and developed recycled water and desalinated water as two new sources of water.

Singapore is now one of the few countries in the world to harvest urban storm-water on a large scale for its water supply. Since 2011, we have increased our water catchment area from half to two-thirds of Singapore's land. The ultimate aim is to increase the catchment area further to 90% of the land surface.

Marina Bay is a good showcase of our expertise in this area, where a single water body now serves multiple functions as water storage, resilience protection against floods, and a community recreational space. The Bay is a fresh water reservoir with a water catchment area of 10,000 ha, or one-seventh the size of Singapore in the heart of the city. The barrage that separates the reservoir from the sea serves as a tidal barrier to prevent flooding in low-lying areas in the city. At the same time, the iconic Bay doubles up as a beautiful waterfront for our new downtown and a venue for leisure and water sports.

Meeting Changing Aspirations

A city is a living machine that evolves continually. In our compact city environment, the complexity is multiplied many times. The work to plan and overcome the challenges of our city never stops.

But the fundamental planning question is about how we can make Singapore more liveable to meet the changing aspirations of the individuals living in the city. When we were a poor economy in the 1960s, the main aspiration was to have a job to provide for the family. But today's citizens have much more complex needs. Besides a good job, they also want time for themselves, time for family, a stronger sense of participation in the community, and active, green, healthy living.

In the last review of the Master Plan in 2013, we posed fundamental questions on how we meet these aspirations in six areas: the economy, housing, community, recreation, transport and identity. The review proposed a well-received plan to bring jobs closer to homes, and to make Singapore a city for all ages that is green, healthy, connected, and strong in community interaction and spirit.

In particular, two key thrusts in the plan will in the long term bring about fundamental changes to enhance liveability.

The first is to accelerate efforts to create new job centres closer to homes, outside the traditional CBD and the industrial area in the western part of our island. The work has already started with some success. In the east, Tampines Regional Centre and Changi Business Park are already established employment hubs. In the west, the Jurong Lake District has been shaping up well since 2008. There are also job clusters at one-north, Paya Lebar Central, and Novena. A new area of focus is the North Coast Innovation Corridor that spans Woodlands Regional Centre and the Punggol Learning Corridor and Creative Cluster. There is an exciting opportunity here to closely integrate the future campus of the Singapore Institute of Technology with a business park for creative high-tech industry. It will provide high-value jobs and opportunities for life-long learning for residents in the north and north-east. When fully completed, the overall effort to bring jobs closer to homes will allow more flexibility to configure future work-life requirements, and will be an important contributor to quality of life.

A second key thrust is to enhance mobility options in the city. Singaporeans are by now familiar with the much publicised effort to invest aggressively in public transport infrastructure. The plan is to double our rail network by 2030 so that eight in ten households can reach a train station within a ten-minute walk. There has also been ongoing effort to enhance the overall public transport capacity with more trains, buses and increased frequencies. We have at the same time announced a National Cycling Plan to build a network of cycling paths to provide a greener, healthier mobility option. When the infrastructure is in place, we can aim for a "car-lite" alternative, where we place emphasis on mobility solutions rather than private car ownership. It will give us a very different city that prioritises the public realm for people and quality of life.

Beyond these fundamental changes, the Master Plan also continues the ongoing efforts to build more inclusive, greener, and active public spaces to encourage community interaction and participation. This is an area that we have done well in in our town planning, but which we will continue to innovate to adjust to the changing demographics in our society. With an ageing population, we will have to put in more effort to make our living environment more age-friendly, and provide facilities to enable our seniors to age-in-place. Kampong Admiralty, which is being developed, is a good example of the ongoing experimental efforts to encourage social interactions and active living through design and integration of communal spaces. When built, it will be a one-stop hub with social and healthcare facilities, dining and retail outlets, wide community spaces, generous green features, and studio apartments all under one roof.

In other incremental ways, we are test-bedding exciting new ideas in new development precincts such as Marina Bay, Jurong Lake District, and the Punggol Eco-Town. This precinct development approach allows us to integrate solutions across developmental agencies to produce much better outcomes with new or existing technology. In successive precincts, we are setting ever higher benchmarks to make them more liveable, more inclusive, and more carbon-friendly through better urban planning and designs, better technology, and better community involvement efforts.

Singapore in Another 50 Years

As we celebrate Singapore's 50th anniversary, a natural question to muse over is what Singapore will look like in another 50 years. Clearly, the future is for us to create. The lesson from the past is that Singapore's future success will depend largely on our continued ability to plan and innovate for the long term to offer an attractive liveable environment to attract ideas, technology, and capital. Innovation is not just about having good ideas. It is also about our collective resolve to take hard decisions to do the right things for the long term, and for future generations.

There are many challenges that we will need to address, such as maintaining Singapore's economic relevance to the rest of the world, the changing demographics and expectations of the population, climate change, resource scarcity, etc. Incremental efforts at innovation will not be sufficient in the long term, since there is a limit to how much we can continue to optimise solutions in an environment of finite space. We will need to explore new paradigms to reshape the city, and to rethink the way we live, work and play. In this regard, the current advancement in disruptive technology in a wide range of areas offers new exciting opportunities. The current progress in autonomous vehicles, for instance, will make it possible to totally re-imagine how we plan, develop and manage mobility in the near future.

This need for continuous innovation and rejuvenation makes Singapore a well-positioned city for exciting human invention, creativity, and ingenuity. It provides immense opportunities to develop and test-bed new ideas in a compact city setting. However, in our search for solutions, we must always remember that planning for the city is not just about optimising space, resources, and infrastructure. Ultimately, the planning philosophy of our city's founding leaders still rules—it is all about people. Indeed, the success of Singapore as a sustainable compact city ultimately rests on the people's continued commitment to the vision, and our future living environment depends on the choices we make as a society. Key to strengthening our capacity to plan future success will involve harnessing our collective energies to make Singapore not just a sustainable city, but a sustainable home.

CHAPTER 6

Making Singapore a Liveable and Sustainable City: Our Urban Systems Approach[1]

Khoo Teng Chye and Remy Guo

With over five million inhabitants living on 719.1 square kilometres of land, Singapore today is one of only a few cities in the world recognised for achieving high standards of liveability and sustainable development, despite a high population density. This would have been difficult to imagine in the 1960s, when Singapore was plagued by economic woes, poor infrastructure and squalid conditions, with a population of 1.7 million–about a third of the present population. This leap, from a basket case of urbanisation to a thriving global metropolis, was achieved in the space of 40 years.

Today, many highly liveable cities are spread out over large geographical areas with low population density. Cities such as Sydney or Vancouver are often cited. Singapore is one of the outliers that has achieved high liveability with high population density (See Figure 1). Given rapid urbanisation in the developing world, the cities of tomorrow are more likely to be like Singapore than like Sydney or Vancouver. So the lessons learnt from the Singapore approach to urbanisation will be useful to many other cities, especially given the need to reduce urban sprawl and dependence on the car as the major mode of transport.

The CLC Liveability Framework

The Centre for Liveable Cities (CLC) was established in 2008 to capture the explicit and tacit knowledge underlying Singapore's unique urban development

---

[1] This article is adapted from Chapter 1—The CLC Liveability Framework and Chapter 2—Master Planning: Transforming Concepts to Reality in *Liveable and Sustainable Cities: A Framework, Centre for Liveable Cities, and Civil Service College, Singapore (2014)*.

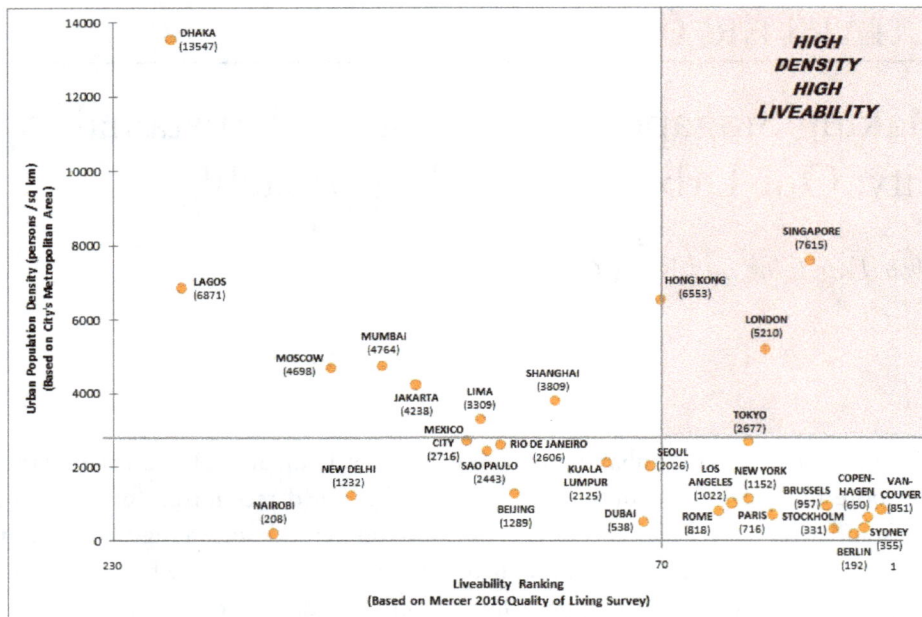

Figure 1.   The CLC Liveability Matrix.[2-4]

experience, and to distil some of the general principles that have guided Singapore's urban planners and policy makers over the years. Our research has included over 230 original interviews with past and present cabinet ministers and senior officials, several of whom are quoted in this article. Through its research, CLC found

---

[2]Metropolitan area data was used consistently for all cities in the matrix. As defined in the 2009 Revision of the UN World Urbanization Prospects report, a metropolitan area is a contiguous area encompassing the city proper and additional surrounding areas that are under the direct influence of the city proper (for instance, through transport links and a commuting labour market). With cities now growing beyond their administrative boundaries into larger metropolitan areas, metropolitan area definitions were felt to be more relevant. This is also a better comparison with Singapore, which is a city-state, not just a city, and has to allocate space for infrastructure, industries, housing estates, defence, etc. Metropolitan areas and the relevant population figures are derived from open source city data available for each city to derive the population density figures.

[3]The Mercer's Quality of Living Survey is used as an indicator of urban liveability as the index is the most comprehensive and widely recognised international measure of Quality of Life/Liveability. The criteria used fall under 10 main categories, with the categories weighted to reflect their relative contribution to overall quality of living. Examples of the categories include political and social environment, medical and health considerations, natural environment and recreation.

[4]Cities included in the matrix represent a good spread of examples from low-density, low-liveability cities to high-density, high-liveability cities. A good geographical spread was taken into account when selecting cities for the matrix.

that Singapore has held three key liveability outcomes constant in its urban development:

(i) A **competitive economy** in order to attract investments and provide jobs;
(ii) A **sustainable environment** because the city has to survive with limited natural resources, especially in terms of land and water; and
(iii) A **high quality of life**, including the social and psychological well-being of the population.

The liveability outcomes are fairly obvious, and can be measured, as has been done in various liveability indices like Mercer's. What is less obvious is how Singapore and other cities maintain these outcomes over time.

Ensuring that these liveability outcomes are sustained, two elements have been vital to successful urbanisation in Singapore. First, it was crucial to have a **system of integrated planning and development** that kept the outcomes of a liveable city constantly in view, over the long term.

Second, subscribing to an **urban governance approach that was dynamic** helped sustain the conditions needed for a thriving liveable city.

Together, these elements form the components of the **CLC Liveability Framework** (Figure 2).

The CLC Liveability Framework aims to provide a lens through which city leaders can view their cities and analyse the actions or approaches open to them to enhance liveability. While the three outcomes–High Quality of Life, Competitive Economy, Sustainable Environment–are highly visible and present useful goals for cities, the mechanisms underlying these outcomes are critical for city leaders seeking to initiate and sustain urban transformation.

Singapore's urban development experience has demonstrated that building a liveable city requires the twin systems of Integrated Master Planning and Development, as well as Dynamic Urban Governance. This chapter focuses on the principles behind Singapore's integrated planning and development system, and provides insights into Singapore's integrated approach.[5]

The Principles of Integrated Master Planning and Development

Integrated planning and development has enabled Singapore to manage development priorities on both in the short- and long-term, in response to changes in a dynamic

---

[5] The scope of this chapter does not cover urban governance. For more insights on dynamic urban governance, please refer to Chapter 1—The CLC Liveability Framework, and Chapter 3—Urban Governance: Foresight and Pragmatism in *Liveable and Sustainable Cities: A Framework, Centre for Liveable Cities, and Civil Service College, Singapore (2014).*

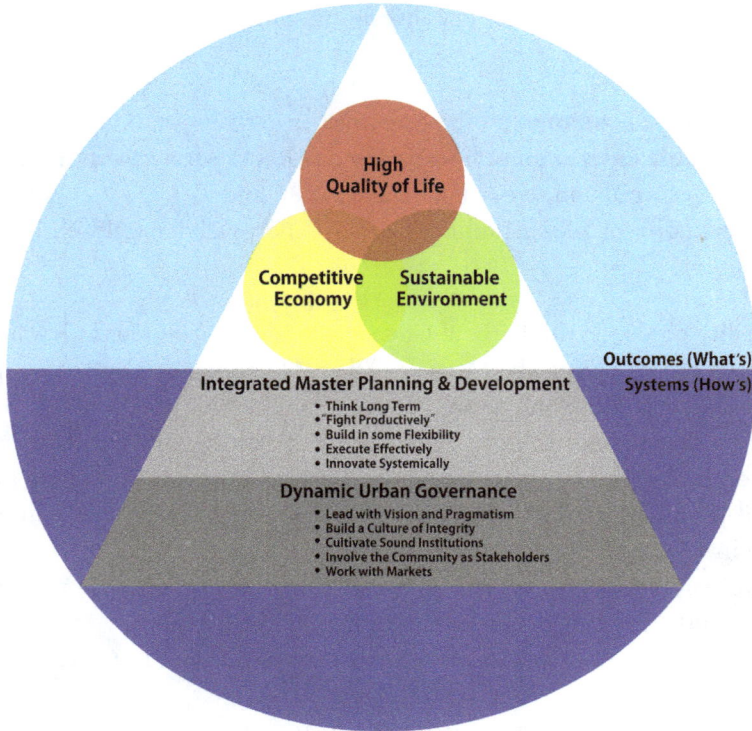

Figure 2.   The CLC Liveability Framework.

political, economic and social environment. Urban policies and programmes among different stakeholders in government are integrated through a common national document, known as the Concept Plan, which lays out strategic land use over a time horizon of 40 to 50 years.[6] More detailed plans for implementation are then derived as statutory Master Plans, which are coordinated across different government agencies.

This transparent and legal planning system is not unlike that of many cities. What differentiates Singapore's integrated planning regime from other cities' is that its plans do not just stay on paper–they are coordinated, implemented and executed through dedicated organisations, with expertise and resources. These powerful executive agencies, for e.g., the Housing and Development Board (HDB), Public Utilities Board (PUB), Land Transport Authority (LTA) and National Environment Agency (NEA), "fight" to achieve their mission outcomes, and are forced to optimise or compromise,

---

[6]The relatively longer planning horizon of 40–50 years is essential to safeguard land for future development purposes in Singapore. For example, when Singapore's public housing authority ramped up its development programme to meet public housing demand in 2012, vacant land had already been safeguarded for housing development since 1991 in the Concept Plan.

given the lack of land and other resources. These productive fights are resolved often by taking a long term view, and trade-offs are made, for example, between development and the environment. Flexibility, innovation and effective execution are often the outcomes when this integrated approach is taken, underpinned by good governance.

Five implicit principles underpin this integrated approach to planning and development[7]:

(1) Think long term;
(2) Fight productively;
(3) Build in some flexibility;
(4) Execute effectively; and
(5) Innovate systematically.

Principle 1: Think Long Term

Land is Singapore's most binding constraint. Urban development in Singapore is subject to detailed and long-range planning to ensure that sufficient land is made available to cater to population growth and economic activity while maintaining a good quality of life. This principle of long-term planning did not emerge overnight, but was established over time as Singapore's planning and development evolved.

Singapore's Historical Town Planning System

Singapore's first statutory Master Plan was modelled on the Greater London Plan of 1944 and adopted in 1958 under the British colonial administration (Figure 3). Designed by renowned British town planner Sir George Pepler and his team, it accounted for population trends, building resources, industrial resources, traffic standards, and redevelopment needs and other concerns. However, premised on a population of two million in 1972—a size that was exceeded by 1970—the 1958 Master Plan was fundamentally static and preservationist. By and large, it was considered unsuccessful even though it had been prepared and administered with due diligence.[8]

Shortly after the Master Plan was approved in 1958, Singapore was granted full internal self-government from the British in 1959. After a short-lived merger with Malaysia, Singapore became an independent republic in 1965.

---

[7] These principles of Integrated Master Planning and Development form part of the CLC Liveability Framework, which distilled the general principles that have guided Singapore's urban planners and policy makers over the years. See Chapter 1—The CLC Liveability Framework by Khoo Teng Chye in *Liveable and Sustainable Cities: A Framework (2014)*.

[8] Steven Choo, "Planning Environment and the Planning Process—A Case Study of Singapore, *UNIBEAM*, 90–96.

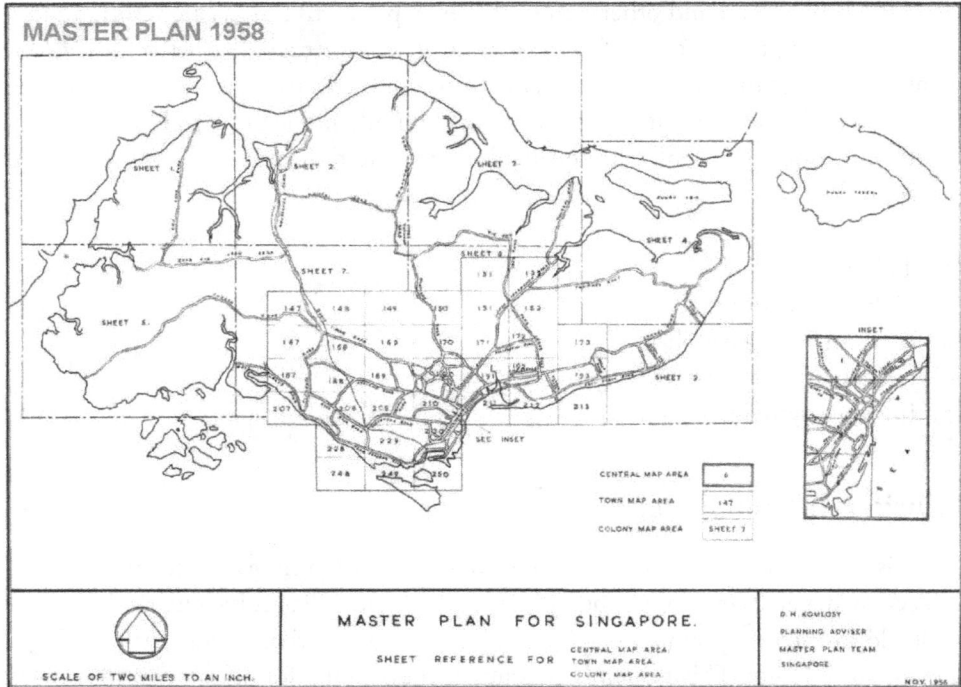

Figure 3. The 1958 Master Plan.

Source: Urban Redevelopment Authority.

As former Minister for National Development S. Dhanabalan recalls, "the top priority when the government came into power was housing the population and building up a manufacturing sector to create employment." Rapid industrialisation, identified as a key strategy for the nascent city-state, meant that land would need to be used for ports, industrial estates, transport networks and other needs more conducive to rapid growth and modernisation. This strategy was at odds with the preservationist mode of the 1958 Master Plan.[9]

The State and City Planning Project—Beginnings of a Long-Term Approach

Upon the Singapore government's request, two United Nations (UN) teams of experts[10] visited Singapore and found the 1958 Master Plan urgently in need of revision.

[9] Pepler's plan was based on a slow and steady rate of urban growth and social change, reliance on the limited private sector for physical development of the city, and the preservation of past institutions.

[10] A 1962 team, led by UN Town Planning Advisor Erik Lorange, made a preliminary survey with recommendations that the 1958 Master Plan needed urgent revision. This was followed in 1963 by a UN team consisting of Charles Abrams, Susumu Kobe and Otto Koenigsberger (the "KAK team").

A "project-by-project" action plan-driven approach was recommended by the UN experts and adopted to drive urban development and growth.

However the government was mindful that a "project-by-project" approach to development could lead to possible negative effects in the long-term. A plan of operations was drawn up in 1966 in preparation for a growth-oriented long term master plan. All physical planning and implementing agencies were consolidated within the Ministry of National Development (MND). An ad hoc organisation called the State and City Planning (SCP) project was formed from a number of departments, with the original Planning Department as the nucleus, serving as a counterpart to the UN team. Work began in 1967 and the SCP plan eventually became the 1971 Concept Plan.

The 1971 Concept Plan—Building Foundations for Long-Term Planning

The 1971 Concept Plan made provisions for a time frame of 30 to 35 years. In addition, the 1971 Plan reflected an understanding that urban planning had to be carried out within an overall framework of social and economic policies. This understanding has since come to characterise Singapore's approach to integrated planning.

The creation of the 1971 Concept Plan had a broader aim of maintaining Singapore's political independence, economic viability and social cohesion amidst a

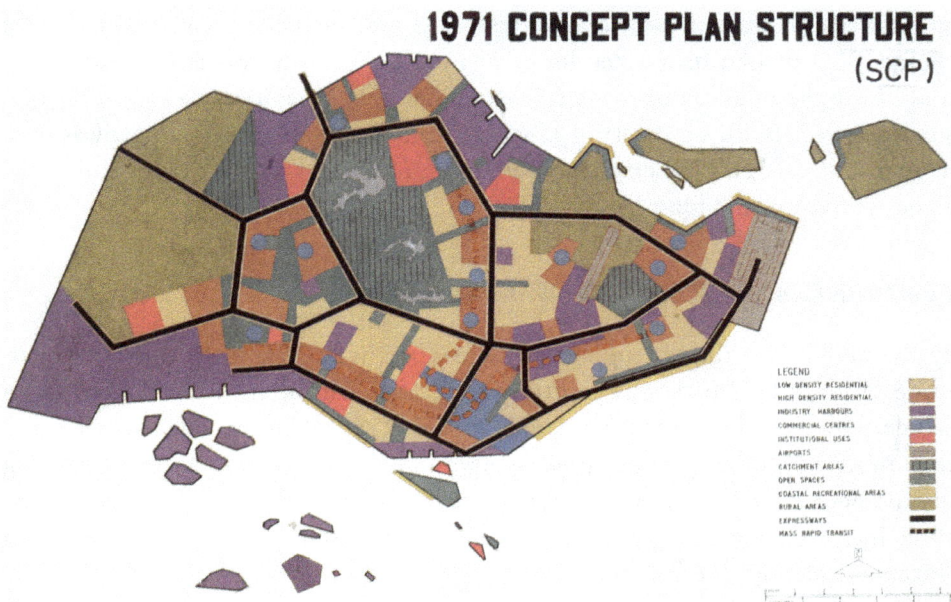

Figure 4.   The 1971 Concept Plan.
Source: Urban Redevelopment Authority.

diverse population. The SCP made specific projections on population, school children numbers, workforce, housing needs, motor vehicle numbers, productivity growth, household income, employment and occupational structure, industrial land requirements, residential land requirements, office space demand and hotel space demand. It also looked at the implications of land use for the transportation network.

Consequently, the 1971 Concept Plan was able to bring greater coherence to Singapore's development, allowing the government to move ahead quickly on building public housing, industrial estates and roads. A key idea in the 1971 Concept Plan was the decision to develop Singapore along a Ring Plan, which addressed both land use and transport system planning. The Ring Plan allowed for staged development, with flexibility to account for changing priorities later on, and integrated plans for an efficient Mass Rapid Transit system and expressways. Much of Singapore's urban structure today—particularly the ring-cum-linear shape—is the outcome of this approach.

The primary mechanism for implementing the Concept Plan was the Master Planning Committee (MPC). Plans from various government agencies had to be submitted to the MPC, which would approve the land use and land allocation for all public sector developments.[11] This enabled development to take place in a coordinated manner. Strategic agencies such as the Housing and Development Board (HDB), Jurong Town Corporation (JTC) and Economic Development Board (EDB) could safeguard land early on for their long-term needs. Major, capital-intensive infrastructure projects that required long lead times of up to 20 years to build (such as power stations, water mains, service reservoirs and incineration plants) could be planned and phased into a development programme. Transportation authorities could time the building of roads to ensure that new developments would be adequately served. Based on the 1971 Concept Plan, the international airport was relocated from Paya Lebar, a fairly central location, to Changi on the eastern end of the island, to free up land for other developments.

The 1991 Concept Plan—The Watershed Plan

By the mid-1980s, the system and processes for physical planning and implementation of plans by the various government agencies had been put in place. After a decade, however, there was a need to review the 1971 Concept Plan to take into account new priorities: demographic changes and economic restructuring, balancing environmental considerations with economic needs, catering to the rising aspirations of an increasingly affluent population with more lifestyle choices, and conserving Singapore's identity and heritage.

---

[11] The Chief Planner (acting on the advice of the MPC) was the authority on public sector developments, with the power to make the final decision resting with the Minister for National Development and the Cabinet.

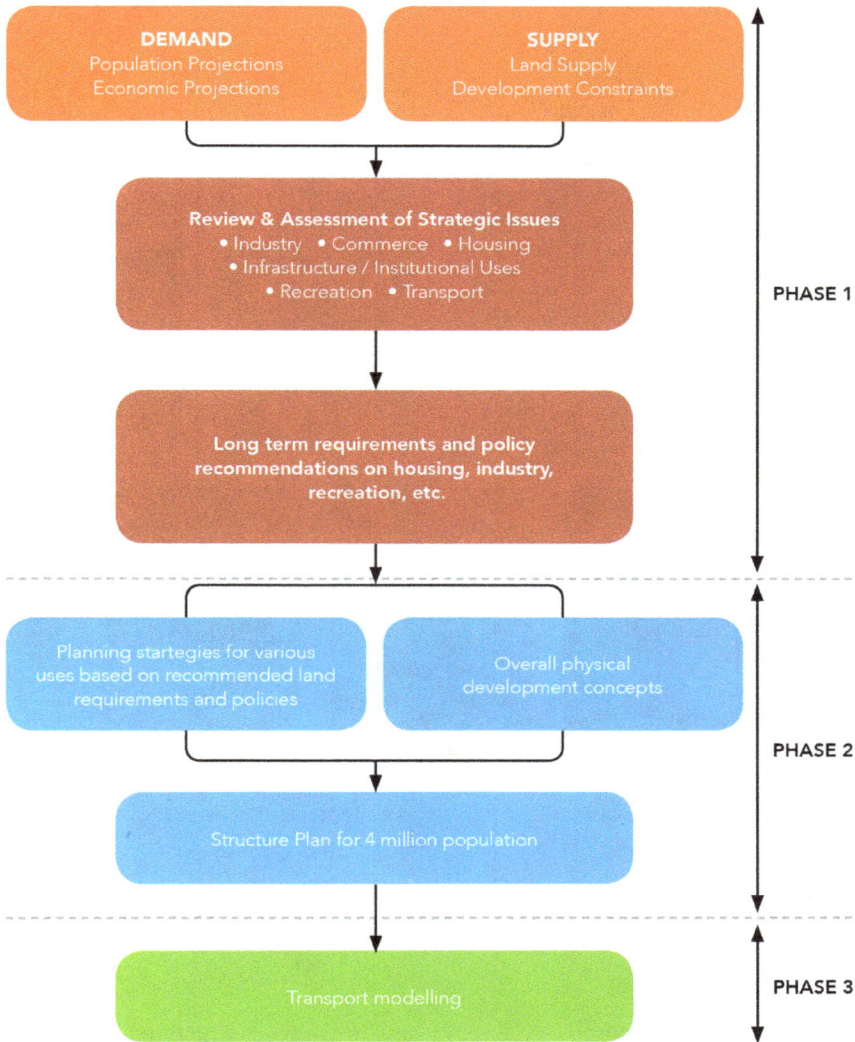

Figure 5.   Three phases of the 1991 Concept Plan preparation.

Source: Singapore-Suzhou Software Transfer Project, 1994, Urban Redevelopment Authority.

Preparation for the 1991 Concept Plan started in the late 1980s. It was the first time the planning authority in Singapore was drafting the Concept Plan on its own. The institutional framework and the processes which were set up to draft the 1991 Concept Plan would serve as the general basis for the drawing up of future Concept Plans.

In many ways, the 1991 Concept Plan was considered Singapore's *watershed plan*—it established a framework for "Year X", envisioning Singapore's physical land

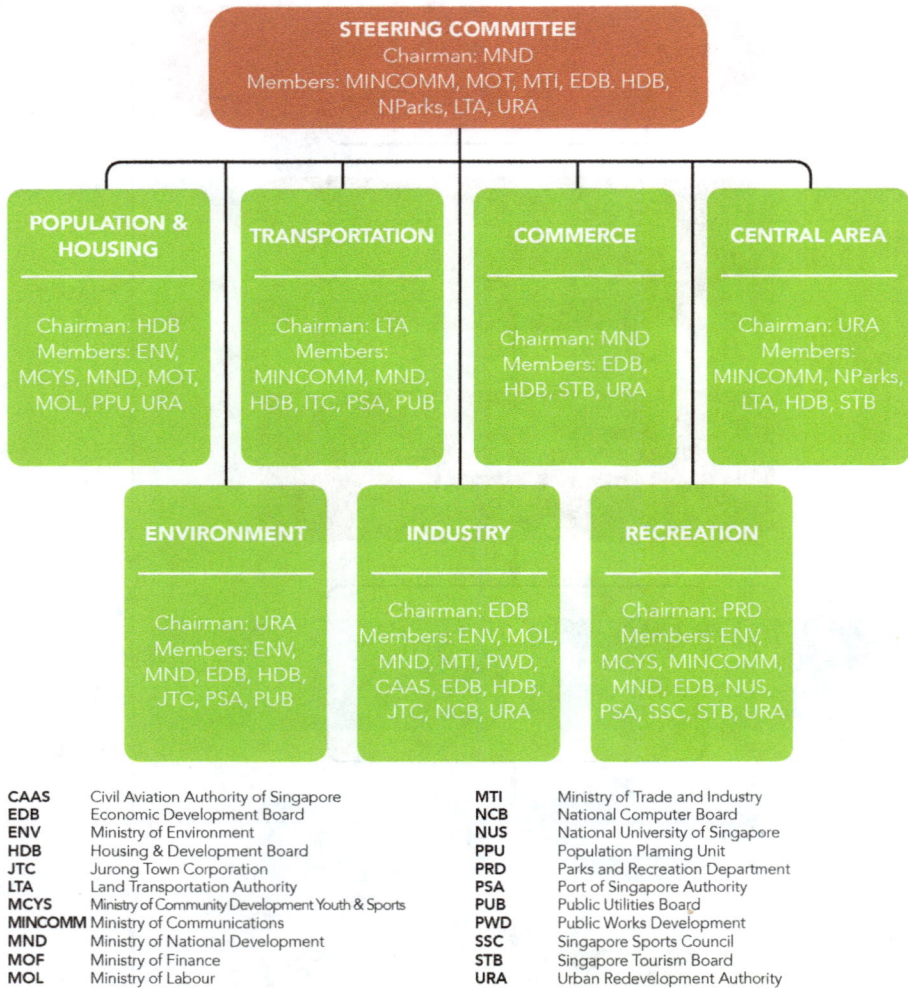

CAAS	Civil Aviation Authority of Singapore	MTI	Ministry of Trade and Industry
EDB	Economic Development Board	NCB	National Computer Board
ENV	Ministry of Environment	NUS	National University of Singapore
HDB	Housing & Development Board	PPU	Population Planing Unit
JTC	Jurong Town Corporation	PRD	Parks and Recreation Department
LTA	Land Transportation Authority	PSA	Port of Singapore Authority
MCYS	Ministry of Community Development Youth & Sports	PUB	Public Utilities Board
MINCOMM	Ministry of Communications	PWD	Public Works Development
MND	Ministry of National Development	SSC	Singapore Sports Council
MOF	Ministry of Finance	STB	Singapore Tourism Board
MOL	Ministry of Labour	URA	Urban Redevelopment Authority

Figure 6.   Preparation of the 1991 Concept Plan—inter-agency structure.

Source: Singapore-Suzhou Software Transfer Project, 1994, Urban Redevelopment Authority.

use structure when the population reached 4.4 million in size. The review process was intense and rigorous, with planners going down to the minutest details.

The planning process (Figure 5) comprised three main phases: reviewing and identifying land use requirements; formulating development strategies and policies; traffic modelling, plan evaluation and refinement. Once the Concept Plan had been revised, there was a review phase, which consisted of monitoring and updating the plan.

An Inter-Ministry committee was formed, with the Ministry of National Development (MND) as the chair (Figure 6). The main committee mapped out the constraints imposed by various major land uses (such as defence, pollutive industries, water and airports), while various sub-committees were tasked with working out the specific policies and directions in the areas of population, housing, transportation, commerce, central area planning, environment, industry and recreation.

A committee comprising all Permanent Secretaries endorsed a set of overarching strategic policy directions on land use planning. Some of these policies included: controlling pollution at source through technology instead of using land as a buffer; locating pollutive installations offshore; having high quality open space instead of increasing the quantity of open space. These policies would guide the land use development of industry, commerce, housing, transport, recreation, infrastructure, institution use and environment.

New ideas were also introduced in some critical areas of land use:

Transport–integrated land use planning

One of the bold ideas articulated in the 1991 Concept Plan was to integrate land use and transport planning, while decentralising commercial activities. In general, many international cities tend to deal with land use planning and transport planning separately. As veteran planner Liu Thai Ker explained, "the purpose of transportation is principally to move people from home, to shopping to commercial centres, to factories, to school…when you don't combine the two (i.e., land use and transportation), you get a lousy urban plan."[12]

When drafting the 1991 Concept Plan, the planners noted that vehicular traffic was particularly heavy during morning peak hours in the east-west direction owing to the concentration of manufacturing employment areas in the western part of the island. There was also heavy travel in the north-south direction, from residential new towns in the northern part of the island towards the city centre, where the majority of commercial, business, and financial activities were located. Planners realised that a more even distribution of housing and jobs would help to make better use of the transport infrastructure and balance transport demand in each direction.

The 1991 Concept Plan thus introduced a key policy direction to decentralise in order to ease traffic congestion in the city centre. Establishing public transit as "the first organising principle" of Singapore's urban system, "the planning and allocation of the most intensive and activity-generating uses were at the most accessible locations by mass transit."[13] This gave rise to the "constellation"

---

[12] Liu Thai Ker, interview by the Centre for Liveable Cities, Singapore, June 29, 2011. Liu is currently Director of RSP Architects Planners & Engineers (Pte) Ltd. He held previous appointments as Chief Executive Officer of the Housing and Development Board, and Urban Redevelopment Authority.

[13] John Keung, interview by the Centre for Liveable Cities, Singapore, June 27, 2011. Keung is currently Chief Executive Officer of the Building and Construction Authority (BCA). He is also the Co-Executive

concept and development of regional centres (see Principle 3: Build In Some Flexibility).

Industry development–new ideas

By the mid-1980s, EDB was already promoting Singapore as a place to do business. The manufacturing sector focused on high value-added sectors such as biotechnology, pharmaceuticals, chemical industries and R&D. In line with this economic restructuring, older industrial estates that were lower value-adding and land-intensive industries were scheduled to be phased out or rejuvenated.

These in-depth studies culminated in major strategies to develop technology corridors that would have business parks located near major tertiary institutions, along major transportation corridors and near regional centres. Other strategies included reclaiming offshore areas (i.e., Jurong Island) for the co-location of pollutive industries such as petroleum and other chemical industries.

Housing strategies–quality homes

While the 1970s and 1980s saw massive public housing construction by HDB, further housing demand was projected in the 1991 Concept Plan due to projected population growth and declining household size. An additional 1.35 million dwelling units were estimated to be required.

To accommodate the 1.35 million dwelling units required, several strategies were introduced in the 1991 Concept Plan. These included: (i) phasing out industries and other less suitable uses within prime residential areas; (ii) safeguarding offshore islands as a contingency land reserve to meet long-term housing demands; (iii) carrying out further land reclamation with interesting profiles to create high quality waterfront housing; and (iv) upgrading and improving the living environment of existing HDB estates to be comparable to private residential developments.

Recreation policy–enhancing a Garden City

Since independence, Singapore has adopted a policy of greening the city. The 1991 Concept Plan review sought ways to further pursue this. A key strategy was to provide a variety of open spaces that would be well distributed, ranging from regional

Director of the Clean Energy Programme Office, Chairman of BCA International Pte Ltd, a board member of BCA and member of the Supervisory Board, Solar Energy Research Institute of Singapore. He held previous appointments as Deputy Chief Executive Officer (Building) of the Housing and Development Board, Director of Strategic Planning in the Ministry of National Development, Deputy Chief Planner (Planning Policies) in the Urban Redevelopment Authority and later, as its Deputy Chief Executive Officer (Development Control and Corporate Development).

parks to town parks and neighbourhood parks, a riverine park and beach areas along the waterfront. Nature reserves and ecologically important sites such as Labrador Nature Reserve Park and Bukit Timah Nature Reserve were also to be preserved.

The 1991 Concept Plan integrated each of these major critical land uses at a national level, taking into account the policy directions and goals of each critical use. The thrust of the 1991 Concept Plan was publicised through an exhibition in 1991, which sought to explain to the public how Singapore's urban planning could affect them in the future.

Principle 2: Fight Productively

Each of the various government agencies in Singapore has a directive to solve specific urban issues: housing, industrialisation, water supply, recreation and so on. Given Singapore's land scarcity, it is inevitable that competing claims for land use will arise.

One point of contention raised in the 1991 Concept Plan Review had to do with industrial and housing development encroaching on protected water catchment areas. A 1983 policy decision stipulated that the land area to be developed by the public and private sectors would be restricted to 34.1 per cent of the unprotected water catchment area, covering a total area of 6,945 ha. The major concern then was that development would increase the risk of contaminating Singapore's water resources. However, Singapore was urbanising so quickly that this ceiling of 34.1 per cent was breached by 1991.

Following the review, URA and HDB estimated that an additional 1,855 ha of land in the unprotected water catchments would be required in the long term, based on a projected population of five million. However, while there was the need to accommodate population and economic growth, there was also a need to ensure that development would not compromise the quality of the city-state's water.

PUB and the Ministry of Environment (ENV) engaged a consultant in 1996 to study the impact of urbanisation on unprotected catchments and the allowable urbanisation level in each water catchment. They found that Singapore's water pollution control efforts had been effective, and that the water quality in unprotected catchment reservoirs had not deteriorated significantly despite development in the catchments over the years.

Various options were presented to the Cabinet. In 1999, following a joint proposal by MND, ENV and the Ministry of Trade and Industry (MTI), the Cabinet lifted both the urbanisation cap and population density limit, subject to the continuation of stringent water pollution control measures. Future development would no longer need to be curtailed as long as pollution control measures were implemented rigorously and effectively.

This ability of different government agencies to iron out their differences and not dig in their heels on a position has been instrumental in finding solutions that benefit Singapore.

Having in place a rigorous process to settle policy differences is critical to good urban governance. The implications of different options should be analysed by professionals who have the experience, the competencies, the qualifications and the right capabilities",[14] taking into account different perspectives, and presented at different levels of government before final decisions are taken. The point is to carefully scrutinise all the available options, in order to come to a full understanding of the implications of any decisions made.

Principle 3: Build In Some Flexibility

Singapore learnt from the first 1958 Master Plan that a static blueprint plan would not be effective in the light of changing circumstances or inherent assumptions. As it is impossible to predict and anticipate trends accurately over several decades, the planning process includes a built-in review mechanism. The Concept Plan is reviewed every 10 years, while the Master Plan is reviewed every five years. The ability to change or adapt plans if they are not working as intended has been a critical factor in Singapore's urban development success.

To alleviate traffic congestion in the city centre, the 1991 Concept Plan introduced the "constellation concept" (Figure 7). The concept involved the creation of commercial nodes outside the city centre, including regional centres at Tampines, Jurong, Woodlands and Seletar, together with smaller sub-regional and fringe centres. More areas for housing were allocated in and around the city centre, while industrial estates and commercial centres were planned in the north and north-east to create more jobs in those areas.

However, the requirements of Singapore's economic structure limited the scope for decentralisation. The petrochemicals and pharmaceuticals industries were key economic activities. Given their polluting nature, there was little choice but to locate them in the west, on offshore islands away from housing areas.

Likewise, financial sector players wanted to be located in "Grade A offices" within the more prestigious Central Business District with a "high contact" environment. Thus, while the development of commercial centres such as Tampines Regional Centre and Novena Fringe Centre allowed some commercial activities to be decentralised, there was still a need to plan for the majority of office space to be located in the city centre. Developing a critical mass of high quality office space in the city centre was also seen as important in projecting Singapore's image as a financial hub and vibrant global city. Consequently, the 2001 Concept Plan refined the decentralisation strategy proposed in Concept Plan 1991 to retain the majority of office space within the city area.

---

[14] Lim Hng Kiang, interview by the Centre for Liveable Cities, Singapore, April 13, 2012. Lim is currently Minister for Trade and Industry. He held previous appointments as Deputy Secretary for the Ministry of National Development, Chief Executive Officer of the Housing and Development Board, Minister for National Development and Minister for Health.

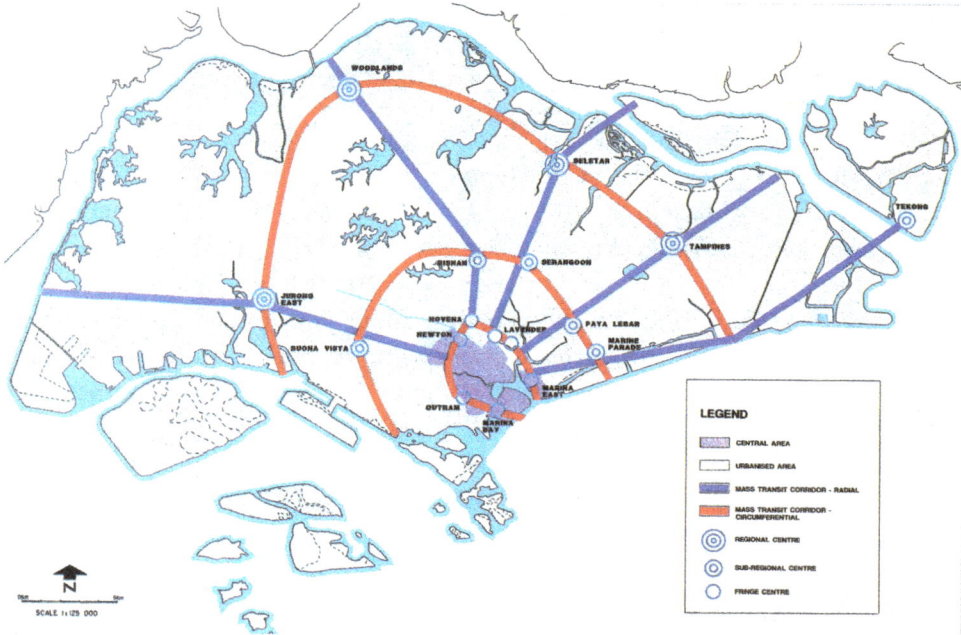

COMMERCIAL CENTRES OUTSIDE CENTRAL AREA

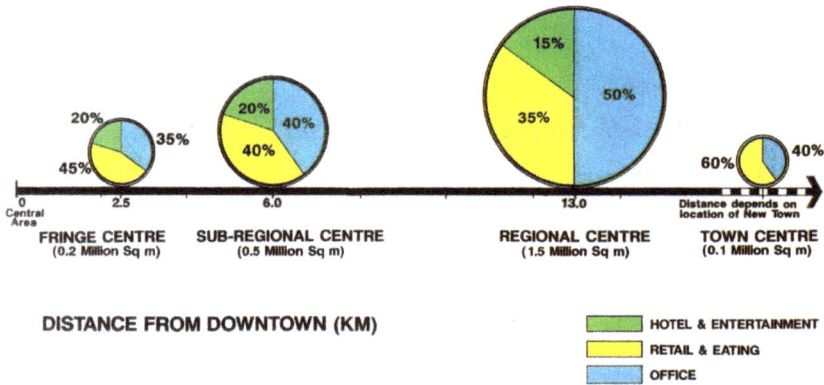

DISTANCE FROM DOWNTOWN (KM)

Figure 7.   The 1991 Concept Plan–constellation concept.

Source: Urban Redevelopment Authority.

There is also flexibility within the system for considering proposals which may not comply with existing guidelines. This is done through the statutory process of ad hoc alterations to the Master Plan for major departures, or waiver of certain guidelines when a proposal merits special consideration. The key has been to strike a judicious balance between controls and flexibility.

Principle 4: Execute Effectively

Implementing Through Action-Oriented Government Agencies

Government agencies' emphasis on effective action has played a pivotal role in implementing Singapore's urban development plans. Singapore at independence was faced with an acute shortage of housing and employment. The political leadership tackled these two issues through urban development. While the Concept Plan laid out the structure and shape for the development of Singapore, the success of translating the plan into reality lay with the various policies and programmes of government agencies and departments such as the Housing Development Board (HDB), Economic Development Board (EDB), the Jurong Town Corporation (JTC) and the Public Works Department (PWD).[15,16]

These public agencies were highly effective in developing the needs of the city in Singapore's early years. By the end of 1965, HDB was building flats at a rate of 12,000 units per year. In 1968, nearly 0.75 million people, or 36% of the population, lived in public flats. Veteran planner Liu Thai Ker recalls that by 1985, Singapore had become "the first Asian city that was free from slums and squatters".[17]

Over time, other government agencies and departments have been formed to effectively execute the different facets of urban development within Singapore. The Urban Redevelopment Authority was formed as an independent statutory board under MND in 1974 to redevelop the Central Area and resettle residents affected by redevelopment.

Implementing Through the Private Sector—Sale of Sites and Central Area Redevelopment

The private sector also played an important role in implementing development plans through the Sale of Sites mechanism. The programme began in 1967, when the Urban Renewal Department (which was later to become the URA) released the First Sale of 13 sites in the Central Area for public tender. The private sector would contribute financial resources and expertise to undertake development. Special financial concessions were offered to attract developers.

With the success of the initial sale sites, state land across the island began to be regularly released for sale to the private sector for development, subject to planning

---

[15] Economic Development Board, *Annual Report 1968* (Singapore: Economic Development Board, 1968), 17–18.

[16] Tan Jake Hooi, "Metropolitan Planning in Singapore", *Australian Planning Institute Journal* 4 (1966), 111–119.

[17] Liu Thai Ker, interview by the Centre for Liveable Cities, Singapore, June 29, 2011. See earlier endnote for Liu's current and past appointments.

guidelines. The enacting of planning intentions through the market has since become an established approach in Singapore's urban development.

Greater Transparency—Reform of the Master Plan and Development Control System

For the market to be the primary mechanism for realising the Master Plans, a transparent planning system is crucial. But the degree of transparency Singapore has today was not always the norm.

From 1960s to 1980s, the government prepared various non-statutory plans to guide permissible forms of development, and to serve as a basis by which private sector planning applications were evaluated. However, most of these plans were for internal development use and were known as "bottom-drawer" plans.[18] The public and private sectors were not always aware of these plans nor the intended use of a parcel of land as the Master Plan could be imprecise on a site's specific location. Applications that varied from the Master Plan were evaluated on different guidelines or policies.[19] This lack of transparency—in the allowable use, intensity and design considerations—led to cumbersome decision-making processes, where "every development application submitted by the private sector required an individual decision... and (had to) be decided by the Minister".[20]

[18] Leung Yew Kwong, *Development Land and Development Change in Singapore* (Singapore: Butterworths, 1987), 26.

[19] John Keung, interview by the Centre for Liveable Cities, Singapore, June 27, 2011. See earlier endnote for Keung's current and past appointments.

[20] Lim Hng Kiang, interview by the Centre for Liveable Cities, Singapore, April 13, 2012. See earlier endnote for Lim's current and past appointments.

A number of changes were made in the late 1980s to early 1990s to streamline the arbitrary forest of rules"[21] within the urban planning system. The following are some of the key changes introduced during that period.

Creating a Forward-Looking Planning System—Development Guide Plans (DGPs)

Following the completion of the 1991 Concept Plan, a series of forward-looking development guide plans (DGPs)[22] were prepared and released to keep the public informed on the type of developments they could have for certain sites. The DGPs translated the broad intentions of the Concept Plan to highly detailed local plans and technical guidelines. The government began releasing the draft DGPs to the public in the early 1990s. By 1998, all 55 DGPs were completed and gazetted, collectively forming the new 1998 Master Plan.

Reviewing Development Controls—Changes to Development Charge

Development controls—which ensure that all properties are developed and used according to the Master Plan—were also made more transparent.

A more open system for calculating the development charge[23] was introduced in 1989. Previous methods of calculating the payable development charge varied in terms of how the intensity for residential and non-residential developments was measured. From the point of view of the private sector developer, the system was complicated and lacked transparency.

A revised system of calculating the development charge based on fixed rates was introduced in September 1989. This system defines Singapore by sectors and included a table which showed the values of different uses categorised by geographic sectors. The charges are reviewed every six months to account for changes in property values. Since the rates for the development charge are published, developers can estimate the full development charge payable even before submitting their plans for approval.

---

[21] Khoo Teng Chye, interview by the Centre for Liveable Cities, Singapore, September 19, 2011. Khoo is currently Executive Director of the Centre for Liveable Cities, Ministry of National Development. He held previous appointments as Chief Executive of PUB, Singapore's National Water Agency; Chief Executive Officer/Chief Planner at the Urban Redevelopment Authority; Chief Executive Officer/Group President of PSA Corporation; President and Chief Executive Officer of Mapletree Investments and Managing Director (Special Projects) of Temasek Holdings.

[22] The planners divided the entire island into five regions (north, north-east, west, central and east) and 55 planning areas. Each area had a Development Guide Plan (DGP).

[23] The development charge, originally modelled after the British betterment levy, is a tax that is levied when planning permission is granted to carry out development projects that increase the value of the land, for instance, re-zoning to a higher value use or increasing the plot ratio.

Amalgamation of Planning and Development Functions within URA

The revised system needed a new organisation to operate smoothly. In 1989, the Urban Redevelopment Authority Act was amended to merge the URA, MND's Planning Department (including development control functions) and the Research and Statistics Unit. Explaining the amalgamation in Parliament, S. Dhanabalan, then Minister for National Development, said that "the planning and development control functions will be centralised under a single authority…With the amalgamation of URA's expertise in Central Area planning, particularly in urban design and Planning Department's expertise in strategic planning, there will be better co-ordinated planning for the whole island."[24]

Critically, Dhanabalan also pointed out that the physical development of Singapore in the future would increasingly be undertaken by the private sector. The public sector would guide the course of Singapore's physical development rather than become involved in the direct implementation of projects.[25]

This new mandate allowed the URA to focus on its core planning and development functions. Incumbent Chief Planner Lim Eng Hwee has noted that the uniqueness of the URA is in having multidisciplinary expertise", reflecting the coordinated, integrated nature of the Singapore system as a whole, where agencies "work together as a whole-of-Government."[26]

Principle 5: Innovate Systematically

Innovative thinking, coupled with engineering expertise, has been crucial in ensuring that urban policies and programmes make Singapore's 719.1 square kilometres of land area liveable.

For example, manufacturing businesses brought in by EDB required large parcels of land. Given the limited land available in Singapore, sprawling manufacturing developments are not feasible. JTC came up with the idea "stack-up factories", designed with large ramps allowing container trucks to access factories located at the upper floors of a development. At the same time, JTC ensures that land is productively used

---

[24] S. Dhanabalan, Urban Redevelopment Authority Bill, Parliament no. 7, Session 1, Vol. 54, Sitting 5, August 4, 1989.

[25] Prior to the merger in 1989, the URA built and managed developments within the Central Area. These include resettlement centres constructed to house displaced businesses and residents due to redevelopment plans. The implementation of these developments was in addition to URA's planning and development functions for the Central Area.

[26] Lim Eng Hwee, interview by the Centre for Liveable Cities, Singapore, June 2, 2011. Lim is currently Chief Planner and Deputy Chief Executive Officer of the Urban Redevelopment Authority. He has previously served in the Ministry of National Development and the Ministry of Trade and Industry, overseeing urban development and economic development policies and initiatives.

by industries. Lim Hng Kiang, Minister for Trade and Industry, noted that "every time the lease period of the land is renewed, we ensure that the value-added per hectare of land is raised. Otherwise, other industries that can contribute more to the economy for the same parcel of land will be allocated the parcel of land."[27]

Another example of innovation is in the use of Singapore's drainage corridors to link up a variety of open green spaces. "The concept was to develop a green network linking the coastal parks to the Central Catchment…so that residents in private and public housing have access to this green network."[28] Today, these green connectors are known as park connectors, and are managed by the National Parks Board (NParks).

PUB and NParks have also introduced the Active Beautiful and Clean Waters (ABC Waters) programme, converting concrete drainage canals into people friendly public spaces through innovative designs, while retaining drainage and flood control functions. These include naturalised rivers which would meander through parks and housing areas and provide recreational spaces for people. Such "rivers" also help improve water quality and contribute to biodiversity in urban areas.

Conclusion

Over the years, Singapore's urban planning system has built in a long-term perspective of development needs through the Concept Plan. At the same time, the Master Plans allow for a significant degree of flexibility and detail to guide development and implementation, refined through regular review processes. Thinking long term fosters the discipline of considering far-reaching implications of current development trends. This allows areas of concern to be identified upfront and addressed well ahead of time, helping to make the most of Singapore's scarce land resources.

Singapore's experience speaks of an emphasis not just on planning with foresight, but on the effective implementation of plans made as well. This has taken a high degree of political will over time, the cultivation of effective and action-oriented institutions, timely legislation, as well as a sound, transparent market-based approach to development. Together with a dynamic system of urban governance, Singapore's integrated approach to planning and development is the key element to sustaining and enhancing liveability in a high density context.

---

[27] Lim Hng Kiang, interview by the Centre for Liveable Cities, Singapore, April 13, 2012. See earlier endnote for Lim's current and past appointments.
[28] John Keung, interview by the Centre for Liveable Cities, Singapore, June 27, 2011. For Keung's present and past appointments, see earlier endnote.

CHAPTER 7

The Evolution of HDB Towns

Cheong Koon Hean

PLANNING OF HDB TOWNS

Introduction

The public housing programme implemented by the Housing & Development Board (HDB) over the last 55 years has provided affordable housing and a quality living environment for the people of Singapore. Today, more than 80% of the Singapore resident population lives in about 940,000 HDB flats across the island. More than 90% of the resident households live in home ownership flats.

Establishment of HDB

HDB was formed in 1960, after Singapore had attained internal self-government in 1959. It took over from its predecessor, the Singapore Improvement Trust (SIT), and was tasked with solving a housing shortage that was exacerbated by a fast growing population.

As many people were living in slums and squatter housing then, the new Government and HDB had to tackle the challenging task of providing proper homes equipped with basic facilities. Hence, HDB was vested with the authority from the Government to carry out land acquisition, slum clearance, town planning, building and development, and management of infrastructure. Given this mission, HDB formulated its first five-year building programme which targeted to build more than 50,000 flats from 1961 to 1965. Within five years, HDB built 44,345 flat units, more than the 23,019 units which its predecessor, the SIT under British rule, took to build over some 30 years.

The focus of HDB's first building programme then was on providing basic and functional low-cost housing, clustered in small estates (like Queenstown, Kallang and Macpherson) near the city where land was available. Basic amenities and facilities like markets and shops were provided to serve residents living in these estates. For example, in Queenstown, housing designs were kept simple and utilitarian, and slab blocks of 1-, 2- and 3-room flats were provided with piped water and electricity.

Toa Payoh—HDB's First Comprehensively Planned Satellite Town

Toa Payoh was the first comprehensively planned satellite town entirely planned and built by HDB. Planning was based on the "neighbourhood principle" where several neighbourhoods were grouped around a town centre. Each neighbourhood had its own Neighbourhood Centre, community facilities, and primary and second-ary schools. In planning for the town, planners and architects also introduced more variety in the buildings, both individually and in their layouts. For example, building heights varied from 6 storeys to 25 storeys, lending diversity to the town's skyline. The taller blocks of 25 storeys were used to mark strategic points in the town.

The Toa Payoh Town Centre was planned with facilities that would cater to some 200,000 people: with a projected 120 shops, department stores, two theatres, a library, a clinic and community institutions. It was built on 16 hectares of relatively level land with a layout that housed shops on the ground floor of low-rise slab blocks. The shops were planned to face another row of shops so that a main thoroughfare could be created through the continuous wide central pedestrian mall. The shopping pedestrian mall was meant to create a seamless "shopping parade" leading to the major areas where the market, library, emporium, and post office were located.

In addition, the largest bus terminal in Singapore was planned for the town. Greater attention was also given to the provision of better social, recreational and sporting amenities including a sports complex with a running track, football pitch and swimming pools.

Industrial land was also provided so that factories like Philips, Fairchild and General Electric could employ residents living nearby. This would help make Toa Payoh a self-sufficient town.

Toa Payoh was planned with a ring road to allow traffic to circulate easily to every part of the town and at the same time discourage through traffic (Figure 1).

The construction of Toa Payoh began in 1965. By 1970, 23,900 flats had been completed for some 120,000 residents; and by 1977, 36,600 flats had been com-pleted, thus bringing the initial phase of development of Toa Payoh to a close.

Prototype New Town Model

In the early 1970s, HDB's emphasis was on increasing the public housing supply to meet the rising housing demand. Once the immediate housing needs were met by the mid-1970s, the next phase of development shifted from building as many flats as quickly as possible, to improving the quality and amenities of HDB towns and estates. New towns, with their town and neighbourhood centres, were developed according to the earlier New Town Structural Model which was developed in the late 1960s as seen in the development of Toa Payoh (Figure 2).

This model of new town development was characterised by more purposeful and systematic town planning, as exemplified in the construction of Ang Mo Kio which

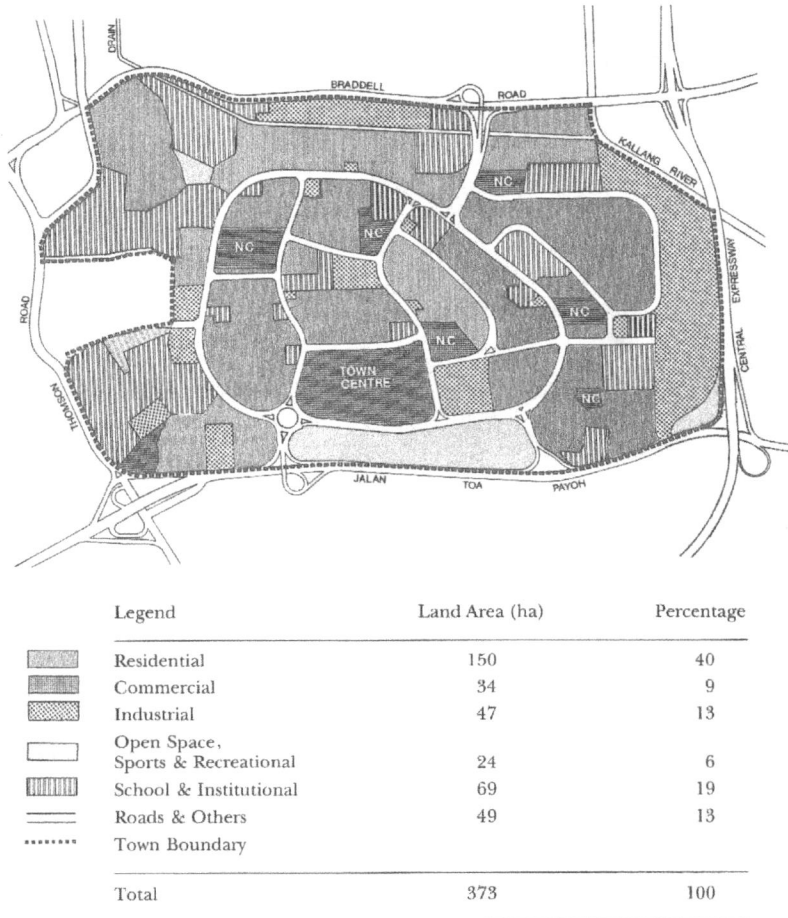

	Legend	Land Area (ha)	Percentage
	Residential	150	40
	Commercial	34	9
	Industrial	47	13
	Open Space, Sports & Recreational	24	6
	School & Institutional	69	19
	Roads & Others	49	13
	Town Boundary		
	Total	373	100

Figure 1. Land use plan and road network of Toa Payoh Town (1985).

began in 1973, followed closely by Bedok and Clementi. The hierarchy and distribution of activity nodes such as the town centre, neighbourhood centres and sub-centres were clearly spelt out. There would also be light and clean industries on the fringe of the town.

It was also a standard practice to carefully juxtapose low rise, low intensity land uses in the midst of high rise, high density residential developments. Low rise developments such as schools, community centres, sports facilities, neighbourhood parks were distributed throughout the residential areas to relieve the impact of the high rise, high density public housing environment.

In the late 1970s and 1980s, HDB developed more towns such as Yishun and Bukit Batok. Within these towns, HDB incorporated additional design considerations, including more 'human scale' development, street architecture and natural landscaping. Open space guidelines and pedestrian path systems were also introduced.

Figure 2.   New Town Structural Model.

Enhancing the Living Environment and Adding Variety to HDB Towns

Steps were taken in the 1980s to add variety and foster a stronger identity for HDB towns, so as to enhance the living environment. Town planning was carried out with emphasis on urban form, new town structure, hierarchy of uses, and the provision of regional facilities such as regional parks and open spaces.

During this period, the "precinct concept" was established to provide a more conducive setting for community interaction. The neighbourhoods were further broken down into several smaller housing precincts, comprising about 400 to 800 flats each, so as to provide a more conducive social setting for neighbourly interaction and community bonding. A wide variety of recreational facilities, like playgrounds, fitness corners, multi-purpose courts and reflexology paths, were located at each precinct centre. To facilitate community interaction, precinct pavilions were also provided. Examples of the precinct planning concept can be found in Bishan, Pasir Ris and Tampines.

At the block level, neighbourliness was fostered through having a smaller number of flats on each floor, served by a shorter corridor as compared to the early blocks of the past. The roofscapes of blocks were enriched in unique ways to give towns an identifiable character, as exemplified in the pitched roofs of blocks in Bishan. Towns were also developed along different themes, for example, the identity and architecture of Pasir Ris took inspiration from the surrounding beach and sea elements, reflecting a resort by the sea.

Emphasis was also placed on retaining significant natural features of a new town site. For example, a rocky outcrop and pool at Bukit Batok were retained to complement the urban ambience. More greenery was also included throughout each town. In addition, landscaped areas were introduced between two new towns to act as 'separators' so as to better define the visual identities of the two towns. To this end, Bishan Park, wedged between Bishan and Ang Mo Kio, functioned not only as a recreational space, but also as a 'threshold' for those travelling across one new town to another.

In the 1990s, greater emphasis was placed on creating a quality living environment with character by building up the identities of precincts, neighbourhoods and towns. Landmark buildings, landscaping, open spaces and special architectural features were incorporated to achieve a strong visual identity for new towns such as Sembawang and Sengkang.

HDB also tapped on private sector expertise to meet the rising expectations of flat buyers. The Design and Build Scheme, launched in 1991, allowed private firms to develop public housing projects while working within cost and design guidelines. The first Design and Build project was in Tampines Neighbourhood 4, and its hexagonal layout made it an iconic project in Tampines.

Introduced in 1995, the Executive Condominium Housing Scheme offered flats which were designed and built by private developers, but sold with initial eligibility and ownership restrictions, such as an income ceiling for buyers. After 10 years, the conditions would be lifted, and the development would attain private housing status.

HDB town centres saw the sprouting up of new air-conditioned shopping complexes like Northpoint in Yishun. The multi-storey complexes, compared to the low-rise developments of earlier town centres in Toa Payoh and Ang Mo Kio, marked a shift towards a more vibrant and diverse retail environment in HDB town centres.

Estate Renewal

In the 1990s, HDB focused on upgrading its older towns/estates to a standard closer to the newer ones that were built. This led to the launch of various programmes to renew the heartland.

a) *Main Upgrading Programme (MUP)*

The MUP, a plan to comprehensively upgrade the older HDB flats and living environment, was unveiled in 1990. The MUP offered improvements within the flats which included the upgrading of toilets and bathrooms, addition of a utility room or balcony, and replacement of old soil discharge stacks. Externally, there were enhancements to the playgrounds, covered walkways and landscaped areas.

The upgrading plans were drawn up in consultation with residents and the Adviser to the grassroots organisations for the precinct; and HDB would proceed only if at least 75% of the eligible flat owners voted for the programme. Flat owners only had to pay between 7% and 45% of the bill for the upgrading works, depending on their flat type and the upgrading package they voted for, with the rest borne by the Government.

The MUP was well-received, with a total of about 131,000 flats benefitting from the programme from 1990 to 2007.

Figure 3.   Before MUP: Boon Lay Gardens   After MUP: Boon Lay Gardens (2006).
(2001).

b) *Interim Upgrading Programme (IUP)*

The MUP was to be the precursor to more upgrading programmes, each with a different focus. The IUP was launched in 1993.

Under the IUP, the town councils would improve common areas in the blocks and precincts. This included new coats of paint for blocks, new lift lobbies, modern playgrounds, covered walkways and study corners. For IUP to proceed, at least three quarters of flat owners had to support the plans. From 1993 to 2001, more than 150,000 flats benefitted from the IUP.

c) *Lift Upgrading Programme (LUP)*

The LUP was introduced in 2001 to offer direct lift services to flats, where technically and economically feasible. Besides providing speedier and more convenient access to homes, the lifts also benefit the elderly, families with young children, and the less mobile. The scope of works include the upgrading of existing lifts, provision of a lift landing on every floor and addition of new lifts and lift shafts.

Over 13 years (2001 to 2014), HDB has brought lift access to some 5,000 blocks, benefitting over 500,000 households.

d) *Interim Upgrading Programme Plus (IUP Plus)*

The IUP Plus was introduced in 2002 to replace the IUP. It combined two programmes: IUP and LUP. Similar to the IUP, the IUP Plus was targeted at blocks built between 1981 and 1986. With the combined programme, HDB flat owners did not have to wait for two separate programmes which would have been carried out at different times.

e) *Home Improvement Programme (HIP)*

In 2007, the HIP replaced the MUP in response to calls for more flexibility in flat improvement works. Residents could choose from a list of optional improvements with corresponding adjustment in co-payment. HIP also helps flat owners deal with common maintenance problems related to ageing flats, such as spalling concrete, in a systematic and comprehensive manner. It focuses on the interior of the flats, as compared to the MUP which provided enhancements to both flats and common areas.

HIP works are categorised into Essential, Optional and Enhancement for Active Seniors (EASE) Improvements. The Government fully funds the essential improvements and subsidises between 87.5% and 95% of the cost of optional and EASE improvements for Singapore Citizen households. More help is given to smaller flat types. Residents pay only for the items they opt for under the optional and EASE improvements.

f) *Neighbourhood Renewal Programme (NRP)*

In 2007, the NRP replaced the IUP Plus. It focuses on precinct- and block-level improvements and is carried out on a larger scale across two or more contiguous precincts. This enables resources to be pooled and a wider range of facilities to be provided. Common areas in HDB neighbourhoods are enhanced with covered linkways, drop-off porches, playgrounds and fitness corners, etc.

NRP's key feature is the programme's active engagement of residents, who collectively decide, through mini-exhibitions, surveys, dialogues and town hall forums, on the improvements they want in their neighbourhoods.

As these improvements are made to the common areas in HDB neighbourhoods, the Government funds the entire bill of the upgrading works.

g) *Selective En-Bloc Redevelopment Scheme (SERS)*

SERS was launched in August 1995 as part of the Government's continual effort to renew old HDB towns and estates. Selected old blocks of home ownership flats with redevelopment potential are acquired under the Land Acquisition Act for redevelopment. The residents are given the opportunity to move to new flats with fresh 99-year leases at subsidised prices and a better living environment served by modern facilities.

SERS owners are paid the market value of their existing flat at the time of announcement and reasonable expenses (comprising of a removal allowance and stamp/legal fees for buying a replacement flat equivalent to the existing flat) incurred arising from a change in residence. Residents taking up a new flat at the

Figure 4.   SERS: Former Block 79 Toa   SERS: Current Blocks 79A-E Toa Payoh
Payoh Central (1972).   Central (2007).

designated site can also jointly select flats with their family members and neigh-bours (up to six households) under the Joint Selection Scheme, enabling residents to retain kinship and community ties built over the years.

After the residents are resettled into their new homes, the old flats are demolished to make way for new developments; helping to rejuvenate the old towns, as well as revitalise the demographic and economic profiles of the residents as younger residents move in to these towns.

To date, more than 39,000 households in 79 sites have benefitted from SERS (Figure 4).

Remaking Our Heartland—Blueprint for Renewal

The Estate Renewal programmes have served to rejuvenate and renew selected precincts of HDB towns and estates over the years. Beyond the upgrading/redevelopment of individual housing precincts, HDB launched a new initiative, the "Remaking Our Heartland (ROH)" programme, to renew and remake the HDB heartland in a more comprehensive way. Prime Minister Mr Lee Hsien Loong announced this new initiative in 2007. With the new ROH blueprint, Singapore's public housing estates are expected to be transformed over the next 20 to 30 years.

ROH 1

Bold new plans and programmes were formulated by multi-agency teams to remake estates and towns in every age band—"Young Estates" where development commenced in the 1990s and is still on-going, "Middle-Aged Estates" where flats were largely built in the 1980s and "Mature Estates" where flats were largely built before the 1980s. As part of the ROH plans, Punggol, Yishun and Dawson were chosen as examples of how young, middle-aged and mature towns/estates could be transformed.

a)   *Yishun Town—"A vibrant hub and great outdoors"*

The town centre in Yishun would be revitalised with a new extension to the current shopping hub, a new library, a new hospital and improved connectivity.

A new mixed development would also be built at the Town Centre which includes residences, commercial retail space, a bus interchange and a town plaza. The plan also included improved pedestrian and cyclist access to recreation and commercial areas in Yishun.

b) *Dawson Estate—"Housing-In-A-Park"*

For Dawson Estate, a new "Housing-In-A-Park" vision was introduced. Housing would be seamlessly integrated with landscaping, community greens and complemented with amenities such as shops and F&B facilities.

SkyVille @ Dawson and SkyTerrace @ Dawson were two Build-to-Order (BTO) housing developments designed to realise the "Housing in a Park" vision. These two projects are set in a scenic park-like environment, where greenery is brought to the residents' doorstep and extended to mid-levels of their blocks in the form of sky gardens which provide good views of the surrounding area (Figure 5).

HDB piloted two new schemes; the Flexi-Layout Scheme at SkyVille @ Dawson to cater to different family needs, and the Multi-Generation Living Scheme at SkyTerrace @ Dawson to facilitate multi-generation living.

The heritage of Dawson is also not forgotten. The gallery at SkyTerrace @ Dawson showcases memorable buildings and events in the rich history of Queenstown and the Dawson estate. At SkyVille @ Dawson, heartland heritage is integrated into the design of the new developments in the form of mural walls which traces memories of the past.

Figure 5.   SkyTerrace @ Dawson and SkyVille @ Dawson (2015).

c)   *Punggol New Town—"A Waterfront Town of the 21st Century"*

The ROH plans for Punggol included the development of a new and vibrant Town Centre, with a mix of commercial, entertainment as well as cultural and recreational uses. A new 4.2 km man-made waterway meandering through the town was introduced to connect the Punggol and Serangoon reservoirs, opening up opportunities for waterfront living and water-based activities (see Box Story: My Waterway@Punggol). A variety of waterfront homes, both public and private, will be built along the waterway from which residents will enjoy scenic views of the waterway.

My Waterway@Punggol

My Waterway@Punggol is Singapore's first man-made waterway. The 4.2 km waterway connects Sungei Punggol and Sungei Serangoon, which were converted into freshwater reservoirs to increase Singapore's water catchment area. The waterway, which was completed in 2011, not only creates an attractive and vibrant waterfront living environment for the residents, but also serves as a platform to explore urban solutions to enrich the biodiversity and maintain good water quality standards along the waterway, as part of HDB's efforts to enhance sustainability and liveability for Punggol Town.

Punggol Waterway (2012).

ROH 2

Plans for ROH 2 were announced in 2011, covering Hougang town, East Coast (specifically Bedok town) and the Jurong Lake areas. The key thrusts for these towns and areas were positioned under four common themes of "Rejuvenation of Town Centre"; "Outdoor Recreational Choices"; "Improved Connectivity"; and "Heartland Heritage".

a)   *Hougang—"Colours of Hougang"*

Hougang town's rich history and heritage played a prominent role in the ROH proposals. For example, a key idea was to transform Upper Serangoon Road, a century-old road, into a distinctive Heritage Corridor.

Other proposals included rejuvenating the town centre with an integrated mixed development as well as strengthening pedestrian connections between major recreational nodes. New housing developments would be built and the existing Neighbourhood Centres, rejuvenated.

b)   *East Coast Area—"Gateway to the East Coast"*

The plans included the extensive rejuvenation of Bedok Town Centre with the introduction of a new mall and air conditioned bus interchange, a hawker centre and the development of Bedok Integrated Complex (Figure 6). There is also a new town plaza with a heritage corner, and improvements made to the pedestrian mall in the Town Centre. The neighbourhood centres in Bedok Town

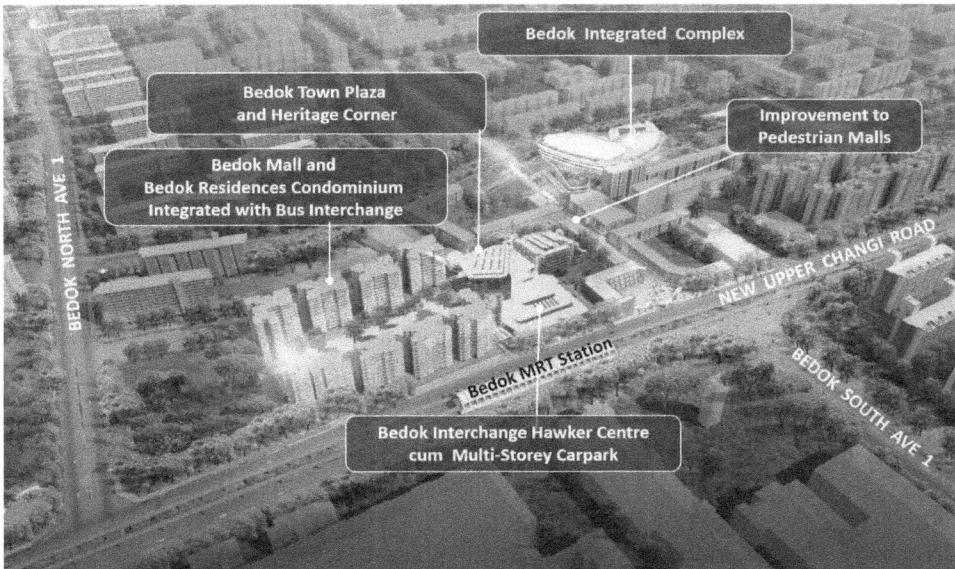

Figure 6.   Artist impression of the new hawker centre and town plaza at the rejuvenated Bedok Town Centre.

are also rejuvenated to benefit both the residents and retailers. A heritage trail which highlights the heritage sites will deepen residents' knowledge on the history in the East Coast area. A comprehensive cycling network will improve overall connectivity within the town with a dedicated cycling and pedestrian path providing additional convenient access to East Coast Park and Bedok Reservoir Park.

c) *Jurong Lake Area—"Our Jurong Lake Story"*

Developed as an industrial town in the early 1960s, Jurong played a key role in Singapore's early industrialisation efforts. Since then, Jurong has grown into a modern and bustling town. ROH aims to bring new life into the Jurong Lake area. There are plans to make the Jurong Lake District and Pandan Reservoir a choice leisure destination; to rejuvenate the HDB heartlands and neighbourhood centres in the area; and to create a new Jurong Regional Centre with food & beverage, commercial, office, residential and hotel developments for business travellers and tourists. In addition, Jurong East Town Centre will be rejuvenated into a vibrant hub with places for community bonding, including a heritage corner. A comprehensive cycling network will also be put in place, providing residents with better connectivity around the area.

ROH 3

In 2015, Toa Payoh, Woodlands and Pasir Ris were selected for a makeover under ROH 3. For this latest ROH programme, a ground up approach was adopted. Planners engaged the public through focus groups first to source for more feedback and ideas. Detailed planning proposals would subsequently be developed and exhibited for further comments by stakeholders and residents.

A New Generation of Public Housing— HDB's Roadmap to Better Living

HDB ramped up its building programme from 2010 to 2015 (launching more than 100,000 units) due to a surge in demand for public housing. This provided an opportunity for HDB to develop a new generation of public housing which continues to be highly liveable and pleasant, even as densities within towns increase with a growing population. The new generation of public housing should also cater to changing lifestyle needs and rising aspirations. HDB launched its Roadmap to Better Living in 2011, setting out its key development focus for the next 10 to 15 years. The three thrusts of the Roadmap are to build well-designed, sustainable and community-centric towns.

Thrust 1: Well-Designed Towns

To meet the need for more public housing, new areas have to be opened up for development. HDB responded by formulating master plans for the next phase of development for Punggol, Bidadari and Tampines North. To achieve 'better-designed' towns with a high quality environment, three key ideas will lead the way:

a) *Develop distinctive districts and neighbourhoods*

HDB aims to create more distinctive identities for a new generation of towns in green field sites and when large areas in older estates are rejuvenated. To do this, HDB will capitalise on heritage and place character as well as give greater focus to urban design to shape the towns. New building typologies and flat layouts will be explored to meet changing lifestyle needs and to add more interest to the townscape.

More tropical green and blue water elements will also be weaved into planning and design. The green mantle within our towns will be increased and sky gardens and terraces selectively introduced to provide residents with more places to relax. HDB will also focus on developing community centric public spaces to encourage community interaction.

b) *Seamless connectivity*

HDB aims to develop a 'car-lite' environment by encouraging the use of public transport. Wherever possible, the new areas will be well-served by a rail network and be well-connected by buses. Recognising that some may still need to use a car occasionally, HDB is working with LTA to introduce more car sharing schemes as well as the use of electric vehicles. The potential of introducing autonomous vehicles in the future in selected areas will also be explored.

A comprehensive cycling network will be weaved into HDB towns to encourage cycling. The cycling network will also link to parks and park connectors. Towns will be planned to be even more pedestrian friendly with conveniently connected pedestrian paths, covered linkways and second storey connections (where suitable), which connect precincts and also lead directly to aboveground MRT/LRT stations.

c) *Vibrant community spaces to encourage community activities*

HDB is mindful that it is not building just physical flats, but entire towns that should support the flourishing of communities. As such, the planning will include more community spaces to facilitate interaction and activities. These include large plazas for group gatherings to more localised 'community living rooms', and intimate spaces at the void decks or landscape decks that encourage residents to linger and make conversations with friends and neighbours.

Thrust 2 : Sustainable Homes with Abundant Greenery

As the largest housing developer in Singapore, HDB needs to play its role as an environmentally responsible developer which adopts sustainable solutions for its developments and towns.

Figure 7. HDB Sustainable Development Framework.

Sustainable Development (SD) Framework

In 2011, HDB drew up a holistic and comprehensive SD framework encompassing environmental, social and economic dimensions (Figure 7).

The SD framework sets out 10 key desired sustainability outcomes with broad strategies to achieve them. To achieve social sustainability, strategies such as community bonding activities will encourage stronger social integration, sense of ownership and identity among residents. Economic sustainability strategies focus on creating economic vibrancy, and business diversity through provision of commercial facilities within HDB towns. The environmental strategies are wide-ranging and focus on reducing carbon emissions; optimising the use of resources; and achieving effective water and waste management. This will provide a clean, safe, healthy and comfortable living environment.

Under each strategy, initiatives like solar energy, rainwater harvesting, energy efficient lighting and enhancement of greenery have been successfully tested in Punggol, and are also being rolled out progressively to all new developments in other towns.

Thrust 3: Community-Centric Towns

The third thrust of the Roadmap is to develop community-centric towns where Singapore's multi-racial, multi-cultural society living in high-rise, high-density housing can live and work in harmony. Other than the public housing policies, this can be achieved through good physical design where there are areas for the community to meet and mingle like common greens, playgrounds, hawker centres, and other amenities. Another avenue is to have community building programmes that would promote neighbourliness, expand residents' social network size and provide opportunities for community participation.

Homes of the Future

Punggol

In line with the key thrusts of HDB's Roadmap for Better Living, HDB unveiled the next chapter of Punggol's development in 2012. Working together with partner agencies, HDB's vision for the next phase of Punggol's development will be guided by five new key ideas:

Signature Waterfront Housing Districts

Punggol residents can look forward to seven different waterfront housing districts— Waterway East and Waterway West, Northshore, Matilda, Punggol Point, Crescent

---

Sustainable Development

From the onset, HDB has been mindful that public housing should be sustainable environmentally, economically and socially.

To this end, HDB flats have been designed for natural ventilation, with the aim of reducing household energy consumption through reduced usage of fans and air-conditioning. Similarly, HDB blocks are typically oriented to minimise solar heat gain. Conscious efforts have also been made to incorporate greenery into towns, to provide visual relief from the urban landscape and reduce ambient temperature.

To ensure economic sustainability, programmes have been implemented to enhance the business vibrancy of commercial and industrial developments in HDB towns.

Efforts have also been made to foster cohesive communities in HDB towns. Social and recreational spaces and facilities, ranging from void decks and playgrounds, to commercial centres and parks, have been carefully planned and provided. Neighbourhoods have always been planned and built with a good mix of flat types, to ensure good social interaction among residents of different backgrounds and to foster ties among them.

Environmental Sustainability: Treelodge@Punggol

Treelodge@Punggol, completed in 2010, is HDB's first eco-precinct. The precinct has various green technologies and solutions to enable residents to lead a

---

(Continued)

Sustainable Development (*Continued*)

more eco-friendly lifestyle. These include skyrise greening to reduce heat build-up; LED lighting, Elevator Energy Regenerative System (EERS) for lifts and solar PV panels to reduce dependence on grid electricity; centralised chutes for recyclables to encourage recycling efforts; and rainwater harvesting systems to promote water conservation. With the encouraging results achieved in Treelodge@ Punggol, a standard suite of eco-features is now incorporated in all new public housing developments.

Treelodge@Punggol

and Canal Districts (Figure 8). Each district will have its own distinct character, created to give residents a stronger sense of attachment to their neighbourhoods. This is also in line with the Roadmap's first key thrust to develop well-designed towns.

Punggol Downtown: A New Destination for the North-East Region

Punggol's vibrant mixed-use town centre will be extended to the north-east to form the new "Punggol Downtown". There will be more civic spaces, such as the Punggol Town Square, as well as mixed uses to inject greater vibrancy into the new downtown area.

An Even Greener Punggol

Even as Punggol urbanises and develops, residents at Punggol can look forward to a greener town. More green parks and corridors will be integrated with the waterfront promenades. As HDB's first Eco-Town, Punggol continues to serve as a good

Figure 8.   Signature waterfront housing districts in Punggol.

platform for the pursuit of green initiatives and sustainable solutions, in line with the second thrust of developing sustainable towns.

The existing My Waterway@Punggol and the Punggol Waterway Park will be enhanced, with green spaces expanding towards the north. Collectively, these open spaces, in which the town centre, SAFRA Punggol clubhouse and Punggol Regional Sports Centre are located, will form the 'Green Heart' of Punggol.

Emanating from the 'Green Heart' towards the Coastal Promenade and the park in Coney Island would be 'Green Fingers'—green linear corridors that can be used for recreational activities such as jogging, cycling and brisk walking. One of the main 'Green Fingers' is the Old Punggol Road, which will be pedestrianised and kept as a 1.5 km long linear Heritage Trail connecting Punggol's 'Green Heart' to the seafront at Punggol Point (Figure 9).

Environmental Modelling: HDB's Centre for Building Research has, over the past five years, built up extensive capability in environmental modeling of microclimatic conditions. Such computer modeling is carried out to assess the environmental impact of the plans formulated for Punggol and to guide urban design. Detailed simulations are carried out to identify wind corridors, solar hotspots, and land traffic noise contours at the town, district and building levels (Figure 10). These simulations provide planners and architects with useful insights and enable them to adjust the design and placement of building blocks and green spaces to optimise wind flows, improve thermal comfort and deploy suitable mitigating measures to enhance the living environment.

Figure 9. 'Green Heart' and 'Green Fingers' in Punggol.

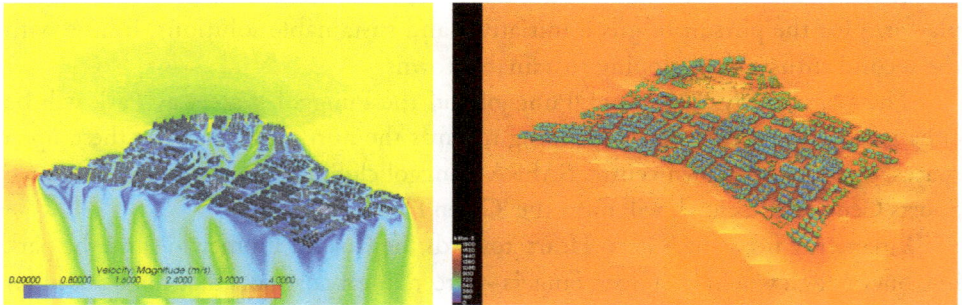

Figure 10. Modelling results (from left to right): Punggol Eco-Town wind flow simulation and solar irradiance analysis.

Biodiversity Index: Working with other agencies and institutes of higher learning, HDB is developing a Biodiversity Index for its towns. Further research will help HDB draw up a Biophilic Masterplan for Punggol, with a focus on urban greenery, harmonious eco-systems and greater biodiversity.

Great Places for the Community

As Punggol moves forward in the development of its 'hardware', the importance of building cohesive and resilient communities is not forgotten. In line with the third thrust of the Roadmap to develop community-centric towns, more civic and recreational spaces will be created to provide the physical setting for community gatherings and events.

For example, a new town square will be developed in the heart of Punggol, including a community club and hawker centre.

Moving Around Punggol

As Punggol's development unfolds and the community grows, there will be a need to improve the connectivity within Punggol. The transport infrastructure will be enhanced, and cycling tracks will be built in tandem with new roads to encourage clean commute.

Bidadari Estate

HDB's development plans for Bidadari Estate were announced in 2013. Located in the central region of Singapore, Bidadari Estate is envisioned to be "A Community in a Garden", a tranquil urban oasis where residents can relax and connect with family and friends in a garden-like setting.

Distinctive Districts, New Housing Typologies and Market Square

HDB has planned four distinctive districts to cater to Bidadari's unique site topography and wooded context (Figures 11). Each of the districts will incorporate new housing forms, comprising linear, tower and terrace forms. The building forms have been developed to respond to Bidadari's unique terrain and characteristics. The entire estate will be complemented by a mixed-use Market Square commercial cluster.

Figure 11.   The four districts in Bidadari.

Environmental Modelling: In the planning of Bidadari Estate, environmental model-ling tools are used to simulate climatic conditions so that key wind corridors can be preserved to harness maximum windflow through the estate. Subsequently, planners and architects will use the findings to refine the placement of blocks and units to opti-mise wind flows through the precincts. This helps to achieve a more sustainable design as a cooler living environment can be achieved using natural ventilation.

Green and Blue Elements

Bidadari is better known for its rolling and undulating topography, and picturesque wooded landscape, which has evolved naturally over time. The rich greenery provides a welcome relief to the residents living around the area, who have been using the space for recreational activities such as strolling and jogging.

The Bidadari community will also enjoy a green estate—even as Bidadari becomes urbanised—through the planning for a new 10-hectare Bidadari Park. Located at the heart of Bidadari Estate, the new Bidadari Park will form the new green lung. Mature and heritage trees to be retained will be integrated into the park. Several 'green fingers' and a greenway will connect the key public spaces within Bidadari, bringing greenery to more corners of the estate (Figure 12).

Figure 12.   Artist's impression of the Bidadari Park with Alkaff Lake.

Complementing Bidadari Park will be Bidadari greenway that traverses the full length of the estate from Bartley Road to Upper Serangoon Road. The greenway will weave through the estate and enable the residents to safely cycle and walk around the estate. Rest spots, commercial and social communal facilities will line the greenway, creating opportunities for more community interaction.

The existing Memorial Garden, which commemorates the heritage of the Bidadari Cemetery as well as many of our prominent pioneers, will also be integrated within Bidadari Park to bring Bidadari's heritage closer to residents and visitors.

Pneumatic Waste Conveyance System (PWCS)

PWCS will be implemented in Bidadari Estate to collect household waste for disposal. Using vacuum suction, household waste will be transported through underground pipes to a sealed container where the waste will be collected periodically by trucks. As a closed system, the PWCS will result in a cleaner environment with less odours, compared to open refuse collection. In addition, refuse trucks need not travel to every block to collect the refuse, hence making the estate safer and quieter.

Tampines North

Tampines North is an integral part of Tampines Town located in the eastern region of Singapore. The vision for Tampines North is "Tampines in Bloom: Budding Communities within a Green Tapestry".

The shape of Tampines Town can be understood anatomically as a 'leaf' structure, with various connectivity layers representing leaf veins. These connectivity layers include the rail, road, park connectors, water bodies, and pedestrian circulation networks.

Tampines North will be a natural extension of the existing Tampines Town, akin to the growth of the leaf with budding new shoots. Overall, the central green spine and the secondary veins are analogous to the structure of the leaf, extending out from the existing Tampines Regional Centre through Sun Plaza Park into the North. The development of Tampines North as a final piece of jigsaw will complete the mosaic of Tampines Town (Figure 13).

The proposals for Tampines North, unveiled in 2013, aim to capitalise on its existing greenery and convenient proximity to the Tampines Regional Centre. The vision is to create an attractive living environment, with emphasis on liveability, imageability, connectivity and sense of community. The key strategies are as follows:

Community Boulevard Park for All: Anchored by two major parks

Two major boulevard parks will be created for the community. The main park will be located centrally amidst the new public housing developments. Planned as a meandering linear park of varying width, it will form the green spine for Tampines North. The park will be lined with a range of activity nodes and recreational facilities for both the young and old, and will be seamlessly connected to the housing districts around it.

Figure 13.   The leaf-shaped structure of Tampines Town, with Tampines North at the tip.

The other proposed major park, conceptually conceived as a "Quarry Park", is located to the north of Sun Plaza Park. There could be opportunities to bring back the heritage element of Tampines (historically known for its sand quarry activities) in the re-creation of a quarry pond with an urban sandy beach for residents' enjoyment in the unique park environment.

Green Tapestry: Greenery permeating through the housing
districts connected to the Boulevard Park

A comprehensive network of public spaces and connections will be put in place to form the "Green Tapestry" in Tampines North, linking the various public spaces, commercial cum social community facilities, and major activity nodes together (Figure 14). This will allow activities to spill over and be integrated with the linear green. Green fingers, in the form of green laces, will extend outwards from the main boulevard park to link up to the rest of the public spaces within Tampines North. Complementing the green laces will be a seamless pedestrian and cycling network that will weave through the various housing districts.

Green Living Rooms at the Doorstep: Inter-precinct
greens with facilities and community spaces

Within the housing districts that are further away from the boulevard parks, inter-precinct greens with facilities and community spaces will be provided at the door-steps of the housing blocks.

Figure 14. An aerial view of Tampines North.

New Shopping Facility at Tampines North Hub:
A commercial and transport hub where the North congregates

A mixed development comprising both commercial and residential uses, integrated with a bus interchange, a plaza square and a green arcade will be introduced in Tampines North. The main boulevard park will thread through this commercial hub, bringing residents and visitors conveniently to the new commercial centre of Tampines North.

Four Distinctive Housing Districts: Thematic housing
typologies and attractive streetscapes

Four housing districts will be introduced in Tampines North: Park East District, Park West District, Boulevard District and Green Walk District. The themes for the various housing districts will provide opportunities to differentiate the character of each district. A combination of different housing typologies will be explored in the housing districts.

Smart HDB Towns

In line with the announcement of Singapore's aspirations to become a 'Smart Nation' in 2014, HDB will tap into significant innovations in Information Communication Technology (ICT) to develop smarter HDB towns—making them even more liveable, efficient, sustainable and safe (Figure 15).

Figure 15.   HDB's approach towards smarter towns.

The Smart HDB Town Framework maps out how the 'Smart' element can be introduced in HDB towns and comprises two layers: a) Enabling Infrastructure Layer; and b) Application and Service Layer. It focuses on four key dimensions: Smart Planning, Smart Environment, Smart Estate, and Smart Living.

Beyond the technology, Smart HDB towns will have the citizens at the heart— the technology will be people-centric, with focus to improve the quality of life for residents.

Going forward, HDB will be piloting selected Smart initiatives in two 'living laboratories" at Yuhua, an existing town and at Punggol Northshore, a greenfield site, to assess their viability and suitability, before extending them to other HDB towns.

Key Challenges and the Road Ahead

Today, more than 80% of Singapore's resident population lives in public housing. Remarkably, more than 90% of the flats are owned by the residents. This high level of home ownership did not come easily and was largely due to the Government's strong commitment to 50 years of the Home Ownership Programme.

HDB's comprehensive approach in building entire townships, and not just housing, has brought about a comfortable and convenient lifestyle for its residents. HDB towns are comprehensively planned and weave in amenities such as health and elder care services, child care centres, schools, sports facilities and shops, bringing them to the doorstep of the residents. Industrial developments, business parks and commercial developments located nearby provide employment.

HDB towns are well served by public transport, enabling convenient connectivity within the town and to the rest of Singapore. Through the implementation of various policies and programmes, residents of different ethnic and income groups live together, thereby fostering community bonds in Singapore's multi-racial and multi-cultural society. HDB towns today are recognised internationally as a good example of affordable housing and good living, garnering numerous global awards, including two from the United Nations.

Nonetheless, HDB cannot rest on its laurels. Going forward, socio-economic and demographic changes will pose new challenges. As a global city subject to a highly volatile global economic environment, HDB has to continue to ensure that its housing remains affordable. Its resident profile will change—not only will there be families to take care of, there will be an increasing number of elderly as the population ages, each with their own needs. Ethnic diversity will become more complex, with more new citizens and foreigners living in the midst of what is traditionally the heartland core. With a wealthier and well-educated citizenry, aspirations and expectations will rise further, even as densities are likely to increase to cater to a growing population. Creating highly liveable and sustainable towns will become more challenging in view of land and resource constraints.

In addition, even as we build new generation towns, the upgrading and rejuvenation of existing towns must continue, especially where many residents prefer to age in place.

The constant evolution of HDB in its planning, development and renewal of towns gives assurance that HDB is keenly aware that it must keep pace with the changing housing needs and aspirations of Singaporeans. Building on more than 50 years of public housing experience, it is in a good position to further develop and experiment with innovative plans and design ideas. It is already expanding its Research & Development scope and will harness the potential of technology to develop new urban solutions. With creativity, perseverance and an unwavering commitment to the mission of providing homes for Singaporeans, HDB can define new frontiers in the public housing landscape in the years ahead.

References

HDB (Housing & Development Board) (1966) *50,000 Up: Homes for the People*, HDB 5th Anniversary Publication. Housing & Development Board, Singapore.

HDB (Housing & Development Board) (1970) *First Decade of Public Housing*, HDB 10th Anniversary Publication. Housing & Development Board, Singapore.

HDB (Housing & Development Board) (1985) *Housing a Nation*, HDB 25th Anniversary Publication. Housing & Development Board, Singapore.

HDB (Housing & Development Board) (2010) *Our Homes—50 Years of Public Housing*, HDB 50th Anniversary Publication. Housing & Development Board, Singapore.

HDB (Housing & Development Board) Annual Reports, Singapore.

Ministry of Culture & National Development (1970) *150 Years of Development*, Singapore.

CHAPTER 8

Transportation: Mobility, Accessibility, and Connectivity

Mohinder Singh

This chapter discusses the role of transportation planning in urban development and the fundamental principles that have underpinned Singapore's land transport policies and key developments since 1965.

Introduction

The Singapore of the 1960s had rudimentary public transport services and severe traffic congestion in the city. Today, Singapore has a well-developed road network with good traffic speeds and accessibility to a multi-modal public transport is universal. Like their counterparts elsewhere, the transport planners in Singapore walk a tightrope of balancing competing objectives which are amplified further by the limited land. Yet, Singapore has avoided the many negative consequences seen in major cities of rapid urbanisation and rising affluence, such as traffic congestion and air pollution.

The transformation of the transport system was a series of incremental changes as well major turning points which led to relatively much larger and lasting changes. At the same time, there were a few key constants in the form of underlying principles which informed the transformation of transport from the 1960s to today.

A Brief History of Land Transport Planning

Transportation in the Early Days

The Public Works Department (PWD) was formed in 1872 and took charge of building roads, bridges and pedestrian walkways as well as all other public facilities such as schools, hospitals and libraries. Many of the early roads were built to serve the British military installations on the island. The first traffic lights were installed in 1948 at the junction of Serangoon Road and Bukit Timah Road. Even as late as 1965, a journey from town to Changi was a "big drive" through seemingly endless vistas of villages and plantations.

Public transport was neglected. The birth of public transport could be dated to 1905 when the electric tram arrived; succeeded by trolley buses in 1925 when the Singapore Traction Company (STC) was set up with a 30-year monopoly to operate trolley and motor buses within the city. However, enforcement was weak—and numerous privately-owned bus companies started providing bus services. These bus companies competed for business and took only popular and profitable routes, leaving many areas uncovered, affecting the population living in these areas especially outside the city. By the 1940s, STC was facing serious operating problems and making a loss because of the intense competition from the private bus companies.

By mid 1950s, the bus situation had deteriorated further and was distinguished both by poor service and high labour unrest. Buses were badly maintained and broke down often. Schedules were erratic due partly to drivers who often went on strike to demand for higher pay and better working conditions. A combination of poor pay and working conditions, high union agitation and weak regulatory oversight led to frequent stoppages, paralysing the whole bus system on which the majority of people depended for their daily travel.

In April 1955, the workers of the Hock Lee Amalgamated Bus Company went on strike, supported by Chinese school students. The next month, on 12 May 1955, later known as "Black Thursday", a major riot involving more than 2,000 people broke out. Four people—two police officers, a student and a press correspondent—died, and more than 30 were seriously injured.

The next year, in January 1956, the "Great STC (Singapore Traction Company) Strike" took place. Lasting 146 days, it severely crippled Singapore' public transportation system.

Public transport was thus in a state of chaos with poor regulation. Commuters had to contend with unsafe bus services, haphazard bus routes and service disruptions that occurred on almost a daily basis because of buses breaking down due to poor maintenance or because of frequent strikes. This was also a turbulent time for Singapore with communist agitation and strong anti-colonial feelings among the people. While the government commissioned a study which resulted in the 1956 Hawkins Report recommending the merger of the various bus companies into a single nationalised corporation, this was not implemented, possibly because the colonial government may have felt this would cause stronger disturbance under the prevailing situation.

Beginning of Land Transport Planning

This sorry state of transport in the 1950s was a result of neglect in transport planning since it was viewed as something of low priority. There were no formal transport studies done, and any traffic measures implemented were focused on facilitating car movements, improving parking and reducing traffic offences, rather than meeting transport needs of the people. The colonial government's primary role was in vehicle licensing and road widening, while public transport planning and operations were left to private bus companies.

An analogous situation prevailed with urban planning. While Singapore had in 1958 its first statutory Master Plan, which regulated land use through zoning, density and plot ratio controls, the planning at that time was focused on public housing and industrial development to cope with massive shortage of proper housing and severe unemployment. No transport plans were developed as part of the urban planning process.

The problems that Singapore's transport then faced were not untypical of those presently experienced in many developing cities such as traffic congestion, inadequate and inefficient public transport services, poor infrastructure maintenance and lack of government plans and enforcements. These were perpetuated with the uncoordinated land transport policies implemented by different agencies due to the absence of an authority to oversee holistically transport planning and development.

The 1960s saw an era of great change for Singapore as population grew and rapid development took place. The need for a reliable and efficient public transport system became more compelling, but had hitherto received little or no systematic planning. The public had to put up with a myriad of timetables, routes and fares by the different bus companies. The lack of any form of integration resulted in long and inconvenient journeys. In order to maximise profits, buses were not regularly maintained by the operators and often broke down. As an alternative to the grossly inadequate public transport system, "pirate" taxis were rampant. These taxis were not regulated and drivers often tried to take as many passengers as they could to increase their incomes, paying little attention to service quality and safety.

After separation from Malaysia in 1965, Singapore found itself thrust into an uncertain era marked by economic and social challenges, fostering a sense of urgency and vulnerability which prompted the Government to take decisive actions and a strong interventionist approach to secure economic development and social stability for the new nation's survival.

Long-term Integrated Planning

Long-term forward looking planning is now firmly entrenched in Singapore's land use and transport planning process. Under this approach, an overall concept plan is prepared for the long term together with the supporting transport master plan which is integrated with the urban development plan.

However, this was far from the case in the 1960s. The limitations of the 1958 Master Plan and rapid development in the 1960s prompted the call to develop a more concrete and comprehensive land use and transport plan. This led to the Government commissioning the State and City Planning (SCP) study to map out urban and transport planning. Thus was laid the foundation of Singapore's first integrated land use and transport master plan.

State and City Planning (SCP) Study

Work started on the four-year SCP study in 1967 with the help of the United Nations Development Programme. The task force of the SCP study was formed by staff from the Planning Department in the Prime Minister's Office, Housing and Development Board (which then included the Urban Renewal Department—forerunner of the present Urban Redevelopment Authority (URA)) and the Public Works Department's (PWD) Roads and Transportation Division.

The SCP study marks an important milestone in transport planning in Singapore. It was the first time that the land use and transport planners worked jointly to develop an integrated urban plan to guide Singapore's physical development. Moreover, it enabled planners to integrate transport and land use planning in the early years before Singapore became more urbanised. Hence, basic infrastructure such as road networks and MRT lines could be laid down and safeguarded, and long-term policies could be implemented to cope with future growth.

The SCP study led to the birth of the SCP Plan in 1971, or otherwise called the 1971 Concept Plan—Singapore's first integrated land use and transport development plan. The 1971 Concept Plan mapped out the basic framework for physical planning in Singapore along designated corridors projected to the year 1992 for a population of 3.4 million. It laid out the future road and rail networks between zones of high traffic generation. This marked an attempt to integrate transport policy and infrastructure planning with economic and social development. It set the stage towards thinking of transport as linking people to employment, services, recreation, and community development.

The 1971 Concept Plan

In developing the 1971 Concept Plan, the SCP study looked at various options of organising land use (Figure 1). Transport modelling and simulation studies were done to help identify the optimum land use dispositions from the transport viewpoint. Apart from population and employment projections, the transport studies looked at parameters such as the growth of car ownership, expansion of the road network and improvements needed for public transport to meet the higher travel demand with economic growth and population increase.

The eventual concept plan structure (Figure 2) adopted a "Ring Concept Plan" by organising land use into high density satellite towns surrounding the central

IDEAS PLANS

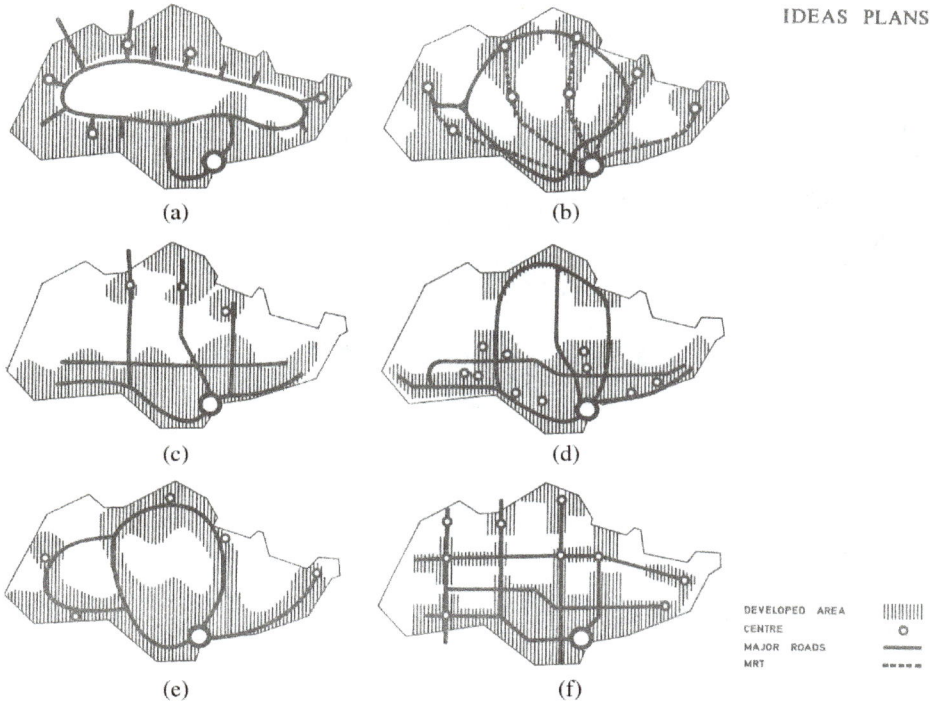

(a)

(b)

(c)

(d)

(e)

(f)

DEVELOPED AREA
CENTRE
MAJOR ROADS
MRT

Figure 1.   SCP Ideas and Plans for alternative development strategies.

Source: SCP Report.

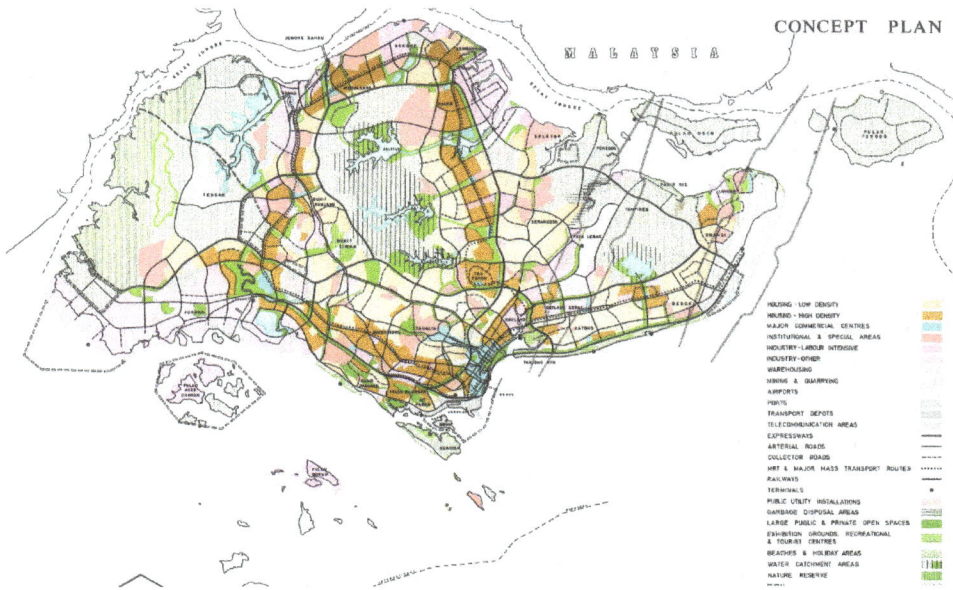

CONCEPT PLAN

MALAYSIA

Figure 2.   SCP Concept Plan 1971.

Source: SCP Report.

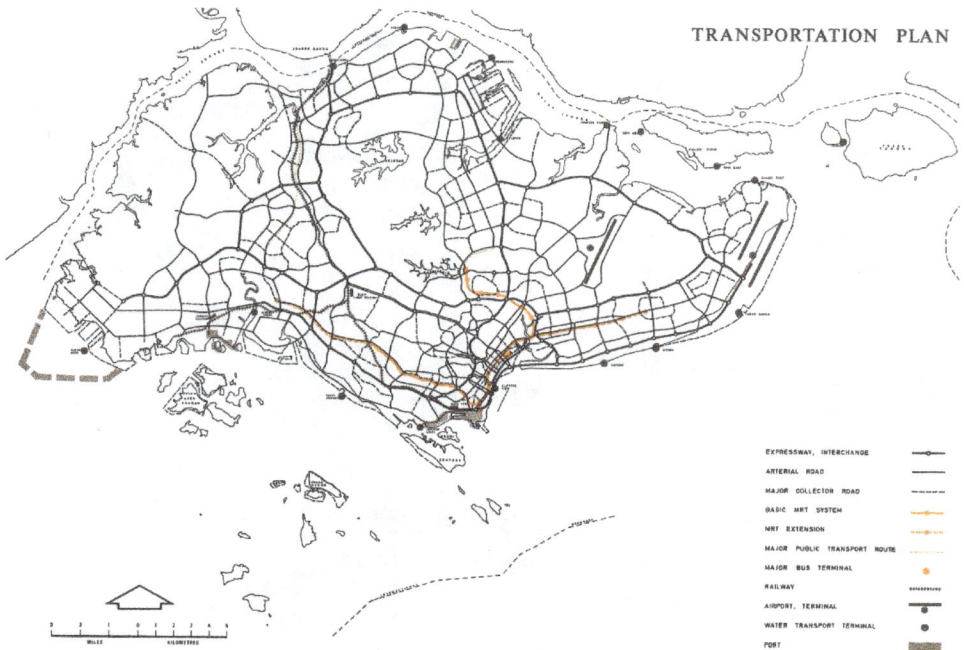

TRANSPORTATION PLAN

Figure 3.   SCP Transportation Plan.
Source: SCP Report.

catchment area and a broad band of development along the east and west coasts, with a planned transport system linking them. An MRT network along the development corridors was envisaged comprising a North-South Line from the city centre to the north and an East-West Line from Jurong to the east. A road network, comprising a high-capacity expressway system and major arterial roads, was conceived. These two plans—an expanded road network and a mass rapid transit (MRT) system—formed the key elements of the transport layer plan (Figure 3) of the 1971 Concept Plan, and facilitated advanced planning and safeguarding of transport corridors and systematic expansion of transport infrastructure in tandem with land development and traffic growth. Arising from the Concept Plan, there was extensive development of the road infrastructure from about 800 km of roads at the end of 1960s to nearly 3,000 km by 1990.

The focus on long-term planning meant that the government had identified broad strokes of transport (and land) development in 1971, with main priorities of a) reducing and managing road congestion, b) increasing road infrastructure, and c) enhancing the public transport system, including MRT lines, to solve Singapore's transport problems and plan for the future.

Reorganisation of the Public Transport Industry

The bus industry underwent major restructuring in the 1970s from a free market of many players into a consolidation of operations into a small number of companies. This came after the setting up of a Transport Advisory Board in 1968 whose findings were used to draft the 1970 Government White Paper titled *The Reorganisation of the Motor Transport Service of Singapore*. Various problems of the bus operations associated with poor quality of service, inefficient management and lack of coordination were highlighted in the report. The White Paper marked the overhaul of bus transport service, where the 10 bus companies were merged into three companies with clear territorial demarcations—(1) Associated Bus Services Pte Ltd served the western sector of Singapore, (2) United Bus Company served the northern sector, and (3) Amalgamated Bus Company served the eastern sector, while STC (Singapore Traction Company) served the southern sector.

At the same time, the bus network was revised along with a uniform fare structure for all three merged companies and the STC. However, STC, which was not affected by the physical reorganisation, went into financial difficulties and eventually ceased operations. This was largely because much of the concessions it previously enjoyed were removed when fares were standardised and it was exposed to competitive pressures. The failure of the STC led the government to review the future of bus operations, and the three remaining bus companies merged to form the Singapore Bus Service (SBS) in 1973.

Although consolidation into one company was intended to bring economies of scale and greater operational efficiencies, this did not materialise. The new management of SBS was still using management methods previously adopted for small bus companies. These problems persisted, and in 1974 led to the government appointing a team of government officials to SBS to revamp its operations and improve organisational efficiency. The Government Team of Officials (GTO) was a multi-disciplinary team of about 100 civil servants, police officers and military personnel.

This resulted in improvements in productivity and profitability. In 1978, SBS was listed on the stock exchange. SBS continued to improve its operations reducing costs as well as raising the quality of service, such as the introduction of air-conditioned buses in 1984, semi-express services and one-man operated services in 1985. However, insufficient peak hour capacity continued to be a problem. Attempts were made to augment peak hour capacity by allowing licensed private hire buses to operate. In May 1982, a second bus company—Trans Island Bus Services Pte Ltd (TIBS)—was formed to grow the bus fleet and provide some form of competition and service benchmarking for SBS. Competition led SBS and TIBS to consider many cost cutting measures such as the use of higher capacity double-decker buses, the adoption of a hub-and-spoke system with the introduction of feeder services in new towns and the conversion of all services to one-man operation.

The dramatic changes transformed the bus industry from a free-wheeling market to a centrally planned and regulated market with some limited competition.

The 1970 Government White Paper also impacted taxis. The taxi industry in 1950s and 1960s was also a free-wheeling one, lightly regulated. Because of high unemployment, many wanted to be taxi drivers and private cars also ferried passengers. There was a rapid increase in "pirate taxis" or private cars operating as taxis without licences. Many pirate taxi drivers were employed by gangster-like owners who controlled fleets of up to 100 vehicles. These pirate taxis had poor service standards, posed road safety problems and charged their own fares. Nevertheless they served a public need as the public bus services were then grossly inadequate. The fleet of licensed taxis was low, much less than the number of pirate taxis.

The government essentially declared war on pirate taxis syndicates through measures such as raising diesel taxes, and stronger enforcement like the suspension of pirate taxis drivers' licences for one year if caught and denoting pirate taxi operations a seizable offence where offenders could be arrested on the spot and charged the following day. At the same time, the government facilitated the setting up of NTUC Comfort in 1970 to provide employment opportunities for the former pirate taxi drivers. Taxi services were more strongly regulated and measures were introduced to root out the pirate taxi services. Pirate taxis died a quick death and in their place, in addition to NTUC Comfort, several new companies formed to provide taxi services with uniform fares and quality standards.

Taming Private Transport Growth

The transport studies for the 1971 Concept Plan concluded that a very large road building programme would be needed if car population was allowed to grow freely. Forecasts indicated, for instance, that roads of up to 16 lanes and/or massive viaducts would be needed to handle unrestrained private transport travel, severely marring the cityscape and adversely impacting the environment. The government hence decided to curb private transport demand by increasing the cost of owning and using a car.

To control car population, additional vehicle taxes were imposed on the purchase of cars. Import duties for cars were increased and an Additional Registration Fee (ARF), which was an upfront vehicle ownership tax, of 25% of the Open Market Value (OMV) was imposed on new cars in 1972, and the annual road tax was based on a progressive rate structure such that cars of higher engine capacities were taxed at higher rates.

Over the years, the ARF continued to increase, reaching a peak of 175% of the OMV in 1983. The annual road tax was also raised to twice and then to almost four times the rates in 1972, depending on the engine capacity of the car. There were also other measures like the fuel tax (an ad valorem duty on petrol) and the parking surcharge in the central business district. With upfront vehicle taxes at more than twice the price of a car, Singapore became one of the most expensive places to own a car. In spite of these drastic measures, the car population to increase in the 1970s as Singapore's economy grew.

The other pressing issue was traffic congestion in the city. In order to improve accessibility and ameliorate the severe traffic congestion in the central area, an inter-ministerial Road Transport Action Committee (RTAC) was formed in 1973 to coordinate transport planning measures and formulate transport policies. Comprising technical staff from the Public Works Department (PWD) of the Ministry of National Development and helmed by permanent secretaries of several ministries, the committee highlighted the pressing need for restraints on car use in the central area.

The RTAC examined and experimented with various measures which included staggering work hours, car pooling, tolled roads and parking fees. However, these measures had limited success. The RTAC concluded that more had to be done to mitigate the rapid rise in traffic flow in the central area. In 1975, the government introduced the Area Licensing Scheme (ALS) to restrict entry into the city centre. It was the world's first congestion pricing scheme and remains very much cited by transport experts today.

Area Licensing Scheme (ALS)

Under the ALS, the more congested part of the city was designated a "restricted zone", and overhead gantries were erected at 31 points along the roads into this zone. Non-exempt vehicles were required to display a paper licence on the windscreen before entering the restricted zone. Enforcement officers were stationed (Figure 4) at the entry control points and fines were imposed on drivers found without a valid licence. The licence could be bought on a daily basis or monthly basis and had varying charges for various classes of vehicles. Various shapes and colour coding of the licence helped to make for easier identification by the enforcement officers (Figure 5).

The implementation of the ALS saw an immediate 44% decrease in the number of vehicles entering the city during the restricted hours and greatly improved traffic conditions. A 1976 World Bank survey of public opinions and attitudes to the ALS found that it had improved transport and environmental conditions, and had not adversely affected the business climate.

Changes were made to the ALS over the years before it was replaced by the Electronic Road Pricing (ERP) system in 1998. The operating hours of the ALS were progressively extended, first from the initial morning peak hours, then to include the evening peak hours in 1989 and eventually to whole day between 7:30 am and 6:30 pm and 7:30 am to 2:00 pm on Saturday in 1995. In addition, to ameliorate the

Figure 4.   The Area Licencing Scheme.
Source: LTA.

Figure 5.   Different types of ALS licences.
Source: LTA.

increasing traffic flow into the city, car pools, motorcycles and company cars were no longer exempted from the ALS.

The experience of the ALS led to the implementation of the Road Pricing Scheme (RPS) in 1995. This passage pricing system (as compared with the ALS cordon pricing) was progressively introduced and started with a stretch of the East Coast Parkway before extending to other expressways such as the Central Expressway and Pan Island Expressway in 1997.

Electronic Road Pricing (ERP)

Being manual schemes, the ALS and its RPS derivative for the expressways outside the restricted zone had certain limitations. They were labour intensive and enforcement was onerous as officers had to work amidst the heat, dust and noise of the roadside environment. At its peak, the enforcement personnel had to work long hours and recognise 16 categories of licences. Human enforcement by visual means was prone to error. Furthermore, although traffic conditions fluctuated depending on the hour, day and location, it was technically and administratively impossible to vary the rates at different times of the day and to have "shoulder charging" to smoothen the sharp change in rate from $0 to the cost of the licence which always led to a rush to enter the restricted zone just before or after the restricted hours.

The government therefore decided to replace both ALS and RPS with an automated Electronic Road Pricing (ERP) system. The ERP system was implemented in 1998. It enables more differentiation in charging since different ERP rates can be levied for different locations and time periods. It also charges motorists on a pay-per-use basis. The system is more equitable as motorists who make more trips or drive along more congested rates pay higher ERP charges. It is more convenient for motorists as they no longer have to queue to purchase licenses. It is also less prone to enforcement errors.

The ALS and ERP systems have successfully managed traffic volume entering the city centre over the years (Figures 6 and 7), despite the substantial growth of the vehicle population as well as employment and developments within the CBD during the same period.

The Development of the Road Network

The 1971 Concept Plan prepared under the SCP study laid down a comprehensive road network to support urbanisation and economic development. It included a network of expressways across the island and arterial roads. The road network was sized to meet the constrained demand within the framework of the land transport strategy to manage the vehicle population and demand for road use.

The inherited road network was systematically expanded to serve new areas of development and to increase its capacity. In 1965, Singapore had less than 800 km of roads, much of it of low capacity, occupying only 5% of the land area. Today we have a well-developed hierarchical network of 3,500 km of roads of different capacities.

Figure 6.   Electronic Road Pricing.

Source: LTA.

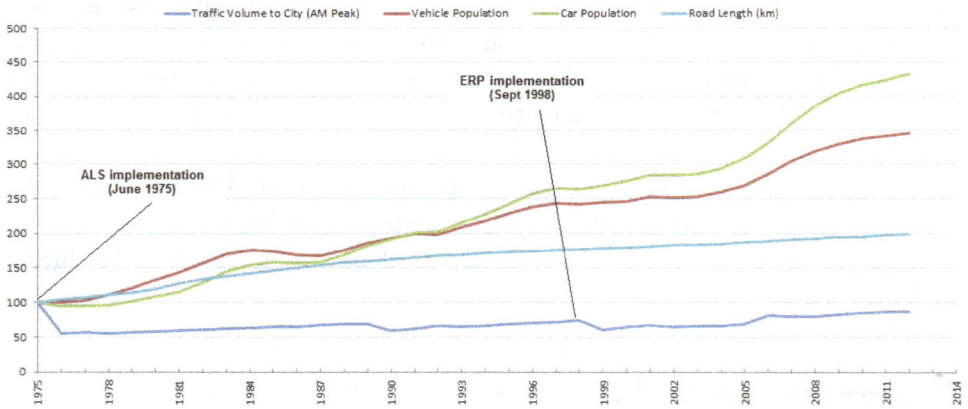

Figure 7.   ALS and ERP keeping traffic volume entering the CBD relatively constant over 30 years.

Source: LTA.

The road network development has not only changed the landscape, but also enabled motorists to move from one point of the island to another in a relatively short time, something that was impossible with the inherited network. Road development also enabled better and more effective routing of buses.

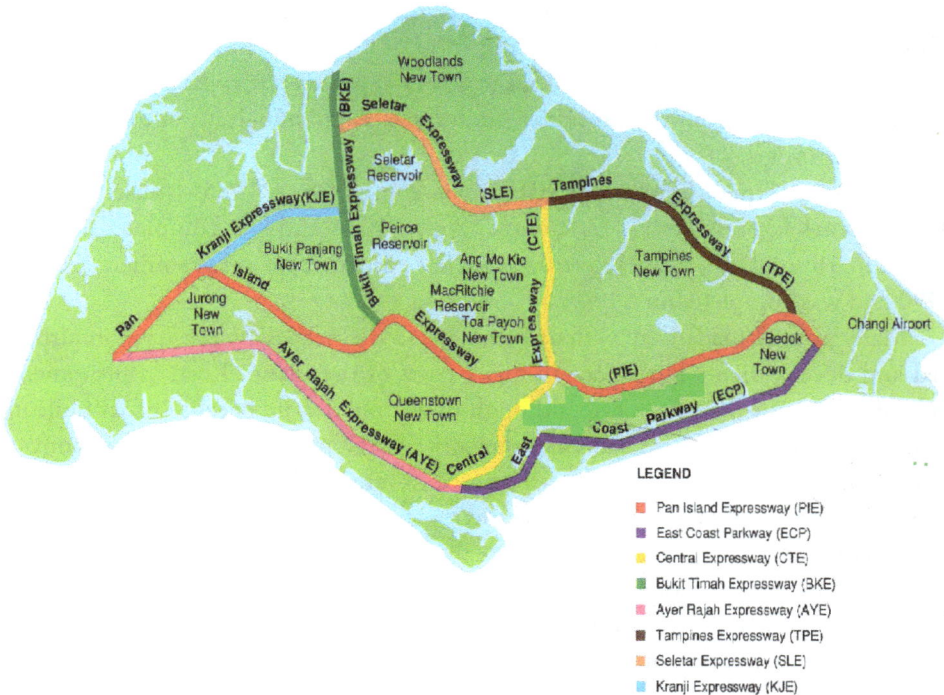

By the end of the 1990s nine expressways will cross the island

Figure 8.   By the early 1990s, eight expressways crossed the island.

Source: The Road Ahead—A PWD Report 1992.

The 1980s could be termed the era of expressways when the Public Works Department (PWD) embarked on the construction of the expressway network laid down in the 1971 Concept Plan. Several expressways were progressively opened to traffic, heralding a new way of faster and high capacity travel across the island (Figure 8). This included the Pan-Island Expressway (PIE), the oldest and longest expressway in Singapore, crossing the island from east to west and making it possible to drive from Jurong to Changi without traffic light interruption. Construction of the East Coast Parkway (ECP) on reclaimed land started in 1976 and the expressway, including the Benjamin Sheares Bridge, was opened in 1981 to coincide with opening of the Changi Airport. Work on the Ayer Rajah Expressway (AYE) started in 1983 and was completed in two phases in 1988. The work included construction of Singapore's first road viaduct, the 2.1-km Keppel Viaduct.

The Central Expressway (CTE) was built in various phases over 10 years from 1981. The last and most difficult stretch was opened in September 1991. Stretching from Bukit Timah Road to Chin Swee Road, the last section of the CTE included the first two expressway tunnels in Singapore. Early SCP plans had envisaged this stretch of the CTE as a largely elevated viaduct in front of the Istana and along Clemenceau Avenue to Chin Swee Road. However, the PWD engineers reviewed that design and took the bold step to put the expressway in tunnels, even though it was much costlier and more complex.

The Bukit Timah Expressway (BKE) was completed in 1985. Construction of the Tampines Expressway (TPE) commenced in 1984 and was completed in three phases in 1996. The Kranji Expressway (KJE) construction programme started in 1990 and was completed in 1994.

Many arterial roads were widened to increase their capacity as Singapore urbanised and developments took place in many parts of the island. Road improvements were also done in the city centre although of a limited scale because of its built up nature and better developed inherited network. Traffic management, such as conversion to one-way streets, implementation of an area-wide traffic control system, removal of on-street parking and side friction such as street hawkers, was done to increase capacity.

Singapore has harnessed technology to maximise the capacity of its road network, to facilitate traffic flow and to help travellers make informed choices of their routes, time of travel and mode of travel. Several Intelligent Transport Systems (ITS) have been implemented over the years. These include the centralised area traffic light control system that optimises traffic light timings and provides "green waves" to facilitate major traffic flows, the Expressway Monitoring and Advisory System (EMAS) to detect and clear incidents along expressways to restore normal flow as quickly as possible, and Junction Eyes cameras for surveillance to assist in traffic management at junctions.

The Great Leap to Trains

The need for a Mass Rapid Transit (MRT) system was examined under the SCP study and proposed in the 1971 Concept Plan. It took the shape of an inverted "T" with an East-West line and a North-South spur on the east of the central catchment.

Feasibility studies were done between 1972 and 1981 to study the necessity of building a MRT system and the routes that the MRT should take. Apart from technical feasibility, the studies looked at costs and benefits and operational viability. It was not until 1982 that the decision to build the MRT was made.

The decision to build the MRT was not an easy one. While transport planners advocated it, the estimated $5 billion construction cost was a hefty sum for Singapore at that time, and the government wanted to examine all alternatives before making a decision to spend that large sum of money. Thus started what has come to be called the "Great MRT Debate", which compared the merits of building an MRT system supported by buses with that of an all-bus system. The Cabinet had differing views of the merits of building the MRT. Various traffic studies were conducted by different consultants, including a team led by Professor Hansen of Harvard University (known as the Hansen Review Team) which recommended that a restructured all-bus system deploying a large number of high-speed point-to-point services would suffice to meet travel demand well into the 1990s. The debate between a rail-based and a bus-based system was aired on national television on 1 September 1980 among members of the Cabinet. Following this, it was decided that further quantitative studies were needed to establish the cost and benefits of the all-bus system and the MRT proposal. This was done under a Comprehensive Traffic Study (CTS) which reported that an all-bus system was not practicable as it would impose severe restrictions on other road users while not providing comparable service to the rail-based system, confirming the need for an MRT to meet future demand.

Eventually, in 1982, the government approved the MRT at an estimated $5 billion. Construction commenced swiftly in 1983 under the newly formed Mass Rapid Transit Corporation (MRTC) which took over the roles and responsibilities of the former Provisional Mass Transit Authority (PMRTA). Four years later, on 7 November 1987, the first section of the North-South Line consisting of five stations over 6 km was opened, heralding the arrival of MRT travel to Singapore. This was soon followed by the East-West Line in 1989, which together completed the basic system, also now known as the Compass Line. It consisted of interchange facilities between the two lines at two stations in the city centre, at City Hall and Raffles Place. With an initial rail network of 67 km and 42 stations (of which 15 were underground), the system was designed to have 40% of business areas as well as 30% of residential areas within the catchment of the MRT. The East-West Line was extended to Boon Lay in 1990.

In 1996, the Woodlands Line was completed to serve Woodlands Town and complete the MRT loop around the central water catchment. The extension of the MRT to Woodlands helped in the take-up of housing in the new town, which was then considered remote from the city.

Planning of the North-East Line (NEL)

In the 1980s, the North-East Sector Study (NESS) was undertaken to look into housing development in the northeast region of Singapore, hitherto not slated for public housing. Two new towns, Sengkang Town and Punggol Town, were planned to serve housing needs into the 1990s and beyond. As part of this planning process, transport studies were undertaken to identify the transport infrastructure needed to serve the planned developments.

Two major transport proposals were identified—a new MRT line called the North-East Line (NEL) running from the city to Punggol and a new expressway called the Paya Lebar Expressway. Engineering feasibility studies were done for both and their routes were safeguarded for implementation when the towns are developed.

Multi-modal Integrated Planning—The 1990s

Towards a New Transport Model

With the entry of the MRT, the structure of Singapore's public transport changed. The MRT network would form the backbone of the public transport system, serving the heavy transit corridors primarily for longer-distance travel. This would be supplemented by trunk buses and feeder buses in a concept known as the "Hub-and-Spoke" model. Under this model, buses would serve residents in the new towns and link them to the MRT station and bus interchange at the town centre.

With public transport slated to play a bigger role in the way people travel, the government reviewed the policies to manage private transport demand at the other side of the travel equation. In 1990, the Vehicle Quota System (VQS) was introduced to limit the growth of the vehicle population to a more sustainable level. In spite of high ownership taxes introduced in the 1970s, car population had continued to increase rapidly with greater affluence. The VQS allowed the vehicle population to be restrained to a level that could be sustained by the capacity of the road system. Under the VQS, a person who wishes to buy a new car had to first obtain a Certificate of Entitlement (COE). The COE quota is auctioned publicly so that those who want to own a vehicle can decide for themselves how much they are willing to pay for the certificate. An Off-Peak Car (OPC) scheme was implemented (replacing the Weekend Car Scheme) from October 1994 to allow people to own cars at lower cost. This was aimed at balancing the need to discourage the use of cars during peak hours while meeting aspirations of people to own cars.

On the road use front, the Electronic Road Pricing (ERP) system replaced the ALS in 1998.

Formation of Land Transport Authority (LTA)

As Singapore's land transport system grew more complex, the 1990s saw a new era of integrated transport management with the merger of all land transport functions into a single land transport agency. In September 1995, the Land Transport Authority (LTA) was formed with the merger of the PWD's Roads & Transportation Division—responsible for the planning, design, construction and maintenance of roads, pedestrian and commuter facilities, the Mass Rapid Transit Corporation (MRTC)—responsible for the planning, building and regulation of the MRT system, the Registry of Vehicles (ROV)—in charge of the administration, regulation and enforcement of land transport policies and rules, and the Land Transport Division of the Ministry of Communications—responsible for formulating land transport strategies and policies.

The merger formed a single agency to coordinate planning for public and private transport infrastructures, formulate vehicle restraint policies, as well as evaluate trade-offs between alternative infrastructure and policy options.

White Paper on Land Transport (1996)

In 1996, soon after its formation, the LTA published the *White Paper for a World Class Land Transport System* which spelt out the transport vision for Singapore and transport policies to achieve the objectives. The White Paper emphasised the importance of a comprehensive rail network as in other developed cities like London, Paris and Tokyo and set out a new funding framework for the rail system under which the second set of operating assets would be paid through a combination of farebox revenue covering the historical cost of the first set of operating assets and government co-financing for the inflationary component.

The White Paper signified the government's commitment to expand the rail network as quickly as possible to enhance the public transport experience. The new funding criterion helped bring forward the construction of the North-East Line (completed in 2003) and the Circle Line (fully completed in stages by 2011).

The White Paper established three principles for the financing of the rail system. These were:

(a) Fares have to be realistic and revised periodically to adjust for justifiable cost increases;
(b) Operating revenue must be able to cover operating costs; and
(c) There must be a sustainable policy on asset replacement.

The public bus system is financed along similar lines where fares and other operating revenues must cover the operating costs, including the cost of the buses. The government builds and maintains all related infrastructure including roads, bus interchanges and bus shelters.

The Turn of the Century—2000s to Present

The turn of the century saw further developments in land transport. While the four strategic thrusts—integrating land use and transport planning, providing a quality public transport system, optimising the capacity of the road network, and managing demand of road use through ownership and usage measures—continue to underpin transport, the emphasis on public transport was strengthened.

With the renewed emphasis on public transport, plans were laid to expand the MRT network. The North-East Line (NEL) opened in 2003 to serve the growing new towns of Sengkang and Punggol in the northeast region of Singapore. The North-East Line was the first driverless MRT line and the forerunner of subsequent MRT lines. Construction of the Circle Line (CCL) was commenced and completed in stages by 2011. While the previous MRT lines were radial lines to connect different parts of Singapore to the city centre, the Circle Line was an orbital line that greatly improved the connectivity of the rail network in addition to serving areas along its route. It allowed commuters to transfer to the other lines without entering the CBD stations such as Raffles Place and City Hall which were getting congested because of the large number of transferring commuters.

The 2000s saw a large increase in Singapore's population since the 1996 White Paper was released. The population and economy had become more diverse and expectations had risen with increasing affluence. Following a year-long review and consultation, the LTA released the *Land Transport Master Plan: A People Centred Land Transport System* in early 2008.

Land Transport Master Plan 2008 (LTMP 2008)

The *Land Transport Master Plan 2008* set out the vision for a more people-centred land transport system that would meet the diverse needs of an inclusive, liveable and vibrant global city. The Master Plan identified three key strategic thrusts that would shape land transport policies and development, namely, Making Public Transport a choice mode, Managing road usage, and Meeting the diverse needs of the people.

Achieving the vision meant transforming the public transport system to make it more attractive to the people and competitive with the car. That meant addressing issues of long waiting times, long journey times and overcrowding by increasing supply and strengthening the integration of the public transport system. Buses and the rail network had to be well integrated as a unified system from the commuters' perspective where transfers are seamless and convenient, services are easily accessible, reliable and comfortable, journey time is competitive relative to cars, and fares remain affordable.

To enhance the integration and efficiency of public transport services, the Master Plan advocated that the Land Transport Authority (LTA) take on the role of a central bus network planner, and plan the public transport network from the commuters' perspective focusing on their total journey experience. The hub-and-spoke system would be enhanced so that the bus and rail services work in partnership. To facilitate transfers, a distance-based through-fare structure would be adopted so that commuters are charged a fare based on the total distance travelled in a journey, without incurring a transfer penalty when they switch between buses or between the bus and MRT.

The Master Plan advocated expanding the rail network, doubling it from the then 138 km to 278 km by 2020. This required major investments in new lines and extensions, namely, the Thomson Line (TSL), the Eastern Region Line (ERL), the Tuas Extension to East West Line (EWL), and the North-South Line (NSL) Extension in the Marina Bay area (Figure 9). This expanded and denser network would extend the reach of the MRT to many more people and places. Within the Central Area, a commuter would be able to access an MRT station within five minutes' walk on average.

To meet the diverse needs of society, greater attention would be paid to the social role of transport in providing access to amenities and opportunities for the community, comprising the low-income groups, the elderly, and wheelchair users, families with young children, pedestrians and cyclists, while at the same time taking care of the environment. All new and existing MRT stations would be accessible to persons with disabilities/impairment, with additional lifts installed at some stations so that commuters can avoid long detours to reach the entrance with a lift. The public bus fleet would progressively be replaced with low-floor wheelchair-accessible buses with the aim of having all public buses wheelchair-accessible by 2020.

The Master Plan recognised the increasing popularity of cycling and planning for it as a non-motorised transport option to bring commuters to transport nodes by providing better bicycle parking facilities at MRT stations, allowing foldable bicycles onto buses and trains, leveraging on the park connectors to provide cycle paths, and installing appropriate road signs to alert motorists to the presence of cyclists along frequently used routes.

New Rail Financing Framework

The expansion of the rail network involves significant financial investment. In 2010, a new rail financing framework was put in place to facilitate the expansion of the rail network in a financially sustainable manner. As the rail network is expanded, future lines will be more expensive to build, operate and maintain as they will be mostly underground. On the other hand, the current network generates higher fare revenue as the lines serve more built up and heavier demand corridors. Hence, to sustain the pace of rail expansion, the financing framework was revised to allow for a network approach, instead of a line by line approach, for evaluating new lines. The new framework takes into account the "network effect" of building new lines as they also add to the ridership of existing lines. This allows future new lines to be implemented earlier, so long as the entire rail network remains financially viable.

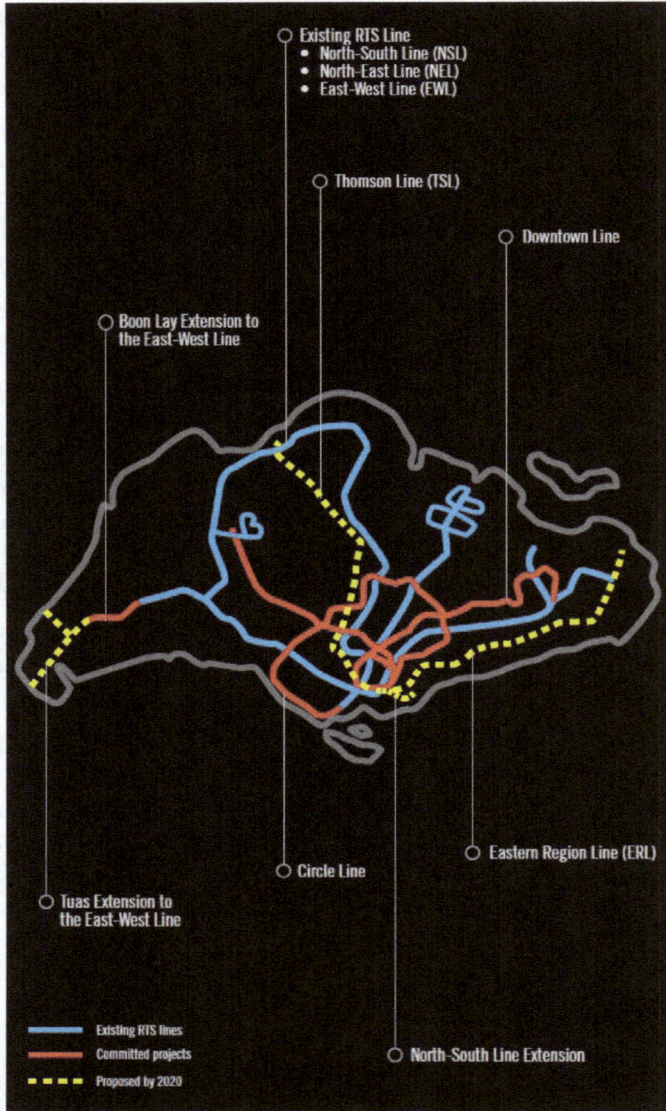

Figure 9.   Existing and proposed rail lines in the Land Transport Master Plan 2008.
Source: LTA.

Bus Service Enhancement Programme (BSEP)

In 2012, the government announced the Bus Service Enhancement Programme (BSEP) to expand the bus fleet to cope with overcrowding of public transport as a result of rapid population growth. The BSEP is financed by the government through a Bus Service Enhancement Fund (BSEF) towards the purchase and operation of 1,000 new buses to substantially increase bus capacity over a short period to reduce overcrowding and waiting time for buses.

Towards Greater Contestability in the Public Transport Industry

In 2010, a step was taken to inject greater contestability to the rail industry to ensure operators continue to operate efficiently and improve service standards to benefit commuters. The licence period for new rail lines, starting with the Downtown Line, was shortened from the existing 30–40 years to about 15 years. A shorter licence period enhances the level of contestability as the operator faces the prospect of competition at the end of its licence term. It also gave the LTA greater flexibility to review licence conditions or appoint a new operator if the incumbent operator had failed to maintain good performance.

Under the new model, the government, instead of the operator, owns the rail operating assets so that it has greater flexibility to decide on purchase of new trains and operating assets to keep pace with growing ridership. To ensure that the operating assets are well maintained, operators are required to adhere to a rigorous set of Asset Management Requirements for maintaining them during the licence term. The takeover of the operating assets represents a move to reduce the barriers to entry into the rail industry and facilitates the injection of greater contestability in the market.

In 2014, the government announced the restructuring of the bus industry from the privatised model to a "Government Contracting Model". Bus contracting will be implemented in phases over several years for smooth transition to the new model.

Under the new model, the LTA will contract operators to run bus services through a competitive tendering process. Bus services will be bundled into a number of packages with stipulated service standards like headways and bus operators will bid a fee to operate these services. Fare revenue will be retained by the government while the operator will be paid a fee. The government will also own the bus infrastructure, such as depots, and operating assets such as buses.

The new model represents a sweeping change from the previous model, since the 1970s, under which the two operators (SBST and SMRT) are awarded rights to plan and operate services in their designated geographical areas subject to regulatory oversight by the Public Transport Council (PTC). The bus planner's role will now be done by LTA while the operator will run the services according to the prescribed standards. It will allow the operator to concentrate on running the prescribed services in the most cost efficient manner while the LTA will plan the services to meet commuter needs.

Future of Land Transport

LTMP 2008 reiterated the fundamental land constraint of Singapore and the pivotal role of public transport in Singapore's mobility system. In 1997, 67% of the trips during the morning peak hours were on public transport; that fell to 63% in 2004 and to about 59% in 2008. This was because car usage grew much faster than public transport ridership between 2004 and 2008, at 31% compared to 16% for public transport ridership. LTMP 2008 aspired to reverse the trend and increase the use of public transport with more rail lines and trains, and improved bus services. The results of the 2012 Household Interview Travel Survey (HITS 2012) showed an improvement in the percentage share of public transport trips during the morning peak hours to about 63%, suggesting that the initiatives were working in the right direction.

The environment and commuter expectations and norms are changing as Singaporeans aspire to a higher quality of life. The trade-offs between using land for roads and other purposes will become more crucial in future. In planning the transport system, it will be imperative to balance the necessary build-up of capacity with liveability and sustainability considerations. The *Land Transport Master Plan (LTMP 2013)* launched in October 2013 sets out the vision for the future land transport system. From the consultation process that took place for preparing the plan, three areas were identified that commuters value most about the transport system.

- **More Connections**—connect people to more places where they work, live and play.
- **Better Service**—improve travel reliability, comfort and convenience.
- **Liveable and Inclusive Community**—the system should be planned and run with the well-being of our diverse community at heart, and afford greater consideration to how it enhances our common living space.

More connections

A more comprehensive rail network that will keep pace with travel growth and serve new developments will be built as the backbone of the public transport system. This will make it faster and more convenient for commuters to take the train to reach their destinations. By 2030, the rail network will increase to 360 km and eight in ten households will be within a 10-minute walk of a rail station. By that time, it is expected that 75% of all journeys in peak hours will be made using public transport, up from 63%. Even with an extended rail network, buses will continue to play an important role in the public transport system, albeit their function will evolve as more long distance trips are made by rail. Under the Bus Service Enhancement Programme (BSEP), more than 40 new bus services will be added to enhance bus network connectivity, including City-Direct services that connect major HDB towns to the city area, making use of expressways.

More walking and cycling routes will be developed to connect to the rail network. A new Walk2Ride Programme will significantly extend the sheltered linkway network to connect public facilities and amenities, offices and residential developments to all MRT stations, bus interchanges, LRT stations and bus shelters with very high usage. By 2018, more than 200 km of sheltered linkways will be built, more than four times 2014's 46 km.

To facilitate cycling, LTMP 2013 proposes to extend the cycling path networks to all HDB towns. By 2020, the network of dedicated off-road cycling paths will be longer than 200 km. Integrated with the Park Connector Networks (PCN) developed by the National Parks Board, (NParks), this will provide cyclists with a comprehensive island-wide cycling path network that will be about 700 km in length.

Better service

To shorten waiting times and reduce overcrowding, the capacity and reliability of both rail and bus systems will be enhanced. The signalling system for the first generation North-South and East-West MRT lines will be upgraded so that trains are able to run at 100-second intervals during peak hours, down from 120 seconds today.

More buses will be on the roads. 90% of all bus services must operate within 10- to 12-minute intervals, up from 80% today. This will rise to 95% for feeder buses services which must run at scheduled intervals of 10 minutes or less.

Liveable and inclusive community

People use the land transport system to access essential services, amenities and opportunities. The system should, therefore, be inclusive by taking into account the needs of different groups of people, such as the elderly, the less mobile and families with young children. The public transport system should be barrier-free, and our roads safer.

Importantly, the transport system should also be designed to support a high quality of life within our densely built-up environment. This would include designing more car-less or car-free zones to allow more public spaces to flourish and bring more vibrancy to the city.

Conclusions

Singapore's land transport has been dramatically transformed from the early days of rickety buses, pirate taxis and badly congested roads. The approach to transport and how transport has in turn shaped urban development in a compact and efficient manner is widely regarded as a success story. This has not come about by chance but through the sustained implementation of sound policies suited for our circumstances and constraints. While many rapidly-growing cities around the world have followed the car—oriented development pattern resulting in their sprawling urban scape, Singapore's transport planners and the country's political leaders had the foresight and tenacity to follow a development path of greater sustainability. Three key principles which underpinned our policies and infrastructure development are worth highlighting.

First, Singapore's overall urban strategy was guided by an integrated transport and land use planning approach, starting with the 1971 Concept Plan prepared under the State and City Planning (SCP) Study. This was long before the concepts of transit-oriented development (TOD) or sustainability became "fashionable", and was driven primarily by the need to optimise our limited land, but also demonstrated the foresight in those early days to plan long term to achieve sustainable outcomes.

Second, Singapore took early steps to slow the growth of motorisation. Additional taxes were introduced to increase the cost of private vehicles in the 1970s and a Vehicle Quota System (VQS) was put in place in 1990 to regulate the growth of vehicle population. A comprehensive road network was built to meet the constrained demand to prevent traffic congestion. As the world's first city to manage traffic with road pricing, Singapore implemented the Area Licensing Scheme (ALS) in 1975 to restrict traffic entering the city centre, the forerunner of the Electronic Road Pricing (ERP) system implemented in 1998.

Thirdly, and most importantly, measures to restrain the ownership and usage of private transport were supported by strategies to develop public transport as the backbone of Singapore's land transport system. The government has invested, and continues to invest heavily, in public transport infrastructure. The rail network is planned to span 360 km in length by 2030 such that eight in ten households are within walking distance of a rail station. More buses will be put on the roads under the BSEP.

Looking Ahead

The future challenges facing Singapore's land transport will include the ones which it has grappled with over the last 50 years: limited land, growing population, rising travel demand, but as well new challenges such as the changing demographics and rising public aspirations. These will have significant impact on Singapore's land transport policies and will require our transport planners to constantly innovate in anticipation of and in response to changing situations.

As a thriving first-world city, our people will expect to get to more places faster and in greater comfort than before as the rail, bus, cycling and sheltered walkway networks are enhanced, and demand a high quality of public transport service. New options such as car sharing and bike sharing schemes will appear and widen the range of transport modes and travelling experience. Walking, cycling and other sustainable modes of transport will become more important through creating a safer and more conducive ecosystem for these modes. Bestowed with the advantage of a compact environment and a world-class public transport infrastructure, Singapore is well placed to build on its excellent urban legacy for a "car-lite" future in which public transport and active mobility such as walking and cycling take dominance, with progressively lesser reliance on private cars.

References

Centre for Liveable Cities, Land Transport Authority, *Transport: Overcoming Constraints, Sustaining Mobility.* Singapore: Centre for Liveable Cities.

Chew Hock Yong, *Enhancing Travel Experience.* Singapore: LTA Academy, *Journeys 2013.*

Chin, Hoong Chor. "Urban Transport Planning in Singapore." In *Planning Singapore: from Plan to Implementation, by Belinda Yuen.* Singapore: NUS Press, 1998.

Crooks Michell Peacock Stewart, *The United Nations Urban Renewal & Development Project Report.* Singapore, 1971.

'Hock Lee Bus Strike and Riots.' http://infopedia.nl.sg/articles/SIP_4_2005-01-06.html

Land Transport Authority, *Integrated Land Use and Transport Planning.* Singapore: LTA Academy 2011.

Land Transport Authority, *Land Transport Master Plan 2008.* Singapore: Land Transport Authority, 2008.

Land Transport Authority, *Land Transport Master Plan 2013.* Singapore: Land Transport Authority, 2013.

Land Transport Authority, *White Paper: A World Class Land Transport System.* Singapore: Land Transport Authority, 1996.

Lee Kuan Yew School of Public Policy, *The Singapore MRT: Assessing Public Investment Alternatives.* Singapore: National University of Singapore, 1993.

Lew Yii Der and Maria Choy, *An Overview of Singapore's Key Land Transport Policies: Optimising under Constraints.* Singapore: LTA Academy, 2009.

Public Works Department, *The Road Ahead: Land Transport in Singapore.* Singapore: Public Works Department, 1992.

Sharp, Illsa, *The Journey: Singapore's Land Transport Story.* Singapore: SNP Editions, 2005.

Watson, P.L. and Holland, E.P. 1978. Relieving traffic congestion: The Singapore Area Licensing Scheme. World Bank Staff Working Paper No 281. World Bank Washington.

CHAPTER 9

Industrial Planning in Singapore

Tang Hsiao Ling

'60s—'70s : From Jurong Swampland to Singapore's 1st Garden Industrial Township

Singapore's economy was heavily dependent on entrepôt trade prior to the nation gaining self-governance in 1959. With the need to address unemployment issues, and compounded by the lack of natural resources, Singapore's first Finance Minister, Dr Goh Keng Swee, pursued an ambitious industrialisation programme as the main driving force for the nation's economic growth and transformation into a modern city-state.

After the new Singapore government came into power, it approached the United Nations to help revive the flagging economy. In 1960, Dr Albert Winsemius, a world-renowned Dutch economist, led a team from the United Nations Development Programme (UNDP) to assess Singapore's economic potential. This move resulted in the production of the Winsemius Report, which was to play a pivotal role in initiating Singapore's industrialisation programme. The Report highlighted the need to increase the level of manufacturing to support export-oriented industrialisation and steer economic growth.

Two key proposals in the Winsemius Report were the formation of the Economic Development Board (EDB) to implement the industrialisation programme and promote economic growth; and the development of industrial estates, particularly in Jurong, to provide the infrastructure required by the industrialists. In 1968, two other key state institutions were created from EDB's original functions. The Jurong Town Corporation (JTC) was formed to carry out estate development and management of the Industrial Facilities Committee, providing industrial land and infrastructure to investors, whilst the Development Bank of Singapore Limited (DBS) took over the industrial financing functions.[1]

---

[1] Centre for Liveable Cities, Singapore Economic Development Board, JTC Corporation. Industrial Infrastructure: Growing in Tandem with the Economy. Cengage Learning Asia, 2012.

The development of Jurong Industrial Estate was critical to alleviating the problem of mass unemployment in the '60s, facilitating the quick start-up of businesses to ramp up the economic growth and create a large supply of jobs. JTC developed the blueprint of the Jurong Industrial Estate by preparing land, factory buildings, housing and recreational facilities and played the master developer role. This included providing the necessary infrastructure for facilitating businesses, preparing land-based factories for companies requiring larger facilities; and also building industrial spaces in the form of Flatted Factories for companies that needed smaller production spaces for their businesses. What started out as a dream is today a major industrial node in Singapore, a key contributor to the city-state's total manufacturing output and employment.

Case Study—Jurong Industrial Estate

Jurong, a 5,000 hectare-area in the western region of Singapore, was known as the 'lost region' filled with rural hills, mangrove swamps, thick forests and a few *kampongs* for fisherman and farmers. As Jurong was the least populated area on the island with deep waters at the coastline that made it ideal for a port, the area was found to be a suitable site for the development of a large-scale industrial town. The bold and ambitious plan to create Jurong as the birthplace of large-scale industrialisation was considered a risky venture as this was an unknown rural territory then. Our then Finance Minister Dr Goh Keng Swee, who had the courage to dream big, famously joked that if Jurong failed, it would go down in the history books as "Goh's folly".[2]

Planned as the first industrial garden township in Singapore, JTC had envisaged Jurong to not only house industrial factories to provide large scale employment but also to be an attractive new urban area in the West of Singapore with supporting landuse that includes residential, educational, recreational and communal facilities served by a good infrastructural and transport network.

There were three main planning zones in Jurong: the Residential zone to provide flats for workers and executives, shophouses and motels for visiting industrialists; the Light Industries zone for the 'clean' industries; and the Heavy Industries zone for the 'dirty' industries. The factories in the early days included a large variety of industries ranging from manufacturing of fish hooks and coin minting, to food and textile production, metal and machinery components production, and ship building.

(Continued)

[2]Centre for Liveable Cities, Singapore Economic Development Board, JTC Corporation. Industrial Infrastructure: Growing in Tandem with the Economy. Cengage Learning Asia, 2012.

Case Study—Jurong Industrial Estate (*Continued*)

Figure 1. Aerial view of Jurong in the 1960s when it was occupied by forests, hill and swamps.

Figure 2. Mr Lee Kuan Yew (then Prime Minister) and Mr Hon Swee Sen (then Chairman of the Economic Development Board) surveying earthworks in Jurong in the 1960s.

(*Continued*)

Case Study—Jurong Industrial Estate (*Continued*)

Figure 3. Following the successful transformation from swampland to a modern industrial estate, Jurong attracted numerous investments from MNCs and local companies, creating more jobs and increasing exports.

There was a slow start in development in the early years and growing scepticism on the success of Jurong, and upon its formation in 1968, JTC accelerated its building and development programme to drive the transformation of the industrial landscape. The ramped up development of Jurong contributed significantly to the labour market with demand for factories wholly- or partly-owned by Singaporeans, or owned by companies with capital from abroad.

Mr Woon Wah Siang, JTC's first Chairman, was a key driver in the early developmental years of Jurong Industrial Estate. He projected that the township would ultimately house 700 factories and 80,000 workers within an area of more than 4,800 hectares[3]. Mr Woon also saw Jurong's potential as a community for people from all backgrounds, living in a variety of homes from low cost flats to penthouses, semi-detached houses and bungalows, meeting the needs of a balanced population from top executives to workers.

JTC owned most of the real estate in Jurong. For land allocations, leases were typically for 30 or 60 years. JTC also designed and built land-based standard factories ranging in size from 9,390 sq ft to 35,000 sq ft and also high rise flatted

(Continued)

---

[3]Chase Manhattan Bank (Singapore). Jurong Singapore. Chase Manhattan Bank (Singapore), 1973.

Case Study—Jurong Industrial Estate (*Continued*)

factories to accommodate the needs of the lighter industries[4]. In earlier days when the main concern was to fill up the vacant land and provide a quick solution to unemployment, Jurong had welcomed all types of industries. After these key concerns were addressed in the initial phase, Singapore was able to become more selective, and moved towards cleaner and more skill- and capital-intensive industries, in keeping with the broad industrial development policy.

Changes in policies also encouraged the establishment of private enterprises, both locally and overseas, and assistance was given to companies wanting to set up new factories. Restrictions were lifted on foreign investors keen to do business in Singapore, and government loans were available for private enterprises for initiating and expanding businesses. This business-friendly approach helped to create jobs at a quickened pace for Singapore's fast-growing population and provided a conducive environment for economic diversity and growth.

Figure 4.   Land-based standard factories catered to needs of companies in the heavier general industries whilst high-rise flatted factories were provided for small and medium-sized industrialists requiring space for their businesses.

(*Continued*)

---

[4]Chase Manhattan Bank (Singapore). Jurong Singapore. Chase Manhattan Bank (Singapore), 1973.

Case Study—Jurong Industrial Estate (*Continued*)

Developed as a mixed-use township, a diversity of uses was injected in close proximity to the industrial zones to create a self-sufficient estate. A wide array of amenities was provided to cater to the needs of the young and old and from the blue collar to the white collar workers. Facilities such as Jurong's Sports Complex and a bowling alley provided recreation for the fit and young burgeoning workforce, whilst playgrounds and crèches were built for the children of the growing young working population. All the amenities were supported by a reliable network of electric power, telecommunications, domestic water, industrial water, and modern sanitation laid right up to factory gates. There was also a railway link from Jurong to West Malaysia for the transport of manufactured goods and materials, and even helicopter service and explorations into hovercraft service to serve the commuters[5].

Figure 5.   Jurong was planned as a pleasant working environment with amenities and parks such as the Chinese Garden, which was opened in 1975.

In particular, an extensive Green Belt consisting of Jurong Park around Jurong River and the Japanese Gardens, manmade lakes with islands and the golf course formed a park area eight times the size of the Botanical Gardens[6]. This provided a lush landscape respite for residents beyond Jurong, for the enjoyment of the whole nation. The Jurong Bird Park boasted the highest man-made waterfall and possibly the largest walk-in aviary in the world. Next to Jurong Bird Park is one of

(*Continued*)

---

[5] Chase Manhattan Bank (Singapore). Jurong Singapore. Chase Manhattan Bank (Singapore), 1973.
[6] Chase Manhattan Bank (Singapore). Jurong Singapore. Chase Manhattan Bank (Singapore), 1973.

Case Study—Jurong Industrial Estate (*Continued*)

the preserved hillocks, Jurong Hill, with a lookout tower that offered expansive views of Singapore, Malaysia and Indonesia. The Hill also housed a restaurant frequented by workers in the area.

Completed in 1973, the Jurong Town Hall was JTC's original headquarters in the '70s. It became the heart of the town, with an impressive view of the industrial area. Standing on an 80-foot hill, it signified Jurong's dignity as a modern garden industrial town, overlooking 280 hectares of Jurong Park.

Figure 6.   Jurong Town Hall, JTC's first headquarters, opened in 1975 and was gazetted as a heritage building in 2015. Today, it remains a key landmark in Jurong that symbolises Singapore's economic and industrial progress.

'80s—Moving Up the Value Chain & Creating New Land

Creating Conducive Business Park for High-Technology Industries

In 1980, as the economy moved into a capital intensive and high-technology phase of industrialisation, JTC revealed a 10-year Master Plan that highlighted opportunities for new industrial landscapes and infrastructure that would be needed to support higher value industries. EDB was attracting multinational corporations involved in R&D and high-tech activities specialising in the financial, educational, lifestyle, medical, IT and software sectors. There was a need to create new industrial typology—the Business Park with clean and conducive office-like settings, which could accommodate a combination of manufacturing activities and high-end services.

Singapore Science Park I was launched in 1980 as a science and technology hub in a park-like setting, located in close proximity to the National University of Singapore to facilitate synergies and collaboration between industry and academia. This was followed by Singapore's first Business Park, the International Business Park in 1992, which provided a vibrant site for knowledge-based activities, as well as Changi Business Park in 1997, which today remains a conducive work environment for high-technology businesses, data and software enterprises, R&D divisions of multinational companies and knowledge-intensive enterprises.

Expanding our Land Resource through Land Creation

Singapore's economy had taken on a vigorous programme of industrialisation by the 1980s, requiring large expanses of industrial land parcels that drew down on the limited land resource. It became apparent that more land would be required to facilitate the nation's rapid economic growth. To cope with the land crunch, Singapore looked into extensive major infrastructure efforts of land reclamation from the sea depth of 13 m at Tuas that would serve as an extension of the Jurong Industrial Estate. A major reclamation project was the 'Tuas Hockey Stick'—named after its shape—that increased Singapore's industrial land supply by 600 hectares.[7]

Later in the 1990s, the goals of land reclamation went beyond adding land mass to the mainland to reclaiming and amalgamating seven offshore islands to create a petrochemical hub. The formation of Jurong Island demonstrated how clustering related companies within a sector, in this case the oil and gas sector, can reap economies of scale and provide business and logistics synergies leading to a vibrant, interdependent and competitive industrial ecosystem.

Figure 7.   To meet the increasing demand of industrialists, reclamation works at Tuas for the biomedical industry were completed in 1988 and the site is today the location for Tuas Biomedical Park.

---

[7]Michelle Lee Twan Gee. The Making of Jurong Island—The Right Chemistry. Epigram Pte Ltd, 2000.

'90s—Industry Clustering & Raising Land Productivity

Promote Synergies and Collaboration through Industry Clustering

The vision outlined in the 1991 Strategic Economic Plan was to achieve "the status and characteristics of a first league developed country", resulting in the need to move Singapore's economy upstream to ensure its competitive edge. The Cluster Development strategy was critical in identifying mutually supporting industries to form clusters and compete on that basis. Targeted development plans could be applied to individual high-growth industrial clusters, tapping the eco-system's capabilities and shared facilities, with spin-offs that would increase Singapore's competitive edge and also add value to potential investors. Industry integration would also bring about economies of scale across companies in the value chain and provide the option for industrial premises or non-essential services to be outsourced to third parties so companies can focus on their core businesses.

By clustering the industries in one location, companies could then share resources and facilities, resulting in the optimisation of our precious land resource. To meet the particular industry needs of the identified Clusters, JTC developed and designed new specialised industrial parks including Tuas Biomedical Park for the biomedical cluster, Airport Logistics Park for the air logistics cluster and Jurong Island for the chemical cluster.

The Jurong Island project is a successful case study of industrial clustering. Jurong Island was planned to house a cluster of chemical companies that functioned as one mutually supportive ecosystem with a viable business proposition. A specialised integrated network of infrastructure and service corridors, as well as facilitating companies to do businesses with one another literally at their doorsteps, provided an attractive industrial environment that has also helped these companies to reduce costs and improve process efficiencies.

Case Study—Jurong Island

In the late 1980s, Singapore's Gross Domestic Product was largely dependent on electronics, chemicals and oil refining. With the decline of the electronics sector, EDB had decided to actively ramp up the promotion of chemical projects and raise Singapore's competitiveness against regional countries who were building their own refineries.

The search for a suitable site went beyond Singapore's mainland and into the untapped islands to the south of Singapore. The palm fringed islands where

(Continued)

Case Study—Jurong Island (*Continued*)

Jurong Island is currently sited used to be occupied by sleepy fishing villages with Malay-style wooden stilt houses. By the early 1970s, three oil companies, namely Esso Singapore Pte Ltd on Pulau Ayer Chawan, Singapore Refining Company on Pulau Merlimau and Mobil Oil on Pulau Pesek had decided to house their facilities on the three islands. With these prominent petrochemical companies already on site, there was a great opportunity to tap the growing eco-system and build a chemicals hub around them. This triggered the bold plan to reclaim and amalgamate the seven islands in the area, Pulau Ayer Chawan, Pulau Ayer Merbau, Pulau Seraya, Pulau Merlimau, Pulau Sakra, Pulau Pesek and Pulau Pesek Kechil. Assigned this monumental task, JTC studied the amalgamation plans extensively and completed the concept plan for this major undertaking in the late '80s.

Figure 8.   The idea of amalgamating seven offshore islands into a chemicals hub known as Jurong Island was mooted in the 1980s and JTC was appointed to undertake the ambitious reclamation project in 1995.

The funding to amalgamate the islands and the causeway linking Jurong Island with mainland was obtained in 1993 and reclamation work started shortly. The major infrastructural works that were closely supported and monitored by government agencies involved millions of tons of sand from different sand suppliers, and required coordination between hundreds of contractors, as well as existing and new tenants.

One of the major challenges of amalgamating the islands in the '90s was the need to carry out reclamation in close proximity to existing companies on site, without disrupting their operations. This involved meticulous planning on the sequence and rate of reclamation, including relocation of existing marine services such as jetties to ensure the existing refineries' operations would not be interrupted. To overcome the logistical challenge of bringing in large volumes of sand,

(*Continued*)

Case Study—Jurong Island (*Continued*)

deep water wharfs had to be developed to receive 'Very Large Crude Carriers' right at the door step of Jurong Island for the direct service of the refineries.

Once the sand supply was available, reclamation was then planned on a Just-In-Time arrangement to meet the projected demands, where the land profiles could be tailored to the needs of individual companies. To make it economical to import sand over such long distances, JTC had to develop new loading and unloading methods and measurement protocols so that sand could be delivered for the very first time in bulk carriers.

Whilst most of the reclamation works on the island had been completed by 2008, existing petrochemical companies had started looking at expansion plans by then. This made reclamation even more technically challenging as works had to be carried out in a very tight environment. The works were completed expeditiously to meet the increasing industry demand and to ensure continuation of the companies' operations. To minimise disturbances to the natural environment, tight controls in the form of an Environmental Monitoring & Management Plan were also put in place to monitor, give feedback, forecast and provide early warnings when a certain environmental threshold was exceeded.

As part of the works needed to cater to companies' expansion plans, some of the road infrastructures had to be modified, without affecting the traffic flow on the island. This was also particularly difficult as there was a need not only to divert utility lines that were laid along the roads, but also the need to divert the pipelines that delivered products from one company to the other.

Whilst there were many challenges faced in installing the required infrastructure and services from the mainland to serve the developments, Jurong Island has since built up multiple integration levels. A Plug and Play system has optimised industry integration and business synergies with the provision of common service corridors that enable chemical companies to buy feedstock and sell finished products efficiently. The service corridors also give companies access to essential services and utilities such as steam, cooling water, fire fighting water and waste treatment services. The industrial symbiosis interlinking production processes has led to a decrease in storage needs and transport costs, contributing to savings for companies in capital outlay and operational costs. Shared resourced have also contributed greatly to environmental sustainability, and reduced the heavy vehicular traffic on the island.

The island today houses international companies such as BASF, Celanese, ExxonMobil, DuPont, Mitsui Chemicals, Singapore Refining Company, Shell

(*Continued*)

Case Study—Jurong Island (*Continued*)

and Sumitomo Chemicals. There are also local companies such as Chemical Industries (Far East), Rotary Engineering and Poh Tiong Choon Logistics all of which started as family-owned businesses and prospered through investing in state of the art facilities on the island. By 2014, there were more than 50,000 people working on Jurong Island at over 100 companies, which together had invested over $47 billion in Singapore.

JTC continues to pursue research studies and innovation projects to achieve greater sustainability, and to maximise the reuse of seabed materials removed because of reclamation and maintenance dredging. To expedite reclamation works, new technologies such as the use of air and sea drones have also been harnessed for more effective monitoring and surveying. The efforts towards providing quick availability of land and the ability to customise the reclaimed land to specifically suit companies' needs, remain Jurong Island's competitive advantages over other countries. With continuous initiatives in test-bedding and driving new solutions, Jurong Island is a living project in which the infrastructures and working environment are continually being enhanced and renewed to be the the petrochemical destination of choice.

Increasing Land Productivity through Landuse Policies and Products

With the industrial contribution to the nation's Gross Domestic Product at approximately 25% expected to be maintained, industrial uses needed a ready supply of land and space. In 1997, JTC drew up an Industrial Plan for the 21st Century (IP21) to increase land productivity through intensification of industrial landuse, with the tagline "Better Use of Land. More Room for Growth". To ensure that there would be affordable land supply for future industrial growth, multi-pronged strategies and initiatives were introduced in the form of incentives to improve land productivity, policy changes to encourage better use of land and measures to aid redevelopment and rejuvenation of estates.

Minimum plot ratios were stipulated as part of land allocation criteria for new companies and lease extension was offered to existing industrial companies as an incentive to further intensify their existing developments. Companies who had underutilised their land were allowed to return their sites at minimal cost, and rules were relaxed to allow greater flexibility in subletting spaces that were safeguarded for future expansion.

To facilitate more optimal use of available land, existing older estates with low land utilisation and inadequate supporting facilities were placed under a redevelopment plan. En-bloc redevelopment schemes were also deployed to acquire land from sunset industries with low value-add, and from companies who were sub-optimising their land parcels at low plot ratios. The unexpired tenures of leases were bought back and affected tenants were offered priority allocation and compensation packages to help them relocate. The estates were then comprehensively redeveloped by enhancing the infrastructure and reallocated to industrialists who could achieve increased economic productivity per unit of land and produce higher value-added products. Tukang, an industrial estate in Jurong, was one of the areas slated for rejuvenation. It used to house textile, plastics and metal fabrication industries. Today, it is known as Tukang Innovation Park, catering to R&D activities and companies involved in leading-edge technology.

Financial assistance schemes and grants were provided to encourage companies to undertake industrial engineering or process re-engineering projects that would achieve land savings or increase land productivity and defray the costs incurred. The JTC Land Productivity Awards were also introduced in 1998 to recognise companies that achieved more than 50% increase in land productivity above the industry average.

As part of IP21, new building typologies catering to the operations of land-based companies and addressing the need for land intensification were also introduced. The stack-up factories—Woodlands Spectrum 1 and 2—were a result of a revolutionary concept of stacking the traditional land-based factories to create multi-storey factories. Vehicular ramps allowed heavy trucks and 40-footers to access factories on

Figure 9. New industrial development typologies that met the operational needs of the industrialists in innovative ways were introduced to increase land productivity.

the upper levels, providing the higher units with the same convenience as those on the ground floor. This increased land productivity by two to three times compared to the traditional low-rise factories, utilising the land to its full potential to stretch the scarce land resource.

2000s—Creative Use of Land and Space

Vibrant Mixed Use Spaces for Knowledge-Based Industries

To remain competitive in a maturing economy amidst globalisation and technological advances, Singapore needed to diversify its economy through entrepreneurship and creative industries. This led to the creation of an "enterprise ecosystem" in which large companies and innovative start-ups could come together to generate new knowledge and capabilities. Singapore also started to pursue innovation-driven industries, like bio-medical science, life sciences, information communications (infocomms) and media, clean technology, and environment and water management.

As part of the 2001 Concept Plan, URA instituted a new zoning system that was "impact-based" where different non-pollutive businesses could be housed within a single development. The liberalisation in land zoning created great opportunities for a new typology of mixed-use environments and buildings, in which one could work, live, play and learn.

Conceived in 2000, one-north was a development that aimed to secure Singapore's competitive edge in the region as a key technopreneurial and knowledge-intensive research hub. Planned as an inclusive urban work-centric neighbourhood, one-north is a mixed-use development that seeks to attract international and local talents such as innovators, technology entrepreneurs, business consultants, media artists, and scientific researchers. The integrated industrial landscape serves to support the new knowledge-driven clusters of Biomedical Sciences, Infocomm Technology (ICT), Media, Physical Sciences and Engineering.

Case Study—one-north

Covering nearly 200 hectares, one-north lies at the heart of Singapore's technology corridor, which stretches from the edge of the Central Business District on its eastern end to the Nanyang Technological University on its western end. The greater one-north area consists of National University of Singapore (NUS), Singapore Polytechnic, National University Hospital, neighbouring residential estates, as well as established R&D facilities at Singapore Science Parks I, II and III.

(*Continued*)

Case Study—one-north (*Continued*)

Departing from the earlier planning models of the science parks or business parks in the '80s and '90s, which involved mainly mono-landuse planning concepts, the development of one-north was Singapore's first experiment at developing work-centric and knowledge-based industry clusters in an urbanised mixed-use environment. In developing one-north, JTC played the central role in providing key infrastructure to support projects by stakeholders and government agencies, such as A*STAR, EDB, SPRING, MDA and IDA as well as private companies.

The development of one-north also adopted a new private-public partnership model. Under this initiative, JTC was involved in about 20% of the overall oversaw as a strategic developer, whilst the private sector oversaw the remaining majority of the developments. This has led to an interactive dynamic in which JTC and the developers engaged in ongoing dialogues involving active participation from both parties in the evolution and creation of innovative spaces.

Four main planning strategies guided the one-north master plan and formulated the subsequent Planning Design Guidelines:-

(i) Fine-grained mixed use

  The master plan aims to provide the intensity and diversity of uses necessary to sustain an innovative community through a vertical and horizontal mix of work-live-play-learn components. An optimal mix of the key programmes—research, commercial, educational, residential, and recreational—was introduced to create the social, cultural, and economic vitality.

(ii) Seamless connectivity

  Served by two major MRT stations, Buona Vista Interchange and one-north station that could potentially be supported by a secondary People Mover System, public transport nodes are planned to be readily accessible within 200 m of walking distance. As a fenceless development, one north achieves seamless pedestrian connectivity through a network of 24-hour through-block links and covered linkways. As a major green relief, the one-north Park provides a linear open recreational space that interlinks the one-north districts. The entire one-north is also equipped with high-speed wired and wireless internet connection.

(iii) Constant rejuvenation

  To maintain long-term sustainability, a continuous process of rejuvenation and renewal is a critical response to the ever-changing land demands. The majority of land parcels in one-north is zoned 'White', which allows for a

(Continued)

Case Study—one-north (*Continued*)

more defined landuse to be determined only as and when the plots are ready to be launched. This approach also offers the flexibility for quick adjustments to prevailing market demands as the project evolves, and to inject new programmes over time to continually meet the needs of the working community.

(iv) Unique identity

The master plan draws on the site's intrinsic strengths, and seeks to relate its urban form to its existing topography and undulating ground form. Public spaces are interwoven with the dense and bent-gridded urban fabric providing green relief as well as activity spaces for the community. The existing green ecology is preserved as much as possible through tree protection and a replacement scheme, and the historical significance of the conserved colonial buildings revitalised through adaptive reuse and sensitive insertion of infills.

The districts in the first phase consist of Biopolis, Fusionopolis, Mediapolis and Vista. Biopolis is the pioneer development at one-north that focuses on biomedical R&D facilities and it has been regarded as a successful model for promoting research collaboration and knowledge exchange. Fusionopolis is dedicated to R&D in the Infocomms, Media, Science and Engineering industries. Mediapolis is a vibrant media ecosystem with activities from incubation and R&D to content production and distribution. Vista, which is at the head of one-north near the Buona Vista MRT interchange, is envisioned to be a world-class business centre in one-north as well as a residential and entertainment hub.

Figure 10.   one-north came into fruition in the early 2000s, creating an ideal work, live, play, learn environment for knowledge workers in the biomedical sciences, infocomm and media industries.

(*Continued*)

Case Study—one-north (*Continued*)

one-north is currently moving towards its second phase of development at the south of the estate which would open up further opportunities to integrate with the Science Park and NUS.

JTC is also continuing to venture into the testing of new products at one-north, the most recent development being the JTC Launchpad@one-north, a close collaboration between JTC, SPRING, the Agency for Science, Technology and Research (A*STAR), Infocomm Development Authority (IDA), Media Development Authority (MDA) and National Research Foundation (NRF) to promote entrepreneurship within the estate. The reuse of existing flatted factories and the introduction of infill buildings provided an ideal nesting ground for a vibrant community of start-ups and incubators in the biomedical sciences, info-comm, media, electronics and engineering industries. JTC Launchpad@one-north already houses about 500 start-ups and 2,000 talents that will feed into the community within one-north, adding new energy and ideas to the one-north eco-system. With the close proximity of the A*STAR research labs, NUS and international institutions such as ESSEC in one-north, we are beginning to see a natural increase in the number of collaborations between these organisations and the starts-ups and a rise in the licensing of A*STAR technologies by start-ups and the spinning-off of new start-up companies by graduates of the institutes of higher learning (IHLs).

Figure 11.   JTC Launchpad@one-north as an initiative to promote entrepreneurship amongst start-ups.

(*Continued*)

Case Study—one-north (*Continued*)

> Moving forward, with the diverse presence of strong industry clusters and the growing critical mass of vibrant communities, one-north will continue to present viable opportunities as an experimental platform to test and fine-tune innovative planning and developmental concepts.

Explorations in Underground and Air Rights Developments

Besides intensifying use on available land and reclaiming new land to stretch scarce land resource, JTC has also ventured into alternative space creation in Underground and Air-Rights Developments to explore untapped resources to expand potential space resource.

Case Study—Jurong Rock Caverns, Underground Science City at Kent Ridge Park and Air Rights Developments

With increasing demand for oil storage, JTC looked beyond the conventional way of creating more industrial space by unlocking the potential of subterranean space beneath the sea. Surveying more than 100 m below ground surface, a ground-breaking solution was devised for the possible storage of large amounts of oil within huge underground rock caverns. An area beneath Jurong Island's Banyan Basin, Singapore's energy and chemicals hub, was identified as a suitable site for the caverns as its location complements the petrochemicals hub and will support companies such as Chevron Philips, ExxonMobil and Shell.

Jurong Rock Caverns (JRC) is today Southeast Asia's first underground liquid hydrocarbon storage facility. At 130 m beneath Banyan Basin on Jurong Island, JRC is the deepest underground public works in Singapore to date. By utilising subterranean space for storage, JRC has ensured the security of the products in storage and also freed up approximately 60 hectares of usable land for higher value-added activities such as petrochemicals manufacturing.

To tackle this engineering challenge, JTC brought together an international team of experts and specialists and looked into cutting-edge construction methods to construct the five nine-storey-high rock caverns, with 9 km of tunnels and an integrated network of pipes with supporting utilities. The Caverns will have the capacity of approximately 600 Olympic-sized swimming pools of liquid hydrocarbons such as crude oil and condensate. With large amounts of rock and earth dug up as part of the preparation for the rock caverns, plans were afoot for this material to be re-used as reclamation fill for Jurong Island.

(*Continued*)

Case Study—Jurong Rock Caverns, Underground Science City at Kent Ridge Park and Air Rights Developments (*Continued*)

Figure 12. Jurong Rock Caverns (JRC) exemplifies JTC's efforts in overcoming land constraints by going into great subterranean depths, freeing up surface land for more productive economic activities to support and sustain the growth of industries.

Construction for the first phase of the underground development at JRC began in 2007 after six years of conceptual planning. It was completed after a period of eight years. This capacity is expected to double with the completion of the second phase. The pilot JRC project exemplified Singapore's efforts in overcoming land constraints to sustain the long-term growth of the economy, and spearheaded a new paradigm that triggered explorations into the resource of other potential spaces at great subterranean depths.

Another project being explored is the Underground Science City located below Kent Ridge Park, envisioned to be an extension of the existing eco-system at one-north, Science Park I, II, III and National University of Singapore. By leveraging the existing research centres in the surroundings, the Underground Science City that will be made up of 40 rock caverns will be developed into a fully self-sustaining underground facility for R&D activities and data centres. It is also expected to house up to 4,200 scientists, researchers and other professionals.

(*Continued*)

Case Study—Jurong Rock Caverns, Underground Science City at Kent Ridge Park and Air Rights Developments (*Continued*)

On the other hand, as part of land creation, Air Rights Developments are also being explored above major infrastructure to fully utilise typically unused air space above roads for new developments. By creating elevated infills that can span across existing thoroughfares, a range of land uses such as commercial, institutional, business park and other industrial spaces can be introduced to support neighbouring communities. Besides contributing to land savings, Air Rights Developments will also significantly improve connectivity between spaces previously segregated by the infrastructure.

With a significant percentage of land area used for major roads and infrastructure in Singapore, there is also a strong opportunity to make use of these areas, resulting in potential land savings. Decking over these major infrastructures would also improve on above-ground vehicular and pedestrian connectivity, providing seamless integration between developments with potential synergies currently segregated by these roads. The elevated structures that can span across major expressways and roads can also support infills of a range of different land uses such as commercial, institutional, and industrial which could serve as an attractive addition to the surrounding developments.

Figure 13. Air Rights Development over major road infrastructure.

The concept of Air Rights Developments can also be extended to the introduction of new infills over existing industrial developments and even over port

(*Continued*)

**Case Study—Jurong Rock Caverns, Underground Science
City at Kent Ridge Park and Air Rights Developments (*Continued*)**

or transport facilities. The former would allow for intensification of landuse on sites with retained usable buildings that could be adaptively re-purposed, both retaining the heritage value of the older industrial building typologies and promoting a more sustainable way of development. The latter proposal would give enormous opportunity for logistics intensive-industries to tap onto the major transport node.

2010 and Beyond—New Directions in Industrial Planning

The industrial sector is projected to remain as an important pillar of Singapore's economy and will continue to require a steady supply of land and space. Today, 13% of the island's total land mass is allocated for industrial use. Moving forward, as the conventional means to increase our industrial land supply become less viable, there is a need to also source for more creative and cutting-edge solutions to alleviate our industrial space constraints.

With the projected increase in Singapore's population up to the range of 6.5–6.9 million by 2030,[8] there will be competing landuses within a denser built environment. This also means that industrial land will be planned in closer proximity to urban and suburban areas, residential areas, water catchments as well as parks and recreation areas. The challenge will increasingly be how different land uses can be seamlessly integrated within a compact setting, whilst maintaining a high level of liveability and sustainability in a thriving urban environment.

As Singapore's economy transited through the labour-intensive, skills-intensive, capital-intensive, knowledge-intensive and innovation-driven phases from the '60s to the present day, the industrial infrastructure provision and policies have also evolved progressively to follow economic trends. Understanding the changing economic trends, moving towards innovating new land solutions and building innovative space products will be key to helping our industrialists grow their businesses in a conducive and future-ready environment.

Whilst industrial estates used to be planned as mono-landuse districts and as silos away from residential estates, there will be opportunities to bring jobs with better working environments closer to homes. More integrated mixed-use developments will be

---

[8] National Population and Talent Division. A Sustainable Population For A Dynamic Singapore Population White Paper. National Population and Talent Division., 2013. http://population.sg/whitepaper/resource-files/population-white-paper.pdf.

created with work-live-play-learn-make activities, where industrial buildings, business parks, offices, retail shops, residential homes, recreational facilities, educational institutions and communal amenities can be interwoven seamlessly within a vibrant and liveable environment.

Active programming and place-making initiatives will also be needed to bring together the different communities within such districts, encouraging interactions and collaborations between workers, academics and residents from within and beyond the industrial estates to serve the needs of the greater population. To facilitate last mile transport, these mixed-use nodes will also be planned with seamless connectivity through a network of covered walkways and cycling paths, linking the major transport nodes to amenities and work places.

JTC has embarked on the planning and development of the next mixed-use district, Jurong Innovation District (JID) which covers 600 hectares including Nanyang Technological University (NTU), CleanTech Park, and the surrounding area of Bulim, Bahar and Tengah. JID presents a unique opportunity to transform our manufacturing landscape and serve as a new model for the future of work, live, play, learn and create. New growth areas for advanced manufacturing, robotics, urban solutions, cleantech and smart logistics would be housed in JID, where the entire value chain of R&D, design, prototyping, production and supply chain management could be hosted. The district will also provide a living lab for innovators, makers, entrepreneurs and new businesses, which could be housed in the JTC Launchpad @ JID, targeted for completion in 2017. The district would be an open, smart and liveable environment where students, researchers, industry professionals and entrepreneurs can co-create new ideas, products and solutions that could be prototyped, test-bedded and manufactured.

To address the issue of land scarcity and further optimise landuse, there is also a need to encourage companies to move from land-based facilities to occupying building space. JTC is looking into creating more next-generation industrial spaces that can achieve higher land productivity and also help enterprises enhance their

Figure 14.   Artist impression of a cross-section in Jurong Innovation District.

Figure 15.   New building typologies that include JTC Space @ Tuas, JTC Food Hub @ Senoko and JTC Space @ Tuas Biomedical Park.

competitiveness and increase their productivity. New building typologies that feature shared facilities and flexible design for both generic and specialised industrial spaces for specific industries will help companies to reduce their upfront capital investments and operating costs. Some new industrial developments would include the JTC Space @ Tuas, the first integrated development incorporating ramp-up and flatted factories units above land-based factories catering to a diverse range of industries including oil and gas, precision engineering and general manufacturing; the multi-tenanted JTC Food Hub @ Senoko where companies can benefit from a shared cold room and warehousing facility; as well as JTC Space @ Tuas Biomedical Park that provides a convenient "one-stop-shop" with shared facilities and amenities for both manufacturers and vendors to enjoy shorter turnaround time and enhanced operational efficiency .

New technological advancements will be critical in driving industry transformation at an estate and building level as well as further optimising land through sharing and consolidation of functions and services. Smart technology will act as the horizontal enabler that ties the different planning and design initiatives together, providing real-time updates and information to the stakeholders and greatly improving on the responses to problems and opportunities on the ground. The new industrial districts would also serve as a fertile testing ground for experimenting with and prototyping of new technologies and innovations that could be key enablers in resolving the challenges of evolving industrial trends. The new innovative solutions could be co-developed by industrial partners, academics and even the end-users and rolled out for implementation if proven to be successful.

To further optimise on our available land, old estates can be rejuvenated through land recycling as an approach to maintaining a steady stream of land supply for economic growth. There will also be a rising need for redeveloping brownfield sites and exploring the reuse of landfills for industrial development.

As industries become cleaner and less pollutive in their operations, environmental sustainability will be a key planning strategy for industrial parks, where integrated green and blue features would serve not only as visual relief but also function as grey water treatment or phytoremediation purposes within these industrial settings. The next generation of industrial parks are planned to be future ready to perpetuate Singapore's continued quest to attract quality regional and international investments. Besides creating functional workplaces for the many more jobs that will be created, these future-ready industrial estates will also be well integrated with the surrounding urban fabric, and provide an open and dynamic environment for the greater community.

CHAPTER 10

Greening Singapore: Past Achievements, Emerging Challenges

Tan Puay Yok

Introduction

Singapore is an unusually green city. As a high-density, high-rise city, as well as a country with one of the highest population densities in the world, the competition for land should normally mean that the cityscape is overwhelmed by buildings and infrastructures, as one would commonly see in cities of similar built and human densities. Instead, the pervasive presence of greenery in the city-state makes it rather distinctive when compared to cities such as Seoul, Hong Kong, New York City, Shanghai, as well as many rapidly urbanising mega cities in Southeast Asia. Its greenness has over the years, led to it having a reputation as a green city, a Garden City that is recognised by visitors to the city (Hui and Wan, 2003). It has also attracted opinions that "… the place really does live up to its reputation as the Garden City of Asia, or indeed the world …" (Kingsbury, 2012), and that "… there are a few dense cities in the world that can claim of a better record of greening the city than Singapore …" (Beatley, 2012). There are anecdotal accounts that the architect Norman Foster views the distinctive closed canopy of trees lining the expressway from the airport to the city centre, rather than its architecture, as the iconic feature of the city. The green environment is similarly appreciated by locals. Perception studies of Singapore residents conducted over the years highlight the importance of greenery to residents. For instance, parks and greenery are regarded as one of the top five most important factors affecting quality of life in Singapore, and more than 90% of Singapore residents feel that greenery contributes to Singapore's identity (URA, 2010). Singapore residents also have a high level of satisfaction on the overall greenery in Singapore (81% in 2007 are satisfied) (MOF, 2010).

Collectively, such information suggests that the urban vegetation of Singapore has not only shaped an image of the city — it has also forged an image that has become a common identity that Singapore residents associate with. Interestingly too, a recent survey conducted showed that more than half of respondents preferred the "preservation of green spaces over infrastructural development, compared to the 19 percent who picked infrastructural development" (Chang, 2013), suggesting that a progression

177

from an awareness of presence of greenery, to a wide-spread appreciation of its benefits, and now to an identity that should be treasured and protected could already be in motion within the citizenry.

How green is Singapore? It is useful to get a perspective of this through a quantitative comparison. A common indicator for comparing the presence of greenery is vegetation cover, which is the vertically projected percentage of land that is covered by greenery when viewed from the top. Vegetation cover includes greenery contributed by trees, shrubs and ground cover for all urban greenery forms, such as parks and other forms of green open spaces, roadside vegetation, as well as spontaneous vegetation such as primary and secondary forests, marshland and mangrove forests. Across cities of different population densities, a general pattern can be observed, which is that cities with high population densities tend to have lower vegetation cover (Figure 1). Singapore's vegetation cover of around 40% in 2011 stands out as an anomaly among cities with population densities higher than 6,000 persons per square kilometre. This is evident in aerial images of different parts of Singapore. Despite its high built densities, there is a general pervasiveness of greenery even in built-up areas of Singapore (Figure 2a, b).

It will be difficult to imagine that the remarkable extent in the physical greening of Singapore has occurred without considerable planning and efforts amidst conflicting demand for land and other resources. Such a competition is experienced in all expanding cities, but is particularly acute in a city-state like Singapore. A full appreciation of the challenges faced requires cognisance of the socio-economic and socio-political context of Singapore during the initial era of nation-building between the 1960s and 1970s. Active greening started at a time when Singapore was beset with

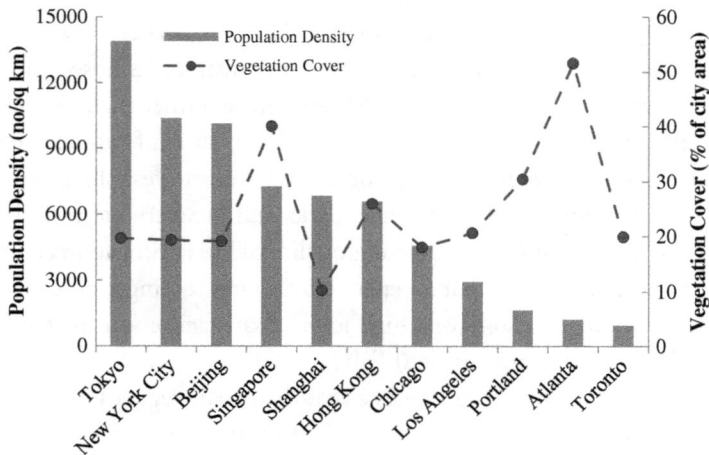

Figure 1. Comparison of vegetation cover in cities with a range of population densities. Vegetation cover data are from Tan *et al.* (2013) for Asian cities, and Nowak and Greenfield (2012) for tree and shrub cover of North American cities. Vegetation cover data for Singapore for 2011 was obtained from Auger (2013).

Figure 2.   Aerial images of built-up areas in Singapore showing a diversity of green spaces such as roadside vegetation, parks and green open spaces, and rooftop greenery. Images courtesy of the Urban Redevelopment Authority.

numerous social, economic and environmental challenges after it had gained self-government from British colonial rule in 1959. It was widely acknowledged that Singapore then faced serious environmental, economic and social challenges as a young nation (Tortajada *et al.*, 2013; CLC and HDB, 2013; Teo, 1992). Some of these include severe housing shortages and appalling living conditions in the city centre that housed 60% of the population on 16% of the land area (Neville, 1969; Hassan, 1969). Singapore was in fact, said to have the largest slums in Southeast Asia then (Yuen, 1996). Environmental pollution due to unregulated discharges from farms and industries into waterways was also a major concern, with the Singapore River and Kallang River as prime examples of severely polluted major waterways up to the 1970s (CLC and HDB, 2013). Other than areas in Tanglin and Stevens Road and others which were traditional enclaves of the British, the city centre and adjacent urban areas were also largely devoid of greenery (Ghani, 2011). To have achieved the level of greening that it enjoys now despite the attention needed on considerably more urgent and critical problems, as well as competition for resources required to deal with them, suggests that there was a purposeful policy to drive urban greening for the past 50 years, and a set of enabling factors that have led to its success.

What might these be? Given that Singapore's population is projected to continue to increase substantially over the next 20–30 years, the twin pressures of urbanisation and increase in population density will be expected to exert downward pressures on existing vegetation, including remnant pieces of secondary forests that have regenerated from forest clearings over the past 50–100 years. How could Singapore reconcile the need to both conserve these spaces and yet also set aside land resources to support other social and economic developments? The objective of this chapter is to discuss the key dimensions of the urban greening of Singapore, taking a look at past trends and current events, and offering perspectives for the future. The first part of the chapter presents a synthesis of the key factors that were important in enabling the successful implementation of an urban greening programme. As Singapore steps into its next 50 years of development, there are also emerging challenges that reflect the physical constraints it faces, an evolving government-civil society relationship, and a citizenry which is increasingly active in projecting its views on greenery conservation matters. A fresh mindset towards the management of its green spaces will be needed. The second part of the chapter describes these challenges and provides several perspectives on dealing with these emerging issues that could well shape the character of the Garden City over the next 50 years.

Greening as a Cornerstone of Singapore's Urban Development

It has been suggested that most economies in the world have gone through a phase of "pollute first, clean up later", starting with Western countries in Europe and the USA, and in more recent decades, exemplified by the severe environmental degradation in China that accompanies its rapid economic development (Azadi *et al.*, 2011; Liu, 2010). This is also now similarly experienced to varying degrees in many developing countries in Asia. This development pathway of an early dominance of pollution, to be replaced by subsequent efforts in environmental improvement and protection has also been suggested to be unavoidable up to a certain threshold of economic and social development (Azadi *et al.*, 2011). While it has been said that Singapore actively avoided such a short-sighted policy of "develop first and clean up later" from the onset of nation building (CLC and NEA, 2013), the suite of environment issues described earlier would indicate that it had similarly experienced a phase of unregulated urban development and a proliferation of pollutive manufacturing industries, cottage industries and farms, which were preceded by massive deforestation that had led to drastic ecological transformations of the city. With the onset of more systematic land use planning, particularly commencing with the 1971 Concept Plan in which concrete environmental planning and guidelines were introduced (Lin, 2007), a more systematic approach towards planning for both growth and environment took shape. In addition to the focus on pollution control, a strong emphasis on greening the environment was also instituted into its overall urban development plans (Ghani, 2011). The key architect of the greening programme was the late former Prime Minister, Lee Kuan Yew. Much has been written about his role and his vision of a verdant Singapore, with detailed descriptions of the prime motivations for greening Singapore, chronological development and milestones (e.g., see Ghani, 2011; Koh, 2000; Koh, 2007; Neo *et al.*, 2012; Tan *et al.*, 2013). The author proposes that from amidst the key events, actors and agents in the greening programme of Singapore, a set of key success factors can be identified as useful learning points on the implementation of one of the most successful urban development programmes in Singapore's history. These are described below.

A Top-down Vision and Political Support

Leading changes starts with a vision. In the case of Singapore, Lee set out to differentiate Singapore from other Third World countries through his vision that Singapore must be a clean and green city. During the rapid industrialisation and urbanisation period of Singapore which started in the late 1950s to early 1960s, he had observed that only "one tree was planted for every 10 felled for building sites" (cited in Neo *et al.*, 2012) and was determined that greening the city should be pursued concurrently with its economic and urban development. While the key driver for this push has usually been interpreted as economic in nature, there was evidence that his vision for a green Singapore also stemmed from an early belief in the importance of greening to the quality of the environment. So while Lee said that "after independence, I searched for some dramatic way to distinguish ourselves from other Third World countries" and "settled for a clean and green Singapore" (Lee, 2011) to give Singapore its competitive advantage in attracting investors, he also believed that "planting more trees would encourage cloud formation and retain moisture so that the city could be a pleasant place to live in" (cited in Neo *et al.*, 2012). To Lee, "if you get the placed greened up, if you get all those creepers up, you take away the heat, you'll have a different city" (cited in

Han *et al.*, 1998). The latter remarks are not different from current scientifically-based paradigms of urban greenery and urban hydrology as essential means of moderating the urban climate for urban dwellers. His views were however, made 30–40 years before advances in scientific knowledge and empirical verification allow a more informed science-based approach towards city design and planning. Regardless of the motivations, the vision for a clean and green Singapore in an era where there were arguably no good examples the city could adapt and learn from must be credited as the principal driving force for the range of policies and programmes initiated to achieve this vision. In Lee's words, greening Singapore was treated as a key component in the "overall scheme of things—it's not a side issue" (Chuang, 2009).

The importance of personal interest and the top-down approach in monitoring progress cannot be understated. Lee took a personal interest in greenery and environmental issues to make sure government ministries and officials took the tasks of environmental transformation of Singapore seriously (Han, 2011). It directly translated into political support to make available various resources that are needed to carry out the implementation work, key of which must be the financial means of implementation. It was said that Lee in the 1970s had directed the Ministry of Finance to significantly increase the budget of Parks and Recreation Department (PRD), the government agency responsible for carrying out greening operations, reversing earlier difficulties encountered by PRD for additional budgetary allocation (Ghani, 2011). The notion that the nation must invest adequately to green the city as urbanisation proceeded was also reflected in the statement by Lee in 1980: "the challenge for Parks and Recreation is to give that touch of quality and originality in maintaining a balance of flora and fauna in our city, despite the bulldozer, despite the reinforced concrete structures and tarmac-ed motorways. Both brain power and aesthetic senses, and more resources are keys to success" (cited in Lee, 2011). Indeed, despite large population increases over the five decades, per capita expenditure on parks and greenery management did not decrease, but had increased more than 50-fold between 1970 and 2010 (Figure 3a). Total expenditure was $396 million in 2010, which had doubled from 0.4% in 2000 to 0.85% in 2010 as a percentage of total annual government expenditure (Figure 3b). The decision to proceed with the construction of Gardens by the Bay in the late 2000s as the single most costly greenery project requiring unprecedented capital investment and recurring maintenance budget, and which came with a large opportunity cost of forgone real estate development, illustrated that such a financial commitment continues today even when Singapore was already known as a Garden City. This would not have been possible or easy in an environment of perpetual competing needs within the government budgetary allocation processes in both lean and good years, if not for the fact that greening is treated a key priority in urban development. This was directed by vision and backed by political support, as dictated by the top echelon of decision making in the government.

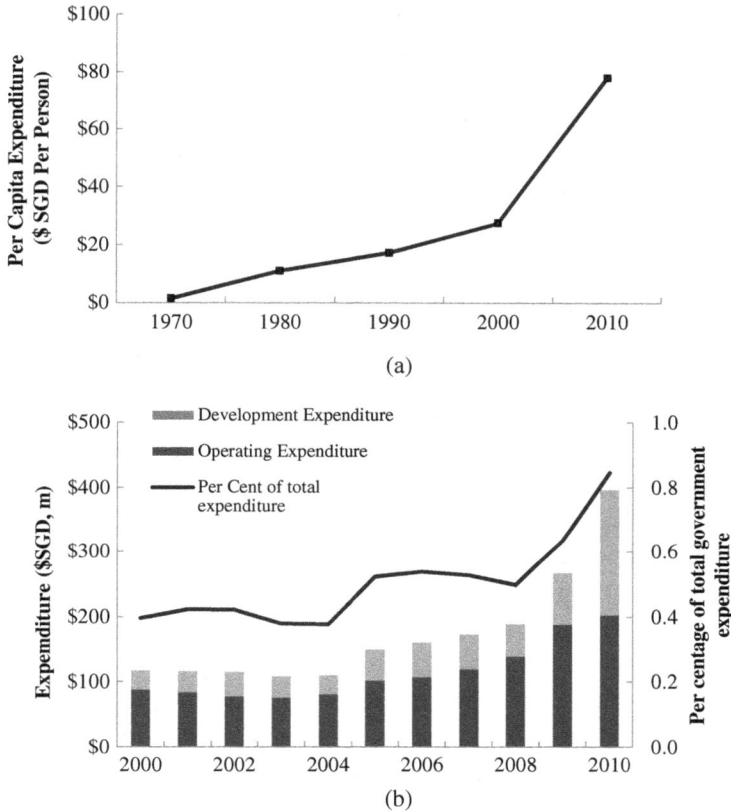

Figure 3. (a) Decadal changes in per capita expenditure, and (b) operating (including manpower) and development expenditure on parks and greenery management. Expenditure data was derived from MOF and population data was derived from DOS (MOF; DOS, 2012).

Legal Framework and Planning Policies

In addition to financial resources, for a city with Singapore's land limitations, the other key resource for greening is land. Between the 1960s and early 1990s when high-rise greening was still hampered by lack of awareness and adequate technological solutions, greening Singapore inevitably involves competition of land at the ground level. It requires trade-offs to be made between providing spaces for greenery and other land needs, particularly in the later years where expanding infrastructure and building developments in an already dense city heighten the tussle for space in a largely zero-sum game of land allocation. In this operating environment, the legal framework, and planning policies including regulatory requirements and guidelines on land allocation would have been critical for both empowering officials who had to green the city, as well as to enable a systematic process of safeguarding land dedicated for greenery through planning approval processes. The legal framework enables institutions to be set up and greening provisions to be enforced. (Refer to Koh, 1995 and Koh, 2007 for an extensive chronological description of the legislations that were enacted to enable greenery provisions to be effected and implemented greenery to be protected. The relevant acts and their key provisions are summarised in Table 1.)

Several key regulatory provisions which the author believes to be of prime value are described here. The first is the "green buffer" policy which requires a three- to five-metre verge to be set aside for tree planting on the sides of developments fronting a public road. This requirement, which is specified in the Parks and Trees Act, effectively ensured that other than public green spaces, land within developments also contribute to the overall greenery of the city. In addition to the green buffer, tree planting is also required on a peripheral planting verge two metres wide on the other sides of a development. This not only adds to tree cover, but also helps to ensure an adequate separation of buildings. This, together with the green buffer and physical buffer (physical setback of the building line from the development boundary) contributes to the creation of open spaces within developments to avoid an overly dense built environment. The green buffer also has two additional impacts. Firstly, planting provision within the green buffer in effect creates a second layer of greenery parallel to the roadside greenery, forming an increased visual depth of "borrowed greenery" for pedestrians and motorists. Secondly, the physical setback provides important aerial space for trees to develop full canopies, the lack of which due to inadequate building line setback is a major barrier to optimal tree provision in a densely built-up environment (Tan *et al.*, 2013).

The second important regulatory provision is the provision of dedicated planting verges along roads, which was implemented as a standardised code for road construction in the mid-1970s. Depending on the types of roads, a two- to four-metre planting verge is mandated for tree planting as part of the road reserves, including a centre planting strip for major roads and expressways. The impact of this is that in the 1960s and 1980s, when built-up areas in Singapore expanded rapidly, roadside greenery was systematically introduced throughout the city concomitant with land development. To date, it is estimated that more than 90% of all roads in Singapore have roadside vegetation (NParks, 2012). Tan *et al.* (2013) argued that these two regulatory policies have in effect, created a consistent urban form which is extensively replicated throughout the island (Figure 4). The role of systematic roadside greening role is seldom recognised but is key towards creating the perception of pervasive greenery in Singapore today through leveraging on the extensive road network. As the land uptake for roadside greenery is also relatively low at 3.7% of Singapore's land area, roadside greening is thus an effective way of creating the ambience of green, particularly as most residents will inevitably experience the street in their everyday living (Tan *et al.*, 2013).

Table 1. Summary of various acts and legal provisions on greenery matters in Singapore. Information is extracted from Koh (1995), Chun (2006) and Lin (2007).

Act and Other Legal Provision	Year Passed	Main Provisions
Part V of Local Government Integration Ordinance	1963	• To restrict the felling of trees exceeding five feet in girth • To require land occupier to clear land for planting of trees and shrubs in land adjoining, abutting or near to designated public road.
Trees and Plants (Preservation and Improvement of Amenities) Act	1970	• To restrict the felling of trees exceeding five feet in girth • To require land occupier to enhance the amenity of land adjoining public roads
Parks and Trees Act	1975	• To restrict the felling of trees on any vacant land above girth of one metre • To require the provision and maintenance of trees and plants in developments • To require the provision of open spaces in developments • To enable setting of rules for the control and management of public parks on the preservation and protection of flora, fauna and other property • To enable setting of rules for the regulation and prescription of the standards of planting, aeration and maintenance of trees and plants
National Parks Act	1990	• To designate the Singapore Botanic Gardens, Fort Caning Park as National Parks. The Nature Reserves and parks of the Public Utilities Board Catchment Area come under the ambit of the Act. • To provide for the protection and conservation of animals in National Parks and Nature Reserves.
Parks and Trees (Preservation of Trees) Order	1991	• To designate two areas of Singapore as Tree Conservation Areas and to make it an offence to cut down a tree with a girth exceeding one metre without approval from authority
Parks and Trees Act	2005	• Revision to Parks and Trees Act 1975. New provisions are highlighted below. • To provide for designation of Heritage Roads. • To increase the maximum fine for a range of offences committed in national parks, nature reserves and tree conservation areas • Enhancement of the effectiveness of National Parks Board

(a)

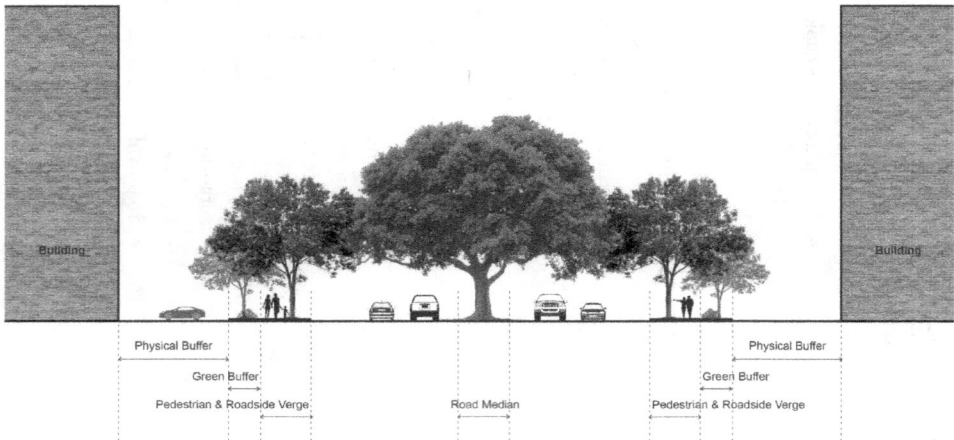

(b)

Figure 4.   (a) Typical roadside greenery that is extensively replicated throughout Singapore, with building setback from the plot boundary, and roadside planting consisting of side verges and a centre planting strip; (b) the standardised road planting code for the above planting scheme adopted in the early 1970s.

The third policy, the Landscape Replacement Policy, is a more recent development implemented by the Urban Redevelopment Authority in 2009. It was introduced as part of the set of development control guidelines called Landscaping for Urban Spaces and High-Rises (LUSH) under the provision of the Planning Act. The policy requires developers to replace all of the green area that has been lost from the site due to the development to other areas within the site, at intermediate terraces within the building or on the roof. This policy was initially applied to areas within the Central Area, but has since June 2014 been extended to regional centres and growth areas such as Jurong Gateway, Kallang Riverside, Woodlands Regional Centre, Punggol Creative Cluster, Tampines Regional Centre, and Paya Lebar Central, as well as commercial and residential developments within 19 town centres. Together with other requirements in LUSH, this policy has since 2009 added 40 hectares of green space in developed areas, not inclusive of green buffer and peripheral planting areas (URA, 2014). While 40 hectares over five years is low in comparison with all developed areas in Singapore over the same period, it nevertheless represents the next best or only available option of compensating for the loss of green spaces when developments are inevitable. With time, this policy should become a key factor which enables the amount of greenery to keep pace with the increase in glass, steel and concrete surfaces in the city.

Dedicated Institutions

If metaphorically, a vision of Singapore being a Garden City is a destination, the legal framework and supporting policies will be the vehicle that facilitates the journey, and dedicated institutions the driver who operates and steers the vehicle. It is suggested here that dedication, both in the sense of having specific institutions tasked with implementing greening policies, as well as having capable personnel dedicated to the cause of greening Singapore, is the third major factor that has enabled a successful greening programme. Between 1960 and 1996, a total of eight organisational changes were made on the key institutions that were responsible for the implementation of national greening policies (Table 2), perhaps more so than any single governmental function over the same period. It highlighted that there was high-level and active monitoring of the programme, such that as priorities of the programme changed and gained complexities, organisational changes were made to provide administrative depth, resources and organisational effectiveness. The formation of the Parks and Trees Unit in 1967 and its subsequent merger with the Parks Division from the Parks and Recreation Division a year later for instance, arose from the need to coordinate and plan greening efforts, which prior to its formation, were undertaken by the Roads Department, Parks Division and Housing and Development Board (Neo et al., 2012). The elevation of the Parks and Recreation Division to a full department (Parks and Recreation Department) within the hierarchy of the Ministry of National Development in 1976 also meant that early in the journey of greening Singapore, there was a single dedicated institution with more influence than in the past in promoting greening policies and programmes within national and urban developmental plans. The importance of this coordinated administration was also recently recognised by the Hong Kong Government, which formed a new Greening, Landscape and Tree Management

Table 2. Key institutions responsible for greening Singapore from the 1960s. Note that greenery planning also involved coordination with other past and current agencies such as the Urban Renewal Department (now the Urban Redevelopment Authority) and Primary Production Department (now Agri-Food and Veterinary Authority of Singapore). Information is extracted from Neo *et al.* (2012) and Wong *et al.* (2014).

Institution	Year
Parks and Recreation Division was set up in the Ministry of Labour	1960
Parks and Recreation Division was transferred to Ministry of Social Affairs	1963
Parks and Trees Unit was set up in Public Works Department	1967
Parks Division from Parks and Recreation Division at Ministry of Social Affairs was moved to Public Works Department and merged with Parks and Trees Unit to form Parks and Trees Division	1968
Parks and Trees Unit merged with Singapore Botanic Gardens to form Parks and Recreation Division within Public Works Department	1973
Parks and Recreation Division elevated to Parks and Recreation Department within the Ministry of National Development	1976
National Parks Board formed within the Ministry of National Development	1990
Parks and Recreation Department merged into National Parks Board	1996

Section in its Development Bureau in March 2010 to provide central coordination of the government's greening, landscape planning and design efforts across different agencies with greening operations (HKSAR, 2014).

The formation of Parks and Recreation Department in Singapore as a dedicated organisation also led to important positive gains, such as the ensuing availability of resources, recruitment of staff with specialist training in silviculture and horticulture, as well as the setup of dedicated research functions such as in soil science, plant nutrition, plant pathology and physiology (Neo *et al.*, 2012). It also meant that the technical competencies required to support greening operations were accumulated over time, instituted as best practices and retained as institutional knowledge within a single organisation. Over time, a wealth of expert knowledge is accumulated. Indeed, as an organisation is only as good as the personnel within the organisation, the focus on technical competencies early in the rapid phase of greening has also been credited as an important success factor, with overseas training being put in place as early as 1970 (Wong, 2014). The emphasis on staff development and technical competencies as a foundation for organisational excellence continues today. Several generations of staff have benefitted from scholarships for higher degrees provided by the Parks and Recreation Department and the National Parks Board, which helped to increase the technical competencies and foster new strategies for the organisation. Many of the beneficiaries also now hold leadership positions within the organisation. Their contributions and those before them can in turn be attributed to early policies on dedicated institutional and human capital development.

Emerging Challenges

Greenery in cities changes over time. Decadal changes in the greenery of 286 Chinese cities (Zhao *et al.*, 2013) and 386 European cities (Fuller and Gaston, 2009) show that these occur in a complex fashion dependent on size of cities, state of compactness, urbanisation and population changes. It will be unusual for greenery in Singapore to remain static. Studying patterns of green spaces changes, in relation to environmental, social and economic drivers, provides a better ability to predict future trends and determine the nature of interventions needed. These are the subject of current studies in the National University of Singapore, and it is clear from some of our studies that recent changes in greenery point to emerging challenges for Singapore. These are briefly discussed below.

Managing Pressures of Population Growth and Urbanisation

Population growth and urbanisation are the two main key drivers affecting land use changes in cities worldwide. Singapore is not immune to such effects. There are telling effects of the pressures of population growth and increasing urbanisation on greenery in Singapore over the years. Between 2007 and 2011, vegetation cover had significantly declined by 7% from 47% (Yoshida, 2012) to about 40% (Auger, 2013). Assuming that changes took place over five years, this represents an average loss of about 1,000 hectares of vegetation cover per year, a rather alarming loss for a small city. Over the same period, population went up by 0.724 million, an increase of 16%, whereas population density increased by 14%. So while it has been extensively reported in the past that Singapore's vegetation cover had increased between 1986 and 2007 despite population increasing by one million, for instance in Yoshida (2012) and numerous official presentations and reports, vegetation cover changes are clearly not just dynamic; they can suffer from large changes. The key question is what the trajectory of change for Singapore over the next ten to twenty years will be, given that population and population density will continue to increase, and that these factors generally drive down vegetation cover (Figure 1). Competition for urban spaces due to road widening and other land development and redevelopments have also led to mature tree population declining steadily for over a decade from 2003, a trend that will require considerable efforts and time to reverse (Tan *et al.*, 2013). Another consequence of population growth is its effect on the park provision ratio (PPR), which is the amount of park area per 1,000 person (ha/1000), used as a planning parameter in national land use planning. PPR has increased from 0.13 ha/1000 in 1971, to 0.36 ha/1000 in 1977, and to the current 0.8 ha/1000 with the Concept Plan Review in 1989 (Wong, 2014). For the past 15 years however, Singapore has notably not achieved its target PPR (Figure 5) even though park area and park area as a percentage of Singapore's land area have both increased. This is clearly an effect of population growing faster than the provision of parks.

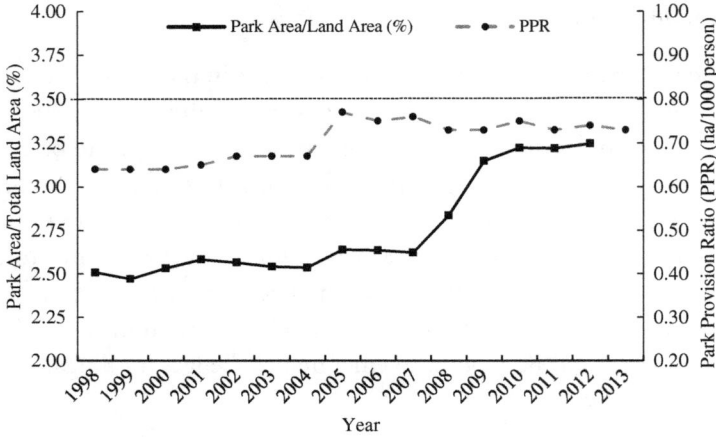

Figure 5. Changes in the park area as a percentage of Singapore's land area and park provision ratio (PPR). The dotted line shows the target PPR of 0.8 ha/1000 used as a planning parameter. Park area and PPR were obtained from NParks and MOF (NParks; MOF).

The consequences of population growth and urbanisation over the finite land area of Singapore and the challenges imposed on greenery provision for environmental and recreational needs have to be better understood. As a city state that has placed greenery and green opens spaces as key to urban liveability and its image, Singapore needs to decide how trade-offs between competing land uses should be made. A focus on innovations in the design of the built environment, for instance, with regards to blurring of public and public spaces, and the design of multi-functional spaces, should also offer potential for mitigating the consequences of space competition. For the latter, an example is the push towards the incorporation of greenery on buildings in Singapore in the form of "skyrise greenery", which thus far has been a success achieved in slightly more than a decade (Tan, 2013). The means to sustain the momentum will be important.

Dealing with a Wicked Problem

Not only is the amount of greenery changes a concern, changes in the composition of greenery is also now emerging as a contested issue. A close examination of the greenery that has been lost between 2007 and 2011 showed that a substantial proportion resulted from the clearing of young secondary forest and scrubland over a wide range of sizes (unpublished data). In effect, the greenery type in Singapore is gradually shifting to an eventual dominance by managed forms of green spaces such as parks, rooftop gardens, roadside vegetation, internal green spaces in developments, etc., with a concomitant reduction in spontaneous vegetation largely due to deforestation of young and old secondary forests. For the latter, many of these patches have been regenerating for 50–100 years from abandoned cultivated land or cleared primary forests, and with time, have gained important ecological, biophysical and social values. The consequences of losses are the subject of a study in progress, but suffice it to say, these losses should not be ignored. This is also because while prominent sites such as Bukit Brown and Bidadari cemeteries have already caught the civic society's and government's attention because of their prominent heritage and biodiversity values, there are numerous small patches across the island that have been silently, but permanently removed from Singapore's landscapes. These are irreversible changes.

From a social engagement perspective, these landscape changes are also opportunities to shape the nature of engagement between civic society and the government on issues of environment. Over the past five years, clearing of wooded areas or secondary forests has resulted in public petitions to reconsider redevelopment plans, mostly without success. While the proliferation of such "green petitions" over the past three to five years has also been suggested to point to the growing level of civic consciousness in Singapore, there are by no means, any indication of a dominant or shared viewpoint across sections of the society (Chua, 2012). Groups within the community may for instance, argue that biodiversity-rich cemetery sites should make way for the living, while others take an equally strong position on the need to conserve the biodiversity and heritage values of these sites (Goh, 2014a; Chew, 2014). Conservationists may also not agree among themselves on types of secondary forests that are worthy for conservation (see Wee, 2013; Ho, 2013). It is suggested here that the socio-ecological impacts of deforestation issues encountered manifests characteristics of "wicked problems", and should be managed as such. Wicked problems are those which are indeterminate, intractable, and have irreversible consequences (Xiang, 2013). They have since their identification in the 1970s, been realised to be a ubiquitous phenomenon in socio-ecological systems. Past and current losses of greenery in Singapore show some of these characteristics. For instance, the separation of the two forest reserve fragments due to the construction of the Bukit Timah Expressway in the mid-1980s has irreversible consequences, not just for the ecology of the forest, but also in the civil society-state relationships that have in the past been said to be plagued by mistrust and antagonism because of the such significant incidences (Goh, 2014b; Lim, 2013). Questions of legality of the state's actions (Yeo, 2014) and threat of legal action (Chua, 2013a) add complexities to governance issues and can deepen the current chasm. A wicked problem is also a problem that does not disappear because it surfaces in another form. A new proposal by the Land Transport Authority to tunnel through a fragile and biologically important part of the Central Nature Reserve surfaced in 2013 (Chua, 2013b), almost 30 years after the separation of the two forests fragments. There is therefore no real solubility to the issue.

As Xiang (2013) pointed out, the process of working with wicked problems is "fundamentally social" and cannot be solved by individual scientific disciplines. A technocratic approach to argue for the merits or lack of the conservation of such spaces will no longer be adequate. The common argument not to conserve such secondary forests (see Chua, 2013a) because they are biodiversity-poor is inadequate because it ignores the potential of such spaces. It ignores possible ecological restoration interventions to enhance forest succession and biodiversity potential, possible design innovations that move away from current construction norms, the social and heritage attachment communities have on such spaces, and above all, that communities should be engaged for their views of the type of environment they want as a crucial process of developing bonds with their living spaces. Given the impending loss of more such wooded areas and secondary forests with the new Master Plan 2014, new approaches for dealing with such deforestation are urgently needed before they disappear forever from the landscape of Singapore.

Conclusion

Visionary foresight, political support, laws and institutions have enabled Singapore to avoid the blighted urban landscape that typifies many rapidly urbanising cities. While growing consciousness of the multiple values of urban greenery has now enabled greenery to be placed as a key component in strategic and sustainable development plans of many cities, greening an already built-up city is fraught with challenges (Tan *et al.*, 2013). Its focus on greening over the past five decades has placed Singapore in a very strong position to leverage on its achievement to move into new frontiers of urban greening and ecology, particularly in the burgeoning field of urban ecology (Tan and Hamid, 2014; McDonnell *et al.*, 2009; Pickett *et al.*, 2011). It should however be critically aware of the emerging challenges that are both environmental and social in nature. The downward pressures of increasing population growth and urbanisation on amount of greenery have clearly emerged over the past five to seven years. The shifting composition of its greenery, particularly in the loss of wooded areas and secondary forests to developments, has also surfaced as a wicked problem, and needs to be managed as such. A new mindset and approach, particularly in the use of social processes such as participatory and community planning, should be key, and offer the potential for greenery and the environment at large to also help forge community identity, network and bonding so crucial to a young nation stepping into its next 50 years of development.

Acknowledgement

I thank R. Samsudin for producing the graphics in Figure 4(b).

References

Auger, T., Living in a Garden — The Greening of Singapore. 2013, Singapore: Editions Didier Miller. 200.

Azadi, H., G. Verheijke, and F. Witlox, *Pollute first, clean up later?* Global and Planetary Change, 2011. **78**(3–4): p. 77–82.

Beatley, T. *Singapore — City in a Garden, in Biophilic Cities 4 June*. 2012. Retrieved 13 October 2014 from: http://biophiliccities.org/blog-singapore/.

Chang, R., *Majority of Singaporeans want slower pace of life*, in *The Straits Times 26 August*. 2013, Singapore Press Holdings: Singapore.

Chew, K.C., *Preventing a grave error: to save Bukit Brown from "an irreversible act of destruction", a political leader should step in before it is too late, writes Chew Kheng Chuan (Perspectives)*, in *The Business Times 22 February*. 2014, Singapore Press Holdings: Singapore.

Chua, G., *Green petitions a sign of growing civic consciousness*, in *The Straits Times 30 August*. 2012, Singapore Press Holdings: Singapore.

Chua, G. *Fight to save forest patch hots up; Pasir Ris Heights group protests against plans to build school*, in *The Straits Times 9 January*. 2013a, Singapore Press Holdings: Singapore.

Chua, G., *Nature Society suggests different route for MRT line; Cross Island Line works put nature reserve 'at risk'*, in *The Straits Times 19 July*. 2013b, Singapore Press Holdings: Singapore.

Chuang, P.M., *Make S'pore stand out with greenery: MM Lee; Show Investors that it's a well-organized place, he says*, in *The Straits Times 7 May*. 2009, Singapore Press Holdings: Singapore.

Chun, J., *Enhancing the garden city: towards a deeper shade of green*. Singapore Academy of Law Journal, 2006. **18**: p. 248–263.

CLC (Centre for Liveable Cities) and HDB (Housing & Development Board), *Housing Singapore — Turning Squatters into Stakeholders*. Singapore Urban Systems Studies Booklet Series. 2013, Singapore: Cengage Learning Asia Pte Ltd. 48.

CLC (Centre for Liveable Cities) and NEA (National Environment Agency), *Sustainable Environment — Balancing Growth with the Environment*. Singapore Urban Systems Studies Booklet Series. 2013, Singapore: Cengage Learning Asia Pte Ltd. 66.

DOS, *Population Trends 2012*. 2012, Department of Statistics, Ministry of Trade & Industry, Republic of Singapore: Singapore.

Fuller, R.A. and K.J. Gaston, *The scaling of green space coverage in European cities*. Biology Letters, 2009. **5**: p. 352–355.

Ghani, A., *Success matters: Keeping Singapore Green*, in *IPS Update*. 2011, Institute of Policy Studies: Singapore.

Goh, A., *Keeping Bukit Brown cemetery not a wise choice (Editorial and Opinion)*, in *The Business Times 25 February*. 2014a, Singapore Press Holdings: Singapore.

Goh, H.Y., *The Nature Society, endangered species and conservation in Singapore*, in *Nature Contained. Environmental Histories of Singapore*, T.P. Barnard, Editor. 2014b, NUS Press Singapore: Singapore. p. 245–275.

Han, F.K., *et al.*, *Singapore Greening*, in *Lee Kuan Yew: Hard Truths to Keep Singapore Going*. 2011, Straits Times Press: Singapore. p. 334–356.

Han, F.K., W. Fernandez, and S. Tan, *Lee Kuan Yew — The Man and His Ideas*. 1998, Singapore: Times Edition.

Hassan, R., *Population change and urbanization in Singapore*. Civilizations, 1969. **19**(2): p. 169–188.

HKSAR. *Greening Hong Kong in GovHK* 香港政府一站通 n.d., accessed 24 October 2014; Available from: http://www.gov.hk/en/residents/environment/sustainable/greening. htm.

Ho, H.C., *Accomodate natural greenery, don't remove it (Forum Letters)*, in *The Straits Times 17 May*. 2013, Singapore Press Holdings: Singapore.

Hui, T.K. and T.W.D. Wan, *Singapore's image as a tourist destination*. International Journal of Tourism Research, 2003. **5**: p. 305–313.

Kingsbury, N., *Singapore — the Garden City State*, in *Gardening Gone Wild*. 2012. Retrieved 13 October 2014 from http://gardeninggonewild.com/?p=16217.

Koh, K.L., *Singapore: fashioning landscape for "The Garden City"*, in *Landscape conservation law: present trends and perspectives in International and Comparative Law*. 2000, IUCN Commission on Environmental Law: Gland, Switzerland and Cambridge, UK. p. 102.

Koh, K.L., *Singapore: from Garden City to City in a Garden — an aspect of sustainable development?* Bayan The Environment: Policy and Practices, 2007. **5**.

Koh, K.L., *The Garden City and beyond: The legal framework*, in *Environment and the City. Sharing Singapore's Experience and Future Challenges*, G.L. Ooi, Editor. 1995, Times Academic Press: Singapore. p. 148–170.

Lee, S.H., *Singapore's chief gardener*, in *The Straits Times 29 May*. 2011, Singapore Press Holdings: Singapore.

Lim, L., *The way forward for State and civil society; Govt should adopt a ligher touch if groups avoid confrontation and operate within law's framework*, in *The Straits Times 7 September*. 2013, Singapore Press Holding: Singapore.

Lin, L.H., *Land use planning, environmental management, and the Garden City as an urban development approach in Singapore*, in *Land Use Law for Sustainable Development*, N.J. Chalifour, *et al.*, Editors. 2007, Cambridge University Press: New York. p. 374–396.

Liu, J., *China's Road to Sustainability*. Science (New York, N.Y.), 2010. **328**(5974): p. 50.

McDonnell, M.J., A.K. Hars, and J.H. Breuste, *Ecology of Cities and Towns*. 2009, New York: Cambridge University Press.

MOF, *Singapore Budget 2010*. 2010, Ministry of Finance: Singapore.

MOF, *Singapore Budget*. Multiple years, Ministry of Finance: Singapore.

Neo, B.S., J. Gwee, and C. Mak, *Growing a City in a Garden*, in *Case Studies in Public Governance: Building Institutions in Singapore*, J. Gwee, Editor. 2012, Routledge: Oxon. p. 11–64.

Neville, W., *The distribution of population in post-war period*, in *Modern Singapore*, J.-B. Ooi and H.D. Chiang, Editors. 1969, University of Singapore: Singapore. p. 52–68.

Nowak, D.J. and E.J. Greenfield, *Tree and impervious cover change in U.S. cities*. Urban Forestry and Urban Greening, 2012. **11**(1): p. 21–30.

NParks, *National Parks Board Annual Report*. Multiple years, National Parks Board: Singapore.

NParks, *Personal communication with National Parks Board officer*. 2012.

Pickett, S.T.A., *et al.*, *Urban ecological systems: Scientific foundations and a decade of progress*. Journal of Environmental Management, 2011. **92**(3): p. 331–362.

Tan, P.Y. and A.R.B. Abdul Hamid, *Urban ecological research in Singapore and its relevance to the advancement of urban ecology and sustainability*. Landscape and Urban Planning, 2014. **125**: p. 271–289.

Tan, P.Y., J. Wang, and A. Sia, *Perspectives on five decades of the urban greening of Singapore*. Cities, 2013. **32**: p. 24–32.

Tan, P.Y., *Singapore A Vertical Garden City*. 2013, Singapore: Straits Times Press.

Teo, E.S., *Planning Principles in Pre- and Post-Independence Singapore*. The Town Planning Review, 1992. **63**(2): p. 163–185.

Tortajada, C., Y. Joshi, and A.K. Biswas, *The Singapore Water Story — Sustainable Development in an Urban City-State*. 2013, Oxon: Routledge. 286.

URA, *Media Release 12 June 2014. LUSH 2.0 — Extending the greenery journey skywards*. 2014, Urban Redevelopment Authority: Singapore.

URA, *URA Lifestyle Survey 2010*. Retrieved 31 May 2012 from http://spring.ura.gov.sg/conceptplan2011/results/ Report%20-%20Lifestyle%20Survey%20and%20Online%20Survey.pdf.

Wee, Y.C., *Wild growth alone won't make S'pore a global eco-city (Forum Letters)*, in *The Straits Times 8 May*. 2013, Singapore Press Holdings: Singapore.

Wong, Y.K. *et al.*, *Garden City Singapore — The Legacy of Lee Kuan Yew*. 2014, Singapore: Suntree Media Pte Ltd.

Wong, Y.K. *An early vision. Building infrastructure alongside the greenery*, in *Garden City Singapore — the Legacy of Lee Kuan Yew*. Wong, Y.K. *et al.*, 2014, Suntree Media Pte Ltd: Singapore. p. 34–44.

Xiang, W.-N., *Working with wicked problems in socio-ecological systems: Awareness, acceptance, and adaptation*. Landscape and Urban Planning, 2013. **110**(0): p. 1–4.

Yeo, S.J., *Bukit Brown group questions legality of land use masterplan*, in *The Straits Times 5 July*. 2014, Singapore Press Holdings: Singapore.

Yoshida, N., *a+u Architecture and Urbanism Special Edition — Singapore, Capital City for Vertical Green*. 2012, A+U Publishing: Tokyo, Singapore.

Yuen, B., *Creating the Garden City: the Singapore experience*. Urban Studies, 1996. **33**(6): p. 955–970.

Zhao, J., *et al.*, *Temporal trend of green space coverage in China and its relationship with urbanization over the last two decades*. Science of The Total Environment, 2013. **442**(0): p. 455–465.

CHAPTER 11

50 Years of Urban Planning & Tourism

Pamelia Lee

In the 1960s and 1970s, Singapore's main focus was to build high-rise flats with modern sanitation for its population. However, by the 1980s Singapore had an oversupply of flats, offices and shopping centres. Attention then turned to tourism which became a key focus and partner in the urban planning of modern Singapore.

The 1980s: Turning the Focus to Tourism

AT LAST THE WINDS OF CHANGE[1]

The beginning of the decade was poised to see tremendous changes on the local scene. New hotels had been built in the 1970s but there were no new attractions—only some tired old ones. The Singapore Hilton, Shangri-La Hotel, and the Mandarin Hotel had all opened their doors, followed by the Oriental, the Marina Mandarin and the Pan Pacific. The only new attractions introduced by the STB[2] were the Handicraft Centre in 1976 and the Rasa Singapura Food Centre and the Instant Asia Cultural Show in 1977. The government's investment in attractions had not matched the private sector's investment in hotels. In the 1970s we liked the idea of being "Instant Asia". We promised visitors the chance to experience all of Asia in one-stop. We also expected instant action and change. In early 1984, Singapore saw a flood of even more hotels in the pipeline and anticipated a serious oversupply of hotel rooms. This caused a chain reaction. First to react were the hotel general managers, most of them foreigners, who saw a fight for the same tourists or market share. Then, the hotel owners, most of them local developers, who saw bank loans piling up and room rates coming down. Finally, the bankers recognised that the whole industry needed a solution that only the government could provide. For the first time, the STB research department got phone calls from bankers asking for hotel and visitor projections. Singapore is a small place, hence within a short time the jitters of the marketplace reached the ears of the government. At that moment, the light of attention focussed on tourism and the highest powers of government stepped in to resolve the problems of the travel industry.

---

[1] Indented text is from *Singapore, Tourism & Me, by Pamelia Lee.*
[2] The Singapore Tourism Board

"The Singapore Government is very concerned about the slowing down of the Singapore economy, therefore ways and means to stimulate the economy, especially the construction industry, are being sought. Facilities for tourist and tourist attractions have been found to be the primary underdeveloped area. The means for support at very high levels, never seen before, will be forthcoming. The Singapore Government will be encouraging construction and growth in this area involving hundreds of millions of dollars, to be spent on tourism related developments. This business climate is becoming more obvious. As large construction firms and architects find themselves with less work, many of them are seeking business opportunities."

(*Source*: Excerpt from author's speech on 1st Update Seminar on Development Projects to Government Officials, 26 October 1985.)

The Need to Plant Seeds

This was the turning point when the STB changed its focus by adding product development to its role. By the 1980s the charm of Singapore had indeed diminished. Hence, the world of tourism in Singapore changed dramatically. While in the 1960s and 1970s the focus was on marketing Singapore overseas, suddenly in the 1980s we started to look inward.

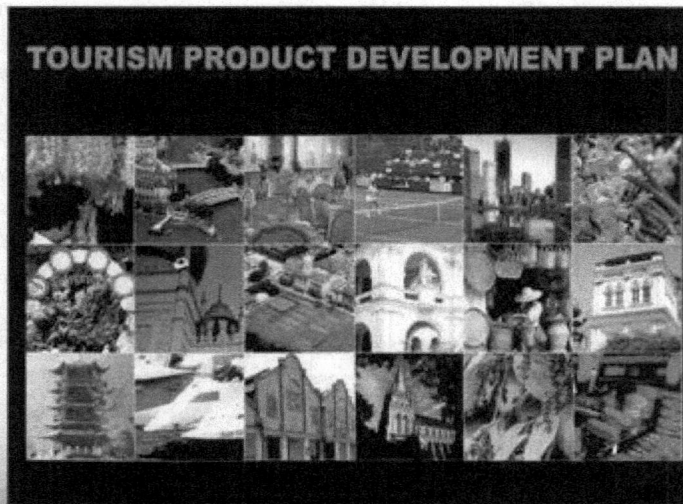

Figure 1.   The Tourism Product Development Plan (1986 to 1990) was the first tourism masterplan of the Singapore Tourist Promotion Board (now the Singapore Tourism Board). S$1 billion was committed to this plan, which involved the conservation and revitalisation of selected historical sites and the development of new attractions.

"Like other developing nations, we also watched the charm of our old city disappear and diminish, bit by bit. For along with the rows and rows of shophouses that were lost, the bulldozers also demolished the very special elements that made visiting Singapore a charming and unique experience. In recent years, we have often been described as a city without a soul: modern, efficient and hygienic, but lacking in grace, refinement and charm."

(*Source*: Excerpt from author's Presentation to UK Parliamentarians, 25–29 April 1987.)

Taking Care of Your Own Backyard First

Instead of limiting ourselves to tourism attractions, like the Handicraft Centre, the Rasa Singapura Food Centre, and the Instant Asia Cultural Show, the STB started to enhance areas in Singapore that did not come under the STB's purview. The festive light-up of Chinatown, Little India and Kampong Glam were introduced. In 1984, we introduced the festive lights along Orchard Road and called it Christmas at the Equator.

An All-Important Tourism & Urban Planning Partnership

The all-important partnership of tourism and urban planning came about during a time of crisis when the economy was slowing down and tourist attractions were lacking. The tourism industry was pleased at last to have a place at the table with urban planners. And presumably the urban planners found the inputs of the tourism industry fresh, creative, and bold yet practical.

Actually, we realised at the time that the quality of a visitor's experience in a city depends heavily on the big as well as the small decisions made by our urban planners. While we in the tourism industry may not use the correct technical urban planning term, we can tell you what works for tourism and what foreign visitors like and dislike. Hence, one could say, "the lines that a planner draws, his sensitivity to plot ratio, set back, and what it takes to achieve a human scale make a big difference to the eventual experience of every visitor who comes to Singapore. And, it makes an even greater difference to locals who "live their whole life experiencing the footprints that our urban planners conceive and build".

It is important that urban planners and the tourism industry work together as partners. Planners need overseas visitors to use what they design, and the tourism industry needs our planners to provide all the things our industry needs.

And as we live in a world of rapid change, both sides need a clear vehicle for regularly scheduled communication to ensure that Singapore can be one of the first in the world to catch changing trends.

Ideas that are good on paper but do not work on the ground must be avoided. Hence, the inputs of travel industry members, more specifically people who work close to the ground, such as guides, tour bus drivers and the visitors themselves need to be sought. Early discussions and an open specific channel for regular discussion will ensure more win-win solutions versus a we-lost-the-chance scenario. This formula will transform Singapore into a city with a difference in the eyes of all visitors, and of course locals who are often visitors or tourist in their own country.

Singapore is Different Things to Different Visitors

Regional Visitors: Not all overseas visitors come to Singapore for the same reason. In other words, Singapore is different things to different people. For those who come from neighbouring countries in the Southeast Asian region, a visit to Singapore is a visit to "the big city", a place where they can find the latest in fashion, fancy dining or world-class cultural and sporting events. This is similar to what London, New York and Paris offer visitors from neighbouring countries.

For a regional visitor in search of big city amenities, Orchard Road is ideal with large, but not overwhelmingly large, hotels and shopping centres, plus a private hospital within walking distance. Furthermore, it takes only a short walk to buy the latest brand-name handbag or jewellery piece to take home. In urban planning terms, Orchard Road offers a cluster of desirable and needed facilities all within easy reach.

Cultured European Visitors: Seasoned, well-travelled visitors from Europe have the latest brand-name collection at home, so they come to experience multi-cultural Singapore, i.e., Chinatown, Little India, Kampong Glam, our Colonial Heart and our museums. French and Italian visitors love to stay in old shophouses within our historic districts. And the British love to stay in grand historic hotels, such as Raffles Hotel and Goodwood Park Hotel. (These hotels also happen to be a favourite venue for Singapore weddings. Young Singaporeans like capturing a special moment in time surrounded by old-world charm.)

Many & Most Visitors: Many consider Singapore's fines for littering, spitting and smoking "scary". Most find Singapore wonderfully compact and convenient. Almost everyone likes our food. And everyone loves our greenery, cleanliness and safety, including our green buildings, made lush with walls of cascading plants and roof tops where greenery camouflages M&E "guts" or necessary back-of-the-house equipment. In urban planning language, we can say that they all marvel at Singapore's bold measures to be a modern, well-planned city that works.

First-Time Visitor Groups: They come in large numbers, it may be their first trip out of their country, and they all come to see if Singapore is the Asian wonder they have heard about. For many, it may be the only trip they will ever make to Singapore. In the 1970s, it was the Japanese who took countless pictures in front of Singapore's British Colonial buildings. At that time, the Singapore Tourism Board promoted Singapore using a picture of the Padang with some young Japanese office girls carrying shopping bags filled with brand-name goods. Tea at the Raffles Hotel was a "must". And to show we welcomed them, Singapore introduced signage in Japanese.

Then for a very short spell it was the Koreans, and now it is the Chinese.

The Chinese come in huge numbers, and they have developed a pattern of their own. Simply put, the local ground handling travel agent gets paid next to zero or nothing at all for handling the group. He has to recover his expenses and make his profit from the commission that he gets when the visitors on his tour package go shopping. The Chinese visitor is therefore taken to all the "free" attractions, such as Mount Faber and the Botanic Gardens. A ride through Sentosa and Marina Bay is included. According to people who know this market, "Despite the emphasis on shopping, visitors from China go away quite pleased with their stay in Singapore". The pattern explains the frequent requests from Singapore's tourism industry for proper and more places to park their tour buses at all our free attractions and wherever there is a shop that caters to such tour groups.

Tomorrow's Hip and Trendy Traveller: Such visitors are "citizens of the world", as they do not come from any specific country or region. They travel light, achieve what they want to achieve in a short time, and then leave right away. They expect fast Wi-Fi connections, quick meals, and reasonably-priced hotel rooms, preferably near the shopping or business districts. A "keep our world green" policy is something they expect. In urban planning terms, this group will tolerate a smaller hotel room foot print, and, interestingly, the lobby need not be on the ground floor.

Still Other Travellers: Countless other visitors come because we are an airline hub. And then there are those who come to simply see if Singapore is indeed the modern miracle everyone talks about.

Travellers by and large: They love the fact that Singapore is so compact. Sadly, most people find Singapore uncomfortably hot and far too humid, an "abrupt" place that is also expensive, especially when it comes to beer and wine!

Given the fact that different visitors come for different reasons, one wonders how the pencil lines defining zones, density, plot ratio and land-use as drawn up by our urban planners, positively or adversely impact the quality of what a visitor experiences today.

Singapore's Urban Planning History & the Winds of Change

Singapore Inherited a Wonderful Legacy

The legacy that the British left us is still enjoyed by residents and tourists today—a wonderful town plan, beautiful colonial buildings, very good systems and the English language. Visit Penang in Malaysia and indeed other British colonial cities as far away as the West Indies, and you will find the same footprint. There is the Padang, a big open green space or a "commons" framed with an old boys' club, a city hall and other government buildings, and a church. Nearby is the harbour as well as an esplanade or seaside promenade. Today, our Padang continues to thrive. Although the Japanese occupied Singapore from 1942 to 1945, they left the colonial buildings intact. Singapore gained independence, but left these obvious symbols of British colonialism intact. And the biggest threat of all, the growth of the almighty car was controlled and diverted to a bridge to protect the Padang.[3]

After 50 Pioneering Years—This is What We Created

The first thing a visitor to Singapore experiences is Changi Airport. It is also the last thing he experiences. Visitors are impressed with Changi's efficiency, amenities, ease of movement, and speed. They like the fact that there is good shopping, free luggage trolleys, clean toilets, as well as a good range of other amenities—even a free city tour.

Although Changi is rated efficient and convenient, the industry worries that the airport will lose its appeal if it grows too big. They wonder how older travellers and those with young children will cope with movement within Changi. Hence, the industry wonders if our future airport will include innovative internal transport.

Once a visitor exits Changi Airport, he has the joy of experiencing an impressive straight and level road that links Changi to the rest of Singapore. This highway, the East Coast Parkway, is the result of sound planning. More specifically our planners designed a long straight road with no level change and no stops. Furthermore, they made sure we would enjoy patches of greenery and views of the sea! And, we are grateful that our small yet dense city does not have a skyline marred by "a labyrinth of ugly spaghetti highways" or tiers of highways as found in other big and dense cities throughout the world.

Hence, to give visitors a good impression, we always encourage them to go by East Coast Parkway instead of the Pan Island Expressway, as although the ride may be slightly longer, it offers an immediate dramatic view of Singapore. And when we explain that this highway is built on reclaimed land, their amazement turns to deep respect for Singapore's forward thinking.

After 15 minutes, a surprise awaits the arriving visitor. A dramatic scene change takes place, as instead of just greenery, Singapore River with its collection of historic Colonial Government buildings and little shophouses become visible. Then, the skyline of modern Singapore with its towering buildings, such as Asia Square and Ocean Financial Centre, comes into full view. Nearby is a generous patch of reclaimed land waiting for the future growth of our tiny island republic. In the distance is a view of Singapore's tourism icon, the Merlion, our famous deep harbour, and with it, a 24-hour operational container port.

---

[3] *Ibid.*

A closer looks reveals Singapore's sensitivity to the conservation of its heritage. Namely, old Clifford Pier, the Waterboat House, Fullerton Hotel (the old General Post Office), Raffles Place and Telok Ayer Market. All these landmarks, solidly built during Singapore's Colonial era, were quietly saved and systematically put to appropriate adaptive reuse. The word "quietly" is used, as there was a time when not everyone in the Singapore Government was keen on conservation. Also, if our Urban Planners did not have the strength to hold on or fight, buildings such as the old general post office could have ended up as the office of the Ministry of Foreign Affairs or Economic Development Board, which would have restricted public access. Now, this grand old building is an elegant hotel which has brought new life to the entire waterfront. Visitors as well as locals are now able to feast in its grand atrium.

As for new and old Singapore, our Colonial Heart sits in interesting contrast to Marina Bay, our new tourism belt. Old Singapore and new Singapore are different and distinct, yet both are visible in one swift panoramic view. Balancing development in this area took great skill, foresight and the ability to imagine how scale perceived on paper would end up "when actually built". Many things could have gone wrong, as on the one hand you have the gentle historic Empress Place and the Padang, and on the other you have the towering buildings of Marina Bay with bridges of heavy steel nearby. Careful thought went into all aspects. For example, to ensure our sea frontage would not get blocked by a wall of buildings, the developer of Fullerton One was asked by the Design Review Panel that URA set up, to keep a viewing channel open so that the ocean would remain visible from Collyer Quay.

Our Government agencies are always trying to find ways to improve the city and the experience of visitors and residents alike. Decades ago we introduced temporary festive lighting, and later permanent lighting of our historic buildings. The permanent buildings that we lit up are Empress Place and City Hall, then we got the private sector to light up CHIJMES and Fullerton Hotel.

To give our city a greater buzz, we have introduced decorative lighting to give our historic districts a festive air for every major festival. Singaporeans cannot imagine our city without its annual decorative lights, as we have come to expect it as a normal part of our city life.

The way in which Singapore decorates its historic areas for major holidays is a multi-pronged effort. In most countries it is the merchants who get together to decorate a street. In Singapore our net is cast wider. While the National Parks (NParks) gave their full support, it also came up with strict instructions on how to protect tree trunks and branches. The Land Transport Authority (LTA) advised on height clearances so that double-decker buses could travel smoothly. When new lamp-posts were installed, they kindly ensured the new lamp-posts would not only be strong enough to carry decorations but also serve as a power source. Now this small city comes alive throughout the year: Christmas, Chinese New Year, Deepavali, Hari Raya and

Figure 2.   The shopping mall orchardgateway straddles both sides of Orchard Road and is linked by a glass bridge.

National Day. A small city with so many happenings throughout the year—all this is possible.

Reversal is Possible

The amazing thing is that Singapore's urban planners were able to turn back the clock some 40 years, so that Orchard Road now pleases the pedestrian once again. In other words, one can walk the full length of Orchard Road using wide, tree-lined pedestrian malls without dodging cars as they step in and out of buildings and shopping malls. This reversal of Orchard Road wherein the pedestrian instead of the car has become king once again has happened before our eyes. Indeed, urban planners the world over will come to study how Singapore achieved this. How did Singapore manage to reverse road patterns, and make the pedestrian king again? How were the roads department and the property owners convinced to make this dramatic change? Were there trade-offs? Was a stern hand needed or very strict enforcements? How did it impact property values? In the eyes of urban planners, the impossible has become possible. Likewise, underground links and dramatic sky bridges now make it possible to cross Orchard Road, a five-lane highway that runs in the heart of this tourism-cum-shopping belt, without the worry of cars. This is a good example of how Singapore continues to improve and reinvent itself.

Singapore's Historic Districts

Singapore's planners in the 1980s drew generous lines. Hence, today, Chinatown, Little India, and Kampong Glam are good-sized historic districts. In Singapore, visitors get to enjoy not only one street, but also a collection of streets and multiple rows of shophouses. Internal roads within Singapore's historic zones have controlled traffic, so a visitor does not have to dodge cars or buses when walking within these historic districts. Additionally, external or periphery roads are designed so taxis, private cars and tour buses have a designated place and visitors have easy access to whatever mode of transportation they prefer. We are also grateful that the stepping of building heights took place so our historic areas enjoy light and air and are not overwhelmed by surrounding high-rise buildings. And we are so glad that familiar places still exist and are recognisable!

When the first lines were drawn demarcating Chinatown as a whole zone, the urban planners remarked, "In other countries Chinatown is just one or two streets, that is why they need a gate to demarcate Chinatown." A good example is Grant Ave, San Francisco. In the case of Singapore, we have saved a whole zone and that zone blends nicely into surrounding zones, such as the financial district. So we don't need a gate to identify Chinatown!

Given the fact that different visitors have different preferences, would Singapore's report card get high or low ratings for what it has achieved and possibly lost over the last 50 years of rapid development? At this juncture, we need to also think beyond the fundamentals of defined zones, density, plot ratio and land use as drawn up by our urban planners. After 50 years of development, Singapore is ready to also address practical creature comforts and creative edges. Practical creature comforts could be as simple as safe and pleasant places to board a tour bus, conveniently located toilets and covered walkways. Creative edges should force us to search for and take advantage of any possible beautiful or nice element that a visitor could enjoy, be it the roof line of an old shop house, the bark of a tree or light astutely placed to guide our view, and then there is always the possibility of the art work of a Singaporean artist.

Singapore's Report Card

Clifford Pier & Singapore River

Fifty years ago, Singapore was a famous port town. Clifford Pier bustled with passengers and sailors coming and going. Change Alley was on every map, and Singapore

River was rich with daily economic activity. Then came the jumbo jet age and containerisation. Our world has changed dramatically. Today, the tourism industry thanks the Urban Redevelopment Authority (URA) for not only preserving Clifford Pier, but also guiding its adaptive reuse into a place for casual and fine dining in an old world setting. So, while we still miss the hustle and bustle of seeing sailors and money changers come and go, today we go to Clifford Pier to enjoy fine dining and the occasional wedding when young Singaporeans make new memories in an old world setting.

As for the Singapore River, gone are the bumboats laden with towering piles of rubber and weatherworn coolies. Also gone are the offices of the rich merchants, who would systematically count their wealth in the piles of rubber sheets moving past on bumboats. Today, instead of the offices of rich rubber merchants, we find pubs and restaurants. Instead of bales of rubber, we find bumboats carrying visitors, both Singaporean and from overseas. The bridges built when Singapore was a British colony are now nicely lit. If you look carefully, you can find some cute statues of children and a typical Singapore cat at play.

Our Famous Historic Hotels

We saved Goodwood Park Hotel, Raffles Hotel and Majestic Hotel. Fullerton Hotel, formerly the General Post Office, and Fullerton Bay Hotel, formerly a marine police pier, came as a great bonus! We did not just conserve these "grand dames", we also managed to protect their surroundings. Hence, today the original Raffles Hotel has an extension that is in keeping with the original hotel, in terms of its massing and form. Without looking at the original plan, few visitors would know what is old and what is the new addition. Saving old Raffles Hotel without having to build a high-rise extension of 20 storeys on the same block is a real achievement that conservations experts would loudly applaud.

However, sadly, we have forever lost the beautiful Adelphi Hotel with its gracious courtyard.

Through a national conservation plan, involving the URA, STB, the National Heritage Board (NHB), LTA and the Land Office, we saved Chinatown, Little India, Kampong Glam, our Colonial Heart, Bugis Street and Tiong Bahru. This conservation momentum also made a difference for Emerald Hill, Neil Road and areas in Joo Chiat. While Singapore was strict about roof lines, facades, back lanes and five-foot ways, it did not protect trades as is done in some other countries. The view of the Singapore Government is to let the private sector adapt itself, in other words, not to interfere with business. At first our foreign consultants were very perturbed, as we would lose the clog maker, the calligrapher as well as all trades that could not survive in a fast-developing world. However, our government was wise, as they knew it would not have been possible to sustain these particular trades as small businesses, in their natural form, in a fast-changing Chinatown.

Today, our historic zones have new business enterprises. While we had hoped, initially we were never 100% sure that new players with appropriately-themed businesses would come to our historic areas. Happily, Chinatown has new restaurants from different parts of China, while Arab Street with the influx of more visitors from West Asia now boasts restaurants from Morocco and Lebanon. Bugis Street continues to sell cheap T-shirts, fruits and amusing gadgets. To our great relief, it is fortunate that most of the new businesses fit and enhance the respective theme of the areas.

The Singapore Botanic Gardens

Today, it is a popular place for early morning *tai chi* sessions, mid-day tours for visitors from China, and in the early evening, residents go there to jog or stroll. While enjoying the beauty of the Botanic Gardens, we must never forget the original British intent which was not to build a pleasure garden but to build a centre for research. And, in the case of Singapore, research was conducted on improving rubber production, a crop that brought great wealth to England.

Visitors, including professional planners from overseas, praise the manner in which we have saved our historic areas. We saved them as thriving, lively zones, rather than as "ghost towns" or museums: Chinatown, Little India, Kampong Glam, our Colonial Heart, Bugis Street, Fort Canning, Botanic Gardens, Chek Jawa, Labrador Park, MacRitchie Reservoir Park and the coral beds and green hills of the Southern Islands. While we did not have to shout about what we did, quietly, Singapore has paid respect to its changing history. We have kept the original names of places, like "The Padang" and "Dhoby Ghaut", and we even kept the statue of Sir Stamford Raffles, who founded modern Singapore.

Look Back to Look Forward: 50 years of Experience Worth Tapping on (1965–2015)

How Exact a Science?

Urban planning and architecture are not exact sciences. Anyone who has planned a zone or built a house or building knows the number of things that can go wrong. Surgeons would find this shocking as in surgery, very clear procedures and steps are laid out. In the case of urban planning and architecture, creativity and a feel of the space being created demand skills and daring of a different kind. Hence, sometimes what we plan on paper does not turn out as we anticipate.

In the 1980s, the Singapore Tourism Board had a strong team of consultants, who came to us through the Pacific Area Travel Association. First there was Robbi

Collins, who made us realise that the Botanic Gardens should be seen, as earlier mentioned, as a place for scientific study. In line with this thinking, one patch of original forest has been preserved just as it originally was. We have in the Singapore Botanical Gardens a living and thriving "museum of plants". Collins also gave us the idea of building a cloud forest, featuring plants that grow near the equator on high mountainous areas. This idea eventually led to the building of the Flower Dome & Cloud Forest at Gardens by the Bay. Also in the team was the famous architect from Hawaii, Pete Wimberly, who gave us the idea that the new extensions of the Raffles Hotel should match the original Raffles Hotel. He kept insisting on the fact that architects should try to hand sketch buildings, instead of simply using a computer to draw. Likewise, photographs may not guide you to see the details. Sketching nurtures the growth of ideas, such as the flow of sunlight during different times of the year, and nearby vegetation and other subtle features come to life. Sketches give architects and planners a deeper feeling of how the end result will look.

Visitors, laymen, as well as architects and urban planners give Singapore high marks for what we have achieved. When they of think how rapidly we have achieved all this, their praise turns to wonderment.

If you are a gifted designer who can translate drawings and calculations into accurate built forms, you must treasure the gift that you have. It is a precious one.

Landmarks are equally important. Sad is the day when locals feel lost in their own city.

Going Back to the Basics—Getting the Fundamentals Right

Visitors, like Singaporeans, love space, greenery, sunlight, clear air, and a human scale. While visitors can choose whether to visit a place, locals have no choice but to live with what we build. They can enjoy the genius of our plans or endure our mistakes.

In the case of Singapore, where development takes place at such a fast rate, the impact of such speedy change is multiplied and intensified. Hence greater caution and heavy doses of astute judgement are needed.

The Great Challenge Ahead for Future Generations of Urban Planners and Architects

The Bad News

Singapore's future urban planners and architects have a very small palette upon which to achieve so much.

The car population will continue to grow, and demands will continue to increase, so the challenge will be even greater than that faced by those before, until someone invents the perfect car that does not pollute or jam our roads.

Visitors will love almost everything the future planners and architects will do, and they will want to do the same in their country, but while the planners and architects can draw up a similar plan for them, and build beautiful models, few can live life according to that grand plan.

Singapore's ageing population will continue to grow, so the city will have to be designed to accommodate them with innovations that have been sorely ignored in the past.

While technology will dominate our lives, the job of keeping a warm human touch over how Singaporeans live will be a great challenge.

The Good News

The urban planners are leaving their future counterparts a beautiful city to build on— a city with few mistakes to correct or clean up, and lots of good examples to follow.

The En-Block Formula of upgrading and renovating will ensure that you future planners and architects have the chance to change or bring new life to Singapore's built up areas every few decades.

A Conservation Formula is in place to preserve Singapore's historic fabric. Hopefully one day Singapore will share the French and Italian approach to conservation, which is to be humble and keep as much of the original fabric and space as possible, which were built for "the weather". At that point, hopefully owners will free the five-foot passage in front of their house or shop, so that pedestrians can walk from one end of a historic zone to another, protected from sun and rain.

It also begs the question, "Can Singapore adapt to change with the speed needed to keep us ahead of the game?" To ensure that Singapore remains a leading visitor destination, urban planners and the travel industry have to anticipate and embrace change even before the need becomes obvious. The tourism industry can give inputs, but the industry needs the planner to bring ideas to life.

Our present planners have left vast expanses of land undeveloped, including the Southern Islands. This means that our future planners will have the opportunity to build new cities with new concepts linked to the fast-changing lifestyle of our citizens. An aerial map will show that development has been concentrated in zones, so future planners will have sizeable zones and big belts of reclaimed land to build on. Imagine the new lifestyle opportunity that the Southern Islands, a cluster of islands near what was Singapore's early harbour, make available for our future planners to develop into a viable lifestyle alternative.

A few words to any young designer: "If you should be given a whole canvas, more specifically the chance to be the Master Planner of a whole new city or a vast piece of unspoilt terrain, may you bring all that you have learnt watching first-hand Singapore change over the last few decades. Under any grand plan is the hard (and rather sad) fact that while plans can be drawn, beautiful plans and models using the latest computer programme, a whole society from top to bottom has to work in unison to make a plan function as designed. The people who live in the beautifully drawn up plan have to be ready to live the lifestyle that the plan promises.

In summary, the good news is that the planners who went before are leaving future generation of planners with an excellent town plan that works and many blank slates for the development of the small red dot called Singapore into a city of innovation and excellence.

CHAPTER 12

Shaping Singapore's Cityscape through Urban Design

Goh Hup Chor & Heng Chye Kiang

Introduction

Singapore's cityscape—a deliberate assemblage of modern skyscrapers, historic character buildings, green spaces, and active waterfront—has contributed to the nation's growing image and distinction as a world-class city. Many tourists, and younger Singaporeans for that matter, might find it difficult to believe that Singapore's signature skyline came into being mostly within the last 50 years. Over a span of five decades, Singapore's land mass has grown at an average rate of 7,540m² per day—a total of some 24% increase in land.[1] Much of the major reclamation works have been ongoing since the 1970s in an effort to extend the foreshore south of the city centre, thus creating prime real estate for high-value and high-density projects. Underpinning this physical manipulation and development of land is a strategic design-led framework which has influenced the urban form and functions of our city.

Urban design is a tool and process for shaping the qualitative texture of a city, producing attractive yet legible urban spaces which, in turn, help to establish a unique place identity for the city as well as create the stage for urban life. In urban design, attention is not only accorded to the overall structure of the city but also the form of buildings, the spaces between buildings, the quality of streets, the connectivity of pedestrian routes, as well as the natural and historical assets of the urban landscape. A comprehensive urban design approach can give a city an intelligible urban language, making the aesthetics and experience of the city memorable and pleasant for both locals and visitors alike. In the case of Singapore, the need for and benefits of an integrated approach to urban design were acknowledged in the 1970s following the initial years of independence.

---

[1] Singapore's land area in 1965 was 581.5 km² [see Chia *et al.* (1988) *The Coastal Environmental Profile of Singapore*, p. 34] and in 2015 it was 719.1 km² [see Statistics Singapore (2016) 'Latest Data'; accessed from http://www.singstat.gov.sg/statistics/latest-data#16].

Singapore's city centre in the 1970s would be unrecognisable by today's standards. Shanty slums, deteriorated shophouses, congested streets, and polluted waterways were the urban challenges which faced our young nation (see Chapter 1 by Alan Choe). The Urban Renewal Department (URD), which operated under the helm of the Housing & Development Board (HDB) between 1966 and 1974, worked in conjunction with the HDB's housing programme. By coordinating the stages of land acquisition, land clearance, and resettlement of affected residents and business owners, vast tracts of prime land in the city centre could be made available for comprehensive redevelopment. The main priority, in those early years of nation-building, was to provide proper homes for Singapore's burgeoning urban population by constructing mass housing in the most efficient and expeditious manner. Urban design, at that time, was limited in scope; nevertheless, the groundwork for the genesis of an integrated urban design framework that would later ensue was provided by earlier site-specific design interventions in the renewal of Singapore's Central Area.

As a result of its increasing role and significance in the transformation of the Central Area, the URD gained greater autonomy in 1974 when it disbanded from the HDB to form an independent statutory board, renamed the Urban Redevelopment Authority (URA), under the Ministry of National Development (MND). Under the newly-formed URA, the Government Land Sale (GLS) programme which existed since 1967 was continued. Through the GLS tender process, a deliberate emphasis on good architectural design emerged alongside greater convictions that design, in its own right, can leverage Singapore's image as a vibrant financial hub. Thus, the start of a comprehensive urban design strategy for the whole of Central Area was sparked.

In this chapter, we aim to uncover the underlying processes and guiding principles of urban design that have contributed to the physical and, in turn, visual transformation of Singapore's Central Area. Moreover, by addressing the significance of urban design from a place-making perspective, we also reveal the key role of urban design in generating a people-friendly city that can be enjoyed by all.

Central Area: Urban Design Vision and Mechanisms

The Central Area,[2] encompassing 2% of Singapore's total land area and characterised by its varied topography and diverse urban fabric, is a complex environment with a unique mix of challenges and opportunities that distinguishes it from other parts of Singapore. One of the key districts of the Central Area, and today the epicentre of Singapore's cultural activities, is the Civic District. Here, the beginnings of Singapore's

---

[2]The URA's planning map of Singapore is divided into five regions: Central, North, North East, East, and West. Each region is further divided into planning areas, totaling 55 planning areas island-wide. Central Region comprises 22 planning areas of which 11 form a boundary known as Central Area.

urban planning and administrative foundations can be traced to historic roads, parks, and buildings established from the era of Sir Stamford Raffles's 1822–3 Plan of the Town of Singapore. In essence, then, the Civic District is arguably the soul of Singapore's city centre as it is communicative of our nation's past and future in both colonial and modern terms. Situated near the Civic District is another significant district—the Central Business District (CBD). Evolving through nearly 200 years from a modest entrepôt to a world financial hub, the CBD of today (a contemporary rendition of its early colonial prototype) plays a significant role in Singapore's survival within the global economy. However, when the 1985 global economic recession arrived on the shores of our city-state, the CBD was first to take a sharp hit, thus prompting the government to reassess Singapore's economic strategies (see Chapter 3 by Philip Yeo). At the same time, the recession created an impetus to re-think the approach of urban design towards rejuvenating the city centre and enhancing Singapore's image as an attractive place to invest and conduct business.

The Structure Plan

In 1982, a comprehensive review was undertaken by the URA for the Central Area (URA, 2011a, p. 6). The aim of the exercise was to create a coherent urban design strategy that would influence the organisation of future growth and development emanating from the Civic and Central Business districts. Given the historical, economic, and cultural significance of these two districts, a thoughtful urban design strategy was needed to rationalise and plan for growth and development that was sensitive to the urban environmental quality of the city centre (see Figure 1). This urban design strategy took shape in the form of a Structure Plan, a tool which helped to guide and coordinate development proposals while identifying patterns and areas for future comprehensive redevelopment, conservation, and pedestrian circulation (URA, 1984, p. 6). The Structure Plan not only considered the intended land uses and development intensities set out by the Master Plan but also, at a more qualitative level, the overall physical form and skyline character of the city centre. In this way, the Structure Plan served as the common language between the various planning agencies by bringing the key urban elements together in a cohesive outline with strategic directions for the future growth and development of the Central Area.

The Structure Plan contained four strategic directions. Firstly, the Structure Plan identified three parallel 'corridors'—Ophir-Rochor Road Corridor, Orchard Road Corridor, and Upper Pickering-Cross Street Corridor—running in the northwest-southeast direction and providing logical links to future developments on the then newly-reclaimed land parcels which were collectively called Marina City (see Figure 2). The three corridors also enabled significant historical terrain to be retained as integral features of the overall cityscape. For example, the Upper Pickering-Cross Street

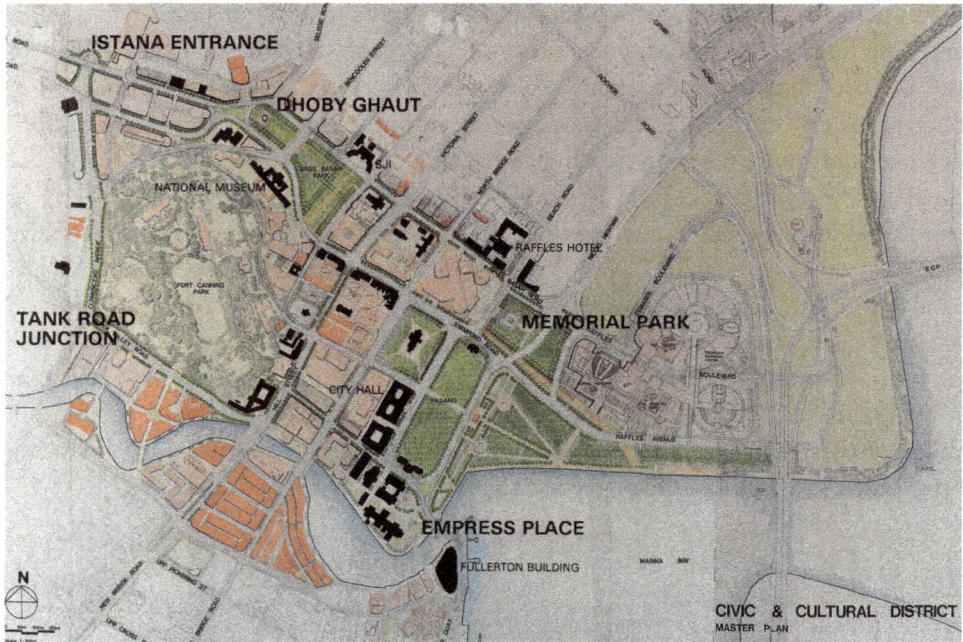

Figure 1.   Civic & cultural district existing condition plan, 1988.
Source: Urban Redevelopment Authority.

Corridor, with its northwest extremity along Havelock Road, passes through two key physical landscape features: the Singapore River on one side and Pearl's Hill on the other. Likewise, the Orchard Road Corridor is flanked by Fort Canning Park to the west and the Istana grounds to the east. The Ophir-Rochor Road Corridor runs laterally along the other side of the Istana grounds.

Bisecting the three corridors in a southwest-northeast direction is the fourth corridor, that is, the New Bridge-Victoria Street Corridor. This corridor is reinforced at several junctions by MRT stations, thus encouraging nodes of high-density developments where accessibility and foot traffic are greatest. At the same time, contiguous street blocks of traditional shophouses with distinct architectural qualities are interspersed between these four corridors, thereby creating an opportunity to bring about a clear pattern of high- and low-rise zones that would contribute to the overall urban form and visual diversity of the cityscape. In this way, the Structure Plan also proposed the selective conservation of heritage districts and buildings with historic and architectural merits.

In this second strategic direction of the Structure Plan, conservation was seen as a parallel effort to complement the nation's drive towards modern city development, where the physical reminders of our historical legacy would lend Singapore a unique personality distinct from other cities. Thus, the Structure Plan identified Chinatown,

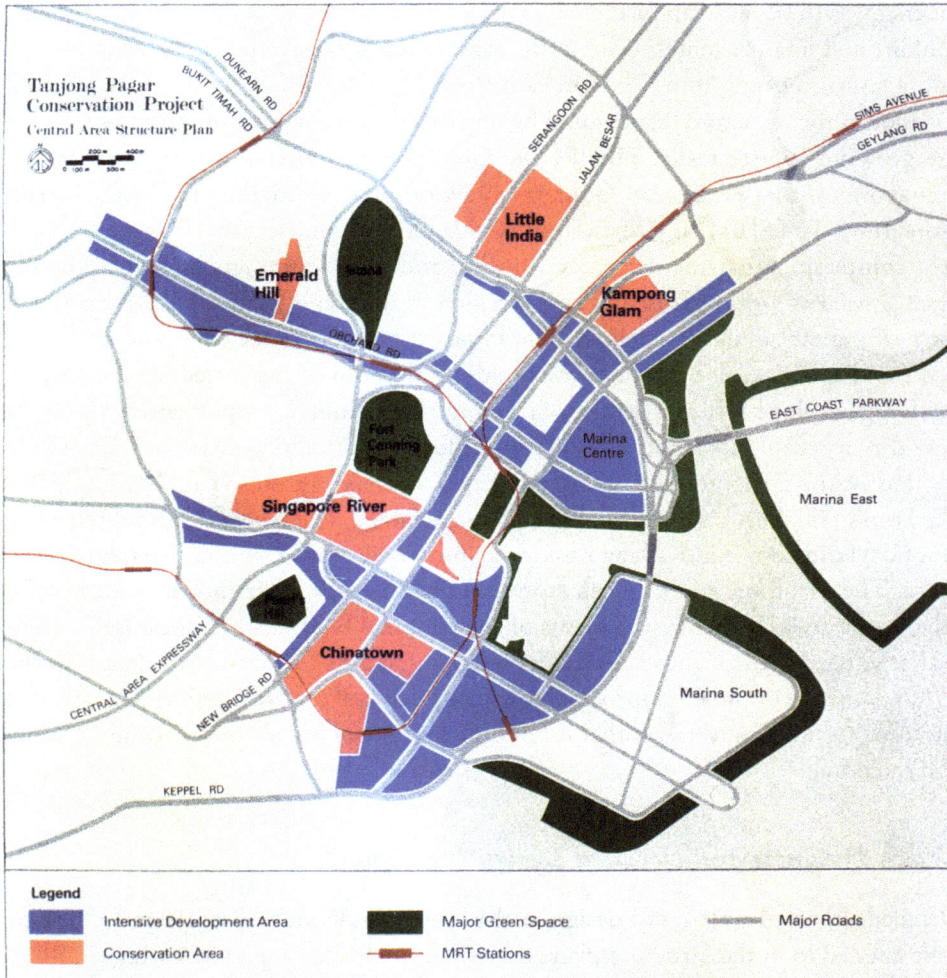

Figure 2.   Central area structure plan, 1986.

Source: Urban Redevelopment Authority.

Kampong Glam, Little India, Singapore River, and Emerald Hill as districts worthy of conservation as they provide the city with character and convey a sense of time and place that is part and parcel of Singapore's social memory. Furthermore, the Structure Plan also suggested that these historic areas, when comprehensively planned and integrated with modern development, can serve as recreational and leisure centres for locals on weekends while benefiting the tourism industry as well.

Thirdly, in addition to identifying areas for conservation, the Structure Plan also specified three districts for concentrated, high-intensity developments that would help boost Singapore's economic growth. Under the Structure Plan, the Golden Shoe

District was to be built-up further so as to increase the supply of office blocks for new banking and financial enterprises; in this way, enabling the young city-state to mature into a global business hub. The Orchard Road District, which doubles as an arterial corridor in the Structure Plan, would be developed into a hotel and shopping belt for the growing tourist trade. Finally, the Golden Mile District—which contained Singapore's initial GLS sites: Golden Mile Complex, Golden Mile Tower, Merlin Hotel (now The Plaza), and Shaw Towers—would continue to grow into a mixed-use area comprising apartments, offices, hotels, and other commercial developments. Here, as well as for other districts and precincts in the Central Area that were planned for new growth, design guidelines were imposed to control not only land usage but also the shape, size, and height of the buildings that can be permitted (also known as 'building envelope'). In this way, the Structure Plan set out a comprehensive vision for how the city would look and feel in terms of form and functionality.

Lastly, the Structure Plan demarcated areas of major green spaces. Existing parks like Pearl's Hill, Fort Canning, and Istana were retained while the waterfront perimeter around Marina Bay and Kallang Basin were proposed as a continuous stretch of green space. The incorporation of green spaces in the Structure Plan and their purposeful relationships with other key elements of the plan had been lacking in earlier conceptual schemes for the Central Area. The burgeoning attention to urban design in the 1980s spurred continued efforts in subsequent decades towards achieving a cohesive cityscape for the Central Area that is not only functional but also aesthetically distinct and memorable.

Urban Precincts and Detailed Design Principles

Detailed urban planning and design at the level of individual districts and precincts were alluded to in the Structure Plan and later formally developed following the 1991 Concept Plan, which resulted in the systematic preparation of Development Guide Plans (DGPs) over a five-year period between 1993 and 1998. The DGPs served as local area plans for each of the 55 identified planning areas in Singapore, providing strategic directions for future urban development through a SWOT (Strengths, Weaknesses, Opportunities, Threats) method of analysis. Today, the Central Area comprises 11 of the 55 planning areas in Singapore: Newtown, Orchard, River Valley, Outram, Singapore River, Museum, Rochor, Downtown Core, Marina East, Marina South, and Straits View. The DGPs also helped to steer development programmes towards a clear set of design principles in order to achieve the outcomes desired for individual planning areas. At the district level, urban design can shape the overall organisation of land, influence the densities at which the land would be developed, determine the massing and heights of future buildings, and identify significant place characteristics, assets, and vistas to be enhanced. However, it is at the precinct level where urban design can have a more direct role to play in choreographing the ambi-ence, experience, and identity of place.

Two precincts in the Central Area have ongoing urban design reviews: Orchard Road and Singapore River. Orchard Road, once a rural road flanked by hillocks of fruit orchards, nutmeg plantations, and pepper farms, is today a five-lane arterial boulevard with commercial developments on both sides creating a continuous shop-ping and entertainment belt. Despite its length of more than 2 kilometres, Orchard Road has a well-defined streetscape unified by roadside tree plantings and wide pedestrian promenades. These features are part and parcel of the overall urban design vision for the precinct, which also includes guiding principles for building setback, public space provision, signage, and lighting. In terms of building setback, a distance of 7.6 to 11.6 metres from the road reserve is consistently applied to determine the building line for both sides of Orchard Road in order to create the effect of a grand boulevard. However, to encourage an interesting variety of building fronts, the urban design guidelines allow up to 40% of the building façade to be recessed from the building line and up to 50% of the podium façade to overhang within the building setback (URA, 2013a). Furthermore, to enhance the continuity of building edges along Orchard Road, all developments are required to build up to the common boundary lines, thus creating party-walls which open out possibilities for both indoor and outdoor pedestrian connectivity.

The urban design parameters for Orchard Road have an impact not only on building form and frontage but also on the experiential quality of the resultant pedestrian promenade and pocket public spaces. As the stage for urban life, accessible public areas can contribute to the vibrancy of the street by providing the space for pedestrian activities, fringe retail, and organised events. Along Orchard Road, selected sites are required to incorporate public spaces within the development's private boundary lines; in this way, creating activity nodes for street life. At the same time, design attention to signage and lighting has also contributed to the day, night, and seasonal ambience of Orchard Road. For example, the annual Christmas Light-Up, a joint initiative of the public and private sectors, transforms the everyday streetscape of Orchard Road into a festive display of lights, decorations, and street installations. Through this combination of urban design and place programming, Orchard Road has successfully built its own image and identity as one of the world's greatest shop-ping streets.

The Singapore River is a legacy of Singapore's beginnings as an entrepôt trading hub. However, with the containerisation of cargo, and as Singapore's economy matured and modernised over time, the Singapore River not only became obsolete as a medium for trade but also began deteriorating after decades of pollution from shipping-related activities and waste discharge from cottage industries further upstream. A large-scale cleaning-up of the urban waterways was initiated by the then

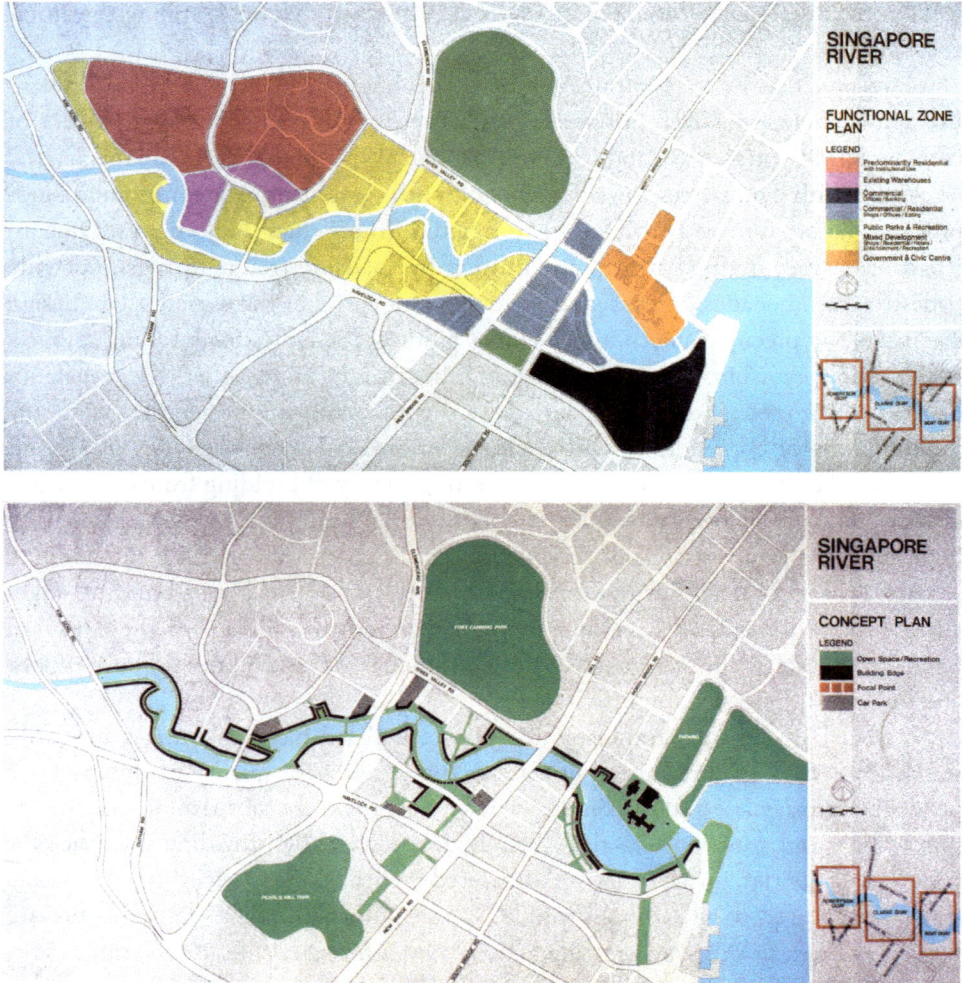

Figure 3.   Singapore river concept plan, 1985.
Source: Urban Redevelopment Authority.

Prime Minister Lee Kuan Yew in 1977. The Clean Rivers Campaign was a 10-year-long effort, after which the URA could develop a concept plan for the revitalisation of the Singapore River. Dividing the Singapore River into three zones—Boat Quay, Clarke Quay, and Robertson Quay—the concept plan gave each zone a different character through its own unique set of design solutions (see Figure 3).

The shophouses and warehouses along the Singapore River were proposed by the concept plan to be retained for adaptive reuse. Adaptive reuse is a process of making an old building or site useable for functions other than its original planning and design intent. In Boat Quay, for example, shophouses have been converted primarily for use as eateries; thereby serving as a popular locale for the office crowds during lunch and dinner, given its proximity to the CBD. Meanwhile, at Clarke Quay, the design goal was to rehabilitate clusters of existing low-rise warehouses of good architectural value. These warehouses, with their larger span, were viewed as ideal for a mix of uses including restaurants, studios, entertainment, and commercial showrooms. It was also proposed that the internal streets be pedestrianised to create an active public realm in the form of an outdoor mall. Finally, given the large land parcels at Robertson Quay, the concept plan recognised the opportunity for new and innovative developments which could integrate the façades of existing warehouses. These developments would accommodate a mix of residential, hotel, entertainment, and cultural uses, thus requiring greater need for comprehensive planning. In order to tie the three distinct zones together to form a common Singapore River identity, three key overarching urban design principles were conceived: (1) to set back buildings away from the river and provide a wide waterfront pedestrian promenade which will form a continuous loop around the river; (2) to control the building height limit along the river banks at four storeys to complement existing conserved buildings and preserve a sense of human scale; and (3) to enable alfresco dining and implement landscaping along the river edge to enhance the ambience and experience of the riverine.

Historic Districts and Design-Led Conservation

The legacies of Singapore's colonial past and cultural diversity can be traced in the physical fabric of our city—that is, in the style of architecture, form of buildings, and character of historic locations. However, prior to the 1980s, early initiatives to preserve select sites of heritage significance were commonly viewed to be counterintuitive to Singapore's economic progress, particularly as urban renewal efforts were simultaneously being carried out in the older districts of Central Area. In 1984, then Second Deputy Prime Minister for Foreign Affairs, Dr. S. Rajaratnam, emphasised the value of creating social cohesion through a shared sense of history and, hence, the importance of conservation in helping to strengthen these links: "A sense of history is what provides the links to hold together a people who came from the four corners of the earth. Because our history is short and because what is worth preserving from the past are not all that plentiful, we should try to save what is worthwhile from the past from the vandalism of the speculator and the developer, from a government and a bureaucracy which believes that anything that cannot be translated into cold cash is not worth investing in" (Rajaratnam, 1984).

Today, there is heightened awareness on conservation issues, yet efforts towards this end are no less challenging amidst the drive for urban growth and development to support an increasing population. Therefore, redevelopment projects with elements of conservation, as exemplified by the China Square Central and Bugis Village schemes, help to elevate the role that conservation plays in not only improving the physical conditions of aged buildings and districts but also strengthening the heritage of place and the diversity of Singapore's social identities. In doing so, strategic conservation actions have the potential to revive the vibrancy in old yet significant areas while celebrating the social and cultural building blocks of the nation. It is important to note as well two key policies that have been instrumental in facilitating conservation efforts in the Central Area.

Firstly, the Control of Rent Act, introduced in 1947 and enacted in 1953, sought to protect tenants from excessive rent increases by unscrupulous landlords during the post-war era when the supply of housing was scarce. The control of rent, however, inadvertently deterred landlords from investing in upgrades to their ageing properties. These properties, predominantly pre-war buildings, began to deteriorate over time. The lifting of rent control in 1988, followed by the gazetting of 10 conservation areas in 1989, motivated more and more private property owners to upgrade and improve the maintenance of their buildings (Dale, 2008, p. 45). Today, there are over 7,000 buildings that have been gazetted for conservation island-wide in Singapore (URA, 2011b, p. 4).

Secondly, the fragmentation of land created by single-lot ownership made amalgamation of land parcels for comprehensive development a challenge. Hence, the Land Acquisition Act (LAA) was introduced in 1967 to enable the government to acquire land from private owners for redevelopment that served a public purpose. The Government Land Sales (GLS) programme is a mechanism for the sale of State-owned land to the private sector at a specified tenure. First launched in 1967 to facilitate urban renewal in the Central Area, the GLS programme has helped to drive economic growth in real estate and property development while also facilitating the implementation of key development plans (URA, 2002). Together, the LAA and GLS programme have created unique opportunities for both conservation and new development, where structures of heritage value are retained on site and incorporated in the tender documents as part and parcel of the design guidelines.

In Singapore, urban conservation not only serves a public purpose in terms of safeguarding significant and meaningful aspects of our built heritage for future generations but also plays a strategic role in shaping the image and character of the city centre. The Structure Plan, which earmarked five areas for conservation, spurred the beginnings of concerted conservation studies by the URA. In 1986, the URA identified six historic areas for preservation through comprehensive planning: Chinatown, Kampong Glam, Little India, 'Heritage Link' (Fort Canning Park to Empress Place), Singapore River, and Emerald Hill Road (Aleshire, 1986). Detailed concept plans were developed for the historic districts and published in 1988; these plans illustrate not only the conserved buildings and monuments but also sites with proposed developments and envelope controls as well as a system of public spaces that include open spaces, plazas, pedestrian

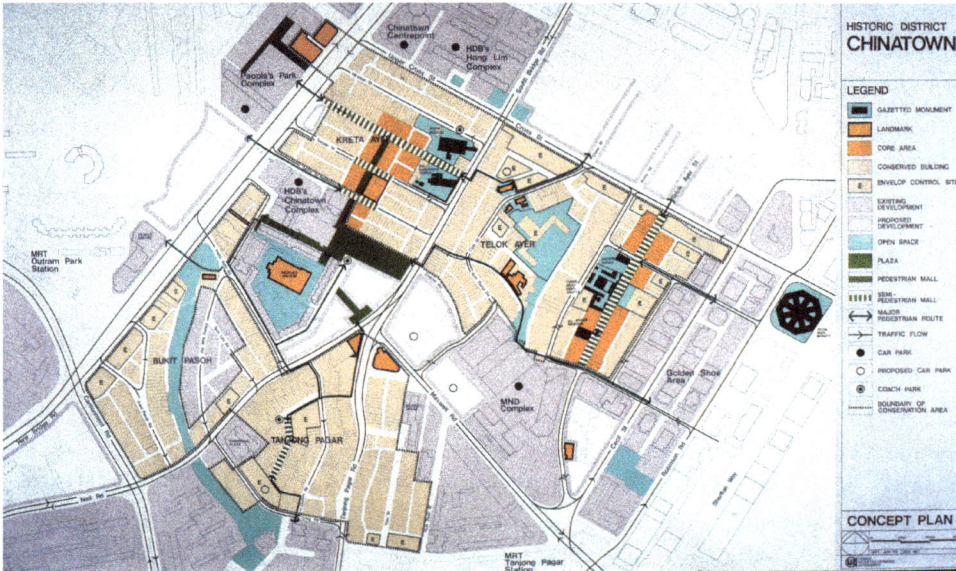

Figure 4.   Chinatown historict district concept plan, 1988.
Source: Urban Redevelopment Authority.

malls, and semi-pedestrian malls (see Figure 4). A significant step in Singapore's conservation history was achieved in 1989 when the initial list of six historic areas expanded to 10—Chinatown (Telok Ayer, Kreta Ayer, Tanjong Pagar and Bukit Pasoh), Little India, Kampong Glam, Singapore River (Boat Quay and Clarke Quay), Cairnhill and Emerald Hill—all of which were gazetted for conservation in the same year. As a lasting result of conservation and urban design efforts over the past 25 years, there are today approximately 5,000 buildings in the Central Area which have been conserved (Boey, 1998, p. 138). Two key approaches to urban design vis-à-vis urban conservation are often well-employed in such areas; they include envelope controls for in-fill developments and adaptive re-use of heritage buildings. These two approaches will be briefly discussed in turn through the the precinct examples of Bras Basah-Bugis and Cuppage Road.

As an extension of the Civic District and Museum Planning Area, the Bras Basah-Bugis precinct has a rich variety of uses, building types, and architectural styles ranging from shophouses to former school buildings and places of worship. In the 1980s, Bugis Street, infamous for its nighttime subculture, was sanitised by the authorities and recreated in the same likeness albeit opposite the original site (Kuah, 1994, p. 178–179). The Bugis area revitalisation efforts received adverse responses from the public, prompting a call for more flexible planning and design treatment towards this unique precinct that would enable arts and cultural activities to emerge and thrive. Given the eclecticism of Bras Basah-Bugis in terms of urban character and grain, the predominant urban design strategy today for this precinct calls for in-fill developments that are compatible with the surrounding context though subject to stringent design controls (URA, 2013b). Small standalone buildings, for example, are generally located on smaller streets with a four-storey building height limit imposed on selected developments along Albert Mall, Waterloo, Queen and Prinsep Streets. Conversely, larger-scale developments are generally located along major arterial roads where, at the Road Reserve line, they are required to build up to two or four storeys. These design strategies help to create a well-defined streetscape, thus complementing the scale of existing developments. At the same time, the diverse yet complementary patchwork of land uses has produced a variety of activities and amenities that relate to or support the growing arts and cultural scene in Bras Basah-Bugis.

Adaptive re-use, as described earlier in the Singapore River example, can also be used as a conservation strategy to revitalise the development potential of an area that is facing decline. Up until the 1970s, the Cuppage Road precinct was an area of deteriorating buildings and incompatible land uses. Apart from existing shophouses, there

Figure 5. Cuppage road redevelopment area and GLS sites.
Source: Huo and Heng, 2007, p. 139.

were also furniture workshops, motor garages, and a market with backlane hawker stalls. With a prime location along Orchard Road, the Cuppage Road area provided possibilities for a synergistic relationship with the shopping belt and thus was earmarked in the 1970s for comprehensive redevelopment under the GLS programme (Huo and Heng, 2007, p. 139) (see Figure 5). The redevelopment plan called for a mix of complementary uses such as hotels, offices, shops and entertainment. Moreover, the plan also resulted in the rehabilitation and adaptive re-use of two rows of Malaccan-style terrace houses with well-preserved architecture and heritage significance. The side street was transformed into a pedestrian mall and integrated into the planned pedestrian network for the larger area. Elsewhere along Orchard Road, adaptive re-use was adopted on Emerald Hill Road in which Peranakan-style shophouses near Orchard Road were converted for commercial use; and, on Tanglin Road, a row of Tudor-style houses were renovated for re-use as offices.

As illustrated by the two approaches described above, urban design seeks to provide solutions that can help achieve a balance between the often conflicting needs of development and environmental quality. Through careful design strategies and guidelines, places and buildings with vernacular characteristics significant to our architectural and cultural history can remain intact while coexisting harmoniously with new modern developments. At the same time, the design controls allow room for flexibility such that private sector developers and architects can explore and express, within the prescribed envelope, their creativity. Often, however, this channel of urban design is typically addressed within the technical tender documents and architectural drawings for the site; hence, the visibility of urban design is usually hidden until the development is completed and experienced first-hand by its users. To this end, urban design is ultimately concerned with the creation of an orderly yet varied and memorable cityscape for public enjoyment.

Urban Design and Early Public Housing Developments in Chinatown

The Central Area is generally guided along three scales of urban design. At the macro level, the Structure Plan has been instrumental in establishing an overall urban design strategy for the city centre and surroundings. At the precinct level, more detailed urban design principles shape the texture and form of the urban fabric. And, for conservation districts and buildings, special urban design guidelines help to ensure harmonious co-existence between old and new developments. In this section, we will discuss the design thinking and logic behind the creation of public spaces and pedestrian linkages at the street block level. Urban design, after all, is as concerned about defining urban spaces for people and their activities as it is in developing the physical aesthetics of the cityscape. Given Singapore's tropical climate, compact urban fabric, and propensity for high-rise, high-density development, it is pertinent that the city be designed for walkability, connectivity, and socio-economic vibrancy. One of the finest examples by which we can observe these intentions at play is the pedestrian and public space networks induced through the early public housing developments in Chinatown. Here, we will examine two early public housing projects: Tanjong Pagar Plaza and Hong Lim Complex.

Completed in the late 1970s, Tanjong Pagar Plaza and Hong Lim Complex provided proper housing in Chinatown after the clearance of slum and squatter settlements; in this way, injecting a live-in residential population to help drive economic activities, particularly at night and weekends when the city became void of the office crowd. Both projects demonstrate how thoughtful urban design solutions, which incorporate quality spaces for pedestrian circulation and street life in areas redeveloped for public housing, can help to enhance the Chinatown historic district within which they are sited. Tanjong Pagar Plaza and Hong Lim Complex are illustrative of the early sentiments towards Chinatown's historic fabric and traditional street activities. In fact, this initial urban design emphasis on the pedestrian and public space networks of the two public housing projects in Chinatown predates the URA's 1986 announcement of six historic areas for preservation, which included Chinatown. Subsequently, the Chinatown Historic District Concept Plan was published in 1988, providing a clear urban design programme towards achieving a cohesive pedestrian network and streetscape in Chinatown (see Figure 4). One year later, in 1989, Chinatown was officially awarded its conservation status; by then, of course, Tanjong Pagar Plaza and Hong Lim Complex were inhabited and operating as integral components of the urban fabric.

Tanjong Pagar Plaza: Internal Courtyards and Gathering Spaces

Tanjong Pagar Plaza, situated along Tanjong Pagar Road between Craig Road and Kee Seng Street, was completed in 1977 by the HDB. The mixed-use development is an example of the HDB's second-generation high-rise, high-density public housing complex typology constructed between 1974 and 1977. The complex comprises five residential slab blocks ranging from 18 to 22 storeys and two point block towers placed above the commercial podiums, which house retail services and public amenities such as a kindergarten, post-office, and banks. A two-storey market and hawker centre are also housed in a separate podium block, though linked to the rest of the complex by overhead walkways.

Set within a historic district of low-rise buildings and shophouses, the lower podium blocks of this public housing project were designed to echo the scale of its urban context. Various functional zones were incorporated into the commercial podium, thus paying attention to the human dimension as experienced from the ground level (see Figure 6). One main feature is the internal landscaped courtyard, which runs the entire length of the commercial podium. Formerly embellished with an ornamental pool and rock gardens, it now has an open plaza with a pavilion in the

Figure 6. Tanjong Pagar Plaza, ground floor plan (top). Hong Lim Complex, boundary of site on bottom left and network of first (yellow) and second (red) storey pedestrian network on bottom-right.

Source: Adapted by Heng Chye Kiang and Chong Keng Hua.

central courtyard as well as gardens with seats at both ends. Public spaces, as such, were not only incorporated in the design of the complex as a means of providing light and ventilation but also to create an informal setting for social gathering among residents and users of the development. By appropriating the scale of the two-storey commercial podiums, adding pedestrian walkways with turfing along the sides, incorporating an internal landscaped courtyard, and arranging the slab blocks perpendicular to the main road in a north-south orientation which reduces the impact of such a high-rise development on the site, Tanjong Pagar Plaza and its internal network of public gathering spaces thus became more approachable and welcoming to the pedestrian on the street.

Hong Lim Complex: Re-engaging the Street

Hong Lim Complex, which is flanked on three sides by Upper Hokien Street, Upper Cross Street, and South Bridge Road, was conceived during earlier phases of the Central Area urban renewal programme. Hong Lim Complex was envisioned to be a mixed-use public housing project arising from redevelopment plans for a precinct of dilapidated shophouses which had been identified for urban renewal (see Figure 6). Over 200 shopkeepers, many of whom had been established in the area for generations, were affected by the redevelopment plans (see also Heng, 2009). Although compensation and alternative commercial space elsewhere were options offered by the State to the shopkeepers, the majority chose to stay on-site through the formation of Fook Hai Development Pte Ltd. In 1970, the URA allocated the group a 2,600m² site which was then developed into a 22,300m² commercial building that is still known today as Fook Hai Building. Completed in 1976, Fook Hai Building comprises a 12-storey tower of office and apartment units on top of a seven-storey podium for retail and office use.

Hong Lim Complex was fully constructed in 1979, three years after the completion of Fook Hai Building. Exemplifying a turn in approach to urban renewal and design response to the urban context, Hong Lim Complex sought to re-engage traditional elements of street life albeit in a contemporary context. In the first instance, the large site was divided into three smaller parcels rather than configured for a single mega-structure. The parcelling of the site not only responded sensitively to the compact urban grain of the surrounding area but also facilitated pedestrian flow between South Bridge Road and New Bridge Road through the pedestrianisation of the former Upper Nankin Street as an internal mall within the complex. The land use and nature of activities along this pedestrianised thoroughfare have persisted despite a major transformation of the built environment. The shops and colonnade at ground level also echo the old five-foot-ways of the surrounding shophouses. Today, the pedestrian street within Hong Lim Complex still flourishes with vibrant street life, thus playing an important role in the Central Area's greater network of public spaces.

Hong Lim Complex consists of five housing slab blocks, ranging from 18 to 20 storeys, situated on four-storey interlinked podiums that house a market, food centre, restaurants, banks, and other amenities. The individual podium buildings were carefully sited in relation to one another, leaving comfortably-scaled street spaces between the blocks which were landscaped for public use. At the same time, vehicular access into Hong Lim Complex was restricted to certain entrances from Upper Hokien Street and Upper Cross Street, and ushered directly into an inconspicuous eight-storey carpark to minimise its impact on pedestrian circulation.

The two public housing projects of Tanjong Pagar Plaza and Hong Lim Complex were initiated during a time of amplified urban renewal efforts in the Central Area. Although the priority then was to resettle urban inhabitants into proper housing as expeditiously as possible, there was also some scope for design experimentation at the site and building level. Such attention to the visual and physical spaces between building blocks and along the street edges, as illustrated by the two urban public housing developments, point to growing efforts by the government then to employ design and spatial strategies in creating quality environments within public housing. These early design interventions and the initial network of public spaces induced through public housing add to an expanding and richly-layered system of urban public spaces, which today includes other networks such as parks, transportation, and conservation areas.

Planning and Designing the Southern Urban Coastline

As a small island-nation, it is a well-known fact that Singapore has limited natural reserves. Land and water, the two essential resources required to sustain urban growth and economic development, have long been recognised for their value as both commodity and asset. Through decades of extensive land reclamation and water impoundment, new terrain and water catchment areas have been created which not only transform the physical profile of the island but also generate opportunities for economic, recreational, and leisure activities.

Historically, land reclamation in the Central Area was undertaken as early as the 1850s when, under the British colonial administration, a seawall was constructed between Fullerton Road and the former Telok Ayer Market (now the site of Lau Pa Sat). This was subsequently followed in the 1880s by more extensive land reclamation that resulted in land created between Telok Ayer Street and today's Shenton Way. Later, the reclamation of Beach Road and the Tanjong Pagar area ensued (URA, 1987a, p. 4). There was a lull period of several decades until the 1970s when two major projects—the Clean Rivers Campaign and Marina City reclamation—were carried out concurrently with the aim of ramping up growth and development along the southern urban coastline. Today, these efforts have resulted in the production of two urban activity areas: Marina Bay and Kallang Basin. In this section, we explore the role of urban design in guiding urban growth and economic development around Marina Bay. More specifically, we will discuss the design vision and land use strategies for optimising Marina Bay's prime location south of the existing CBD.

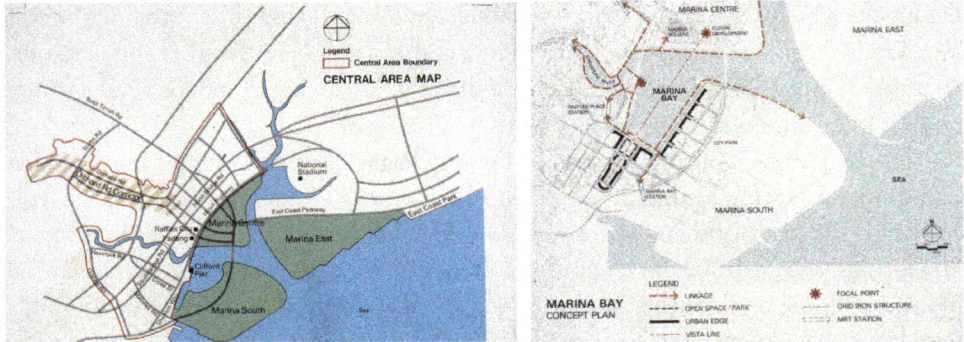

Figure 7.   Marina City Central Area Map, 1987 (left). Marina Bay concept plan, 1989 (right). *Source*: Urban Redevelopment Authority.

Marina Bay: Waterfront Growth and Development

In the 1960s and 1970s, Singapore and Kallang Rivers were areas where few visitors would tread. Polluted with untreated sewage and littered with debris, the two rivers not only posed health and safety risks but had also become eyesores. Left unaddressed, the deteriorating state and condition of these waterways would have stood in the way of economic progress by hindering investment in the city. The call for a massive cleaning-up and redevelopment of Singapore and Kallang Rivers was announced in 1977 by then Prime Minister Lee Kuan Yew. Carried out over 10 years, the ambitious programme involved the installation of proper sewage infrastructure, implementation of a management system to improve water quality, resettlement of squatters, and relocation of cottage industries including duck and pig farms upstream. At the same time, large-scale reclamation had long been underway since 1971 for the creation of Marina City—an area of more than 650 hectares divided into three land parcels that would extend Singapore's urban coastline further south (see Figure 7). Both programmes were concluded nearly simultaneously, with reclamation works ending in 1985 followed by the completion of the Clean Rivers Campaign in 1987. These two programmes then enabled major plans to be rolled out for the newly created land and shoreline around Marina Bay.

Under the Structure Plan, the dual strategic roles of Marina City were, firstly, to accommodate the future expansion of Central Area functions and, secondly, to provide new opportunities for large-scale urban design that would directly and positively shape Singapore's image on the world stage. The first of three land parcels to be reclaimed was Marina Centre in 1977. Planned as an extension of the Orchard Road Corridor, Marina Centre would function as a terminating node of this hotel and shopping belt. Over the decades, Marina Centre has developed into a commercial centre with hotel, shopping, entertainment, and cultural amenities supporting as well as complementing the CBD nearby. Reclamation of the second land parcel, Marina East, was completed in 1985. Although situated furthest from the CBD, Marina East presents the greatest potential for active recreation along its water edge given the continuous seafront that it forms with East Coast Park. It was also envisioned that Marina East would fulfil Singapore's long term needs for housing; thus, current interim uses include recreational facilities such as the Marina Bay Golf Course and Bay East Garden shoreline park.

Lastly, we shall now discuss in greater detail the Marina South land parcel which is sited adjacent to the city core and reclaimed in 1985. Viewed as a significant national asset because of its proximity to the financial, commercial, and tourism activities of the CBD, extraordinary preparation was involved in the planning and design of Marina South (URA, 1987b, p. 5) (see Figure 7). Three key urban design strategies were incorporated in the plans for Marina South. Firstly, a gridiron network extending seawards from the existing street pattern of the CBD creates an efficient circulation system with regular-shaped lots. These prime lots determine more-or-less the extent of future building masses and, hence, the eventual texture of the urban landscape. Secondly, to take advantage of the water frontage around the perimeter of Marina South, visual corridors to the sea were planned and the orientation of the grid maximised so as to create the feeling that developments are surrounded by water. Thirdly, several broad sites were initially held in reserve for large-scale developments which today have been realised: a prominent urban park (Gardens by the Bay), a mixed-use hotel and entertainment development (Marina Bay Sands), and a ferry terminal (Marina Bay Cruise Centre).

Bay for Celebration, Spectacle, and Engagement

Marina Bay has contributed not only to the production of Singapore's urban image but also to the making of a vibrant and memorable landscape. Dubbed as the 'Bay for Events and National Celebrations', Marina Bay is deliberately programmed through planning and design to enable activities that incite festivity and delight (URA, 1987c, p. 6–7). With the city skyline as a backdrop, Marina Bay is perpetually poised as a hosting platform for major celebratory occasions. In recent years, Marina Bay has lived up to its moniker as the Bay for Celebration by serving as the central site and focal point of signature events which include the National Day Parade, New Year's Eve Countdown, and Formula One Night Race.

Marina Bay, together with Kallang Basin, is a vital component of Singapore's central catchment system—as both basins are physically and fundamentally linked in their formation of the Marina Reservoir. On one level, the Marina Reservoir is critical to achieving Singapore's future self-sufficiency in its domestic water supply. On another level, Marina Reservoir contributes to the city's public space network by creating an integrated 'blue' and 'green' landscape that can help to enhance the quality of public urban life. Urban design, in this sense, is an important process which can open out new and exciting possibilities for outdoor activities, both day and night.

More specifically, Singapore's tropical climate calls for special attention towards shading and landscaping for outdoor spaces which, in the context of Marina Reservoir, needs to be achieved without comprising open views across the two water basins and, where possible, outwards in the direction of the sea. Related to climatic and environmental issues is the concern for the pedestrian in terms of safety and comfort. Lighting, seating, and landscaping materials are elements that, when integrated thoughtfully into the overall design strategy, enhance the human experience of public space. The Promontory@Marina Bay, for example, is a green-turfed open space with a hard edge providing ample walkways and seating that juts out into the water. On ordinary days, The Promontory serves as an extension of the waterfront promenade which circuits around Marina Bay and, during special events, it can be transformed into an outdoor stage and activity space.

Similarly, the waterfront promenade forming the inner ring around Marina Bay serves as a seamless and accessible interface between the water on one side and private developments on the other. Additionally, this promenade links several public amenities and attractions in a continuous loop (for example, Esplanade Theatres, Merlion Park, historic buildings at Fullerton Bay and Clifford Pier, Marina Bay Sands Integrated Resort, ArtScience Museum, and so on), thus forming a 'string of pearls'. Furthermore, with ongoing plans to phase out the Tanjong Pagar Port in order to consolidate port activities in the western part of Singapore, there is an opportunity to redevelop the port land for high value-add uses and extend Marina South to this new growth area, thereby forming a 'Greater Southern Waterfront' zone in the future (URA, 2016).

Planning and urban design have transformed the reclaimed land parcels and manmade waterbody at Marina Bay into a congruent landscape that is, at one level, geophysically linked by its water harvesting functions and, at another level, spatially connected by view corridors, circulation paths, and complementary land use patterns. As a new geographical area whose existing coastline was completed as recently as 30 years ago, Marina Bay reminds us of the rigour of research and comprehensiveness of planning required to execute a complex urban project of such scale, coupled with the political courage and will to mobilise the plans.

Designing the City for People: A Comprehensive Public Space Network

Through urban design, the unique and memorable moments of a city can be significantly shaped, created, and enhanced. If carried out thoughtfully, urban design efforts can open out exciting opportunities for diverse modes of street life and place-based experiences; thus, contributing to the vibrancy of the public realm. The different types of urban design interventions covered in this chapter—from the macro

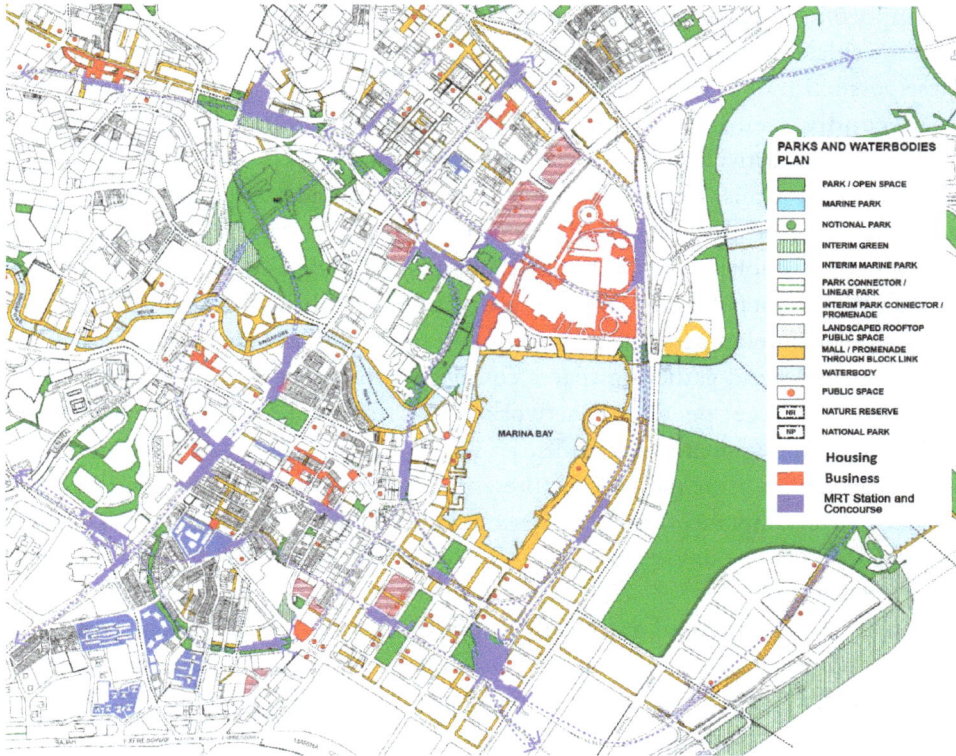

Figure 8.   Illustration of the comprehensive public space network in Central Area.

Source: Adapted by Heng Chye Kiang.

Structure Plan to the micro site-specific guidelines and tender documents—have, over time, produced a comprehensive public space network. This comprehensive public space network is illustrated and updated as seen in Figure 8. From such an illustration, we can better visualise the cumulative layers of urban design interventions while also better understanding the fundamental elements contributing to the visual and experiential congruence of the public space network in the Central Area.

Firstly, pedestrian connectivity is a fundamental element of the comprehensive public space network, as it facilitates access and, hence, use of public space. Moreover, designing for different modes of connectivity affords users with options in terms of mobility, and providing for different levels of connectivity enhances the integrated nature of the public space network. A well-defined circulation strategy incorporating pedestrian paths, roads, and rail lines was initially conceived by the Structure Plan. Over the decades, the circulation strategy has expanded to include new mobility corridors which take advantage of the Marina Bay and Singapore River waterbodies, pedestrian overhead bridges (Jubilee Bridge, The Helix Bridge), and underground linkages (Esplanade Xchange, Marina Bay Link Mall). Today, moving around the Central Area can be achieved by foot, public transportation, or private vehicle—at grade level, above grade, underground, or any combination of these possibilities.

Secondly, well-defined place-based nodes provide points of interest and socio-economic activities along principal pedestrian circuits. These nodes can manifest in various forms, from urban designed precincts and conservation districts to public housing projects which, in and of themselves, contain smaller networks of pedestrian and public space amenities. Tanjong Pagar Plaza and Hong Lim Complex (in addition to Bras Basah Complex, soon-to-be-demolished Rochor Centre, and other similar development typologies), for example, contain an intricate system of pedestrian links and gathering spaces equipped with street furniture—this system feeds into the larger pedestrian network of the surrounding area which includes Chinatown. And Chinatown, as a district which exhibits its own set of conservation and urban design principles, then represents a higher-order node within the grand scheme of the comprehensive public space network. Urban scale, therefore, is another element that affects our cognitive and physical relationship to place and, hence, our experience of the city.

Lastly, environmental assets in the Central Area—such as urban parks and squares, monumental landmarks, and waterbodies—are strung together as part and parcel of a comprehensively-planned, island-wide system of green corridors and connectors. Planning and urban design, for example, have transformed the reclaimed land parcels surrounding Marina Bay into a congruent landscape that is spatially connected by a network of parks, greenways, and view corridors. The Singapore River also illustrates the comprehensive role of urban design in connecting three historic quays along a continuous promenade on both banks of the river. This promenade adds to the public space network with segments that include trees and benches, art installations and sculptures, al fresco dining, and wayfinding boards—all of which play a part in enhancing the environmental quality of the public realm.

The city is a dynamic palimpsest chronicling the evolution of planning and urban design iterations that have, through time, transformed (and continue to transform) the urban landscape. Singapore's urban palimpsest, in spite of its relatively short history, is a dense accumulation of multiple superimpositions and erasures—the result of rapid urbanisation over the past 50 years. Through a close reading of the comprehensive public space network in the Central Area, we glean a better understanding of the hidden and overlapping layers while also recognising the different agendas underpinning and giving rise to the various types and forms of public spaces.

Conclusion

Being small, Singapore needs to be planned well ahead, carefully and creatively. There is long-term benefit in the rigorous process of ensuring that new buildings and future redevelopment schemes relate to the overall cityscape. In other words, beautiful buildings and distinct districts are desirable but only if they fit our city in a meaningful way. Our cityscape should bespeak our multi-ethnic culture and aesthetic values while reflecting our climate and local conditions. Urban design can help to assemble the various elements of a city into a cohesive visual story that relates to the history and aspirations of the people; in this way, enhancing and illuminating the human dimensions of the city.

Today, the signature skyline which many locals and visitors alike identify with Singapore was created not by accident or serendipity but, rather, through decades of thoughtful and meticulous planning and design guided by the strategic directions of a coherent urban design vision. This urban design vision was laid out in the 1986 Central Area Structure Plan. The Structure Plan not only identified the development corridors, conservation areas, and green spaces for their environmental characteristics and economic potential, but also how these assets would relate to one another. Over the decades, Singapore's cityscape has become more richly varied with: the introduction of new modern precincts emerging next to older established areas; revival and rebranding of heritage districts; configuration of a new southern coastline; and integration of a comprehensive pedestrian and public space network. Singapore's cityscape, as familiar as it is to us today, will likely transform over time to accommodate a growing population and promote economic development.

In spite (or perhaps because) of these challenges, there are special features of our city that will remain unique to Singapore for they reflect our heritage, multi-ethnic culture, and tropical setting. It is crucial, therefore, that the urban design strategies for future land uses and intensities help to generate greater diversity (and tolerance) of urban forms, public spaces, and street activities. In this way, a more inclusive cityscape and resilient economy and society can be created—one that enables land parcellation for smaller developments, affordable areas for rich urban life, and flexible land use zones for greater diversity and resilience. With ensuing demographic and rapid technological developments in the next few decades, the practice of urban design will need to be an exercise of sensibility and flexibility in order for the next bold vision to transpire and guide our city confidently into the future.

References

Aleshire, I. (1986) '6 areas to be preserved', *The Straits Times*, 27 December 1986, p. 1.

Boey, Y. M. (1998) 'Urban Conservation in Singapore,' in: B. Yuen (Ed) *Planning Singapore: From Plan to Implementation*, p. 133–168. Singapore: Singapore Institute of Planners.

Chia, L. S., Khan, H. and Chou, L. M. (1988) *The Coastal Environmental Profile of Singapore*. Manila: Association of Southeast Asian Nations/United States Coastal Resources Management Project.

Dale, O. J. (2008) 'Sustainable City Centre Development' in: T. C. Wong, B. Yuen, and C. Goldblum (Eds) *Spatial Planning for a Sustainable Singapore*, p. 31–57. New York: Springer.

Heng, C. K. (2009) 'Continuity and departure: A case study of Singapore's Nankin Street', in: D. Radovic (Ed) *Eco-Urbanity: Towards Well-Mannered Built Environments*, p. 103–111. London; New York: Routledge.

Huo, N. and Heng, C. K. (2007) 'The Making of State-Business Driven Public Spaces in Singapore', *Journal of Asian Architecture and Building Engineering*, 6(1), p. 135–142.

Joshi, Y. K., Tortajada, C. and Biswas, A. K. (2012) 'Cleaning of the Singapore River and Kallang Basin in Singapore: Economic, Social, and Environmental Dimensions', *International Journal of Water Resources Development*, 28(4), p. 647–658.

Kuah, K. E. (1994) 'Bugis Street in Singapore: Development, Conservation and the Reinvention of Cultural Landscape', in: M. Askew and W. S. Logan (Eds) *Cultural Identity and Urban Change in Southeast Asia: Interpretative Essays*, p. 167–185. Geelong, Victoria: Deakin University Press.

Rajaratnam, S. (1984) 'The uses and abuses of the past', Seminar on *Adaptive Re-use: Integrating Traditional Areas into the Modern Urban Fabric*, (Singapore, April 1984).

Statistics Singapore (2016) 'Latest Data'; accessed from http://www.singstat.gov.sg/statistics/latest-data#16

URA (Urban Redevelopment Authority) (2016) 'Greater Southern Waterfront'; accessed from https://www.ura.gov.sg/uol/master-plan/View-Master-Plan/master-plan-2014/master-plan/Regional-highlights/central-area/central-area/Greater-southern-waterfront.aspx

URA (Urban Redevelopment Authority) (2013a) 'Annex A: Urban Design Guidelines for Developments within Orchard Planning Area'; accessed from http://www.ura.gov.sg/uol/circulars/2013/nov/~/media/User%20Defined/URA%20Online/circulars/2013/nov/dc13-15/dc13–15_Annex%20Av2.ashx.

URA (Urban Redevelopment Authority) (2013b) 'Urban Design Guidelines for Developments within Bras Basah Bugis Planning Area'; accessed from https://www.ura.gov.sg/uol/circulars/2013/nov/~/media/User%20Defined/URA%20Online/circulars/2013/nov/dc13–16/dc13–16_Annex%20A.ashx.

URA (Urban Redevelopment Authority) (2011a) 'Conserving The Past', *Skyline Special*; accessed from http://www.ura.gov.sg/skyline/skyline11/skyline11-02/special/skyline%20marapr%20conservation%20supplement%20FA.pdf.

URA (Urban Redevelopment Authority) (2011b) *Conservation Guidelines*; accessed from http://www.ura.gov.sg/uol/~/media/User%20Defined/URA%20Online/Guidelines/Conservation/Cons-Guidelines.ashx.

URA (Urban Redevelopment Authority) (2008) 'Celebrate Life by the Waterfront at Kallang Riverside', *Skyline*; accessed from https://www.ura.gov.sg/skyline/skyline08/skyline08-03/text/07.htm.

URA (Urban Redevelopment Authority) (2002) 'Government Land Sales Through the Years: Remaking Singapore's Landscape'; accessed from http://www.ura.gov.sg/skyline/skyline02/skyline02-04/text/landsales2.html.

URA (Urban Redevelopment Authority) (1987a) 'Marina City: Reshaping the Coastline', *Skyline*, 30, p. 3–4.

URA (Urban Redevelopment Authority) (1987b) 'Marina City: A Peek at What Lies Ahead', *Skyline*, 30, p. 5–7.

URA (Urban Redevelopment Authority) (1987c) 'Panning for Urban Waterfronts at Marina Bay and Kallang Basin', *Skyline*, 38, p. 5–8.

URA (Urban Redevelopment Authority) (1986) 'The Year That Was: Developing the City', *Skyline*, 25, p. 4–7.

URA (Urban Redevelopment Authority) (1984) 'Planning for a Better City: A Challenge for URA', *Skyline*, 11, p. 6–7.

Part 3
Urban Complexities & Creative Solutions

CHAPTER 13

Conserving Urban Heritage: Remembering the Past in a Developmental City-State*

Lily Kong

The history of a city is recorded not only in books, but also in its buildings. While the written word captures the evolution of events and beliefs, buildings embody lifestyles and aesthetic tastes, technology and crafts. Therefore old buildings are more than just bricks and mortar. Old town houses and shops, temples and churches, schools and institutions, are more than utilitarian objects. They also are a record of our ancestors' aspirations and achievements. In Singapore, many of the old buildings embody the visual confluence of our multi-varied ethnic roots. While the majority need some face-lift, they never cease to delight our eyes and enhance the sense of time and place unique to our own city. ... We must realise that photographs and words are no substitute for life-size forms and spaces. For one cannot walk into or around the buildings in these photographs. Meanwhile ageing artisans and their crafts vanish with the passage of time. Buildings demolished are history records gone. While some must make way for progress, some, we hope, will remain to link us with our past.

> S Rajaratnam, then Deputy Prime Minister
> Foreword, Pastel Portraits, 1984

Urban Planning and Development in Singapore: The Place of Urban Conservation

While the history of urban planning in Singapore usually begins by drawing attention to the allocation of quarters for the different ethnicities in 1822, equally conspicuous in such a recounting is the narrative of a colonial cityscape characterised by overcrowded slums, and the efforts of agencies such as the Singapore Improvement Trust (SIT) set up in 1920 to eradicate slums, undertake repairs and redecoration,

---

*This chapter is an abridged version of Kong, L. (2011) *Conserving the Past, Creating the Future: Urban Heritage in Singapore*, Singapore: Straits Times Press.

and build new apartments. The SIT's failure to solve many of the problems of the dilapidated and congested city is as much a part of the narrative, which allowed for the subsequent achievements of the Housing and Development Board (HDB) to be celebrated. The account of efforts to clear the city and modernise the landscape, responsibilities later to be associated with the Urban Redevelopment Authority, is by now, a well-known one.

Amidst the energetic swinging of the wrecker's ball, calls for urban heritage conservation emerged from the 1960s. In 1962, a United Nations Town Planning expert, EE Lorange, was invited to review Singapore's First Master Plan (approved in 1958) and advise on the redevelopment of the city center. Mr Lorange recommended the appointment of three UN experts, namely, Messrs Charles Abrams, Susumu Kobe, and Otto Koenigsberger. They suggested, amongst other things, "an identification of the areas worth preserving, and a programme to improve such areas and make them more habitable" (Abrams et al., 1980). A subsequent report by UN consultants similarly recommended that "some areas of historic import or those which are essentially representative of the colourful and unique character of central Singapore should be carefully conserved" (Crooks Michell Peacock Stewart, 1971). The areas highlighted were Chinatown, Arab Town, the areas between Fort Canning and the Padang, and between Fort Canning and Pearl's Hill.

The earliest concrete steps in saving Singapore's landmarks were effected through the Preservation of Monuments Board (PMB). PMB was established in 1971 in recognition of the need to preserve Singapore's historically and architecturally significant buildings. In 2013, PMB became the Preservation of Sites and Monuments division of the National Heritage Board and has responsibility for: planning, research and publication to extend knowledge on nationally significant sites and monuments; regulatory support to guide restoration, preservation and protection of sites and national monuments; outreach, to promote public interest and awareness in sites and national monuments; as well as to advise the government on matters relating to the preservation of nationally significant sites and monuments. Familiar sites that have been preserved include Telok Ayer Market (or Lau Pa Sat, Hokkien for Old Market), the Old Supreme Court, Sultan Mosque, St Andrew's Cathedral, Sri Mariamman Temple, and Thian Hock Keng. Perhaps less familiar but no less significant are the Old Nanyang University Arch, Macdonald House, and Old Admiralty House.

Apart from the work of PMB, the early "incubation period" of the 1970s and early 1980s also witnessed the rehabilitation of 30 state-owned shophouses on Murray Street and Tudor Court, and the pedestrianisation of Emerald Hill Road. These efforts represent the first steps in conservation in Singapore, giving regard to the protection of buildings of historical, architectural and cultural significance and their traditional settings.

However, awareness of the value of conservation took time to develop. The years of stirring consciousness were long ones, and during those years, many beautiful buildings with historical and architectural significance were demolished. For example,

Bukit Rose, home to four generations of a prominent local Chinese family in Bukit Timah, and the setting for British author Noel Barber's novel *Tanamera*, was demolished for the Casa Rosita condominium. Old China Building, best remembered for its stained glass panels depicting Chinese mercantile activities, made way for the OCBC Centre, and the Old Arcade, built with beautiful Moorish domes in 1909 by the Alkaff family, was razed and replaced by The Arcade in the 1970s.

While proponents of urban heritage conservation have severely criticised the acts of demolition and mourn the loss of such buildings, it was also during this period that the backbone of Singapore's housing shortage was broken. New high-rise apartment blocks representing low-cost options for the majority of the population were built. New spaces of modernity, such as the first shopping complex, People's Park Complex, and new experiments in retail and mixed-use complexes also appeared. Those who defend the actions of the 1970s point to these developments as providing improvements in the lives of Singaporeans. Ironically, some of these outcomes of urban (re)development have themselves become the objects of demolition and redevelopment today, or the focus of debates about conservation. The journey to conservation and the balance with forces of redevelopment over time are clearly not debates that can be settled once and for all, but are historically-contingent moments that call for collective self-reflection. Some of these debates are documented below. They demonstrate the debates that Singapore society engages in, and the choices that need to be and are made—for better, for worse—that reflect the historical specificity, cultural sensitivity, economic contingency and social sensibility of the moment.

Conserving Our Heritage

The Formative Years (1982–1988)

In 1982, as part of the preparation for a new mass rapid transit system, a major urban planning review started. Of significant consideration in this review was the quality of the city's character and distinctiveness of its identity. At the same time, conservation, which was recognised as a handmaiden to tourism, was identified as being vital to the economy. Within this context, decisions were made to undertake large-scale reclamation in the Marina area, next to the financial district, to ensure that Singapore would have sufficient land in the city center for commercial use. In this way, the historic parts of the city center could be kept intact. Thus, in 1986, the URA announced the conservation of seven areas—Chinatown, Kampong Glam, Little India, Boat Quay, Clarke Quay, Cairnhill and Emerald Hill. These plans gained significant impetus from the Tourism Product Development Plan, commissioned by the then Singapore Tourism Promotion Board. The consultants argued that conservation could improve Singapore's economic viability through tourism, and enhance national pride.

The first shophouse conservation project was carried out in Tanjong Pagar in 1987 by the URA, a major development that showed the way in conservation in numerous ways: in technical expertise, economic viability, historical veracity and so on. Following on the heels of this demonstration project, the phasing out of the Rent Control Act in 1988 offered further support for conservation—it allowed pre-1947 houses which had been rented out at unrealistically low rates to raise rents. This made a big difference to conservation, as the earlier low rents made it unattractive for owners to undertake any work on their buildings. Developers welcomed this as an incentive for them to invest in historical buildings. On the other hand, there was also a danger that lifting rent control could drive out the older generation that had lived in those buildings for years, thus disrupting their lives and livelihoods, and jeopardising a sense of community. Clearly, there was a cost to enabling heritage conservation using this approach that would have to be borne by a certain community.

Consolidating Efforts (1989–1992)

In 1989, the URA was formally appointed the national conservation authority and unveiled the Conservation Master Plan. This was followed by the gazetting of the seven areas for conservation announced in 1986, including five other areas: Blair Plain, Beach Road, River Valley, Jalan Besar and Geylang. PMB also added another 10 national monuments to its list of protected buildings. The Conservation Master Plan attempted to be comprehensive in terms of geographical coverage, range of architectural and building types, building assessment method and implementation strategy. Effort was also put into balancing the interests of conservation champions with those of owners who were not keen to keep their buildings because of concerns over costs associated with conservation.

This balance was in part achieved by adopting one policy for the Central Area but a different one for areas beyond the core. Whereas whole districts would be conserved and in-fill developments subject to stringent design control in the Central Area, new developments were allowed to intermix with old buildings in areas outside the city center.

To facilitate the Master Plan, the URA launched the "Conservation Initiated by Private Owners' Scheme" in 1991, which allowed private individual owners to volunteer their buildings for conservation in return for development incentives like bonus gross floor area. Private sector participation in the restoration and rehabilitation of buildings was also encouraged. This was a necessary step, given that about 75% of the conservation areas identified in the Master Plan were privately owned. Private sector participation also allows new ideas, entrepreneurship and financial resources to enter into conservation efforts.

Refinements and Enhancements (1992 to 2000)

By 1992, most of the key areas identified in the Conservation Plan had been gazetted. In 1993, the URA began full implementation of the conservation plan via the provision and upgrading of infrastructure, including sewers, power substations and carparks, as well as walkways, covered drains, and landscaping. The URA also launched *Objectives, Principles and Standards for Preservation and Conservation* to help owners and those involved in conservation work achieve quality outcomes in their conservation projects, and "to share information about how conservation can be done in Singapore" (URA, 1993). The URA also set up a conservation customer service corner to clarify what genuine conservation was as opposed to the restoration of façades, and to offer safety information and advice on building restoration.

In 1995, the URA launched the Architectural Heritage Awards, an annual award to recognise well-restored monuments in Singapore. Information plaques were also introduced to commemorate historic areas, offering information about their historical significance. Storyboards were installed in Kampong Glam, Chinatown, Little India, Boat Quay, and Emerald Hill, Cairnhill and Blair Road.

During this period of implementation, creative ideas were needed to keep a balance between opposing forces of development and conservation. In this respect, the case of China Square exemplifies the imagination and boldness of initiative that characterised this phase. The URA drew up a plan in which streets would be retained, and selected shophouse blocks restored but integrated with new high-rise developments. This allowed the sense of place and history of area to be retained while development could proceed. The area houses new office developments, as well as a combination of old and new mixed-use developments, with shops, offices, and eating and entertainment outlets. Areas along the pedestrian malls and open spaces were designated for outdoor refreshment to add to the vitality and night life of the area. About 200 units—half of the old buildings—were conserved. Urban design guidelines for individual parcels were made known to potential tenderers. During the implementation stage, the URA played a key role in coordinating inputs from other government departments and statutory boards, and facilitating dialogues between private developers, architects and the various regulatory bodies involved. The objective of the URA's coordination efforts was to ensure consistency of design along the mall, despite different portions being constructed by different parties. While some streets and backlanes were glassed over for weather protection, and lifts and escalators were added, one can still experience the feeling of walking through the old shophouses.

China Square thus presents an innovative example of how to achieve the twin objectives of maximising land use to create a modern business city while keeping the historical and architectural heritage.

Greater Public Involvement (2001 to 2010)

The spirit of greater public consultation that had begun especially in the late 1990s was to take full shape in the 21st century, a reflection of larger shifts in society towards a more engaged citizenry, and recognition that the authorities do not have a monopoly of wisdom. These shifts reflected a citizenry searching for a sense of collective past and a shared identity, seeking to make a difference to the future through individual and collective roles.

The involvement of expert groups was clearly signaled by 1999 when a joint review of conservation guidelines was undertaken by the URA and the Singapore Institute of Architects (SIA). This venture into consultation was taken further in 2000, when a Concept Plan Review was initiated. Focus groups comprising citizens from various walks of life (including professionals, interest groups, academia and grassroots) were convened to discuss urban planning issues such as "identity versus intensive use of land" (URA, 2000). Amongst other recommendations, the group suggested more sustained engagement with the public through the establishment of an independent heritage conservation trust.

In response, the Minister for National Development announced the setting up of a Conservation Advisory Panel (CAP) in 2002, to give inputs on built heritage proposals submitted by the URA, propose buildings for conservation, and promote greater public education and understanding of gazetted built heritage (URA, 2002a). The first CAP comprised 15 members from varied backgrounds, including the building industry, media, medicine, education, arts and heritage, and has since expanded to include heritage property owners.

Another outcome of the consultation process was the launch in 2002 of Identity Plans by the URA (URA, 2002b). These plans acknowledged the importance of retaining places with a sense of history and identity. Fifteen areas were identified for study, grouped into four clusters: Old World Charm (Balestier, Tanjong Katong, Jalan Besar, Joo Chiat/East Coast Road); Urban Villages (Anak Bukit, Jalan Leban, Thomson Village, Springleaf and Coronation areas); Southern Ridges & Hillside Villages (Morse Road and Gillman Village areas); and Rustic Coast (Punggol Point/Coney island, Changi Village, Pasir Ris and Pulau Ubin). A Subject Group, with members drawn from different walks of life, was established for each cluster to study proposals in depth, conduct dialogue sessions with stakeholders and consider public feedback.

Consultation now occurred at two broad levels. At a macro level, there is broad consultation regarding which areas deserve to be conserved. At a micro level, there is discussion with individual owners regarding conservation of their units, specific restoration work to be undertaken, and any concerns they may have. The net result of this increase in public involvement was that the number of buildings gazetted for conservation increased by a quarter (about 1,400 buildings), and simultaneously, more buildings were restored (about 4,200 out of 7,000 gazetted buildings).

Conservation Projects

Perhaps the best way to engage in a discussion of how well conservation efforts are progressing is to examine specific projects. Below, I draw examples from historic districts, black-and-white bungalows, and secondary development areas, and foreground different issues and solutions that were at play in their conservation.

Historic Districts

The Historic Districts, originally gazetted on 7 July 1989, comprised Chinatown, Little India, Kampong Glam, Emerald Hill, Cairnhill, Boat Quay and Clarke Quay. Today, the latter two, together with Robertson Quay, form the Historic District called "Singapore River", while Emerald Hill and Cairnhill are part of the residential historic districts. The principles underlying the URA's conservation of historic districts like these are: to retain and enhance the existing activities which are a part of the historical and cultural heritage; to restore buildings of historical and architectural significance; to improve the physical environment; to retain traditional trades while introducing new, compatible ones; to incorporate new features that enhance the identity of the place; and to involve both public and private sectors in carrying out conservation projects (URA, 1995).

Singapore River

The three main areas comprising the Singapore River—Boat Quay, Clarke Quay and Robertson Quay—total 85 hectares and stretch over the 2.9–kilometre length of the river (URA, 1992). Each area contains distinct architecture, differentiated land-use patterns and diverse histories. Near the mouth of the river are several iconic buildings such as The Fullerton Hotel (previously the General Post Office building). Across the river is Empress Place, around which are some of the most historic landmarks of the city—Raffles' Landing Site, Victoria Theatre and Concert Hall, the Asian Civilisations Museum and The Arts House (formerly Old Parliament House).

Most eye-catching are the distinctive godowns and shophouses, vernacular architecture that blends "Malaccan, European, Chinese and Indian styles" (URA, 1991). Besides these heritage buildings, nine unique bridges span the river—from Cavenagh Bridge at the mouth of Singapore River to Kim Seng Bridge almost three kilometres upstream. Beyond Boat Quay, where the river narrows into an "s" bend, is Clarke Quay, flanked by rows of shophouses and some warehouses. Now managed by CapitaLand, a collection of restaurants, clubs and entertainment outlets characterises the area. Further upstream is Robertson Quay, offering a more tranquil ambience with its wine bars, alfresco dining places, hotels and arts establishments, several of which have been adapted for reuse from the warehouses. Examples include the Singapore Tyler Print Institute which houses a printmaking workshop, art gallery and paper mill, and the Singapore Repertory Theatre.

These modern recreational and entertainment facilities mask the early origins of the river and its trade activities, which were dominated by the Hokkiens and Teochews. To accommodate trade and the rapid growth of Chinese immigrants, two- and three-story shophouses were first built in the 1840s, though most were built in the 1920s and 1930s. Many underwent significant renovations after World War II.

The shophouses along the Singapore River have distinctive architectural features designed during Raffles' time. Specific features conceptualised by Raffles include the five-foot ways in front of shophouses which facilitated trade and pedestrian traffic, and offered shelter (Beamish *et al.*, 1985). Many shophouses along the riverfront are also distinguished by their third-story verandahs, which call to mind the viewing galleries of European riverside residences. However, many of the shophouses built from the 1940s to the 1970s were much simpler. Construction was more often in concrete rather than the original timber, and simple rectangular windows lacked plaster decoration.

The godowns were first built during the 1830s along the south bank of the river, often by merchants who had no legal land rights. The early buildings were therefore not architectural masterpieces, but did represent a marriage of east and west. Many were owned by prominent Chinese merchants like Tan Che Sang (one of the earliest merchants from Malacca to come to Singapore in 1819) and Tan Kah Kee. Even the early Europeans owned space, for example, Alexander Laurie (founder of Singapore's first European trading house in 1820) and Riley, Hargreaves & Co.

Due to neglect over the years, the shophouses and godowns became slums, and the waters became polluted. Trading activities led to the development of other related industries such as shipbuilding and repair, which were co-located in the same expanse of river, and added to the pollution. By the 1980s, there were many vacant buildings requiring restoration, and attracting suitable tenants posed a challenge.

In 1986, the STPB-commissioned report made a case for the Singapore River to be a "superb national asset" because it is a "locally used, active, domestic district and a bustling transportation segment" (Lipp *et al.*, 1986). The STPB and the Ministry of Trade and Industry announced their readiness to develop new facilities for entertainment, shopping, hotel and cultural activities to revitalise the area. Since its gazetting as a conservation area in 1989, the shophouses and warehouses have been carefully restored. These efforts have drawn the most public attention in the entire Singapore River conservation exercise.

On the other hand, infrastructural efforts have often gone unnoticed, such as the strengthening of the riverwall and refurbishing of the bridges. Other conservation efforts include the introduction of street furniture (public sculptures and statues) and lighting up the river.

Several conserved buildings along the Singapore River give the waterfront its abiding character. These include the grand old post office which has become Fullerton Building, the Waterboat House, Clifford Pier, Customs House and Change Alley Aerial

Plaza. Conserving these buildings was not straightforward. For example, many developers were keen to buy the land, but none of them wanted the original buildings as they had limited space and no carpark. The case of Fullerton Building illustrates this.

Named after the first Governor of the Straits Settlements, Fullerton Building was the symbol of the colonial government's vision for a classically monumental civic district. Designed by Keyes and Dowdeswell and built in 1928, the building used to house the General Post Office, the Exchange, the Chamber of Commerce and the Singapore Club. The URA packaged the eight-storey landmark with a reclaimed waterfront site across the road to address the issue of limited space and the need for carparks (The Straits Times, 1996). It guided the developer around some constraints such as the tunnel through which mail from ships was brought to the post office. This was eventually integrated into the foyer area of the basement ballroom. Another unique feature of the building is its vaulted coffered ceiling in a fourth-storey room, which was converted into a function room with balconies overlooking the atrium. The rooftop lighthouse that used to guide ships into Singapore's port was enlarged to accommodate a restaurant.

Black-and-White Bungalows

The iconic black-and-white bungalow is so called because the timber structures, windows and doors of these standalone houses are painted black while the infill plaster panels are white. They are characterised by verandahs located along the front and sides of the house, a symmetrical layout with three bays across the front, a carriage porch on the ground floor, minimal ornamentation, and broad, overhanging hipped roofs (Teh *et al.*, 2004). They are essentially single-storey houses raised about two feet from the ground on small pillars or timber posts, which helps to enhance ventilation.

Built from the 1900s to 1920s, these bungalows earned conservation status from late 1991 onwards. The early bungalows are a blend of mock Tudor and Malay kampong houses. Some say they were inspired by the sprawling suburbs of England.

The early bungalows catered to the Europeans, particularly the British colonial officers, and later the rich Chinese too. The black-and-whites thus came to represent social distinction. The distinctiveness of the architectural style was matched by the large compounds surrounding these houses, much of it external garden space. Today, bungalows gazetted for conservation may be found in areas such as Dalvey Estate, Nassim Road, Chatsworth Road, Draycott Drive, Pepys Road, and Mount Faber Road.

733 Mountbatten Road

An example of an award-winning house is 733 Mountbatten Road (URA, 2004). This single-storey Early Style bungalow was built in 1927, with an outhouse added in 1957. In 1999, it was bought by the Ang family, with the aim of turning it into a multi-generational home consisting of three separate wings and a common family wing. The restoration and integration of a new two-storey extension took three years to complete. The restored bungalow was recognised with a 2008 UNESCO Asia-Pacific Heritage Award for Cultural Heritage Conservation, specifically for innovation (UNESCO, 2008). The jury, comprising 12 international experts, found that the contemporary additions had successfully added floor space while retaining the original building. The spatial arrangement and massing of the new building in relation to the historic bungalow also created an appropriate balance between the old and new.

Secondary Development Areas

Secondary development areas are areas outside the central city district which developed partly as a result of the crowdedness of the city center, and which have established their own distinct identities. They represent a significant stage in Singapore's urban development in the 1900s to 1940s, and form the transitional residential areas between homes in the historic districts and residences in the contemporary new towns and suburbs. Secondary development areas are characterised by shophouses and terrace houses, and include areas like Joo Chiat, Balestier and Tiong Bahru.

Joo Chiat

The area called Joo Chiat includes Joo Chiat Road, Joo Chiat Terrace, Joo Chiat Place, Everitt Road, Koon Seng Road and Tembeling Road, plus the stretch of East Coast Road from Marshall Road to Joo Chiat Road. In 1991, 518 buildings in Joo Chiat were gazetted for conservation, and in July 1993, Joo Chiat was designated a "Conservation Area" (URA, 2008). The first phase of gazetting saved the mainly two-storey shophouses and terrace houses of the Transitional, Late and Art Deco styles from demolition.

In the early 20th century, Peranakan landowner and trader Chew Joo Chiat bought the tract of land originally made up largely of coconut plantations (Hamilton, 1995). In the 1920s and 1930s, residences began to appear as the Peranakans moved from the city center to the eastern part of the island on account of crowding. As the area continued to grow as a middle class suburb in the post-World War I years, shops, hawkers and other service providers thrived. The successful traders began to build their own shophouses, and the more decorative and ornate styles apparent today may be attributed to the construction of that period (especially between 1918 and 1930). Another characteristic, particularly of the Late-style Peranakan shophouse, is the narrow and usually elaborate and embellished façade that belies the depth and spaciousness of the residence. Interiors are long and narrow, and in order to ensure there is adequate air and light, airwells were constructed internally. Walls were covered by mosaic and tiles imported from 19th century England; balustrades and doors sported fine wood carvings. Many of the motifs were of mythical figures, flowers and birds.

Conservation guidelines today have allowed some flexibility, even permitting rear extensions of shophouses up to a maximum of five storeys (Teo *et al.*, 1985). Owners of conservation bungalows are also allowed to have new extensions within their compounds subject to planning controls for the area. They may divide the inside areas of their bungalows into apartments for sale or rent as long as the external façades are kept intact.

To attract owners to the cause of conservation, government assistance is offered to owners of conservation buildings in the Joo Chiat and Mountbatten Conservation Areas in these forms: the development charge payable and the provision of carparks and payment of carpark deficiency charges will be waived if conservation guidelines are fully complied with and the conservation work completed in accordance with approved plans. Owners can also apply to the Tenants' Compensation Board to recover their tenanted rent-control buildings; and owners facing difficulty in finding alternative accommodation for their old tenant may approach HDB for assistance (URA, 1994).

The URA-sanctioned possibility of rear extension has given Joo Chiat a new lease of life. Lotus at Joo Chiat is a key example. The development showcases the restoration of a row of 18 two-storey Peranakan shophouses of the Late style fronting Joo Chiat Place. The owner, Casuarina Properties Pte Ltd, chose to keep the entire row and build a new four-storey block with 32 apartments and basement carpark at the rear. The rear of the shophouses was turned into a beautiful second frontage with green-glazed tile canopies and ornamental gateposts. They open onto a beautifully landscaped garden complete with playground, swimming pool and pavilion. The new apartment block has moldings and panels similar in design to those of the shophouses, creating a synergy between old and new.

Another successful attempt at blending the new and the old is the adaptive reuse of traditional shophouses for modern contemporary living. A number of terrace houses on Koon Seng Road have witnessed this trend. Remaining untouched in the front and back according to URA guidelines, these shophouses have been radically reconfigured internally. One such house is 7 Koon Seng Road, where the ingenious synthesis of traditional design and modern décor can be seen in features such as a mini rock-pond in the airwell, a studio tucked into the top floor of the shophouse and abundant use of Malaccan carvings (Seow, 1973).

In 2002, Joo Chiat was identified as a site for further deliberation by the URA. Following consultations, additional shophouses were recommended for conservation. On 1 December 2003, 191 buildings of the simple Modern style were gazetted for conservation.

The URA also undertook detailed consultations with owners of 228 buildings located in the study area in an attempt to convince them to join efforts to conserve their buildings. At the end of the consultation exercise, the owners of 58 buildings agreed to conservation whereas those of 71 buildings objected. No response was received from the owners of 99 buildings. The results of the consultation exercise were then assessed in a comprehensive manner, along with other criteria such as the historical and architectural significance of the buildings, rarity and contribution to the environment. In the end, the URA shortlisted 100 out of the 228 buildings for conservation. These were deemed the most critical to the heritage character of the area.

Controversy, Contestation and Closure

In many parts of the world, urban heritage conservation raises issues that are often controversial, sometimes heavily contested, occasionally without closure. Singapore is no exception. The controversies and contestations bear testimony to the fact that Singaporeans care about their places, have alternative ideas, and are willing to speak up, in order that their voices may be heard. In this section, I will highlight just one case: the highly controversial demolition of the National Library (2004).

National Library

The National Library now stands on Victoria Street, a symbol of the new Singapore, with its sophisticated technology, sensitivity to green architecture, integration of reading material, public talks, research services and more. The plans to demolish its predecessor building, a low-rise red-bricked architecturally nondescript building, had drawn out passionate individuals and civil society groups who protested plans to pull down the building. The myriad views from the public were a demonstration of a sense of place and a sense of identity at its most ardent in Singapore. These sentiments, alas, had to run up against pragmatic planning needs.

The old National Library at Stamford Road was built between 1957 and 1960. Designed by the British architect Lionel Bintley, of the Public Works Department, the reinforced concrete-framed structure with brick walls was said to reflect the red-brick era of British architecture in the 1950s. Not everyone liked it back then though, for some thought it failed to harmonize with the "aesthetically pleasing and dignified National Museum" next to it (URA, 2002c). Nevertheless, the building became a popular destination for young people from the 1960s to the 1980s, especially given the concentration of schools in the vicinity.

In 1987, a Heritage Link Study was commissioned by the STPB, and a panel of foreign consultants was brought in to consider how to revitalise the Heritage Link area, demarcated as the Civic and Cultural District by the URA in 1988. A key component of the widely-publicised plans for the District was the relocation of the National Library. A dialogue with the Minister for National Development was organised on 28 May 1988, where invited professionals such as planners, architects, real estate developers, property consultants and engineers could share their views of the Civic and Cultural District Masterplan (The Straits Times, 1991). During the dialogue, the proposed demolition of the National Library to create a clear view of Fort Canning Hill from Bras Basah Park was discussed.

In 1992, the URA held a public exhibition on the Revised Civic and Cultural District Masterplan, in which a one-way Fort Canning Tunnel was publicised for the first time. The tunnel would enter the hill at the existing National Library site and emerge at Penang Road. Its purpose was to help direct heavy traffic away from the Marina to the Orchard area. Work on the tunnel would begin when the National Library had been relocated to the former Raffles Girls' Primary School nearby.

By late 1998, the Singapore Management University (SMU) had begun to publicise its plans for a new city campus in Bras Basah. It would occupy six parcels of land, including the National Library's Stamford Road site and the former Raffles Girls' Primary School site. SMU organised a public symposium to gather feedback for its campus masterplan. The turnout was overwhelming. Emotions ran high as attendees heard about the definitive decision to demolish the red-bricked building. The next day, the national newspapers carried the headlines "National Library to go" on the front page, together with a special report featuring the views of generations of library users, for whom the building held deep meaning and fond memories (Kwok *et al.*, 2000).

In an effort to provide an alternative, architect Tay Kheng Soon put forward his version of a Masterplan for SMU in January 2000 (Balamurugan, 2004). He proposed sinking Bras Basah Park, retaining the course of Stamford Road, and re-routing the tunnel in order to save the National Library. Various government agencies studied the idea carefully as well as another option of expanding Stamford Road. Each posed challenges which persuaded them that the original solution was still the most practical.

First, keeping Stamford Road, indeed expanding it without building the tunnel, would not improve the traffic and pedestrian friendliness of the area. The road is bounded by the National Museum, and expansion can only be achieved by encroaching into Bras Basah Park, which would require Stamford Canal to be reconstructed and all the existing trees cut down. Even if this were technically achievable, a wider road would not achieve the goal of reducing traffic in the Bras Basah area. The Fort Canning Tunnel, on the other hand, would help divert traffic going to Orchard Road away from Stamford Road, thus reducing traffic volume in front of the museum and SMU. The suggestion to have the tunnel dive more steeply to avoid the foundation of the National Library was evaluated to be technically not feasible as the stretch of road was too short and the library structure was 10 m below ground level, resulting in a very steep gradient that would pose safety concerns.

From February to April 2000, members of the public called for the URA to reconsider its plans to demolish the building. On 7 March 2000, the Minister for National Development Mah Bow Tan announced in Parliament that the National Library building would be demolished (The Straits Times, 1999). In acknowledgement of the groundswell of public sentiment, he assured the House that the URA had not ignored the public outcry, for there had been "extensive public and private discussions on the issue since 1988 when URA formulated the Civic District Master Plan". In fact, he said, there had been general support for removing the library then.

Today, the tunnel is in place and the red-bricked building lives only in memories. The National Library building in Stamford Road closed its doors on 31 March 2004. In an effort to keep alive some of the memories of the National Library, some of the well-loved red bricks were brought to the new building in Victoria Street. The old path from the National Library to Fort Canning and an old gatepost were also kept.

The public outcry over the demolition of the National Library demonstrated how Singaporeans are not apathetic, unconcerned citizens. Whether it is as private individuals, as members of interest groups, or as professionals, Singaporeans stepped forward with views, in order that the place they call home may be shaped the way they think fit. Sometimes, these counter-voices are heard and the views acted upon. At other times, the contrary views are just too different to be accommodated. At yet other times, compromises are made. In a microcosmic way, the negotiations and decision-making in the world of urban heritage conservation reflect a larger social compact evolving, with multiple voices, sometimes testing the limits, tugging at the fringes, but often focused on what is best for Singapore.

A Future for the Past?

With recognition of the importance of heritage comes the responsibility of deciding what constitutes heritage, which buildings and areas deserve to be conserved and preserved, and what can be demolished to make way for new developments. What new uses might old buildings be put to, whose views are to be taken into consideration, and whose responsibility it is to upkeep the buildings—these are all issues that need to be addressed. Further, with a more vocal and engaged citizenry, the task has become more difficult.

The ideals of conserving Singapore's heritage have to be translated into practical actions. The URA's step-by-step approach, honed through the years, is a methodical one. It begins with pilot projects, the successful completion of which injects "a greater sense of confidence among owners, developers and professionals for conservation projects" (Ler Seng Ann, Group Director of the URA's Conservation and Services Department). According to him, these pilot schemes also "demonstrate the proper approach, method and technique for restoration of old buildings, and become benchmarks for the private sector in their restoration works".

Beyond the pilot projects, the URA introduced the Sale of Sites Programme to involve the public and private sectors. Since the mid-1980s, more than 900 conservation buildings have been released for restoration through the Sale of Sites Programme. This was in acknowledgement of the importance of working with the private sector to build a successful conservation programme in land-scarce Singapore. To attract private sector involvement, the government offered incentives, lifted rent control, allowed for change of use, and provided much-needed infrastructure.

In more recent years, URA has also attempted to adopt a more consultative approach, for example, through the use of focus groups to seek public feedback, the establishment of the Conservation Advisory Panel, and the involvement of owners. Beyond the work of conservation itself, URA also seeks to promote the outcomes of conservation, educate the public about its value, and reward those who undertake the conservation and/or restoration work. To recognize efforts, organising exhibitions, talks and the annual Architectural Heritage Awards now constitute part of its work.

Public Sentiment and Professional Evaluation

If the views of Singaporeans, architects and urban planners, tourists and expatriates living in Singapore are anything to go by, there is much support for conservation, though it is often tempered by a sense of pragmatism. There is much admiration for what has been achieved, but not without some dissatisfaction.

Young people, sometimes criticised for lacking in a sense of roots and belonging, have spoken up in favour of conservation often and wholeheartedly, with some claiming that "To know where we're going to, we must remember where we came from". Even stronger evidence of the value placed on conservation buildings may be seen in several examples of young entrepreneurs who have chosen to set up businesses in restored shophouses. In Kampong Glam, beyond the somewhat bohemian Haji Lane, along North Bridge Road, is Jamal Kazura, a revamped traditional Arab Muslim perfumery run by the younger generation carrying on the family business. Their choice of the heritage buildings to bring the old business into the future is premised on an evaluation of the appropriateness of the environment. Similarly, young entrepreneur Kenny Leck and partner Karen Wai chose a shophouse originally built in the 1910s for their book business. Nestled among the century-old clan associations in Club Street, they run BooksActually, one of Singapore's leading independent bookstores. However, the realities of land scarcity and the pragmatism of a people are also often evident, and Singapore's small size and the importance of building our economy are often cited in a bid to understand the need for redevelopment.

The duality of views expressed about whether to conserve or to redevelop is similarly evident in public assessments about the outcomes of conservation. There are certainly appreciative members of the public who applaud the efforts. Some admire the black-and-white bungalows, praising Rochester Park, for example, as "a charming idea". Others appreciate the willingness to conserve where land value is high. Yet others applaud the value that young Singaporeans place in conserved apartments, as in Tiong Bahru, where many have invested time, resources and energy to purchase conservation units and keep faith with heritage in their interior design. And finally, there are those who enjoy the architecture and treatment of the conserved buildings.

But, equally, there are those who are critical. Those disapproving of Chinatown and Clarke Quay, for example, frown on what they perceive to be compromises to the authenticity of the sites. For example,

> Of Chinatown: "Sometimes they spoil the character by giving too much free hand. The net result is a whole splash of colors like rainbow on it. That's not quite conservation. Conservation has got to have a subdued look, like patina on copper, it ages beautifully. The character's not quite there."

> Of Clarke Quay: "…the "eco-umbrellas" … take away from the character of the old buildings around Clarke Quay."

Others complain about the extent of commercialisation, using Chijmes as the example: "It's just way too commercialised. It really changed the character of the place. It used to be like a grand duchess. But with all this commercial activity, there's no meaning and no remaining true to character. Singaporeans need to touch base with their cultural roots." And certainly, there are those who lament the loss of iconic buildings: "They should have kept National Library, National Theatre and the Van Kleef Aquarium which were post-independence Singapore icons."

Enthusiastic, pragmatic, supportive, appreciative, critical—the voices are myriad, whether from individuals, interest groups, or professionals. Perhaps this will always be so to varying degrees, for multiple values will always be at stake.

Celebrating Successes

Notwithstanding local debates, the URA's efforts have won international recognition. In July 2006, the URA's conservation programme won the Asia-Pacific Urban Land Institute (ULI) Award for Excellence. Singapore was the only Global Award winner from the Asia-Pacific region.

The case made for Singapore's award was built on the following submission. First, within a relatively short timeframe of 20 years, Singapore had managed to designate 6,563 buildings for conservation, located in 86 conservation areas, covering 204 hectares of land. The majority of the buildings that were in dilapidated condition have been fully restored while the rest have been kept in good condition. Second, a "win-win situation" had been achieved for all stakeholders. The unique character and beautiful architecture had been kept, while innovative solutions had been found to allow a wide variety of new uses, from residential to commercial, cultural and entertainment. Third, successful public-private partnership had been forged, and a market-oriented approach to conservation had been achieved. Close consultation with professional bodies and the community and a high degree of public support was evident. And finally, the Conservation Programme has garnered international recognition: Brunei, China, Hong Kong, Indonesia, Japan and Malaysia have come to Singapore to learn about its approach. Additionally, Indonesia had specifically asked the URA to conduct a course on conservation for its officials, while Thailand and Cambodia (through UNESCO) invited the URA to share Singapore's urban conservation efforts at their respective conferences.

Given the interest from other countries in Singapore's conservation efforts, perhaps Singapore has the potential to offer a heritage conservation model in the region.

Looking Ahead

Efforts are under way to extend the scope of conservation to include familiar landmarks that possess aesthetic, engineering, design and historical merits. These may include park and garden structures such as gazebos, pavilions and bridges, colonial military structures like forts and gun batteries, and infrastructural or utility structures such as bridges, gates and water towers. One of the most recognised structures is the cast-iron gazebo and bandstand in the Botanic Gardens, most recently named a UNESCO World Heritage Site.

The move elicits a sense that there are few buildings left as obvious targets for further conservation, resulting in the turn towards considering discrete elements of architecture. Individual structures, however, are abundant, and clarity of criteria will be necessary to ensure that not everything is preserved simply because of age. Further, if preservation is to consider the integrity of the surrounding environment, the challenge would be great for small independent structures to be integrated with new developments around them.

Similarly, it is perhaps because most of the notable buildings and areas have already been earmarked for conservation that public attention in the mid-2000s has turned to more recent architecture—large, multi-storey buildings of the post-independence period. While some consider the architecture of many modern and post-modern buildings unremarkable and undeserving of conservation, others recognise them as markers of an era and sites of collective memory. Often, members of the public who appeal for conservation are not the owners who seek to realise or maximise the value of their properties. At the same time, owners of strata title properties often have different views about what to do with the same building.

One example of these dilemmas is public disquiet over a few 1970s condominiums that had succumbed to the en bloc sales fever in 2006 and 2007. Some argued that Singapore would lose its sense of familiarity and identity if even relatively recent buildings were demolished. Yet, to others, keeping individual buildings is not important, particularly when they are not architecturally distinctive, and hold only personal sentimental value. Given myriad views that will inevitably be expressed about any one site or approach to conservation, it is clear that decisions cannot be made on the basis of consensus views.

The URA's task hence is to balance the interests of sectors that value conservation and owners who have a certain right over their buildings and an expectation, for example, to retirement funds that could come with en bloc sales. To address these issues, the URA hopes to encourage more public-private-people sector collaboration.

Still, the big challenge remains of how to handle the conservation of large modern buildings. Here, examples set in other countries may be instructive. In New York City, for example, land values are much higher than in Singapore, but through the vision of enlightened owners like that of Seagram Building (owned by a German American firm, RFR Holdings LLC), the 38-storey monument of the International Style was given a new lease of life. RFR volunteered to conserve the Mies van der Rohe building in 1989, turning it into successful office space with an impressive tenant roster. Another example is Lever House by Skidmore, Owings and Merrill, which became a designated landmark in 1982, and was also bought over by RFR Holdings LLC. RFR announced a US$25-million restoration programme in 1998, believing the building to be a trophy landmark building, deserving restoration. As a result, what was once the headquarters of a consumer giant has now been turned into a successful multi-tenanted building which, together with Seagram, remains an icon for Modernism, not just in New York City but worldwide.

Alternatively, trust funds have been established in various countries, often as community-based efforts, to support conservation. There are different models. For example, the Japan National Trust for Cultural and Natural Heritage Conservation is a non-profit, tax-exempt, public-benefit corporation supported by its members and contributions from industry, government and private foundations, and is under the Ministry of Transport. In the United Kingdom, the National Trust is a registered charity independent of the government, reliant only on the generosity of 3.5 million subscribing members and other supporters. In the United States, the National Trust for Historic Preservation is a private, non-profit membership organisation that includes advocacy and education among its roles. There lies a possibility of an equivalent development in Singapore.

While there remain challenges for the conservation of large modern buildings, it is important not to forget the many smaller, unique buildings that have already been conserved. It is critical to ensure that these buildings are kept in good condition, remain economically viable, and that their social and economic vibrancy is improved. While we need to "make places", we also need to "manage" them. Making places includes restoring buildings and providing supporting infrastructure for them to be physically viable. Managing places means, amongst other things, ensuring that there is interesting information on the history of the building for public consumption, balancing the types of trades to ensure a historically appropriate yet economically viable mix, facilitating a vibrant social calendar, as well as encouraging residents and owners to organise themselves to develop that sense of identity and pride, and foster the viability of trades. Whereas place-making purely in terms of restoring the physical infrastructure has been successfully carried out with many buildings, place-management in terms of cultivating the social, cultural and economic life of place now warrants fuller attention. Indeed, some would argue that a place is not made if it is only physically restored; a place is made if it is lived. This form of place-making cannot be legislated or fully managed. Providing information about the history of places is one thing; getting people to be interested in that history is quite another.

References

Abrams, C., Kobe, S., Koenigsberger, O. (1980) Growth and urban renewal in Singapore. *Habitat International*, **5(1/2)**: 85–127.

Balamurugan, A. (2004) *Singapore Infopedia — National Library Building, Stamford Road*, http://infopedia.nlb.gov.sg/articles/SIP_661_2004-12-27.html, accessed 27 August 2008.

Beamish, J., Ferguson, J. (1985) *A History of Singapore Architecture — The Making of a City*. Graham Brash (Pte) Ltd, Singapore.

Crooks Michell Peacock Stewart. (1971) *The United Nations Urban Renewal and Development Project, Singapore. Part Four: The Central Area*. Crooks Michell Peacock Stewart, Sydney.

Hamilton, S. (1995). Spotlight on Singapore: Houses as History. *Silver Kris, April*, 58–62.

Kwok, K.W., Ho, W.H., Tan, K.L. (eds). (2000) *Memories and the National Library: Between Forgetting and Remembering*. Singapore, Singapore Heritage Society.

Lipp, G.E., Wimberly, G.J., Jenkins, C.H., Collins, R., Sugaya, H.B. (1986) *Tourism Development in Singapore*. Singapore Tourist Promotion Board, Singapore.

Seow, E.J. (1973) *Architectural Development in Singapore*, Unpublished PhD Thesis, University of Melbourne, Melbourne, Australia.

Teh, L.Y., Goh, M., Quah, S.H., Tan, H.J., Bay, P. (eds). (2004) *Architectural Heritage, Singapore: Architectural Heritage Awards 1994 to 2004: Award-Winning Projects by Singapore-Registered Architects*. Urban Redevelopment Authority, Singapore.

Teo, S.E., Savage, V. (1985) Singapore Landscape: A Historical Overview of Housing Change, *Singapore Journal of Tropical Geography*, **6(1)**, 48–63.

The Straits Times, Decision made 'after all options were considered', 8 May 1991.

The Straits Times, Fullerton Building to be redeveloped as top-notch hotel, 27 July 1996.

The Straits Times, National Library building to go, 14 March 1999.

UNESCO Bangkok. (2008) 2008 Jury Commendation for Innovation: 733 Mountbatten Road, http://www.unescobkk.org/culture/wh/asia-pacific-heritage-awards/previous-heritageawards-2000–2013/2008/award-winners/2008jc/, accessed 27 August 2008.

URA (Urban Redevelopment Authority). (1991) *A Future with A Past — Saving Our Heritage*. Urban Redevelopment Authority, Singapore.

URA (Urban Redevelopment Authority). (1992) *Singapore River, Development Guide Plan, Draft*. Urban Redevelopment Authority, Singapore.

URA (Urban Redevelopment Authority). (1993) *Objectives, Principles and Standards for Preservation and Conservation*. Urban Redevelopment Authority, Singapore.

URA (Urban Redevelopment Authority). (1994) *Secondary Settlements—Conservation Guidelines for Joo Chiat Conservation Area*. Urban Redevelopment Authority, Singapore.

URA (Urban Redevelopment Authority). (1995) *Conservation guidelines for historic districts: Boat Quay, Chinatown, Kg Glam, Little India*. Urban Redevelopment Authority, Singapore.

URA (Urban Redevelopment Authority). (2000) *Concept Plan Review, Focus Group Consultation, Final Report on Identity versus Intensive Use of Land*. Urban Redevelopment Authority, Singapore.

URA (Urban Redevelopment Authority). (2002a) *URA Corporate Plan Seminar*, 8 April, URA, Singapore.

URA (Urban Redevelopment Authority). (2002b) *URA launches Identity Plan for 15 areas in Singapore*, http://www.ura.gov.sg/pr/text/pr02–42.html, accessed 15 August 2008.

URA (Urban Redevelopment Authority). (2002c) *Parks and Waterbodies Plan and Identity Plan. Subject Group Report on Old World Charm*. Urban Redevelopment Authority, Singapore.

URA (Urban Redevelopment Authority). (2004) Architectural Heritage Awards—No.733 Mountbatten Road, http://www.ura.gov.sg/uol/publications/corporate/aha/2004/733-Mountbatten-Road.aspx, accessed 27 August 2008.

URA (Urban Redevelopment Authority). (2008) *Areas and Maps: Joo Chiat Conservation Area*, http://www.ura.gov.sg/conservation/jooc.htm, accessed 3 July 2008.

CHAPTER 14

Public Housing and Community Development: Planning for Urban Diversity in a City-State[1]

Tan Ern Ser

Introduction

Over the last 50 years or so, Singapore's population has expanded from 2.07 million in 1970 to 5.47 million in 2014. More spectacularly, between 1990 and 2010, the population grew by about one million or more each decade. Correspondingly, the population density has also more than doubled from 3,538 per square km in 1970 to 7,615 in 2014 (DOS, 2014:v). This growth has necessitated and is reflected in the proliferation of high-rise apartments across the slightly more than 700 square km-island Republic. Most of these flats were built by the Housing and Development Board (HDB), Singapore's public housing authority. Indeed, official figures indicate that close to 82% of Singapore residents, comprising citizens and those granted permanent residency, live in HDB-built flats, while most of the rest reside in private condominium apartments or landed properties (DOS, 2014:v).

Moreover, notwithstanding the "public housing" label, which may convey a negative impression in some other social contexts, an overwhelming 97% of HDB dwellers live in "sold", as opposed to "rental" properties. Some 77% of residents in the "sold" units live in the larger flat type, ranging from four-room to executive apartments (HDB, 2014:15). These figures are the outcome respectively of the government's home ownership policy, as well as a manifestation of residential and social mobility, which has contributed to a visually homogeneous middle-class society in housing terms (Chua and Tan, 1995:4).

---

[1] This is a recast and expanded version of "The HDB Community: A Work in Progress" by Tan Ern Ser which first appeared in *Urbanization in Southeast Asia: Issues and Impacts* edited by Yap Kioe Sheng and Moe Thuzar (2012), pp. 190–204. Reproduced here with the kind permission of the publisher, Institute of Southeast Asian Studies, Singapore, <https://bookshop.iseas.edu.sg>.

However, beyond what is immediately observable, and as one gets closer to the ground and data on the profile of residents, it is obvious that the HDB towns, estates, and precincts house a rather heterogeneous population along the dimensions of ethnicity, religion, and even class. What then are the implications of heterogeneity for community building in Singapore, especially given that we are also dealing with an urban context where casual observations often convey the image of closed doors and lack of social interactions among neighbours, and thereby the apparent absence of community, despite people living in close proximity to one another?

Is Community Possible and Alive in the HDB Neighbourhood?

The transformation of the housing and urban landscape commenced in earnest in the 1960s to handle the massive resettlement of the population from kampongs or villages and overcrowded inner-city neighbourhoods with poor infrastructures and provision of utilities and sanitation amenities. While this programme had vastly enhanced the physical comforts of residents, it also involved the rupturing of old neighbourly ties and community, real or imagined.

Indeed, the notion of "loss of community" has been a common theme in the older sociological literature, both local and international (Hassan, 1976; Delanty, 2003). The feeling of nostalgia about community life during "kampong days", perceived positively to be characterised by communal solidarity, social integration, and sense of belonging and involvement (Hassan, 1976:260), is often captured in—or, more correctly, generated by—local popular drama series and writings. These contain an implicit message that it is worth recovering the traditional community life that was lost with the move from kampongs or villages to high-rise, urban living (cf. Delanty, 2003:25). Perhaps, it is also in this spirit that providing citizens with a roof over their heads has turned out to be not the HDB's only mission; the housing authority also aims at community building, a process which corresponds to and reinforces nation building in post-independence Singapore.

Wong and her colleagues (1997:443) observed that "the HDB's housing philosophy has evolved from the emphasis of the early 1960s on providing basic shelter to the present emphasis on providing a total living environment and supporting community development within the housing estates". They also noted that in "the concepts of neighbourhood and precinct planning, the provision of common spaces such as void decks, playgrounds and segmented corridors, have been introduced in order to encourage social interaction among residents who share common facilities", and that "HDB area officers are being trained in community relations and extensive co-operation is given to grass-roots organisations and voluntary agencies to help nurture a community spirit among the residents" (Wong et al. 1997:444).

But community-building involving the grafting of people from diverse locations into an urban context can be rather challenging, though not impossible. Wong and her colleagues (1997:444) pointed out that the popular perception is that community existed only in the "idyllic" village or small town, while the urban context, characterised by "the size, density and heterogeneity of the city [which] give rise to a generally impersonal competitive environment", spells the demise of community. Such a view is obviously untenable, given the weight of the evidence. They countered that "sociologists and urban anthropologists have long found the persistence of primary ties, informal groups and well-organised neighbourhoods" in the urban environment (Wong *et al.* 1997:444).

Somewhat similarly, Chua (1997:439) argued that while "the generalized sense of community as in the village is no longer possible", it is "now replaced by much more personalized sentiments localised at a particular void deck or in one's routine routes" in the neighbourhood. In other words, community is not quite dead, but merely reduced in scope and sphere of activities in the modernist, urban environment.

Whatever the form that the HDB community may evolve into in the future, we can expect a fair amount of government intervention, given its importance to nation building and social stability and mobilisation, through the HDB, to ensure that town layouts and amenities contribute towards facilitating social interactions and sense of belonging among residents. At the same time, the People's Association (PA), the government organisation responsible for community development, will continue to develop engagement platforms, as well as encourage ground-up initiatives, to promote social cohesion and ownership through creating opportunities for residents to do things together, be it participation in leisure activities or working on group projects to solve municipal problems (PA, 2014:26). However, whether the community building efforts can maintain the high degree of social cohesion that has already been achieved or, better still, even further strengthen the social fabric in a dynamic social landscape, depend to a large extent on the profile and community orientations of HDB residents, among other factors.

A Multidimensional HDB Social Landscape

One key aspect of the HDB's mission is to house a nation, not merely accommodate a population. It is expected to provide affordable housing to citizens, regardless of race and class, and to facilitate home ownership. This has served to "homogenise" Singapore visually, as well as transform Singapore into a showcase of a middle-class society, though, as noted earlier, heterogeneity is what actually characterised Singapore and the public housing, social landscape.

However the heterogeneity can be reconfigured by the people themselves, through a self-selection process, to produce segregated, homogeneous groupings within distinct geographical areas. Such an undesirable possibility prompted the HDB to consciously prevent the formation of ethnic enclaves via the "ethnic quota" policy and of class enclaves by locating mixed flat types within the same estate, precinct, and even apartment block. The HDB neighbourhood is therefore, within the limits imposed by the Singapore demographic composition—such as having a large ethnic Chinese majority—clearly a multidimensional social landscape. Besides being multiracial and multi-class, it is also multi-religious and multigenerational. With the stepping up of immigration in recent years, it has become more multi-national as well.[2]

The HDB towns, estates, and precincts[3] are obviously not all multidimensional to the same degree. For instance, in a comparison of HDB towns in 2008,[4] the Central Area, which is classified as a mature town,[5] was found to have the lowest median household income of S$2,979, while a young town like Punggol had the highest median income of S$6,569 (HDB 2010a:52). This income difference could be explained by the fact that the mature town has a higher proportion of elderly residents, who are likely to have less formal education and be economically inactive, and if employed, more likely to be in low skilled jobs, such as "cleaners or labourers" (HDB 2014:49).

Overall, it can be observed that a large majority of HDB residents live in middle-income housing, defined as "four-room or larger flat type". If we use flat type as a crude indicator of class, it can be inferred that the size of the middle class has grown considerably over the last 20 years, rising from 41.3% in 1987 to 77.0% in 2008 and dipping slightly to or perhaps stabilising at 76.3% in 2013 (Table 14.1).

Table 14.2, focusing on education level, also shows a significant increase in the size of the middle class. The proportion of HDB residents aged 15 or older who have attained polytechnic or equivalent diploma or university qualifications rose from 19.9% in 1998 to 31.4% in 2008 and 42.8% in 2013. The proportion with primary or no qualification was somewhat high at 30.5% in 2008, but declined sharply to 15.3% in 2013.

Table 14.3, focusing on occupation level, corresponds to a large extent with that of educational attainment, given the high correlation between these two variables. It can be seen that the proportion of HDB residents among the ranks of professionals, managers, executives, and technicians (PMETs), which may be classified

[2]A "permanent resident quota" policy was also introduced in 2010 to ensure that "no distinctive enclaves of immigrants" emerge on the HDB landscape (Fernandez, 2011:223).
[3]In this paper, "HDB towns, estates, and precincts" refer to the three levels of neighborhood size and organisation, while the term "HDB neighborhood" is used in a generic sense to refer to any of these levels.
[4]The data reported in this paper are primarily from the HDB Sample Household Survey 2008 and 2013 monographs. Figures on some dimensions found in the former are not available in the latter monograph.
[5]Mature towns refer to those built before the 1980s, while young towns are those developed in the 1990s and where construction of new apartments and amenities is still ongoing.

Table 14.1.   HDB residents by flat type (%).   *Source*: HDB, 2010a:14 and 2014:23.

Flat type	1987 %	1987 Cum.%	2008 %	2008 Cum.%	2013 %	2013 Cum.%
	HDB residents					
1-room	6.3		1.2		1.6	
2-room	7.0		2.2		2.8	
3-room	45.4		19.6		19.3	
4-room	29.0		41.0		41.1	
5-room	9.9	41.3	26.7	77.0	26.6	76.3
Executive	1.6		9.3		8.6	
HUDC	0.8		—		—	
Total	100.0		100.0		100.0	

Table 14.2.   Employed HDB residents aged 15 or older by education level (%).   *Source*: HDB, 2010a:25 and 2014:30.

Education level	1998 %	1998 Cum.%	2008 %	2008 Cum.%	2013 %	2013 Cum.%
	HDB residents					
No qualification	11.8	37.7	8.2	30.5	1.5	15.3
Primary	25.9		22.3		13.8	
Secondary	35.4		32.9		33.2	
Upper Secondary	6.9		4.5		8.7	
Polytechnic	10.7	19.9	15.3	31.4	19.0	42.7
University	9.2		16.1		23.7	
Others	0.1		0.7		0.1	
Total	100.0		100.0		100.0	

as middle-class occupations, has increased steadily from 40.4% in 1998 to 45.2% in 2008 and 50.6% in 2013. The latter figure indicates that one of every two HDB residents is middle class.

In regard to income, the indications for 2008 were that 20% of HDB households had income of S$8,000 or higher, while 25% earned below S$2,000 (Table 14.4). The overall picture shows clearly that there has been significant income mobility, though it also points to one of every four HDB households earning less than half of the median household income, and that 8.5%—many of which were "elderly" households—did not have any earned income.

Table 14.3.   Employed HDB resident aged 15 or older by occupation (%).   *Source*: HDB, 2014:30.

Occupation	1998 %	1998 Cum.%	2008 %	2008 Cum.%	2013 %	2013 Cum.%
		HDB residents				
Legislators, Senior Officials, & Managers	10.9		10.7		13.3	
Professionals	8.5	40.4	11.9	45.2	14.5	50.6
Associate Professionals & Technicians	21.0		22.6		22.8	
Clerical Workers	13.6		12.8		12.9	
Service & Sales Workers	12.7		12.6		11.8	
Production Workers	21.2		15.0		11.9	
Cleaners & Labourers	8.1		10.7		9.2	
Others	4.0		3.7		3.6	
Total	100.0		100.0		100.0	

Table 14.4.   Monthly household income from work of HDB residents (%). *Source*: HDB, 2010a:55.

Monthly household income (S$)	2003 %	2003 Cum.%	2008 %	2008 Cum.%
		HDB Residents		
No earned income	10.2		8.5	
Below 1,000	7.5	30.1	4.4	24.8
1,000–1,999	12.4		11.9	
2,000–2,999	17.8		12.3	
3,000–3,999	15.8		12.9	
4,000–4,999	9.3		10.1	
5,000–5,999	7.1		8.6	
6,000–6,999	6.3		6.2	
7,000–7,999	4.1		5.3	
8,000–8,999	2.0		4.4	
9,000–9,999	2.6	9.7	3.1	19.9
10,000 & above	5.1		12.4	
Total	100.0		100.0	

Tables 14.5 and 14.6 confirm that there is some intersection between age and class, using income and house type as crude indicators. It shows that in 2008, elderly households were more likely to be living in one-room or two-room rental flats, compared with non-elderly households: 14.6% and 2.9% respectively. By the same token,

Table 14.5. Flat type by elderly and non-elderly households, 2008 (%). *Source*: HDB, 2010a:62.

Flat type	Elderly %	Elderly Cum.%	Non-elderly %	Non-elderly Cum.%
1-room	7.0	14.6	0.8	2.9
2-room	7.6		2.1	
3-room	40.3		21.3	
4-room	30.2		39.3	
5-room	12.3	14.9	27.5	36.6
Executive	2.6		9.1	
Total	100.0		100.0	

Table 14.6. Monthly household income (S$) from work by elderly and non-elderly households, 2008 (%). *Source*: HDB, 2010a:64.

Monthly household income (S$)	Elderly %	Elderly Cum.%	Non-elderly %	Non-elderly Cum.%
No earned income	36.3	57.9	2.4	16.6
Below 1,000	7.4		3.0	
1,000–1,999	14.2		11.2	
2,000–2,999	9.5		13.2	
3,000–3,999	9.5		13.9	
4,000–4,999	5.3		11.2	
5,000–5,999	4.4		9.2	
6,000–6,999	3.7		6.7	
7,000–7,999	2.7		5.8	
8,000–8,999	2.1		4.7	
9,000–9,999	1.5		3.5	
10,000 & above	3.4		15.2	
Total	100.0		100.0	

Table 14.7. Monthly household income (S$) from work by ethnicity, 2008 (%).   *Source*: HDB, 2010a:55.

Monthly household income (S$)	Chinese		Malay		Indian	
	%	Cum.%	%	Cum.%	%	Cum.%
No earned income	8.8		6.6		8.1	
Below 1,000	4.2		5.3		4.9	
1,000–1,999	11.3	48.7	15.8	57.8	12.3	51.3
2,000–2,999	11.8		15.2		12.5	
3,000–3,999	12.6		14.9		13.5	
4,000–4,999	9.7		12.4		10.6	
5,000–5,999	8.5		8.8		8.8	
6,000–6,999	6.1		7.4		5.6	
7,000–7,999	5.4		4.1		5.4	
8,000–8,999	4.6		3.2		4.1	
9,000–9,999	3.4	21.7	1.7	9.5	2.2	18.5
10,000 & above	13.7		4.6		12.2	
Total	100.0		100.0		100.0	

57.9% of elderly households were found in the below-S$2,000 income bracket, compared with 16.6% in the case of non-elderly households. Significantly, slightly more than a third of elderly households had no earned income.

Another correlation to note is that between race and class—again using income as a crude indicator of class. Table 14.7 shows that in 2008, 57.8% of Malay households earned less than the median household income, compared with 48.7% for the Chinese, and 51.3% in the case of Indian households. On the upper segments of the income ladder, it can be observed that 21.7% of Chinese households earned S$8,000 or more in 2008, while the comparative figures for Malay and Indian households were 9.5% and 18.5% respectively.

The final diversity to be highlighted here is that of nationality. Currently, about two of every five persons living in Singapore are foreigners, including about half a million permanent residents, but excluding those who have become naturalised citizens (DOS, 2014:v). Unfortunately, I do not have the figures on the nationalities of HDB residents; hence, as a crude approximation, I shall refer to the Census 2010 data, which refer to the entire Singapore population. Table 14.8 shows the significant presence of residents hailing from East Asia (China, Hong Kong, and Macau), South Asia (India, Pakistan, Bangladesh, and Sri Lanka), and Southeast Asia, particularly Indonesia, and 0.7 per cent from Europe, North America, or Australia and New Zealand. The majority of non-Singapore born residents originated from Malaysia.

Table 14.8.   Resident population by place of birth, 2010.   *Source*: DOS, 2010.

Place of birth	%
Singapore	77.2
Malaysia	10.2
China, Hong Kong, Macau	4.6
South Asia	3.3
Indonesia	1.4
Other Asian countries	2.4
Europe	0.4
North America	0.2
Australia and New Zealand	0.1
Others	0.1
Total	100.0

These figures do resonate with casual observations of any heavy human traffic space, such as hawker centres, shopping malls, and bus terminals, in a HDB town regarding the diverse "nationality" composition of residents.

From the above analysis, the image we form of the HDB neighbourhood is that it is largely middle-class—broadly defined to include residents with tertiary qualifications, PMET occupations, or above median level household incomes—with small pockets of low or no earned income elderly households or ethnic minority residents living in one- or two-room rental flats (HDB 2014:xiv). However, the middle class, being a broad category, can be fairly heterogeneous itself.

Does Diversity Spell Social Tension and Conflict?

Having described the multidimensional diversity of the HDB resident population, a critical question to ask is which one of these scenarios best characterises the HDB neighbourhood: prevalence of social tension and conflict involving opposing values and interests; apparent presence of social harmony produced by strong state intervention in society; or the emergence of community brought about by the forging of social ties and the accumulation of social capital across the diverse social landscape?

Data from my (Tan, 2004:36–37) 2001 survey indicate that, among Singaporeans, 85% had "friends from lower income groups", while 11% said they did not. Slightly less impressive were the figures on having "friends from higher income groups". Seventy-seven percent had friends who are of a higher class than themselves, compared with 18% who did not. A high proportion of Singaporeans, 47%, and 60% of those who identified themselves as "lower class", also indicated that "successful people in Singapore tend to look down on the less successful ones".

With regard to inter-ethnic relations, 21% of Singaporeans indicated that they did not have "close friends of a different race". It was also shown that older people are less likely to have "close friends of a different race", compared with younger people. In addition, Singaporeans with lower education have fewer "close friends of a different race" than those with higher education. This finding is also true of the majority Chinese, compared with their counterparts among the ethnic minorities in Singapore, who are more likely to interact across ethnic lines (Tan, 2004: 38–39). The broad picture painted here is reinforced by a more recent survey which indicates that 23% of Singaporeans agreed that they "don't have much in common with Singaporeans of other races" (Tan and Koh, 2010).

The same recent survey also casts some light on the challenges confronting citizen-immigrant integration. It shows that two thirds of Singaporeans felt that the "policy to attract more foreign talent will weaken Singaporeans' feeling of one nation, one people". The proportion with a "negative" inclination towards foreign talent was highest among those in the smaller house type or with low income, declining from 72% among those living in one- to three-room HDB flats to 49% among those residing in private properties.

Singaporeans are somewhat more accommodating towards immigrants when they consider the latter's importance to the economy. Specifically, two thirds of Singaporeans, as reflected in the survey, agreed that the "Government is right to increase the number of foreigners working in Singapore if our economy needs it". However, the proportion who disagreed with the statement was, not unexpectedly, highest among those living in the smaller house type or with lower income, decreasing from 45% among the one- to three-roomers, to 24% among those residing in private properties.

Within the HDB towns or estates, a similar pattern can also be discerned. The proportion of HDB residents who perceived that the foreigners in their midst were integrating well was 44.3%, as compared with 25.9% who thought otherwise. Like the findings from the national survey reported above, HDB residents with higher education, living in larger house types, and younger in age were more likely to perceive foreigners in a positive light (HDB 2010b:66).

Notwithstanding some of the "negative" indicators highlighted above, I would argue that, given what we know of Singapore over the last 50 years, it would not be justifiable to suggest that the country is characterised by, or prone to, class, ethnic, religious, or citizen-immigrant conflict. If anything, the "positive" figures generally outweigh the "negative" ones. This is not to deny that individuals may, to different extents, harbour prejudices and practise some subtle form of discrimination against people of another class, race, age, or nationality, as manifested in snide, even toxic, remarks reflecting negative stereotypes in response to specific events which have "gone viral" on social media; or, occasionally, experience unhappiness over nuisances committed by neighbours (HDB, 2014:23).

However, despite the largely positive atmosphere in the HDB social landscape, it is plausible to suggest that the diversity remains potentially a source of social tension or conflict; hence, the need for vigilance and community building. Take for instance a 25% "negative" figure, as compared to 75% "positive", with respect to how Singaporeans feel about migrants in Singapore. While this is a statistical minority, it can be rather significant, given that it reflects the views of almost 800,000 people, equivalent to the population size of three major HDB towns combined (HDB 2010a:15). This to some extent explains why the state continually emphasises social integration even with the much taken-for-granted prevalence of harmony and stability in Singapore. It should be reiterated that integration is more than just about the absence of conflict, or even the presence of harmony, which could be achieved through coercive measures; rather it goes much further, seeking to promote understanding, acceptance, connection, and collaboration across social divides.

Community Orientations of HDB Residents

Apart from examining the social profile of HDB residents, another dimension which may have a strong bearing on community development in the HDB towns, estates, and precincts is that of their "community orientations". The latter concept "captures" how residents relate to their neighbourhood, including the extent to which their daily routines take place within its boundaries. Specifically, it affects the probability of their developing a sense of belonging, ownership, rootedness, and commitment, and thereby the propensity to contribute to community building.

Sense of Community

Community orientations may be gauged in terms of two dimensions: that of commitment to community, and thereby directly or indirectly contributing to its development; and participation or involvement in daily or community activities as well as neighbourly relations. The HDB Sample Household Survey (SHS) 2013 (HDB, 2014: 15) indicates that an overwhelming majority of residents engaged in less intense forms of neighbourly interactions, such as exchange greetings and casual conversations, while more than half went further to "exchange food/gifts on special occasions", and a third, to "visit one another", or "keep watch over (each other's) flat". The HDB survey also found that the ethnic minorities were more likely to engage in the more intense forms of neighbourly interactions, and that length of residence and age of residents are positively related to increase in mutual help between neighbours (HDB, 2014:21). Another important indicator is that 85.7% of HDB residents interacted across ethnic, nationality, or both ethnic and nationality lines in 2013 (HDB, 2014:19).

Similarly, the sense of community score has remained consistently high, though rising only slightly over the years, from 70.0% in 2003 to 73.2% in 2013 (HDB, 2014:32). Overall, the indication is that there is a strong sense of community in the HDB neighbourhood, whether at the precinct, estate or town level, and that two variables—age of residents and length of residence—have a positive effect on its magnitude.

A Typology of Community Orientations

Besides the broad picture outlined above, it might be useful to develop a typology relating social characteristics and community orientations. I would hypothesise, based on non-systematic observations, that we could identify the following four possible types of community orientations.

Among the HDB residents, probably the least committed to the neighbourhood would be the subtenants and rental tenants, since they are in transition, whether short or long term. However, this orientation does not necessarily render them visually invisible, especially if they are non-Singaporeans and likely to congregate with their fellow nationals in neighbourhood facilities, such as basketball courts, coffee shops, or shopping malls, possibly giving rise to an impression that they constitute an enclave of sort. The high visibility may have the unintended effect of enhancing the "negative" feeling which some Singaporeans may hold towards the foreigners in their midst. But, on a more positive note, there is also a fair amount of interactions between Singaporeans and foreign nationals in the HDB neighbourhood, thereby contributing to some extent to social cohesion and community development.

The second type of orientations is that of non-Singaporean HDB residents, but who are non-tenants, comprising foreign domestic workers. Given the nature of their job, they spend the most time in the estate, and are likely to form their social networks among fellow domestic workers from other households in the neighbourhood. Their daily activities, whether they involve looking after elderly persons, bringing young children to and from kindergarten, buying groceries at the wet market, or taking the family pet for a walk, present many opportunities for interactions with others who frequent or operate in the same public space or route, thereby contributing to community building in the neighbourhood.

The third type relates to that of HDB residents who are elderly persons, housewives, and young children. They may be owners, occupiers, or tenants of a flat. They are likely to spend much of their time in the estate, and have established their own social networks through their daily routines, which may be similar to that of foreign domestic workers, for instance, mothers sending their young children to kindergarten or school, housewives shopping in a nearby wet market or supermarket, elderly persons chatting at the void deck on the ground floor, elderly men having a drink and discussing politics with friends at a coffee shop, or young children, under the watchful eyes of their mothers or foreign domestic workers, using the playground.

The fourth type of orientations is that of older teenagers, and young and working adults. They are likely to spend the least time in the estate due to study or job responsibilities. However, this does not necessarily mean that they would possess the weakest commitment to the community. Moreover, given their educational and occupational profile, they would have the capabilities and, potentially, the commitment to provide leadership in the community-building process. There are indeed some data on social capital in the HDB neighbourhood which indicate that younger residents, households in higher income brackets, and those living in the larger flat types, or with higher educational attainment, tend to score higher on reciprocity and trust, two key components of social capital measures (HDB, 2010b:25–34).

Social Capital in the HDB Neighbourhood

As implied above, social capital is another angle by which to gauge the presence and extent of community. This concept may be operationalised for use as a measure not only of social distance, but, more importantly, also the degree of connection and collaboration among HDB residents. Broadly speaking, to the extent that social capital, embedded in both bonding and bridging ties, is present, we could expect a community in the making populated by residents who possess some sense of identity, belonging, and ownership, and having the potential to produce a secure, stable living environment where residents look out for one another and contribute towards the collective good.

Social capital is therefore an attractive concept from the perspective of housing policy and governance. Not surprisingly, it was given much prominence in the research efforts of the HDB. Its Sample Household Survey (SHS) 2008 report also provides a rather comprehensive definition of the concept as follows:

> "Social capital refers to the accumulation of people's trust, confidence and shared relationships with one another in both formal and informal settings. It has both an individual and a collective dimension… At the individual level, it refers to the resources available to a person, through his networks of relationships with informal groups (e.g., family members, relatives, neighbours, colleagues)…and formal institutions (e.g., community and government agencies)…which can facilitate and enable the pursuit of his objectives. At the community level, social capital refers to the collective strength of individuals' social networks, along with related attributes, which facilitates (and enables) the pursuit of collective or shared objectives" (HDB, 2010b:14).

The SHS 2008 found that, on a scale of 0 ("Not at All") to 10 ("Completely"), HDB residents have mean social capital scores of above 6 (Table 14.9). If we conceive of social capital scores as valid indicators of social health, or the extent to which community is taking shape—and there are strong theoretical and empirical bases for doing so—then we have good reasons to be optimistic that the HDB neighbourhood is becoming more of a community over the years. However, it should be noted that family, kinship, and friendship ties, in terms of trust and reciprocity, remain stronger and more extensive than that of neighbourly ties (Tables 14.10 and 11). In regard to social integration, a positive sign is that 77% of HDB residents are interacting across ethnic and/or nationality lines (Table 14.12).

Table 14.9.   Social capital scores of HDB residents (Mean score).   *Source*: HDB, 2010b:20.

Components of social capital	Mean score
Trust in informal & generalized networks	6.4
Reciprocity in informal & generalized networks	6.5
Confidence in institutions	6.8
Average size of informal networks	61 persons

Table 14.10.   Norms of trust in informal and generalised networks (Mean score).   *Source*: HDB, 2010b:20.

Network	Mean Score
Family members	9.0
Relatives	7.2
Friends who are not neighbours	6.3
Friends who are neighbours	6.1
Neighbours in general	4.9
Overall score	6.4

Table 14.11.   Size of informal networks (Mean number).   *Source*: HDB, 2010b:22.

Network	Mean number of people
Family members	7
Relatives	17
Friends who are not neighbours	24
Friends who are neighbours	6
Neighbours in general	10
Overall score	61

Table 14.12. Interaction with neighbours across ethnic and nationality lines (%).   *Source*: HDB, 2010b:43.

Type of interaction	%
Interacted across ethnic lines	60.3
Interacted across nationality lines	2.0
Interacted across both ethnic and nationality lines	14.7
No interaction across ethnic and/or nationality lines	23.0

Concluding Remarks

The discussion and findings mobilised above indicate that while the HDB landscape is heterogeneous, with some social divides, it is, by and large, not characterised by social tension and conflict. The harmony has been brought about by policies and measures aimed at promoting social integration through both town designs which facilitate interactions as well as programmes and activities which encourage participation, connection and collaboration. This harmony is undergirded by the core values of fairness and multiracialism, which are regularly reinforced and consistently enforced by a strong state, to prevent any seeds of tension from germinating, let alone taking root. The HDB neighbourhood has therefore been created and nurtured to become an epitome of more than just a decent physical living space, but increasingly a community and an important contributor to nation building in Singapore.

However, notwithstanding the positive report, one should not assume that the community is able to last indefinitely on its own. In the age of globalisation, we can expect changes to the demographic profile, and challenges to our core values. This entails a robust response in terms of strengthening social capital, adaptation to changing conditions, but rejection of values which threaten our social fabric and welfare.

At the same time, if the desire is to build community from the ground up, it makes sense to encourage those with the capacity for leadership to step forward. In my view, this capacity is already present among those with higher educational and occupational attainment, but they may not have the time due to school, work or familial responsibilities. Perhaps, a practical approach is to customise or calibrate the time commitment required to match individual schedules. This facilitates participation from a larger pool, and the possibility that involvement can produce its own momentum for further involvement.

Secondly, allowing for and encouraging voice and civic participation would strengthen sense of belonging and ownership among residents and thereby community. Given the rise in the education level of residents, we would expect the capacity and propensity for civic participation to expand as well. A likely consequence of civic participation is that HDB residents would increasingly see themselves less as customers to be served, but more as empowered stakeholders with a responsibility to serve the community.

Thirdly, strengthening the sense of security among citizens would enhance their acceptance of migrants and foreigners in their midst, thereby contributing to social integration.

Finally, even as Singapore emphasises self-reliance as a value, it is important to pay attention to inculcating mutual support within a caring community as a counter-balance. This is because a community is established on networks of interdependency, rather than a collection of self-sufficient individuals.

References

Chua, B. H. (1997) Modernism and the Vernacular: Transformation of Public Spaces and Social Life in Singapore. Reprinted from Journal of Architectural and Planning Research 51, no. 1 (1991):36–45. In: Ong JH, Tong CK, and Tan ES (eds.), *Understanding Singapore Society*. Singapore: Times Academic Press.

Chua, B. H. and Tan, J. E. (1995) Singapore: New Configuration of a Socially Stratified Culture. *Sociology Working Paper No. 127*. Singapore: Department of Sociology, NUS.

Delanty, G. (2003) *Community*. New York: Routledge.

Department of Statistics (DOS). (2014) *Population Trends 2014*. Singapore: Department of Statistics.

Fernandez, W. (2011) *Our Homes: 50 Years of Housing a Nation*. Singapore: Straits Times Press.

Hassan, R., ed. (1976) *Singapore: Society in Transition*. Oxford: Oxford University Press.

Housing and Development Board (HDB). (2010a) *Public Housing in Singapore: Residents' Profile, Housing Satisfaction and Preferences (HDB Sample Household Survey 2008)*. Singapore: Housing and Development Board.

Housing and Development Board (HDB). (2010b) *Public Housing in Singapore: Well-Being of Communities, Families and the Elderly (HDB Sample Household Survey 2008)*. Singapore: Housing and Development Board.

Housing and Development Board (HDB). (2014) *Public Housing in Singapore: Residents' Profile, Housing Satisfaction and Preferences (HDB Sample Household Survey 2013)*. Singapore: Housing and Development Board.

People's Association (PA). (2014) *Community 2015: Master Plan*. Singapore: People's association.

Tan, E. S. (2004) *Does Class Matter? Social Stratification and Orientations in Singapore*. Singapore: World Scientific.

Tan, E. S. and Koh, G. (2010) *Citizens and the Nation: Findings from NOS4 Survey*. Singapore: Institute of Policy Studies.

Wong, A., Ooi, GL, and Ponniah, R. Dimensions of HDB Community. Reprinted from Aline Wong and Stephen Yeh, eds. (1985) *Housing a Nation: 25 Years of Public Housing in Singapore*. Singapore: Maruzen Asia. In: Ong JH, Tong CK, and Tan ES (eds.) *Understanding Singapore Society*. Singapore: Times Academic Press.

CHAPTER 15

Era of Globalisation: Singapore's New Urban Economy and the Rise of a World Asian City

Ho Kong Chong

Introduction: The Rise of a World Asian City

Fifty years represent a sufficient time period to take stock of the economic changes arising from our plans to create a competitive city, some of which are dramatic, while others represent a more gradual path constructed by putting new pieces in the groundwork laid out by masterplans. Given the general readership of the book, this chapter will endeavour to develop a narrative without an extensive review of the academic literature on the topic.

In addition, my take as a sociologist on urban planning may be different from my co-writers in this volume in several ways. First, urban planning has to be related to the economic planning in city building, with economic planning providing the broad strokes in shaping the Singapore economy and urban planning in facilitating and housing the activities that are the result of economic planning. Second, I see urban planning as a set of trade-offs, developing what is prized, and minimising the costs. Understanding this trade-off is important, so this chapter will provide a context for the reader to understand these trade-offs. A third related point is that the notion of "what is prized" is of course a political decision, but it is a decision made within a certain economic context. The logic which led to a certain course of economic action and which has consequences in terms of the built form of the city is made within a specific historical time period. And so an excavation of this context is important. While Singapore's 50 years of urban planning is largely celebratory, understanding the costs and efforts to minimise this are also important. Lastly, sociologists have been described as people who go to a football game and watch the crowd. This is an apt description for our concern as sociologists is always with society. Therefore, my take on the last 50 years of urban planning is also to see how such plans and its consequences have an influence in the way our society and our city are shaped.

The title and the collection of concepts in it give me a chance to weave a story out of the work which I have already done. First, the notion of globalisation in the Singapore case is really not recent and will require the reader to take a leap back 200 years with Singapore as a port city, since international shipping traffic going through Singapore was part of the globalisation developed during the colonial period. As a port city, Singapore had arguably already achieved "world city" status as an entrepôt along with other strategically-located port cities, and acted as crucial elements in the development of the global economy as collection points for regional produce and distribution nodes for western products. Understanding where we came from is essential as a marker of the changes we have experienced, and so, some focus on Singapore's economic history is necessary.

Second, the idea of Singapore's "new urban economy" is also interesting. We usually think of the new urban economy as giving more priority to services (finance, business services like legal and accounting, real estate) and the chapter will be contrasting this with Singapore's previous economic phases. Lastly, is Singapore a "world Asian city"? Singapore is certainly a world city and while Singapore may be geographically in Asia, our continued openness to global influences and our lack of an illustrious cultural history, make us less of an Asian city.

For the above-mentioned reasons, it is necessary to mark out two earlier phases in Singapore's economic history, namely its development as a port city and later as a manufacturing center. Two other reasons for examining the historical aspect are, firstly, because the previous economic phases are never absent; they continue to be a significant factor even in Singapore's present economic base. Secondly, the reader needs to understand the previous phases in order to have a greater clarity to the "new urban economy" as a contrasting form.

Singapore as a Port City

There are many excellent historical texts detailing Singapore's economic history as a port city. The Dutch already had a presence in Indonesia in the early 1800s but were more interested in developing Indonesia's resources. In contrast, the British focussed on developing Singapore as a free port, with the result that the trade of the Indonesian islands began to centre around Singapore. The 1860s represented a significant decade in the urban development of Singapore for two reasons. The shifting of administration from the East India Company to Singapore being a Crown Colony in 1867 resulted in an expanded government capacity with new legislative and specialised agencies to manage the affairs of the colony, reigning in, but in no way effectively solving the rather chaotic attempts to manage the settlement. The Tanjong Pagar Dock Company had already developed the new harbour in Tanjong Pagar, but as Bogaars (1955: 136) pointed out, "the opening of the Suez Canal (in 1869) revived the flagging trade of the port, and brought in a new era of prosperity: it set the Tanjong Pagar Dock Company firmly on its feet, and within a decade turned attention from the area of the Singapore River to New Harbour: it established a pattern of development which lasted for fifty years".

The following two quotes are useful in giving the reader a sense of the priorities of the colonial government:

> The British in Singapore measured success by the amount of trade secured and the miles of roads paved. But what about schools, hospitals, and low-cost housing? In the matter of schools and hospitals, the government invoked laissez-faire principles and expected philanthropic contributions from private individuals who had benefited from the free trade system. (Lee, 1989: 40)

> Though the interests of the local manufacturer would be best served by protection, the interference with the freedom of the port which would be involved might be disastrous to the entrepôt trade... The prosperity of Singapore has been built on its entrepôt trade. Industrial development is a later growth and has not begun to approach the entrepôt trade in importance. To disturb this merely for the sake of protecting still problematic industries would be to throw away the substance and grasp the shadow". (quoted in Pang and Tan, 1981: 141)

Edwin Lee's point allows us to understand the strengths of the economic infrastructure. The British approach to urban planning in Singapore was clearly aimed at making sure main source of revenue of the country was not jeopardised, thus resulting in an excellent transportation and communications infrastructure that was in many ways, the most advanced in the region. The economic success of the port was clearly a significant factor in building a set of activities which supported the trade of Singapore: the banks and financing activities, warehousing, import-export businesses, and transportation-related services (including boat building, ship chandlers).

The flip side of Lee's point is also significant, for the indifference of the administration to social policies had meant that different communities had to provide for services such as education and health. Such provision, along with the central role played by ethnic and religious associations, kept affiliation and identification within communities, creating a plural society where people looked inward to their own communities. Thus the state-society relationship in Singapore during the colonial period was characterised by a strong society as individual communities were well organised and had the loyalties of the people, and an indifferent state which saw its responsibilities and therefore directed its urban planning focus on tending to the economic infrastructure, leaving the various communities to fend for themselves.

However, even the best effort of the community was insufficient. The surveys conducted by the Department of Social Welfare in 1947 and 1954 on the residential arrangements of Singapore's central area are worth repeating as an indicator of the congested conditions in the city. In both surveys, the term "space" is used to denote the most congested sleeping arrangement: "places like bunks in passage ways, the tiered bed-lofts common in Singapore, sleeping selves under or over staircases, sleeping arrangements in five-foot ways, kitchens and backyards, and other places used for sleeping without enclosures or partitions" (Department of Social Welfare, 1947: 70). In 1947, the percentage of household using such spaces consisted 21% in ward 1 (the harbour area stretching to west Chinatown), 16% in ward 2 (the rest of Chinatown, including the business district, extending east to Middle Road) and 26% in ward 3 (comprising areas east of Middle road, bounded by Serangoon Road and the Kallang River) (Department of Social Welfare, 1947: 71). By 1954, when the second survey was done, the figures had increased to 38% for wards 1 and 2, while remaining unchanged at 25% for ward 3 (Goh, 1956: 68–69).

The second quote offered by Pang and Tan (1981) reveals just how narrow this economic pre-occupation is. While the port was the main economic activity of Singapore, there had in fact developed a range of manufacturing which consisted essentially of the processing of sub-regional products like timber, rubber and tin smelting, and also basic production of goods such as clothing and furniture making, which were focused on the local and sub-regional market. Rubber-related goods such as shoes and tyres were the only export-oriented products that came out of Singapore in the inter-war years (Huff, 1994: 217–218). The colonial government had considered the possibility of providing some support such as tariff protection for local manufacturing. It is important to locate this set of comments within the context of the 1930s, when the Colonial government had considered manufacturing and industrial development "a later growth", taking the prevailing thought that there is a "natural" economic division of labour between the developed world which should focus on industry and while the colonies supplied the raw materials and agricultural products.

It is significant to note that both the colonial and Singapore governments' approach to governing Singapore were overwhelmingly economic. British intentions for Singapore were economic and economically narrow because they had no other ambition for the colony. When Singapore became independent, the government's intention for Singapore was also overwhelmingly economic because Singapore had to succeed despite its tiny size.

Singapore as a Manufacturing Platform

By the late 1960s, Singapore had achieved what Gamer (1972) called the capacity to plan, having secured the political mandate as well as built the organisational and legal and regulative capacity. The Singapore story on manufacturing, like that of the port city, is a well-trodden path, except that this story is told through the activities of the EDB (Economic Development Board) which focused on investment promotion, JTC (Jurong Town Corporation), responsible for industrial planning and industrial estates, the URA (Urban Redevelopment Authority) which oversaw the movement of old trades out of the Central Area of the City and the HDB (Housing Development Board), that housed people and activities in new towns.

The period from the 1960s to the 1980s was a period of rapid growth and development. The city-state had gone through a make-over with core features such as the port being enhanced, the congestion and mixed development of the city centre being removed, and a comprehensive transportation network which linked the new towns in the suburban fringes of Singapore through a concerted planning and implementation which is well documented in the preceding chapters.

The manufacturing phase in Singapore's development is significant for several reasons. First, it was a very different system of economic organisation and consequently a different economic globalisation process. While the colonial period involved trade between Europe and the Far East, in contrast, the manufacturing that occurred from the 1960s was driven in part from European, American and later Japanese manufacturers seeking low cost production sites away from their increasing expensive home countries. The nature of this production had advanced to a point where parts and components could be produced in different parts of the world and assembled somewhere else and sold worldwide, adding increased complexity to logistics and transportation. This new process of organising industrial production resulted in what Froebel and associates (1981) termed as the "new division of labour". Singapore was able to tap into this newly emerging system by offering a production site with relatively low cost and productive labour source and efficient transport infrastructure developed during the colonial period as a port city. This new way of organising production meant a new transnational management system embodied in multinational companies, with their multi-product, multidivisional structure dominated global production (Hymer, 1972) and brought a transnational class of managers and professionals to Singapore as overseers of various production activities. The new system of global production meant an increase in movements of components to different factories around the world. While all merchandise during the colonial period was carried through ships and therefore facilitated by ports, the manufacturing that occurred involved air-cargo in addition to shipping, since the electronic components and products were high value items which could be air-lifted. Therefore, airport capacity was increased to supplement this type of traffic.

Second, this new system of industrial production of which Singapore was now a part of also resulted in a new spatial economic organisation. The centre of entrepôt trade activities was concentrated in the Tanjong Pagar and Singapore river area with the merchants, shipping companies, banks, docks and godowns located there. By the 1970s, the enhanced capacity for planning and implementation, and the coordination between different government agencies created three types industrial sites. The site of major heavy industrial activities was located in Jurong Industrial Estate. The planning of this estate in 1960 by Dr Goh Keng Swee, who was Finance Minister at that time, was visionary if we mark 1960 as the beginning of the shift from port-related activities to manufacturing. At that time, the creation of the estate was tantamount to the assumption that if we were to build a hotel, the tourists would come. The pessimists of the day labelled Jurong Industrial Estate "Goh's Folly", but by 1976, 650 factories were located in Jurong.[1] Besides Jurong, smaller types of industrial estates developed throughout Singapore, partly in response to resettling the local economic activities. So, for example, boat building activities which had concentrated in the Tanjong Rhu and Kallang basin were moved to the newly-built Kallang Industrial Estate in the 1970s. Various motor vehicle repairs were relocated to the Sin Ming industrial estate, also built in the 1970s. A third type of industrial estate was the light non-polluting manufacturing activities such as electronics and these were located at the periphery of New Towns so that the factories could tap into the resident labour pool in these new towns. By 1972, 22% of Singapore's manufacturing workforce was located in the nine industrial estates within public housing estates (Pang & Khoo, 1975: 242, 246).

The third significant impact brought by the industrial phase was the changes to the labour force. The rapid growth of Singapore's manufacturing industry was not matched by domestic labour growth. Rather than lose momentum, and also to keep the better paying managerial jobs in manufacturing in Singapore, the policy to use foreign workers on short term work permit schemes was created. This policy brought in cheap labour from the surrounding region as a solution to the chronic labour short-age that had started to build up in the 1970s. This dependency on a foreign workforce has over time increased and broadened beyond the industrial sector to fill areas of work which local workers shunned. Foreign workers have become an everyday reality.

Singapore's New Urban Economy and Consolidation as a Global City

Unlike the shift to manufacturing where there was a bold and decisive step based on the advice of Dr Albert Winsemius and under the direction of Dr Goh Keng Swee, the policy shift to services was more gradual. Manufacturing continued to yield good returns to Singapore and it made economic sense to keep a viable industrial base in Singapore through technical upgrading of production facilities as well as to attract new higher value-added and skill-intensive manufacturing like chemicals and pharmaceu-ticals. Manufacturing also involved management, financial and business functions to support production operations. And so when rising manufacturing costs drove produc-tion out of Singapore, the realisation was that Singapore needed to hold on to and become a base for strategic control, innovation and key operations (MTI, 1986, 1991).

---

[1] http://www.nas.gov.sg/archivesonline/article/in-memory-of-dr-goh-keng-swee.

By the 1990s, Singapore had already built up a strong set of business services. Good land-use and transport planning had ensured a wide array of office facilities and an excellent airport hub, essential elements for a service economy (Ho, 2000). A 2001 study of firms with regional headquarters highlighted good quality business services as a key reason for companies choosing to site their regional headquarters in Singapore (Yeung, Poon and Perry, 2001). It is also important to note that aside from production-based administrative centres, there are also consumption-type sales and distribution centres. As the growth of the middle class expands in Southeast Asia, Singapore will also most likely be the regional centre of companies wanting to expand their brand presence in this region.

The growth of the services economy in Singapore can be noted from number of employees in services in contrast to manufacturing. The manufacturing industry, which was dominant in the 1970s and 1980s, had already started weakening (in terms of employment) by the 1990s. In 2001, 19.5% of the resident labour force was employed in manufacturing. This share declined rather dramatically over the decade and in 2013, only 13.6% of the resident labour force was employed in manufacturing (Figure 1). In contrast, three sub sectors of services recorded steady growth: the social services (which incorporates personal and community services) share of the total resident employed labour force grew from 20.4% in 2001 to 23.6% in 2013; the business services share of employment grew from 12.6% in 2001 to 14.2% in 2013; and the financial services (which included insurance services in 2009 and 2013) expanded from 5.6% in 2001 to 7.2% in 2013.

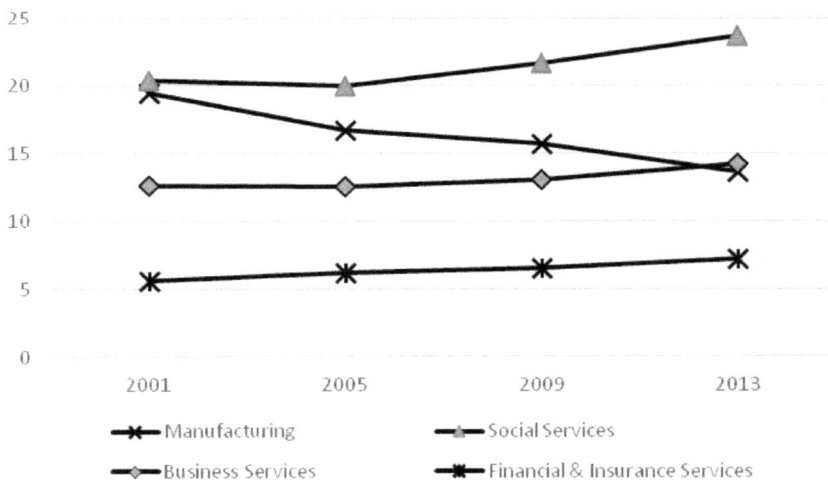

Figure 1.   Sector Employment Shares (%) 2001–2013.

Note: Employed Singapore residents.

Source: Singapore, Department of Statistics, Yearbook of Statistics Singapore, various years.

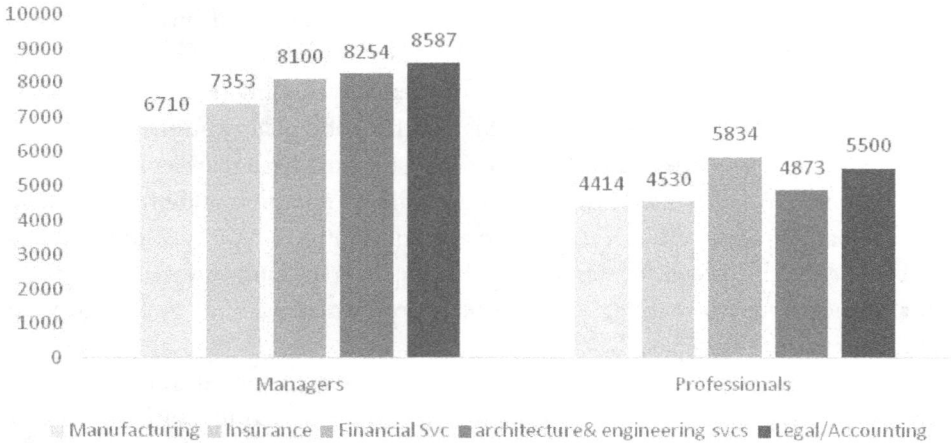

Figure 2. Median Monthly Gross Wage of Top Occupations in Manufacturing and Key Service Sectors (2011).

Source: Singapore, Ministry of Manpower, Report of Wages in Singapore, 2011.

It is important to understand how Singapore's shift to a new services economy has changed the complexion of the city. As manufacturing presence declined and the services economy took root in Singapore, a key change was the rise of income levels at the managerial and professional ranks. Figure 2 shows the managerial and professional monthly wages in manufacturing and four other services sector: insurance services, financial services, architectural and engineering services, and legal and accounting services. Figure 2 also indicates that the managers and professionals of these selected sub sectors earn significantly more than those in manufacturing.

Alongside the increased propensity to spend with increased income levels of managers and professionals in service occupations is the link between consumption and services work. The nature of client-based work in services work requires the need to style the self when taste and decorum is linked to work performance. Advertising services represent perhaps one extreme of such styling work as the following quote from a Hong Kong advertising firm creative director illustrates:

"Of course, it is important to dress decently for my job, because what I sell are ideas, my brains… It is not the same as selling a fax machine or a microwave oven, where the consumer can check out the product, and hold it in his hands and look at it before deciding to buy it. For advertising, if you cannot show the client you have good taste, how can they trust you enough to put their products into your hands? (field material from Chan, 2000: 121–122).

While this need to style the self is of a varying intensity depending on the particular nature of services, the nature of client-based work in the service industry means that self-presentation is essential, along with the need to entertain clients as part of work, and the acquisition of taste and cultural capital as prerequisites in relating to affluent clients.

It is this nature of services work, along with the increased incomes at the top end of services industry occupations, which is at work in reshaping the consumption terrain of the city. Services, with its need for self-presentation coupled with the ability to spend, results in the opulence of financial services clustered in the central business district from Shenton Way to the new Marina Bay Financial Centre. The design-based services with their sensitivity to aesthetics result in a more refined presentation variety and are located smaller scale clusters in the shop house conservation areas of the Central Core (Ho and Hutton, 2012).

The dominant financial and business services economy forms one of triggers of the new consumption landscape in Singapore. Tourism forms the second pillar of consumption.[2] The F1 night races were introduced in 2008 and the two casino resorts in Marina Bay Sands and Sentosa in 2010. A feature article[3] prepared by three economists from the Ministry of Trade and Industry for the Economic Survey of Singapore 2010 estimated that tourism spending supported about 111,500 jobs in 2010 compared to the average of about 99,800 jobs in 2007 and 2008 and suggested that these new attractions played a pivotal role in boosting tourism numbers and spending (Tan, Kuan and Yong, 2011: 75–76). The rising importance of the Integrated Resorts to tourism can be deduced from the Singapore Tourism Board annual visitors' survey. In 2011, of the visitors surveyed on paid access visits, 10% mentioned the Integrated Resorts, and 29% Sentosa (STB 2012: p.51). A year later in 2012, the Integrated Resorts climbed to the top of the paid access venues with 31% of the visitors, while Sentosa dropped to second place with 20% (STB, 2013: p. 36).

While these three attractions represent the latest additions to a stable of attractions, they are significant not just for the size of investments and the physical scale of the venues, but for the connections these attractions make to the city and to the tourism industry. Since the Singapore F1 event is a night race that occurs in the city rather than on a purpose-built track located outside the city, this event allows for Singapore's night skyline to be broadcast worldwide, thus strengthening the city's marketing efforts. The night is of special relevance as well since the race allows associated late night party activities like food, music, drinks and dancing to be added as a run on to the race. And because the F1 is an event-based attraction, the city takes on a festival atmosphere (despite the usual grouses of merchants and people affected) as roads are closed, the circuit built, and life for that week revolves around this event.

---

[2] See Chapter 11 for a more complete treatment on the tourism industry.

[3] *Source*: http://www.mti.gov.sg/MTIInsights/Documents/app.mti.gov.sg/data/article/24184/doc/Feature%20Article%202_AES_2010.pdf.

The Integrated Resorts represents a constellation of amenities and attractions. True to the idea of an integrated resort, the casino takes only 3% of the Marina Bay Sands's gross floor area and 5% of Resort World Sentosa's gross floor area (Henderson, 2012: 141).[4] The two resorts have added 4,100 rooms to the city's inventory and over 180,000 square metres for meetings, conventions and exhibitions. Each of the resorts has five celebrity chefs anchoring its restaurants (*Inside Asia Gaming*, 2014). Resorts World brought Universal Studios to Singapore. According to Henderson (2010: 254), Universal Studios Singapore has a comparable number of attractions to Universal Studios Orlando, and of the 24 rides, 18 are described as "original or redesigned especially for Singapore". Thus, the entry of Universal Studios to the already well-developed tourism venue of Sentosa significantly added to Sentosa's overall attractiveness to visitors and Singaporeans, providing a fuller array of options for the visitor to Sentosa.

Marina Bay Sands has all the trappings of an iconic building: conceived by a famous architect, the most expensive building at the time of construction, and the world's largest cantilevered sky park on top of the building with views of the city skyline. Most significantly, the site which was given to Marina Bay Sands was meant to highlight the iconicity of the trophy building. It is at one end of the Bay, opposite the Singapore River, sandwiched between Suntec City and the New Financial Centre. With the low rise Gardens by the Bay at its back, the waters of the Marina Bay in front and without any competing building in the immediate vicinity, office workers, visitors and shoppers have an uncluttered view across the Bay. Arguably, in spite of the gaming-related issues surrounding Marina Bay Sands, this structure at the centre of the city represents the jewel centrepiece of the new services urban economy, the pendant with the necklace formed by tourism and business services located at Suntec City and financial services at the Marina Bay Financial Centre.

Singapore, as the export manufacturing platform for multinational companies in the 1970s and 1980s, developed a built environment comprising of industrial estates that was efficient but bland in its outlook. The new urban services economy, with its focus on financial business and tourism, is decidedly more glitzy because it has to be. While the spotlight of manufacturing is in its products, services requires a different outlook. If opulence is required of banking and business services, then taste is necessary for design services, and fun for tourism. The city for services is a city of both day and especially the night as it is a city where entertainment is work and consumption is taken seriously. In a city-state where land is scarce, tourism development is moving into event-based attractions. Mega events like F1 in September create a city of seasons, where residents and visitors alike catch the mood of sporting, music and arts events.

---

[4] In spite of the small percentage of floor area given to gaming, the Marina Bay Sands derives 75% of total revenue from gaming while it is 76.8% for Resorts World (*Inside Gaming Asia*, 2014).

At the same time, Singapore as a world city is inauthentic. The city is up for show because of the innate logic and desire of world city managers to impress as a condition for competition. A city of services is a cosmopolitan city comprising a transnational workforce which coordinates Singapore with other key nodes in the rest of the world, and a city where visitor numbers are significantly higher in the central city. Because of this, heritage assumes a greater instrumental value because projects like Kampong Glam, Chinatown and Little India are always on display to others, as an aesthetically pleasing setting for leisure and entertainment, and as an appropriate location for design and creative services.

While manufacturing resulted in a set of decentralized industrial estates, the new urban services economy of Singapore has re-centred the Singapore economy just like the entrepôt economy in the first 150 years of Singapore's modern history. But while this recentering is similar in terms of importance, it is very different in terms of substance. While the entrepôt economy was a mixed use jumble of activities with a highly congested city core, Singapore's urban planning has created a careful order in its city centre.

One worry is that with the new services economy, which comes with increased flows of foreigners and an internationalised property market, the Singapore central core will become increasingly higher-priced and foreign-owned. Residential properties in the central core are already the most expensive neighbourhoods because of their centrality and the availability of lifestyle attractions and amenities. This area is also increasingly attractive to foreign buyers. Citing a Jones Lang LaSalle study comparing profiles of buyers of non-landed private homes between 2000 and 2007, a *Business Times* article[5] reported that in the Central Core Area, the caveats lodged from Singaporeans declined from 54% in 2000 to 47% in 2007, and those from permanent residents increased from 10% in 2000 to 15% in 2007. The largest change was registered for foreigners (non-residents), increasing from 11% in 2000 to 26% in 2007. Left unchecked, a continuation of this trend will result in a spatial division with the city centre being for the rich and for foreigners, and with the heartlands for locals. Is this an inevitable outcome for successful global cities? An alternative scenario is raised by journalist Melissa Tan.[6] When contemplating the 2013 draft Master Plan to build new housing in two central districts of Marina South and Kampong Bugis, Ms Tan wondered if such residential units could be public housing. Rather appropriately, Ms Tan cited a comment URA general manager Alan Choe[7] made in 1975: "the residential usage proposed in the central area must cater to all social groups". If this progressive inclusive principle is to prevail, planning will have to intervene over the market, placing social value over the economic value of the development.

---

[5] *Business Times*, 2008, "Rising tide of foreigners snapping up S'pore property", 27 March.
[6] *Straits Times*, 2013 "Eye on Singapore: HDB flats in Marina South?", 12 December.
[7] See Mr Choe's contribution in Chapter 1 of this volume.

The Role of Planning in the Transformation
of Singapore's Built Environment

This chapter represents an attempt at showing how the economic emphasis has shifted from the port to the factory and finally to the central business district. Three observations can be made about the relationship between planning and economic activity. Firstly, the shifts in the last 50 years are marked by efficient economic planning working in tandem with urban planning, as new economic activities replace non-viable ones and the built environment is reshaped to house these activities. Thus, within this period, we saw the shift of economic activities from the central city to a decentralised focus on industrial estates and then to the central city again as the financial, business services and tourism centre. Secondly, the planning which is done is informed by a network of Singapore offices overseas charged with economic (including tourism) promotion. The Economic Development Board for example has developed an economic intelligence network in key cities which is capable of discerning new trends and working with overseas clients with the intention of attracting investments to Singapore (Ho, 2009: 129). In the mid-1990s, the EDB had more than twice the number of investment promotion personnel overseas as compared to Australia and almost three times the overseas personnel as Hong Kong (Ho, 2000: 2344). Such an economic intelligence network provides critical inputs to planning, and more so to Singapore's capacity as a world city. Thirdly, being a small city state that is a world city and without a large domestic market, Singapore is prone to the volatility of the regional and international economic environment. It is important to understand that the institutions needed to manage the downturn–institutions are just as important as those that plot the economic path forward. Such institutions include the National Trades Union Congress, which plays a role in job coaching and retraining workers being retrenched. Lastly, I had suggested at the start of the chapter that planning is about proceeding on a path with anticipated gains and this is the portion which receives much publicity and celebration when consequences unfold according to the plan. What is less discussed and celebrated is the point that planning is as much about managing the costs of planned action. Some of these costs are anticipated as trade-offs such as the population debate while others are unanticipated consequences such as foreign workers or the Little India riot incident in December 2013. Planning and city building also then require managing the costs of being simultaneously a world city and a city state.

At an Institute of Policy Studies conference on 30 July 2013, I jotted down a comment Janadas Devan made: "We exist as a city, we survive as a country". Singapore's new urban economy has built on our legacy as a port city. Looking ahead at the next 10 years, as a country without a hinterland, the key strategy of emphasizing services looks to be unchanged as our economic means of existence. Our planning instruments and institutions, developed as they already are, need the type of flexibility necessary to make the necessary directional changes to our sails in order to catch the shifting winds. To survive as a country, our interventions must necessarily be diplomatic in regional and international arenas. Katzenstein (1985) argues in *Small States in the World Market* that participation in regional groupings has allowed small European states to pool their interests, exert a larger voice on a range of collective interests and gain a stronger bargaining position with larger countries. Similarly, Nuemann and Gstöhl (2004: 17) suggest that with more limited material resources, small countries tend to choose diplomatic strategies that "institutionalize rules and norms, such as international law, international regimes, and international institutions".

City building also requires that we mend the cracks and flaws which emerge. As we cross our 50th year of being an independent city-state, it is as apparent in 1965 as it is in 2015 that we have to survive as a country. This will require that we go beyond the necessary but insufficient condition of delivering a good quality of life, to emphasising our identity and bond as Singaporeans.

References

Bogaars, G. (1955) The effect of the opening of the Suez Canal on the trade and development of Singapore. *Journal of the Malayan Branch of the Royal Asiatic Society* **28 (169 pt. 1)** 99–143.

Chan, AHN. (2000) "Middle-Class Formation and Consumption in Hong Kong" in BH Chua (ed). *Consumption in Asia: Lifestyles and Identities*. pp. 98–134. New York: Routledge.

Department of Social Welfare, Singapore. (1947) *A Social Survey of Singapore: A Preliminary Study of Some Aspects of Social Conditions in the Municipal Area of Singapore*. Singapore.

Gamer, R. (1976) *The Politics of Urban Development in Singapore*. Cornell University Press, Ithaca.

Goh, KS. (1956) *Urban Incomes and Housing: A Report on the Social Survey of Singapore, 1953–54*. Singapore: Government Printing Office.

Henderson, JC. (2010) New Visitor Attractions in Singapore and sustainable destination development *Worldwide Hospitality and Tourism Themes* **2(3)**, 251–261.

Henderson, JC. (2012) Developing and Regulating Casinos: The Case of Singapore *Tourism and Hospitality Research* **12(3)**, 139–146.

Huff, WG. (1994) *The Economic Growth of Singapore*. Cambridge: Cambridge University Press.

Hymer, S. (1972) The Multinational Corporation and the Law of Uneven Development. In: J.N. Bhagwati (ed), *Economics and World Order from the 1970s to the 1990s*, pp. 113–40. Macmillan, London.

Frobel, F., Heinrichs, J., Kreye, O. (1980) *The New International Division of Labour*, Cambridge University Press, Cambridge.

Lee, E. (1989) The Colonial Legacy. In: KS Sandhu & P. Wheatley (eds). *Management of Success*, pp. 3–50. Institute of Southeast Asian Studies, Singapore.

Ho, KC. (2000) Competing to be Regional Centres: A Multi-agency, Multi-locational Perspective *Urban Studies* **37(12)**: 2337–2356.

Ho, KC. (2009) Competitive Urban Economic Policies in Global Cities: Shanghai Through the Lens of Singapore. In XM Chen (ed). *Shanghai Rising: State Power and Local Transformations in a Global Megacity*, University of Minnesota Press, Minneapolis.

Ho, KC, Hutton, T. (2012) The cultural economy in the development state: a comparison of Chinatown and Little India districts in Singapore. In: P Daniels KC Ho & T Hutton (eds). *New Economic Spaces in Asian Cities*. pp. 220–237. Routledge, London.

Hymer, S. (1972) The Multinational Corporation and the Law of Uneven Development. In: J.N. Bhagwati (ed). *Economics and the World Order*. pp. 113–140. Macmillan, London.

Katzenstein, PJ. (1985) *Small States in World Markets*. Cornell University Press, Ithaca.

Ministry of Trade and Industry. (1986) *The Singapore Economy: new Directions*. Singapore National Printers, Singapore.

Ministry of Trade and Industry. (1991) *The Strategic Economic Plan: Towards a Developed Nation*. Singapore National Printers, Singapore.

Nuemann, IB., Gstöhl, S. (2004) Lilliputians in Gulliver's World? Small States in International Relations, Centre for Small States Studies, Institute of International Affairs, Iceland, Working Paper 1-2004. *Source*: http://rafhladan.is/bitstream/handle/10802/5122/Lilliputians%20 Endanlegt%202004.pdf?sequence=1.

Pang, EF., Khoo, HP. (1975) Patterns of industrial employment within public housing estates. In: SHK Yeh (ed). *Public Housing in Singapore*. pp. 240–261. Housing and Development Board, Singapore.

Pang, EF., Tan, A. (1981) Employment and Export-led Industrialisation: the experience of Singapore In: R. Amjad (ed). *The Development of Labour Intensive Industry in ASEAN Countries*, pp. 141–174. Geneva: International Labour Office.

Tan, HL., Kuan, ML., Yong, YW. (2011) Contribution of Tourism to the Singapore Economy, feature article in *Economic Survey of Singapore 2010*, Ministry of Trade and Industry. *Source*: http://www.mti.gov.sg/MTIInsights/Documents/app.mti.gov.sg/data/article/24184/doc/ Feature%20Article%202_AES_2010.pdf.

Singapore Tourism Board, *Annual Report on Tourism Statistics* 2011 and 2012.

Yeung, HWC., Poon, J., Perry, M. (2001) "Towards a Regional Strategy: The Role of Regional Headquarters of Foreign Firms in Singapore", *Urban Studies* 38(1): 157–183.

Newspaper and Magazine Articles

Business Times, 2008, "Rising tide of foreigners snapping up S'pore property", 27 March.

Inside Asia Gaming, 2014, "Winning Big Beyond the Casinos… In Singapore You Bet", 14 October.

Straits Times, 2013, "Eye on Singapore: HDB flats in Marina South?", 12 December.

CHAPTER 16

Towards Greater Sustainability and Liveability in an Urban Age

Heng Chye Kiang and Yeo Su-Jan

Introduction

From the bustling agoras and marketplaces of a bygone era to the pulsating business districts of our modern times, cities have long been recognised as the economic engines of nations. Much of this economic growth is, and will continue to be, contingent on city-to-city trade, commerce, and investment activities. Over the past 50 years, a digital revolution has created a borderless platform enabling cities separated by long distances to network and conduct business in real-time while also demonstrating their economic might in front of a captive global audience. Furthermore, the expansive scale and extensive reach of today's digital world make it possible for information and ideas to flow across societies and cultures. The most dynamic and vibrant cities, therefore, are not only economic epicentres but also innovation hubs for knowledge and enterprise. In short, globalisation and urbanisation are parallel megatrends at the forefront of world development in the 21st century—and both phenomena have equally significant impacts on the sustainability and liveability of planet Earth. These impacts are further amplified by the rapidly expanding global population that may reach almost 10 billion by 2050 (UN, 2015a).

Today, urban areas accommodate more than half of the world's population with one in every eight urban dwellers living in a megacity exceeding 10 million inhabitants. In 1950 there were only two megacities on the planet, compared to 20 and 28 megacities in 2000 and 2014, respectively. By 2030, it is projected that there will be 41 megacities in the world (UN, 2014a). For Asia, this growth amounts to 44 million new inhabitants moving into the cities every year or, in other words, an increase of 120,000 people per day (Roberts and Kanaley, 2006). Linked to this simultaneous expansion of population and urbanisation are critical environmental challenges that implicate not only the development of cities in Asia but also, and ultimately, their liveability. With a focus on the Asian region and, in particular, Singapore, this chapter examines the impact of globalisation and urbanisation in Asia, identifies Singapore's early initiatives towards sustainability, discusses the key sustainability issues of the 21st century, and explores homegrown innovations for long-term urban resilience and liveability in our own city-state.

Asian Cities in a Global Urban Age and the Urgency of Sustainability Planning

As the most populous continent with a current population of 4.3 billion people, Asia accounts for 60% of the world's 7.3 billion inhabitants (UN, 2015b). In 2010, the global rate of urbanisation tipped the scale for the first time in human history, thus marking the prevalence and propulsion of cities. Today, Asia represents 53% of the world's urban population; by 2050, it is projected that Asia and Africa will constitute close to 90% of the world's urban population (UN, 2014a). Between 2000 and 2010, 29,000 square kilometres of land in the 'East Asia region'[1] was converted for urban use (WBG, 2015)—that is, developed for roads, housing, industry, and supporting infrastructure to accommodate a burgeoning urban population. This 2.4% average annual rate in the expansion of urban land within a decade suggests that more, rather than less, urbanisation in Asia is likely to occur in the near future. For the most part, the rate of urban population growth in Asia is driven by unprecedented levels of rural-to-urban migration as migrants relocate to urban centres with the hopes of accessing better opportunities in employment, healthcare, education, and living conditions. China, for example, is actively ramping up urbanisation, driven largely by government-led investment, in order to meet the target of a 70% nation-wide urban population by 2025 (Johnson, 2013).

In both advanced and emerging cities of Asia, wealth creation through the sale and development of land has helped to boost construction and real estate activities and, thus, public investment capital and economic progress (Lin, 2010). Meanwhile, the aspirations and consumption practices of a rising urban middle class have placed greater pressures and demands on cities. From the desire for home and car ownership to the preference for branded and imported goods, the sophisticated and discerning tastes of the professional working class in Asia have a significant impact on urban development and, in turn, the environment. Car-oriented suburban growth, luxury single-family housing, gated communities, internationalised retail and entertainment precincts, and 'iconic' mega projects are some of the prevalent urbanisation trends shaping the physical landscape of Asian cities. These trends have also added challenges in terms of social inequality, creating in some cities a wide income gap made visible by

[1]The World Bank defines East Asia as comprising of Brunei Darussalam, Cambodia, China, Indonesia, Japan, the Democratic People's Republic of Korea, the Republic of Korea, the Lao People's Democratic Republic, Malaysia, Mongolia, Myanmar, the Philippines, Singapore, Thailand, Timor-Leste, and Vietnam (see World Bank Group, 2015, p. 7).

spatial segregation with the urban poor often left out of adequate and affordable housing, that is, relegated to the urban periphery or informal slum settlements.

This urban economic divide coupled with a lack of proper planning can have long-term, adverse impacts on the environment. In Asia, cities consume 80% of the region's energy and generate 75% of carbon dioxide emissions (ADB, 2015). Indeed, rapid and poorly-managed urbanisation are factors that can intensify climate change risks and place urban populations in potentially vulnerable situations. Jakarta, Manila, Mumbai, Wuhan, and New Delhi—which are among the fastest growing cities in Asia—have the lowest sustainability ranking (outperforming only Nairobi) in a list of 50 world cities, according to the 2015 Sustainable Cities Index developed by Arcadis (2015). Furthermore, a widening urban economic divide creates inequality in terms of who is able to access information and resources that promote awareness about sustainability issues. The unrestrained urban expansion in Asia, therefore, presents a real urgency to re-examine the methods of growth vis-à-vis sustainability and liveability.

Today, 16 of the 28 megacities worldwide are located in Asia with Tokyo (38 million), Delhi (25 million), and Shanghai (23 million) topping the list in terms of urban population (UN, 2014b). As might be expected, the Asian continent has the highest overall population density at 135 persons per square kilometre of total surface area (persons/km²), compared to Africa (37 persons/km²), Europe (32 persons/km²), Latin America and Caribbean (30 persons/km²), North America (16 persons/km²), and Oceania (4 persons/km²) (UN, 2014b). It is commonly agreed that the form and growth of a city can have an impact on sustainability, yet there are conflicting viewpoints regarding high-density and compact development as the best (or only) way forward towards achieving a sustainable urban future (Dempsey and Jenks, 2010; Heng and Malone-Lee, 2010; Heng and Zhang, 2010; Neuman, 2005). In this respect, some of Asia's highly-dense, modern, and economically developed cities could offer insightful lessons to advance our understanding of sustainable urban development. While cities may present many problems, they are also centres for innovation and influence where concerted efforts can make a positive global impact towards sustainability.

Singapore, as we shall illustrate in the following section, ventured on a sustainability journey decades before the seminal 1987 Brundtland Commission Report elevated sustainability at the apex of a worldwide environmental agenda. As an island-state with a miniscule land area in a developing region, Singapore's scarce supply of land and natural resources have made it necessary for the country to plan strategically and long-term for sustainable growth and, ultimately, survival.

Singapore's Quest for Sustainability and Liveability: The Early Years

Singapore is ranked the 10th most sustainable city in the world by Arcadis (2015) and rated as the most liveable city in Asia for international assignees to the region by

ECA International (2015). Employing methods and indicators that can differ widely from index to index, such surveys require critical reading. Nevertheless, the reports effectively draw attention to the cities which they feature, such as Singapore's efforts in the areas of environmental sustainability and urban liveability; these efforts pre-date the recent surge of concerns on climate change and quality of life issues. The vision for a sustainable and liveable city has always been at the forefront of Singapore's growth agenda since the earliest beginnings of the Republic's independence.

In 1965, Singapore was in a fragile state of affairs having emerged from almost 150 years of colonial rule to then be removed from the Federation Government of Malaysia and with an uncertain-looking future. The political leaders and state government of the newly-formed Republic embarked on their first of several arduous and urgent tasks—to alleviate Singapore from poverty by raising living standards and increasing social mobility through housing and job creation. The path to Singapore's transformation from a Third World to First World nation required thinking about sustainability from the very start and in every aspect of development: economic, social, and environmental. As an island with a small territorial size, Singapore's first sustainability challenge was the utilisation of land. In order to ensure that the limited land supply can accommodate long-term population growth and support the needs of future generations, strategic planning and careful management are the key strengths in Singapore's management of this precious resource. Four specific policy areas have been particularly foundational and instrumental in contributing to Singapore's sustainability and liveability goals.

Firstly, Singapore's public housing programme has enhanced urban liveability and promoted social sustainability (see also Chapter 14 by Tan Ern Ser for the impact of public housing on community development). In terms of social equity, the home ownership rate in Singapore is among the highest in the world at 90.3% as of 2014 (DOS, 2015). Public housing appeared in colonial Singapore during the 1930s under the administration of the Singapore Improvement Trust (SIT). The SIT was replaced by the Housing & Development Board (HDB) in 1960, after which building efforts were ramped up to provide proper and adequate housing to what was then a largely poor population. In the first Five-Year Plan (1960–1965) the HDB completed nearly 55,000 public housing units (HDB, 2014/15), exceeding the SIT's total of some 23,000 units during its 32 years of existence (Liu, 1985). Over the decades, public housing has accommodated generations of families with initiatives and incentives enabling grandparents, parents, and children to live within close proximities. Singapore's public housing adopted a 'new town' development model comprising high-rise blocks spatially arranged into self-sufficient neighbourhoods served by a central commercial core. Public housing, therefore, has facilitated urban density by accommodating greater numbers of people in a compact and land-efficient manner; in this way, reducing travel distances by enabling residents to work, live, and play within proximity to their homes. At the same time, urban density and compactness make more viable the integration of an efficient and effective public transportation system, thus reducing reliance on private vehicles as the dominant means of daily commuting.

Secondly, the 'Garden City' and 'Clean Rivers' campaigns, launched in 1967 and 1977, respectively, demonstrate the early attention given to environment and water issues. The population boom after the Second World War outpaced planning projections outlined by the 1958 Master Plan, resulting in unfettered urban growth, congestion, and unregulated practices such as unscrupulous littering and improper waste disposal. The 'Garden City' initiative aimed to not only improve the aesthetic image of the streetscape but also counteract the environmental impact of urbanisation. Some of the pragmatic advantages of tree plantings in Singapore's hot tropical climate include: provision of shade, minimisation of heat island effect, reduction of traffic noise, containment of dust pollutants, and concealing otherwise imposing concrete structures such as retaining walls. The tree-planting programme was first initiated in 1963 by the then Prime Minister Lee Kuan Yew. In 1967, Singapore's greening efforts were formalised through an official declaration of the 'Garden City' vision and establishment of a Trees and Parks Unit within the Public Works Department. By 1970, new trees and shrubs in excess of 55,000 and 340,000, respectively, had been planted (PWD, 1971, p. 27). Today, greening efforts continue in Singapore with new emphasis on community gardens, recreational greenways, and biodiversity; thus, giving Singapore the renewed moniker of 'City in a Garden'. The 'Clean Rivers' 10-year programme for the revival of the Singapore River included resettlement of households and industrial enterprises. Here, earlier decades of indiscriminate sewage dumping by households and cottage industries in unsewered premises along the river banks made the waterways a toxic breeding ground for disease. The Singapore River clean-up was the impetus that led to a comprehensive, island-wide modern sanitation network and treatment system which was implemented completely in 1997 (CLC & CSC, 2014, p. 147). Although the project timelines for both the 'Garden City' and 'Clean Rivers' initiatives were short-lived, the vision was long-term with the aim to not only improve public health and living standards but also better the image of Singapore within and beyond our shores.

Thirdly, prior to the 1967 State and City Planning (SCP) study, transport planning was virtually non-existent, much less integrated with land use planning (see Chapter 8 by Mohinder Singh). The 1971 Concept Plan concretised the outcomes of the 1967 SCP study with a comprehensive plan in which land was safeguarded for road networks and mass rapid transit (MRT) lines to meet Singapore's physical development demands in the long-term. Besides infrastructure planning, strategic transportation policies are also crucial in the management of traffic given the pace of growth and development in Singapore. Perpetual traffic congestion not only hinders businesses, services, and day-to-day activities that rely on transportation but also, as a result, increases fuel consumption and generates air pollution at the expense of liveability. In 1975, Singapore became the first mover in the world to implement a congestion pricing scheme, the Area Licensing Scheme (ALS). With advancements in technology, the current Electronic Road Pricing (ERP) came into being in 1998. The Vehicle Quota System (VQS), introduced in 1990, is another road use management mechanism which regulates the vehicle population. Transport infrastructure provision and policy have long been key pillars in reinforcing the goals of urban liveability and sustainability; and, at the same time, illuminating Singapore's innovation capabilities for sustainable planning on the world stage.

Finally, at the macro level, comprehensive and long-term planning has played a significant, overarching role in guiding Singapore's sustainability future in terms of resource management, infrastructure provision, and land use distribution for population and economic growth. In 1971, Singapore's first Concept Plan was adopted. Three key strategic thrusts of the 1971 Concept Plan are, today, ingrained features in Singapore's physical landscape: (1) a concentration of developments in a 'ring and line' pattern encircling the Central Catchment Area along which are nodes of high-density satellite towns, and another line of developments along the southern coast from the eastern to western extremes; (2) an integrated transportation network comprising a system of expressways, MRT lines, and gateways such as Changi Airport; and (3) the nurturing of the Central Area into a significant financial centre and tourism magnet for locals and visitors alike. The Concept Plan, reviewed every 10 years, enables a small island-state like Singapore to re-examine the needs of the nation and plan ahead to ensure development is sustainable for future generations.

Within Asia, Singapore has long been viewed as a trailblazer for environmental sustainability—serving as inspiration for other Asian cities. Many of the initiatives and policies which the city-state carried out in the 1960s and 1970s were relatively uncharted for their time, that is, a time before 'green' became trendy. Arriving at such critical crossroads required courageous visions, strong political will, and committed government support. In the mid-1970s, for instance, Singapore took a stance on upholding strict pollution standards when Japanese firm, Sumitomo, established a petrochemical plant on Pulau Ayer Merbau (today reclaimed as part of Jurong Island) (CLC & CSC, 2014, p. 10; Ng, 2012, p. 63–64; CLC, 2010, p. 75). At a time when the young island-state was vying for foreign direct investments, the government's uncompromising perseverance towards environmental sustainability was an exceptional manoeuvre but one that was viewed as a necessary development strategy for economic growth, rather than a deterrent against it. Sound environmental policies were considered to be equally vital in attracting and retaining investors, businesses, and professionals.

Singapore's early efforts and solutions in sustainability were motivated by and primarily addressed domestic environmental concerns. Today, place-specific environmental problems are no longer confined within national borders as can be observed by the seasonal transboundary haze pollution affecting Southeast Asia. Thus, the infrastructures, resources, technologies, and expertise that Singapore has developed and accumulated over the decades will need to be re-calibrated in order to better understand and confront future sustainability threats concerning human society at a global scale. The next section discusses the major sustainability issues of the 21st century and, turning to the challenges ahead, explores current strides in the domains of government and research to advance knowledge, produce cutting-edge technologies, and formulate new targets for a more sustainable and liveable urban future in Singapore.

Environmental Resilience and Responsibility: Towards a Sustainable Urban Future in Singapore

The two megatrends of the 21st century, which we described earlier as being globalisation and urbanisation, are implicating sustainable development in critical ways that are multi-dimensional and interconnected. At the forefront of the sustainability challenge is energy and climate change. Urbanisation is a resource-intensive process, involving vast amounts of energy to construct buildings, develop infrastructure, and drive industrial output in order to achieve higher standards of development and economic competitiveness. As cities expand to accommodate physical and population growth, their energy demands increase, simultaneously compounded by the day-to-day production and consumption patterns of urban dwellers. In 2013, global CO_2 emissions peaked at a new high of 35.3 billion tonnes (Gt) CO_2 (PBL NEAA, 2014) and, in the following year of 2014, the Earth's average surface temperature was recorded as the highest since the earliest readings in 1880 (NOAA NCEI, 2015). Climate change is increasingly being reported as the cause of extreme weather events over recent years, ranging from floods and storms to droughts and heat waves. Cities, today, are therefore more vulnerable to the heightened frequency and intensity of such natural disasters. The threat of rising sea levels, for example, is a scenario that an island-state like Singapore will need to consider in its capability planning for climate change adaptation.

Another pressing sustainability issue of our times is urban waste and water pollution. Rapid urban migration adds stresses and strains to the carrying capacity of cities, particularly in cities with the lack of resources to cope with rising population numbers. Currently, there are almost 830 million people living in slum conditions where potable water and adequate sanitation are scarce (UN, 2012). Here, a shortfall in the proper technology and infrastructure to handle the disposal and treatment of waste can create serious problems related to environmental contamination and public health arising from unscrupulous dumping of waste and clandestine landfills. At the other end of the spectrum, member nations in the Organisation for Economic Co-operation and Development (OECD) produce approximately 1.75 million tonnes of waste per day, making the developed world the largest generators of waste (Hoornweg *et al.*, 2013). In Singapore, the amount of waste generated and disposed has increased over the decades from 1,260 tonnes per day in 1970 to 8,338 tonnes per day in 2014 (NEA, 2015), thus placing greater demands on the existing waste management system which is further compounded by our land constraints.

Against this backdrop of climate change and environmental pollution, the reliable and adequate production of food is a contentious issue with global demand and supply implications. At the same time, modern agricultural practices and contemporary food consumption habits are increasingly acknowledged as unsustainable, contributing to the exacerbation of food insecurity. Given that only one quarter of the land on Earth is suitable for cultivation (UNEP, 2012, p. 18) and almost 10 billion people are estimated to inhabit our planet by the year 2050 (UN, 2015a), the impetus for a more sustainable approach to food production and consumption will require concerted efforts at a global scale. Cities, in particular and as a start, can make a significant impact on improving the state of the world's food system through advancements in urban horticulture. Singapore relies on imports to meet the food demands of the island's growing population, though the country's global emissions output is currently less than 0.2%. Nevertheless, when environmental calamities and/or uncertainties heighten, this food supply chain would be affected if not disrupted completely. Therefore, apart from shrinking our carbon footprint related to food transport, we also need to consider innovations in self-sufficiency for food security.

The environmental issues affecting the planet today will have dire consequences in the foreseeable future, if the status quo remains. In order to counteract anthropogenic environmental degradation, more and more cities are now exploring two parallel strands of action: resilience and responsibility. Resilience—the ability to adapt and recover in times of adversity and disorder—can be fostered through preparedness. Preparedness, in turn, requires a multi-faceted framework of mechanisms, methods, and data to manage and minimise risks that might threaten the viability of cities. Resilience without accountability, however, is inadequate in driving sustainability. International environmental treaties—for example, the United Nations Framework Convention on Climate Change and its Kyoto Protocol—promote participation and, hence, incite nations to take responsibility in combatting climate change. In this regard, we will now examine six sustainability programmes representing the diverse perspectives and roles of the government and research sectors in Singapore; these programmes collectively aim to enhance our nation's resilience to environmental change while upholding an ethos of responsible urban development.

More significantly, at the crux of these programmes, a triangular relationship is forged between the spheres of design/planning, technology, and behaviour. In short, it is through forward-thinking design/planning, ingenious technology, and responsible behaviour that we can derive more effective solutions to the sustainability problem.

Government Sector

The government sector plays a significant role in promoting sustainability through public policy development, legislation, and setting of national targets; in this way, steering economies, industries, and citizens towards a cohesive agenda or vision with clear sustainability principles. As the key authority that decides how public funds are channelled, the government is a catalyst and provider of sustainability innovation. Such innovation includes infrastructure and technology development for improving environmental performance in areas of, for example, transportation, energy, buildings, and housing. In relation to housing, the HDB formed a Committee of Environment Sustainability in 2005 which involved government agencies, academia, and the private sector in formulating long-term strategies towards sustainable towns and estates (SPH, 2007). HDB's first eco-precinct, Treelodge@Punggol, is illustrative of such an initiative in this direction (see Chapter 7 by Cheong Koon Hean). By leading through example, the government helps to drive behavioural change towards greater sustainability-consciousness within civil society and the private sector. In Singapore, the government has developed several concurrent national-level agendas, three of which are highlighted below. The *Sustainable Singapore Blueprint*, *Smart Nation Programme*, and *National Climate Change Strategy* aim to advance sustainability through environmental goal setting and responsible urban development practices.

Sustainable Singapore Blueprint

The Sustainable Singapore Blueprint is a targets-based mandate developed with feedback from public dialogues, focus group discussions, and surveys; the document sets out environmental goals and initiatives with an immediate timeframe of 10 to 20 years. First launched in 2009, the Sustainability Singapore Blueprint is now in its second run with the 2015 edition led by the Ministry of the Environment and Water Resources and the Ministry of National Development. The 2015 Sustainable Singapore Blueprint presents a national vision towards higher standards of sustainability and liveability revolving around a desired five-pronged outcome: (1) 'eco-smart' housing districts; (2) 'car-lite' environment; (3) zero waste nation; (4) leading green economy; and (5) community stewardship. Identifying key environmental indicators and their levels in the year 2013, the 2015 Sustainable Singapore Blueprint maps out 2030 targets for these indicators that include: increasing the amount of skyrise greenery from 61 ha to 200 ha; extending the length of cycling paths from 230 km to 700 km; doubling the rail network from 180 km to 360 km; increasing the proportion of buildings with BCA Green Mark Certified rating from 21.9% to 80%; and reducing flood prone areas from 36 ha to 23 ha.

Smart Nation Programme

The Smart Nation Programme is a national-level initiative involving government agencies across various sectors from information communication and technologies to transportation and housing. Premised on the 'smart city' concept—where digital technologies are leveraged to enhance the delivery and efficiency of urban services while reducing costs (environmental and economic) and catalysing user participation in the process—Singapore's 'smart nation' vision entails significant cooperation and collaboration between government, industry, business, and citizens. Of interest to note is how the Smart Nation Programme dovetails with the Sustainable Singapore Blueprint, as both agendas are essentially committed to improving the future of sustainability and liveability in Singapore. Two thrusts of the Smart Nation Programme, in particular, address the built environment through their focus on the development of big data and technology-driven innovations towards improving the future capabilities of transportation (Smart Mobility) and housing (Smart Living). The Smart Mobility 2030 plan, jointly developed by the Land Transport Authority and Intelligent Transportation Society Singapore, provides strategies for big data analytics and intelligent transportation system (ITS) applications towards a more integrated, interactive, and sustainable land transport ecosystem. Concurrently, under the Smart Living banner, the HDB has developed a 'Smart HDB Town Framework' that integrates smart technologies in the realms of town planning, environmental monitoring, estate management, and dwelling infrastructure. In 2015, Yuhua was the first live-in public housing estate where Smart technologies were trialled in 10 households for six months (HDB, 2015). The Smart home devices included an 'Elderly Monitoring System' and 'Utilities Management System' to alert of anomalies in elderly movements and utilities consumption, respectively. This demonstration project is currently being expanded to 3,200 households in Yuhua estate (CNA, 2016). Smart technology applications will also be test-bedded in the recently launched Punggol Northshore pre-sale Build-to-Order development, which will feature: a smart car park management system; a smart pneumatic waste conveyance system; sensor-controlled smart lighting in common areas; and a home energy management system.

National Climate Change Strategy

The Inter-Ministerial Committee on Climate Change (IMCCC), a whole-of-government effort on climate change policies, was established in 2007 and is today provided with coordination support by the National Climate Change Secretariat, formed in 2010 under the Prime Minister's Office. The National Climate Change Strategy document, developed by the IMCCC shortly after the 2011 United Nations Climate Change Conference in Durban, seeks to address how Singapore can reduce long-term emissions and enhance energy efficiency while ensuring continued growth and progress. The vision articulated by the National Climate Change Strategy is for Singapore "to be a climate resilient global city that is well positioned for green growth" (NCCS, 2012, p. 12). Achieving this vision, as the document posits, involves a four-pillar approach in addressing climate change. Firstly, Singapore has set the bold target of reducing emissions by 16% below 2020 business-as-usual (BAU) levels.[2] Currently, Singapore has begun implementing policies and measures to reduce emissions by 7% to 11% from the 2020 BAU levels (Ibid, p. 11 & 40). Secondly, in order to enhance Singapore's adaptation measures to climate change, various government agencies alongside the research sector are attempting to bridge knowledge gaps and develop cutting-edge studies on topics such as coastal protection, water conservation, biodiversity and greenery, public health, and urban infrastructure. Thirdly, efforts in curbing climate change could generate economic opportunities for green growth. By tapping on these opportunities, Singapore not only creates an avenue across sectors for financing and trading but also fosters research and innovation in sustainability. Lastly, implementing and achieving sustainability policies and targets require local as well as global partnerships between committed stakeholders, ranging from civil society and government to the corporate sector and international community of nations and organisations.

Research Sector

Enhancing our proficiency in sustainability issues through scientific and applied research in areas such as climate change, land development, and changing demographic trends is an integral component of a comprehensive, national sustainability roadmap. The introduction of new tools and methods, test-bedding of real and hypothetical scenarios, and development of technical expertise are some of the ways through which the research sector can help better enable the government to formulate policies, regulations, and initiatives on sustainability. In 1991, Singapore established the National Science and Technology Board which launched a $2 billion, publicly-funded, inaugural five-year National Technology Plan (see Chapter 3 by Philip Yeo). A total of

---

[2] More recently, in the lead up to the 2020 Paris Climate Change Conference, Singapore has submitted to the UNFCCC Secretariat its intended nationally determined contribution (INDC) to achieve a 36% reduction in its 2005 emissions intensity by 2030. The INDC also states Singapore's intention to stabilise its emissions levels with the aim to peak emissions by around 2030 (see IISD, 2016).

$40 billion over a 25-year span has since been allocated for research and development (R&D) activities to support industry needs (Lin, 2016).

Today, the National Research Foundation, a department within the Prime Minister's Office and secretariat to the Research, Innovation and Enterprise Council, is tasked with setting the national direction for R&D—a direction that includes a renewed focus on sustainability projects under the NRF 'National Innovation Challenge', and developing the R&D capabilities of universities and institutes. Although national- and university-level research centres and institutes focusing in one way or another on sustainability research abound, the following sections describe three research centres located at the National University of Singapore (NUS): *Campus for Research Excellence and Technological Enterprise*, *NUS Environmental Research Institute*, and *SDE Centre for Sustainable Asian Cities* in order to highlight the mission and the kind of research programmes undertaken at research centres at the national, university, and faculty level respectively.

Campus for Research Excellence and Technological Enterprise

Launched in 2006, the Campus for Research Excellence and Technological Enterprise (CREATE) is an initiative under the National Research Foundation to help catalyse new innovations and develop their economic growth potential. Co-located with the NUS University Town, CREATE serves as a hub for inter-national research collaborations and inter-disciplinary research activities. With a focus on four key research areas—environment systems, energy systems, human systems, and urban systems—CREATE research centres are positioned to address climate change through the advancement of scientific knowledge and development of cutting-edge mitigation and adaptation technologies. Some of the novel work conducted at CREATE include R&D in: energy storage systems, electric vehicle technologies, building energy efficiency, water and energy management, and renewable energy. In this way, CREATE not only contributes to but can also leverage on a flourishing R&D ecosystem comprising university research institutes, corporate laboratories, technology incubators, and start-up venture capitalists—all located within geographical proximity to foster partnerships, promote cross-fertilisation of knowledge, and facilitate technology transfer. The future of sustainability planning will indeed be dependent on the capability of cities to harness opportunities derived from technology and innovation.

NUS Environmental Research Institute

As a university-level research institute at NUS with a focus on environmental research, the NUS Environmental Research Institute (NERI) is mandated to coordinate mul-tidisciplinary research and education initiatives involving strategic partners (in higher education, government, and industry—locally and globally) on key environmental issues affecting sustainability in Singapore and elsewhere within Asia. One such partnership is the 'Energy and Environment Sustainability Solutions for Megacities' (E2S2), a five-year research collaboration between Shanghai Jiao Tong University (SJTU) and NUS which was initiated in 2012 through funding by NRF. Taking the two cities of Shanghai and Singapore as case study sites, E2S2 aims to develop and test-bed urban sensing, modelling, and assessment systems so as to better understand as well as address the complex challenges of future cities. This ongoing NUS-SJTU research collaboration recently spun-off a joint research centre at the NUS Research Institute (NUSRI@Suzhou) located at the Singapore Suzhou Industrial Park. The joint research centre is intended to strengthen the R&D capabilities of the NUS-SJTU partnership, while also exploring opportunities for collaborative research, commercialisation, and human resource training in the areas of environment and water. NERI is also equipped with a state-of-the-art laboratory and an in-house research team, enabling the institute to conduct and publish scientific research along four distinct tracks: (i) environmental surveillance and treatment; (ii) environmental and human health; (iii) green chemistry and sustainable energy; and (iv) impacts of climate change on the environment.

SDE Centre for Sustainable Asian Cities

Established in 2009, the Centre for Sustainable Asian Cities (CSAC) is a research centre at the School of Design and Environment (SDE), National University of Singapore, dedicated to the production of cutting-edge knowledge on sustainability issues and solutions with a focus on high-density urban environments in Asia. Working closely with the Ministry of National Development, CSAC complements the efforts at the national level to develop appropriate solutions and best practices for a more sustainable and liveable Singapore. Research conducted at CSAC ranges from studies of high density thresholds, urban metabolism, and urban spaces to that of urban climatic mapping, urban greenery, and the application of green plot ratio. Given the rapid rate of urbanisation in Asia and the enormous challenge faced by Asian cities in balancing urban growth and sustainability, CSAC has created an assessment framework for sustainable development and cities. This framework comprises four key thrusts that can each be readily evaluated by a set of relevant indicators from the slate of 13 themes including economy, environment, resources, people, and governance, etc. These themes are de-constructed to reveal a 'dashboard' of dimensions and key indicators for monitoring urban sustainability (Figure 1). Such a tool would be useful for city mayors, policy makers, and planners in charting their development trajectory vis-à-vis sustainable growth (see also http://www.sde.nus.edu.sg/csac/booklet%20small.pdf).

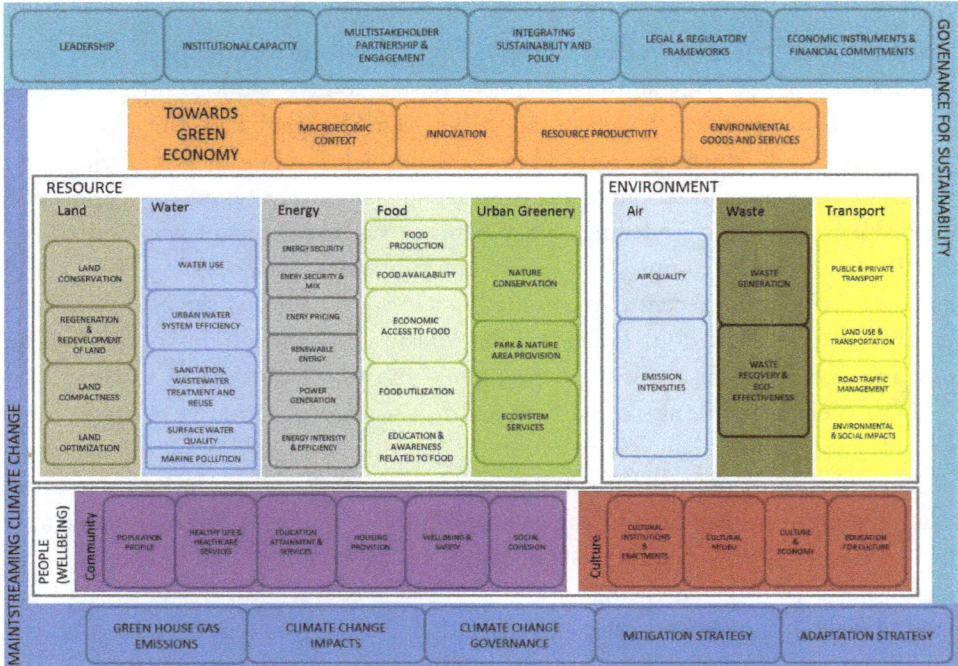

Figure 1. Dashboard for city sustainability developed by C.K. Heng and L.C. Malone-Lee. *Source*: **CSAC, NUS.**

Conclusion

The 21st century represents not only the ascent of a global and digital era but also an era of rapid urbanisation. On the one hand, rapid world population growth has exacerbated (if not created) challenges for the future of sustainability and liveability on the planet. On the other hand, cities can play vital roles as innovation hubs for test-bedding and developing capabilities in design/planning, technology, and behavioural trends towards more effective sustainability solutions. For Asian cities, sustainable urban growth is and will continue to be a pressing issue as 660 million people are estimated to migrate into the cities in the next 15 years; thus, adding to the urban population and intensifying demands on resources and infrastructure. At the same time, it is also within Asia's most advanced cities where high-density urban development has long been practiced and where novel innovations in sustainability planning and building are often test-bedded.

Singapore's urban development, for example, was guided at the very early beginnings of independence by visions and policies that were not only pragmatic but also long-range and sustainable in order to safeguard standards of liveability for future generations. In the ensuing decades, however, Singapore and other urban areas worldwide will need to enhance their resilience to climate change while also shouldering greater responsibilities to reduce their carbon footprints. As a nation with limited land and natural resources, Singapore's greatest contribution towards global efforts on sustainability is in demonstrating the significance of setting bold targets and, more importantly, achieving the targets through: strong leadership and coordination; thoughtful long-term planning; support of R&D initiatives to drive innovation in design/planning and technology; and cultivation of conscientious behaviour among citizens, government, and the private sector. Indeed, the challenges of creating a sustainable urban future are immense and complex; yet, the opportunities have never been greater for cities to drive forward a sound sustainability agenda into the next wave of urbanisation.

References

Arcadis (2015) *2015 Sustainable Cities Index: Balancing the Economic, Social and Environmental Needs of the World's Leading Cities* (Online). Available from https://s3.amazonaws.com/arcadis-whitepaper/arcadis-sustainable-cities-index-report.pdf; accessed on 26 August 2015.

ADB (Asian Development Bank) (2015) 'Asia's booming cities most at risk from climate change' (Online). Available from http://www.adb.org/news/features/asias-booming-cities-most-risk-climate-change; accessed on 16 June 2015.

CLC & CSC (Centre for Liveable Cities & Civil Service College) (2014) *Liveable & Sustainable Cities: A Framework*. Singapore: Centre for Liveable Cities Singapore.

CLC (Centre for Liveable Cities) (2010) 'Lee Kuan Yew World City Prize: Dialogue with Minister Mentor Lee Kuan Yew' (Online). Available from http://www.leekuanyewworld cityprize.com.sg/Dialogue_MM_wcs2010_long.pdf; accessed on 8 January 2016.

CNA (Channel News Asia) (2016) 'Smart devices trial extended to 3,200 households in Yuhua' (Online). Available from http://www.channelnewsasia.com/news/singapore/smart-devices-trial/2724842.html; accessed on 26 June 2016.

Dempsey, N. and Jenks, M. (2010) 'The future of the compact city', *Built Environment*, 36 (1), pp. 116–121.

DOS (Department of Statistics) (2015) 'Home ownership rate of resident households', Government of Singapore (Online). Available from http://www.singstat.gov.sg/statistics/visualising-data/charts/home-ownership-rate-of-resident-households; accessed on 16 June 2015.

ECA International (2015) 'Singapore secures top spot again in global liveability index for Asian expatriates, Bengaluru best of Indian locations' (Online). Available from http://www.eca-international.com/news/press_releases/8130/Singapore_secures_top_spot_again_in_global_liveability_index_for_Asian_expatriates__Bengaluru_best_of_Indian_locations#.Vfu3U9-qqko; accessed on 16 June 2015.

HDB (Housing & Development Board) (2015) 'Yuhua the first existing HDB estate to go Smart' (Online). Available from http://www.hdb.gov.sg/cs/infoweb/press-release/yuhua-the-first-existing-hdb-estate-to-go-smart; accessed on 26 June 2016.

HDB (Housing & Development Board) (2014/15) 'Key Statistics', *HDB Annual Report 2014/2015* (Online). Available from http://www10.hdb.gov.sg/ebook/ar2015/key-statistics. html; accessed on 7 January 2016.

Heng, C. K. and Malone-Lee, L. C. (2010) 'Density and urban sustainability: An exploration of critical issues' in: E. Ng (Ed) *Designing High-Density Cities for Social and Environmental Sustainability*, pp. 41–54. London, Sterling, VA: Earthscan.

Heng, C. K. and Zhang, J. (2010) 'Sustainability in the built environment' in: G. L. Ooi and B. Yuen (Eds) *World Cities: Achieving Liveability and Vibrancy*, pp. 193–210. Singapore: World Scientific.

Hoornweg, D., Bhada-Tata, P. and Kennedy, C. (2013) 'Environment: Waste production must peak this century', *Nature*, 502, pp. 615–617.

IISD (International Institute for Sustainable Development) (2016) 'Singapore submits INDC', *IISD Reporting Services* (Online). Available from http://climate-l.iisd.org/news/singapore-submits-indc/; accessed on 21 March 2016.

Jenks, M., Burton, E., and Williams, K. (Eds) (1996) *The Compact City: A Sustainable Urban Form?* London: E & FN Spon.

Johnson, I. (2013) 'China's great uprooting: Moving 250 Million into cities', *The New York Times*, 15 June (Online). Available from http://www.nytimes.com/2013/06/16/world/asia/chinas-great-uprooting-moving-250-million-into-cities.html?pagewanted=all&_r=0; accessed on 16 June 2015.

Lin, G. C. S. (2010) 'Scaling up regional development in globalizing China: Local capital accumulation, land-centered politics, and reproduction of space' in: Henry W. C. Yeung *Globalizing Regional Development in East Asia: Production Networks, Clusters, and Entrpreneurship*, pp. 115–133. London; New York: Routledge.

Lin, Y. (2016) 'More public money will go to projects that improve Singaporean lives, says NRF', *The Straits Times*, 9th January (Online). Available from http://www.straitstimes.com/singapore/finding-the-right-formula-in-research-funding; accessed on 11 January 2016.

Liu, T. K. (1985) 'Overview', in: A. K. Wong and S. H. K. Yeh (Eds) *Housing a Nation: 25 Years of Public Housing in Singapore*. Singapore: Maruzen Asia for Housing & Development Board.

MEWR and MND (Ministry of the Environment and Water Resources, and Ministry of National Development) (2015) *Sustainable Singapore Blueprint*. Singapore: MEWR and MND.

NEA (National Environment Agency) (2015) 'Solid waste management infrastructure' (Online). Available from http://www.nea.gov.sg/energy-waste/waste-management/solid-waste-management-infrastructure; accessed on 16 June 2015.

Neuman, M. (2005) 'The compact city fallacy', *Journal of Planning Education and Research*, 25 (1), pp. 11–26.

NCCS (National Climate Change Secretariat) (2012) *National Climate Change Strategy*. Singapore: Prime Minister's Office.

NOAA NCEI (National Centers for Environmental Information) (2015) 'State of the climate: Global analysis for December 2014' (Online). Available from http://www.ncdc.noaa.gov/sotc/global/201412; accessed on 16 June 2015.

Ng, W. H. (2012) *Singapore, The Energy Economy: From the First Refinery to the End of Cheap Oil, 1960–2010*. New York: Routledge.

PBL NEAA (Netherlands Environmental Assessment Agency) (2014) *Trends in Global CO_2 Emissions: 2014 Report*. Netherlands: The Hague.

PWD (Public Works Department) (1971) *Annual Report 1970*. Singapore: Government Printing Office.

Roberts, B. and Kanaley, T. (Eds) (2006) *Urbanization and Sustainability in Asia: Case Studies of Good Practice*. Philippines: Asian Development Bank.

SPH (Singapore Press Holdings Ltd.) (2007) 'James Koh to be new HDB chairman', *AsiaOne News* (Online). Available from http://news.asiaone.com/News/AsiaOne+News/Singapore/Story/A1Story20070927-27265.html; accessed on 13 July 2016.

UN (United Nations) (2012) 'The future we want: Water and sanitation fact sheet' (Online). Available from http://www.un.org/en/sustainablefuture/pdf/Rio+20_FS_Water.pdf; accessed on 16 June 2015.

UN (United Nations) (2014a) 'World's population increasingly urban with more than half living in urban areas' (Online). Available from http://www.un.org/en/development/desa/news/population/world-urbanization-prospects-2014.html; accessed on 20 August 2015.

UN (United Nations) (2014b) '2013 Demographic Yearbook, Sixty-Fourth Issue'. New York: United Nations Department of Economic and Social Affairs. Available from http://unstats.un.org/unsd/Demographic/products/dyb/dybsets/2013.pdf; accessed on 25 August 2015.

UN (United Nations) (2015a) 'World population projected to reach 9.7 billion by 2050' (Online). Available from http://www.un.org/en/development/desa/news/population/2015-report.html; accessed on 16 June 2015.

UN (United Nations) Population Division (2015b) *Data Query* (Online). Available from http://esa.un.org/unpd/wpp/DataQuery; accessed on 20 August 2015.

UNEP (2012) *The Critical Role of Global Food Consumption Patterns in Achieving Sustainable Food Systems and Food for All* (Online). Available from http://www.unep.org/resource-efficiency/Portals/24147/scp/agri-food/pdf/Role_of_Global_Food_Consumption_Patterns_A_UNEP_Discussion_Paper.pdf.

WBG (World Bank Group) (2015) *East Asia's Changing Urban Landscape: Measuring a Decade of Spatial Growth*. Washington, D.C.: International Bank for Reconstruction and Development / The World Bank.

Epilogue

Perspectives on the Future
of Urban Planning in Singapore

Challenges for a New Era

Peter Ho

The 1971 Concept Plan that is reflected in the modern city-state of Singapore today was very much a product of its time, when the focus was on creating jobs and housing for a young nation. Nevertheless, the guiding vision of a highly liveable and economically vibrant Singapore remains relevant even now. The need for strong leadership, supported by the necessary plans, policies and legislation that take the long-term view, remains key to the realisation of our vision into the future. But the process of achieving it will be more challenging given Singapore's very different context today as a First World city state.

Firstly, our population is much bigger compared to 1965. As the population continues to grow, the demand for housing, facilities for the people like hospitals and schools, and for transport, will grow in tandem.

Our population is also rapidly ageing. We need to plan and develop infrastructure that creates opportunities for our elderly to remain economically active, socially engaged and mentally alert. This is so that they can age in place within their communities while leading independent and productive lives.

Adding to these challenges are the changing aspirations and expectations of Singaporeans. Compared to the past, many today value the less tangible aspects of life, such as pursuing one's interests, achieving work-life balance, and participating in civic life. All these translate into greater demand for public spaces like parks and greenery, for sports and recreation, as well as for the arts and heritage. Given that there is a limit as to how much more land can be created through reclamation, catering to all these different aspirations and expectations requires us to explore and experiment with new solutions–such as underground space.

Our economy is also changing in fundamental ways with rapid advances in technology. Disruptive technologies like additive manufacturing, robotics and automation are beginning to transform the nature of manufacturing, as well as displace traditional jobs. The distinction between manufacturing and services is blurring as the economy moves towards higher value-added activities like R&D and knowledge creation. The emergence of the sharing economy, facilitated by advances in infocomm technologies (ICT), is changing the way businesses are conducted in a variety of areas, such as car-sharing, taxi booking apps, and short-term/tourist accommodation. Work aspirations are changing too, with more people willing to take the plunge to start their own businesses, instead of working in traditional office jobs. Advances in ICT also facilitate more flexible working arrangements such as telecommuting.

We cannot fully anticipate all future possibilities. But what we can do, and should do, is to ensure that our plans are flexible enough to support changing needs. For example, instead of planning for single-use spaces, we should plan for multiple uses, to facilitate synergies, and to enable uses to be changed more easily.

As our population and economy continue to grow and evolve, travel demands will increase. Today roads already take up 12% of our land area, close to the 14% for housing. This is not sustainable. Instead, we must explore ways to reduce travel, by bringing jobs closer to homes, through a more polycentric network of employment nodes distributed across the island. At the same time, we need to push for greater use of public transport. This means looking at disruptive technology that can offer new car-lite transport options that will require less road space, such as autonomous vehicles, as well as creating an environment that is conducive for walking and cycling. Resilience in our public transport system could be strengthened by supplementing the existing Mass Rapid Transit (MRT) network with new options, such as a bus rapid transit system (BRT).

As a small island city-state, Singapore is vulnerable to the impact of climate change. We are already experiencing more extreme weather conditions in the form of greater rainfall intensity, prolonged dry periods without rain, and more hot days. We need to find ways to maintain a highly liveable environment in spite of such extreme climate conditions. Mitigation measures will have to be introduced to reduce carbon emissions. Our buildings will have to be green and energy efficient. New ways of greening our built environment–such as through more vertical greenery–will have to be deployed. We will have to make space so that more sustainable energy sources such as solar and wind can be adopted.

Conclusions

As our land needs increase with a growing population and an evolving economy, there will be a limit to how much more we can expand our land capacity through incremental and conventional efforts. The philosophy of planning has to shift towards greater flexibility, more sharing of space for multiple uses, and an increased willingness to experiment with new ideas, as we work to realise our vision for Singapore in the next 50 years.

A City in Time for the Future

Low Teck Seng

Singapore's 50-year transformation to a vibrant global city is a testament to leaders who had the foresight and political will to see their visions through. However, the present unique challenges demand shifts in planning processes for Singapore to continue to grow sustainably, bearing in mind the impact that economic progress and population growth have on our urban environment. Integral to these shifts will be our ability to leverage research and development (R&D) to push the boundaries of what it means to maintain Singapore as an endearing home. Three aspects are discussed.

Leadership & Organisation

R&D will play a growing role in developing solutions to meet our national needs. PUB's water story was our national archetype for R&D success: Long-standing water security concerns spurred R&D efforts that established Singapore's international reputation for water reclamation and desalination. However, future urban challenges are less likely to be defined by discrete needs. Instead, they comprise a system of interconnected issues that span the urban and socioeconomic problem-space. Given the increased complexity, Singapore will transit to a R&D strategy coordinated at the ministerial level to address our resource constraints while enhancing urban liveability and sustainability. Our R&D planning teams will ensure cross-domain integration to safeguard against silos and duplicative efforts, while engaging the relevant government bodies to ensure technologies have agency and industry receptacles for deployment. With input from technology roadmaps and stakeholders from industry and academia, Singapore's leadership will spearhead a whole-of-government approach towards strategising our R&D initiatives while ensuring solutions remain impactful.

Human Capital

Singapore will grow local R&D manpower to anchor our core capabilities and hone our entrepreneurial edge. Recognising the need to accelerate capability-building, the concept of a Campus for Research Excellence and Technological Enterprise (CREATE) was endorsed by the National Research Foundation (NRF) Board. CREATE brings together world-class research institutions in one location in Singapore and establishes institutional partnerships so that a strong pipeline of ideas, talent and research capabilities from partner universities increases the vibrancy and diversity of Singapore's R&D ecosystem. Today, CREATE co-locates 16 research programmes where researchers from outstanding universities conduct interdisciplinary research. Additionally, Singapore will engage our scientists, entrepreneurs, venture capitalists and large local enterprises to define pathways to capture economic and societal value. By developing individuals with relevant skills along the innovation value chain, we can extract the benefits from our intellectual property.

Tools

Computer modelling and simulations (M&S) will complement and guide Singapore's R&D thrusts. M&S has traditionally been a tool to study phenomena in isolation. Moving forward, M&S will evolve into a "test tube" for investigating system-of-systems type problems. This will enable us to study non-trivial interactions between nascent technologies, public policy and social behaviour. Resources will then be allocated to develop suitable technologies that deliver results within Singapore's socioeconomic and urban context. A case in point is Singapore's push for solar energy: increasing the share of solar energy requires that we change the way we harness and consume electricity. Planners can leverage the Virtual Singapore 3D platform that is being co-developed by NRF, the Singapore Land Authority (SLA) and the Infocomm Development Authority (IDA), to optimise our solar deployment strategies given our land constraints and dense urban profile. Similarly, economic modelling can shed light on how real-time dynamics of electricity demand and supply can influence consumer behaviour so as to accommodate the intermittency of solar energy. M&S will allow us to holistically assess novel ideas and bring together our best engineers, social scientists and policy makers early in the planning process.

Since independence, science and technology have been integral to Singapore's prosperity. To win the future, Singapore must transform from a technology taker to a technology driver and global thought-leader. The role of government will be to actively nurture a vibrant R&D community capable of meeting national needs where there are no existing solutions, and providing policy makers with indigenous options for sustainable development.

Singapore: The Smartest City on Our Planet

Kishore Mahbubani

Many cities in the world are now aspiring to be "smart cities". Only one city on our planet can aspire to be the "smartest city". That city is Singapore.

Why is Singapore unique? It is the world's only city-state. If the city fails, Singaporeans have no countryside to fall back to. We have no other option to fall back on. We have to keep our little city living and breathing. This is why from very early in our history, our founding fathers recognised that our little city-state could choke and die if we allowed too many cars on Singapore roads. If Singapore were full of traffic jams like Bangkok or Jakarta, its economy would grind to a natural halt. We would die just like any human being who tried to swallow too much.

Reducing Singapore's car population is therefore a matter of life and death for Singapore. It is a necessity, not an option. Yet, Singapore now has an amazing opportunity to turn this necessity into a virtue. We can become the first city in the world to announce a zero car ownership society.

To get to this noble objective, the population of Singapore must accept an undeniable fact. A car is not a god to be worshipped. A car is an instrument to get us from place to place. Human beings rationally change their instruments when technology improves. When I was young, I took rickshaws because they were cheap and reliable. Later I took motorised taxis because they were cheap, reliable and fast.

Today, the best instrument to get us from place to place in a cheap, reliable and fast manner is a smartphone. Virtually, all Singaporeans now own a smartphone. Therefore, what Singapore needs now is a fleet of cars that will respond immediately to their smartphone app and get them from point to point. Our current generation of leaders now have a unique opportunity to match the political courage of our founding fathers who dared to create disincentives for car ownership.

We can match their political courage by now creating a set of incentives to switch away from car ownership. Hence any car that is brought in for use by smartphone apps to get from point to point need not pay the usual additional car taxes or purchase a COE. This would make renting a car for individual rides far cheaper than owning a car. Behavioural economics teaches us that people are smart. With the right set of incentives, they will change their behaviour. With the right set of incentives, Singaporeans will stop worshipping cars and start using cars.

However, the incentives need not be economic alone. Singaporeans are normal human beings. They also have altruistic motives. If they are given a chance to save our fragile planet with no personal sacrifice (and indeed they should gain in economic terms), they will happily do so, especially when they see the world admiring the Singapore population for its boldness. By switching away from car ownership to car-ridership, we would reduce the number of cars on Singapore's roads from 900,000 to 300,000.

When that happens, the seven billion citizens of planet earth will look at us with great admiration and say with greater sincerity and conviction, "Singapore is the smartest city on our planet."

People-Centric Approach
to Urban Planning

David Chan

In recent years, liveability, well-being, quality of life, social capital and other constructs in the social and behavioural sciences have joined traditional planning concepts such as access to amenities, mobility and connectivity to become central considerations in Singapore's urban planning policies. Although the expanded language for urban planning is recent, the people-centric goal of improving life and living in Singapore has always been fundamental for both urban planners and national leaders. This is clear to those who are well-informed of the history and current focus of urban planning and public policies in Singapore. But as we reflect on the future and prepare for it, it is important to have more clarity on what a people-centric approach to urban planning entails.

In a people-centric approach, social and behavioural factors are not treated as "good to have" luxuries in urban planning. Instead, they are recognised as necessities to be incorporated when designing and implementing urban policies and interventions. It means research and development in urban planning should go beyond technical solutions to include social and behavioural sciences. This becomes obvious when we recognise that liveability is about people's evaluations, experiences and encounters when they interact with their physical and social environments

To effectively adopt and apply a people-centric approach to urban planning, I suggest we focus more on three important but somewhat neglected issues. First, we need to understand that the key social and behavioural sciences constructs in urban planning, such as liveability, quality of life and social capital, are inherently multidimensional. Each construct comprises multiple distinct variables that may be related in different ways and to different degrees. Depending on which specific variables we focus on and what metrics we use, the evaluation of the construct and how it applies in Singapore's urban planning can vary widely. The complexity in the construct definition and measurement should not be confused with the practical relevance of the construct to urban planning. The fact that many of these constructs are multidimensional makes it even more important to be evidence-based when incorporating social and behavioural factors in urban planning. Evidence and application must be rooted in the rigour and relevance of the social and behavioural sciences.

Second, when incorporating social and behavioural factors, it is critical to ensure that they adequately capture the experiences of various segments of the Singapore population. For example, the same built environment can impact different groups of people differently or impact people differently over time. Take for instance the Singapore-Kuala Lumpur High Speed Rail terminal station that will be built in Jurong. When it is ready, it could bring about a large transient commuter population in the area, and with it, implications on how to manage emergencies involving a crowd that includes travellers and workers who may be entering Singapore for the first time. They are less familiar with the physical surroundings of the station than the regular commuter living in Singapore. Therefore, the physical layout and urban forms in the surrounding area must be aligned with contingency plans for incident management during train disruptions. This in turn calls for a collaborative approach in urban planning involving different agencies. It also calls for an integrative approach that brings together various experts to better understand how people think, feel and act in different settings, and how these thoughts, emotions or behaviours may differ between groups or change over time. This means having social and behavioural scientists working alongside urban planners and other public service officers, architects, engineers, and physical scientists to enhance people's well-being and quality of life in urban settings.

Third, it is important to anticipate how needs and wants may change over time and across demographic groups. This is especially relevant when using social attitude surveys to gather public sentiments as inputs for town planning. It is unwise to simply take the needs and wants reported in these surveys as given. Instead, it is necessary to think about how they can change, the different demographics, and how environmental change can actually influence people's expectations.

As urban planners and national leaders in Singapore reflect on and prepare for the future, they need to adopt and apply a people-centric approach. As a city-state, Singapore aspires to be both a global city and a cohesive country. Unlike other countries where people can move between cities in the country, Singapore is unique in that people who want a change of living environment would have to leave the country. Singapore needs a living environment and ways of life that will enable more emotional attachment and rootedness to the country, for both citizens and non-citizens.

Singapore: From Liveable to Lovable City

Melissa Kwee

The foremost challenge ahead for Singapore is to create a **loveable** city. Our history has brought us through the challenges of viability–in our founding years, productivity–in our early growth years, and liveability–as we matured and valued aesthetic and sustainable environmental attributes to create the bustling, dynamic destination we are today. I believe that for Singapore to be significant and truly successful, it must be a nation and home we love. The city: ours–by and for the people, both loved and loveable by locals and visitors alike. To be loveable means every person practising the love of neighbour, community and self. This may be more instrumental than social defence and national resilience. The essence of a great city is one that is built upon a collective spirit and common purpose.

How does a city-state like Singapore embrace this next stage and incorporate the principles and posture of love into our planning structures and processes?

I propose three broad guiding principles.

The first is that planning must be based on a conscious examination and co-articulation of our national values in action. Values define a leader, an organisation and a city. If form follows function and values determine our priorities, then the definition of function must be rooted in the values and priorities of its use. In planning, this approach would begin with a reflection of how our spaces carry the look, feel and function of the values of our nation. Truly shared values can only emerge from authentic engagement and participation especially, amongst different voices. Urban leaders are the civic facilitators where they find ways to collaborate, collect ideas and resolve conflicts. Co-created visions are best owned when every stakeholder's interest is heard.

The second related principle is that city-making must become a more participatory and humanised process. We must rethink how processes in themselves could be redesigned to be more relational.

What if citizens and neighbours could re-envision their neighbourhoods and work places? What if you and I were invited to dream together and envisage how new buildings, recreation or services could help communities integrate better, reduce crime or improve a sense of well-being?

Imagine this: our planning systems have been designed to foster empathy and inclusion—from children to grandparents; the able-bodied to the handicapped and socially-estranged. **Anchoring citizen participation in the context of family and relationships may also create a more human-centric and relational view of places and spaces.** Participation is about timely, meaningful, relevant and respectful engagement in a process towards solution seeking for the greater good.

The final principle is to keep iterating at the fringes and core. Iteration improves the accuracy and relevance of any plan towards achieving its ends. It is flexibility and responsiveness, that encompass humility to know that there is rarely a single right answer in nation-building. It drives a freedom to experiment at the fringes with moderate risk. What remains constant is how the changes reflect fundamental values. **<u>In this new world, planning is not purely administrative or analytical but a value-driven, human-centric and a transformational learning journey.</u>**

Accommodating Nature in Singapore

Shawn Lum

Singaporeans are as dependent on nature's services as are citizens of any other country. We need clean air, water, food, and a stable climate as much as anyone else. However, nature and biodiversity confined within Singapore's borders will not determine whether the city-state survives or not, at least not in terms of our immediate, physical subsistence. Singapore's land area and its natural habitats are far too small to provide all of the air, water, and other services for our large population.

This is not to say, however, that nature in Singapore is unimportant. Nature and greenery are synonymous with Singapore, giving the country its distinctive and pleasant ambience, and making the city attractive to visitors and to the thousands of skilled professionals who choose to live here. Nature in Singapore is not a luxury; it is a strategic element that directly contributes to the country's success.

What makes Singapore such a biodiverse city? The island's many parks and nature areas, its generous roadside landscaping, its commitment to tree planting, and its rapidly expanding skyrise and vertical greenery are factors. They are no accident. They are testament to meticulous planning, investment in manpower and maintenance, and thoughtful policy. Good fortune plays a role too.

Singapore is in the wet tropics, a region with nature so exuberant that if enough space is set aside, many kinds of plants, birds, insects, and other wildlife will flourish. Villages, plantations and other human settlements that were cleared a generation ago and set aside as land banks for future development have not been sitting idle. They have been colonised by plants and wildlife. Examples include the species rich former Bidadari Muslim Cemetery and the Bukit Brown Cemetery.

Singapore is able to support its human population by importing food and materials produced elsewhere. Our land area is a bit larger than 700 km^2, but our land requirements are many times that, if one considers Singapore's total resource needs. In a similar way, our enviable biodiversity is made possible in large part by greenery that is outside the formally designated nature reserves/parks/streetscapes system. When "idle" State Land is gradually turned over in the years ahead for development, Singapore's biodiversity will be subject to a simple law of ecology–all else being equal, less land area will translate to lower species diversity. Wildlife thrives wherever there is greenery, and Singapore will have less undeveloped greenery in the future.

A commitment to biodiversity will have to be underpinned by human ingenuity and empathy. We can continue to harbour rich, sustainable natural heritage if we apply ecological principles in a systematic way across the Singapore landscape. For example, we can set aside zones of varying access and recreational use, from wildlife-only areas to ones that are readily accessible. Such zoning should be acceptable to and respected by everyone. If nature becomes part of our way of life, we will cherish it and we will find that it thrives.

Garden City Mega City

Wong Mun Summ and Alina Yeo

Urban planning in 20th century Singapore was strongly focused on land use zoning and largely dictated by industrialisation, population growth, vehicular traffic and roads. The framework of two-dimensional land use parcellation produced a largely segregated city comprised of siloed mono-use buildings and an inherent sense of social alienation. It also resulted in a planning vision encoded in regulations that limit evolving with the times.

The 21st century city needs to respond to pressing current issues – climate change, resource scarcity, rapid urbanisation and digital technology. This is particularly crucial for our land scarce island city-state with limited resources, where compactness–not urban sprawl–is the only option moving forward. The model of cities with hinter lands, as well as those in the temperate west cannot simply be imported into Singapore's unique context. To ride the next wave of our nation's future, Singapore has to innovate from within and pioneer its own solutions.

This calls for a strategic rethinking of urban planning as a 3D matrix rather than a 2D grid. By **Layering Cities**, architecture, infrastructure and urbanism can be integrated in radical ways to produce self-sufficient micro cities, while creating multiple new ground levels that increase urban liveability, foster community, and reinforce human scale. By **Planting Cities**, re-greening of the urban environment can be found in topographic architectural forms and building integrated green screens, sky gardens and sky parks. By designing for **Breathing Cities**, buildings can open up to the climate and nature by adopting sustainable and passive design strategies.

To achieve a 21st century Garden City Mega City, public and private sector mindsets and the methodology for **Rating Cities** must evolve. Buildings/towns should no longer be measured solely in terms of developers' efficiencies, but according to more sustainable and humane yardsticks. **'Green Plot Ratio'**, for instance, measures the amount of landscaped surfaces within a building over its site area, with the aim of reintroducing biodiversity and green relief into the city. **'Community Plot Ratio'**, on the other hand, measures the total amount of community space within a building over its site area, with the aim of encouraging social gathering and human interaction at various scales. To measure the extent to which a building encourages and facilitates the public life of a city, a **'Civic Generosity Index'** can be introduced. This rewards buildings that exhibit good neighbourliness in the way they gift the city visually or spatially. The adoption of "urban ecological" approaches to support wildlife within cities can also be assessed under an **'Ecosystem Contribution Index'**, which measures the degree to which a building supplements a city's ecosystem. To drive sustainability further, a **'Self-Sufficiency Index'** that measures a building's capacity to provide its own energy, food and water can also be adopted.

This notion of a high-density, high-amenity 21st century Garden City Mega City is not a romantic ideal. It is a realistic vision for our urban future, holding the key to a highly liveable, three-dimensionally integrated Singapore that is progressive, sustainable and humane, serving as a model that is applicable even to other Asian Mega Cities.

Top Down Bottom Up?

Tay Kheng Soon

The seeds of the future are always embedded in the folds of the present. Singapore needs to go beyond conventional demographics obsessed with the economics of age dependency. This short essay takes a different perspective by suggesting that there is a possible future that may lie in the seemingly impossible nexus between youthful idealism and angst with aged resignation and faded dreams. It will require an excursion outside of conventional thought though.

Things taken for granted can be shaken by too much wealth or too little. The young grown up in good times are never grateful for what they have. They look for meaning in freedom. Those in retirement where their instincts were grounded in experience oscillate between resignation and unfulfilled dreams they had traded for success. The Internet brings these two perspectives into contact as never before. Viewed from the perspective of orderly administration, this is a problem, but I prefer to see it for its creative potential in making a new narrative of how new capacity can be released. There are spatial implications usually not factored that are being considered here.

The spatial nexus is this: that as people go about the routines of their everyday life, they should affirm old relationships, meet new people, experience new things, get new ideas effortlessly. But this has to be deliberately planned for. As it is, there is no physical network of connections which everyone routinely goes to, like the extensive nervous system of a high-functioning organism. Analogously, where we live, work, study etc., we should experience the currents of everyday life and grow intelligent because of it. The flow and conviviality would then underpin life and generate trust which makes productive social relations all the more productive and possible. But instead of growing such an extensive Nervous System, we have the checker-board zones punctuated by hubs traversed by highways; liveable no doubt, but this spatial arrangement lacks the ***synaptic density*** any intelligent organism ought to have. Emulating the neural network is therefore the inspiration.

For example, once a synapse occurs in the brain, a connection is made between neurons–information flows across. Many synapses linking many neurons make for high-level complex thought. This is the basis for metaphorical thinking–the basis of creativity. Hubs and zones just don't do this–they may be efficient but are not inherently intelligent. We can also take full advantage of augmented reality by linking the physical with the virtual neural network–the Internet! This is the new power that few can do but compact Singapore can!

This is therefore the challenge: not shrink away from radical new thinking. Singapore can pioneer intelligence by design, i.e., by building-in **synaptic density** like that of a well-educated and courageous mind and brain. The design challenge is to dare to insert the required nervous system into every housing estate and eventually the whole island. This is the kind of creative destruction that is needed. Thinking of the whole island as a living organism served by an extensive Central Nervous System is the way forward and this requires a change in the design of schools, community centres, shopping centres, offices, cultural and civic centres! Once these form over time the contiguous synergistic network easily accessible by foot or bike near to residences, Singapore becomes the most intelligent city the world has ever seen!

Education is the social glue that has to be future-ready. This means emphasising the 6Cs. Courage then Curiosity then Creativity then Compassion, Collaboration follows and finally Commitment. This requires a total change of education concept to a curriculum that offers balance between core curriculum and free subject choice options by students. But this means that the design and location of schools has to be very different. Spatially, students are above, all the rest below where the action is. This is place-based learning, I call this a web-like Super School; thus such a school becomes a multi-generational learning facility in which book learning is linked to reality learning integrated into the activity of the Central Nervous System of every community. This is the venue where youthful idealism can be finally aligned with the revived dreams of the old and a new society comes into being![1]

A smart brain is a richly interconnected brain and smarts is what Singapore needs. This is what "future ready" should really mean. There can be no debate that Singapore needs to become much, much smarter as a people not just to survive but to go beyond its current conception in a much-changed and turbulent world. And given the plateau of excellence already created, Singapore can now take off into the world unlimited by its smallness if only it dares. Singapore has to have the gumption to be a torch bearer of a new and better world for it to remain relevant and exceptional! This is my hope.

---

[1] *Please see my YouTube video, Singapore Version 2.0.*

www.ingramcontent.com/pod-product-compliance
Lightning Source LLC
Chambersburg PA
CBHW080548270326
41929CB00019B/3238